T0283568

LEADERS
IN THE
MAKING

LEADERS
IN THE
MAKING

THE CRUCIBLES OF
CHANGE-MAKERS IN HR

ARVIND AGRAWAL
T.V. RAO

BUSINESS

An imprint of Penguin Random House

PENGUIN BUSINESS

USA | Canada | UK | Ireland | Australia
New Zealand | India | South Africa | China

Penguin Business is part of the Penguin Random House group of companies
whose addresses can be found at global.penguinrandomhouse.com

Published by Penguin Random House India Pvt. Ltd
4th Floor, Capital Tower 1, MG Road,
Gurugram 122 002, Haryana, India

Penguin
Random House
India

First published in Penguin Business by Penguin Random House India 2022

ISBN 9780670097005

Typeset in Adobe Caslon Pro by MAP Systems, Bengaluru, India
Printed at Thomson Press India Ltd, New Delhi

www.penguin.co.in

Contents

Foreword

No one doubts that individual leaders matter and collective leadership matters more. We each can name a leader who has shaped our lives and we appreciate the quality of leadership that shapes organizations where we work, live, worship and play.

Being a better leader and building better leadership are well-studied topics (over 4 billion, yes **billion**, Google hits on 'leader' and 'leadership').

Arvind and T.V. bring fresh insights on how to make and become more effective leaders. Their insights are based on exceptional theory (being the leading human thinkers in India for some time), research (in-depth studies of thirty leaders and accessing rigorous research) and practice (coaching and nurturing leaders for decades).

First, Arvind and T.V. highlight the crucibles (or settings) that frame how leaders are both born and bred, defined by their inherent nature and created through nurturing. Family heritage and DNA are the seeds of leadership that shape predispositions about how leaders think, act and feel. Any of us who age increasingly see our parents in the mirror! But, even more, seeds grow and leaders are nurtured by their education, early mentors, first jobs, training, bosses and experiences with challenging problems. Leaders learn by accepting stretch assignments, playing new roles and growing from successes and failures.

Second, HR professionals, who are both leaders and who are often charged with building leadership in organizations, have a unique set of competencies within business, people, personal, professional and social categories. When HR (and other) leaders recognize and master these competencies, they will improve themselves, their organizations and society.

Third, *Leaders in the Making* is amplified with thirty exceptional case studies. The authors' deep dive into these thirty remarkable leaders gives readers an opportunity to not just hear about 'a' leader or to see some statistics on leadership but to see the formative process of leaders being made.

The ultimate takeaway from this outstanding book will be that each reader can be guided to 'develop their own ecosystem of values, their own vision of the functions that they are called to perform in their lives, both professional and social'.

With this book, Arvind and T.V. have continued their legacy of providing ideas with impact.

July 2022

Dave Ulrich,
Rensis Likert Professor,
Ross School of Business,
University of Michigan, and
partner, The RBL Group

Preface

This book is about how leaders are made. What crucible of experiences do they go through during their life journey to evolve as effective leaders? How are they influenced by their parents, schools, colleges, teachers, bosses and other people in the organizations they work with?

To discover the underlying pattern, we have taken a sample of thirty seasoned and very successful HR Leaders (HRLs) in the business context. We started to research, document and draw lessons from those who had influenced these HRLs. By the time we completed the book of case histories of these thirty HRLs, we discovered that the stories go beyond what is traditionally included as HR. It turned out that many of these HRLs have grown beyond HR to becoming business leaders besides CXOs and CEOs. We realized that to be a good CEO or CXO, a stint in HR offers a great opportunity.

We also realized that leaders are leaders not only in the HR profession but anywhere. A leader in any business context goes through a slew of experiences, positive as well as negative. A good leader demonstrates the ability to manage these experiences and learn life-changing lessons. We call these a 'crucible of experiences'. As we were in the last leg of completing our work, Indra Nooyi's autobiography got published. It presents great evidence of the significance of such experiences in the shaping of a great leader. HRLs covered in this book come from some of the most successful organizations in India and across the world. The organizations where our HR leaders worked range from business houses and organizations including Adani, Aditya Birla Group, Ambanis, ITC, Infosys, L&T, Murugappa Group, Tata, TVS and Wipro, in the private sector; American Express, GE, GSK, HUL, P&G, etc., in MNCs; and Bank of Baroda, HPCL, IPCL, NTPC, ONGC, SAIL, etc., in the public sector.

The case studies presented in this book trace the experiences of the leaders from early childhood and cover early schooling, college or university education, first job, subsequent jobs, experiences with peers, bosses, colleagues, and the way they orchestrated various experiences in their life. Insights are drawn from these experiences and the leaders speak about how these experiences shaped them to become impactful professionals. We expect these case studies to not only make for interesting reading but also inspirational reading for all categories of readers. For parents we expect them to provide insights for shaping future generations. For schools and colleges, we expect the case studies to provide insights for designing and creating the curricular experiences. For managers, these case studies provide inspiration and alternative pathways to give the right experiences to their team members and develop them as future leaders. For CEOs and CXOs, we hope this provides insights and strategies for managing people (spotting, utilizing and developing talent) for their business, irrespective of the function they are in. For management students, the case studies are expected to provide insights into leadership behaviour irrespective of the function they are in. Every function, whether it is finance, marketing or IT, or a start-up, manufacturing or services, requires the leaders to work with people. What else can be a greater lesson than the ones offered by those who spent a large part of their lives as people managers and have emerged as great leaders?

We enjoyed interacting and learnt a lot from these leaders. Our research-driven qualitative analysis, presented in three chapters at the end as crucible experiences, competencies and values, has been educative for us as authors. In Chapter 3, we attempted, at the cost of appearing repetitive, crucible experiences from thirty case studies and drew lessons from them. The competency analysis indicated to us that, across the globe, what are considered outcomes of years of research in building the professional base at universities like Michigan and by professional bodies like SHRM, CIPD or NHRDN, can be seen live in our case studies. In this book, for limitations of length, we have given only brief accounts of these models.

We hope that this book will form a basis of offering courses, seminars, conferences and building leaders for the future by various organizations, institutions and professional bodies. We also hope it will serve as a source of inspiration for developing leadership competencies not only in HR but in every other profession and academic discipline. Many of our leaders have come from humble and simple beginnings, and demonstrate that leadership heights can be achieved by one's own effort and commitment to growth using every experience one comes across as bricks of leadership experience to learn and build on. We are conscious that very few women leaders have been covered in this book. This is a serious limitation of the book. In the last couple of decades many more women leaders have emerged and we hope future works on leaders will have a higher percentage of women covered. Lastly, it is our desire and dream that this book will stimulate more research and documentation of the new era leaders and leadership in all sectors in India and around the world. As authors we will be happy to facilitate any effort by industry, institutions and professional bodies.

Arvind Agrawal
T.V. Rao

1

Introduction

Leaders contribute to making a difference in the lives of people and, thereby, to overall societal progress. We start with an outline of the way leaders and leadership are seen in the contemporary business world and other settings. Significant views and viewpoints of some much-respected leaders, authors, researchers and practitioners are then briefly presented as a backdrop against which we have tried to analyse the contributions of the HR Leaders chosen for this book.

Given the evolving business environment, we present a brief discussion on the growing significance of the human resources profession and its leading practitioners. The critical need for effective HR sets the criteria for selecting the HR Leaders who, literally, select themselves with the magnitude of their contribution. We conclude the chapter with an overview of the methodology used to develop the case studies, highlighting the life journey of the HR Leaders, analysing their journeys and highlighting the main lessons from their inspiring stories.

Approaches to Leadership

Jacob Morgan (2020) interviewed more than 140 CEOs around the world for his book *The Future Leader: 9 Skills and Mindsets to Succeed in the Next Decade* and asked each of them to define leadership. He did not receive even one duplicate response from the 140 respondents. Clearly, there are many approaches to leadership. The literature on the subject is enormous and is multiplying every day. We had to select those that we considered relevant and appropriate for management professionals. We were particularly impressed by the following frameworks:

Leaders as institution builders and institutional managers

After years of research on the role of achievement motivation in building entrepreneurship and causing economic development in societies, McClelland and Burnham (1976) formulated the concept of 'institutional managers' (McClelland and Burnham, 1996 and 2003). Institutional managers focus on building power through influence rather than through their own individual achievement. Such managers are the most effective and their direct reports have a greater sense of responsibility. They see organizational goals more clearly and exhibit greater team spirit. McClelland and Burnham outlined the following as characteristics of institutional managers:

- They are more organization-minded and feel responsible for building organizations;
- They strongly believe in the importance of centralized authority;
- They report that they like to work. They seem to like the discipline of work. It satisfies their need for getting things done in an orderly way; and
- They seem quite willing to sacrifice self-interest for the welfare of the organization that they serve.

Institution builders—the Indian context

In the Indian and Asian contexts, Udai Pareek has contributed considerably to our thinking on leadership effectiveness. He first elevated the conceptual position of managers to the leadership level in his book, *Beyond Management*, where he conceptualized institution-builders as people who are even a step higher than managers and leaders (Pareek, 1981, 2002). Pareek identified the following eight main roles of top-level executives for becoming institution-builders:

1. Identity-creating role,
2. Enabling role,

3. Synergizing role,
4. Balancing role,
5. Linkage-building role,
6. Futuristic role,
7. Impact-making role, and
8. Superordination creating role

In another framework, Pareek (1980) offers role-effectiveness as the central concept for being effective in any role that one is performing. He formulates those effective managers make their own roles and ensure self-role integration, proactivity, creativity and confrontation, while simultaneously feeling central to the process, influencing others, growing personally, linking with other roles, and helping and working for superordination.

Leaders as effective people, using their talent to make a difference

The concept of good leaders as institution-builders was further reinforced in India in a recent study by T.V. Rao as a characteristic of super-effective people (Rao, 2015). He defines an effective person as one '. . . who discovers inner talent, uses it to make a difference in the lives of other people in a way that benefits them'. He maintains that the one who discovers talent, puts it to good use and makes a difference in the lives of others, can be considered an effective person. Everyone is born with some inherited talent but in widely varying circumstances, sometimes adverse. Some master these adversities and use their inner talent to push ahead. These people can come from any walk of life. On the basis of his analysis of around seventy effective, very effective and super-effective persons, Rao identifies the following eight qualities as characterizing these persons, based on those common to all effective persons drawn from teachers, social workers, doctors, nurses, lawyers, entrepreneurs, civil servants, development workers, businessmen, managers, chartered accountants, scientists, actors and self-employed professionals, among others:

1. They think differently;
2. They stretch their talent by exploring new vistas and opportunities;

3. They consider values as core drivers;
4. They are compassionate;
5. They live with purpose;
6. They reach out to many;
7. They take initiative and build institutions; and
8. They are integrative; not divisive

Rao's study found super-effective persons to be institution-builders, who continually make a difference in the lives of others.

Building others as leaders

Noel Tichy (1997) maintains that there is leadership talent in everyone. A leader-driven organization is a winning one and has leadership at all levels. Such organizations produce leaders as contrasted with others that are not similarly served by quality leadership. Further, Tichy asserts that great leaders are great teachers. They accomplish their goals through the people whom they teach and they teach them to be leaders, not followers. Winning leaders create energy in others and they motivate with their enthusiasm and actions, stretch goals and inspire ambitious effort.

Great leaders make a difference

Zenger and Folkman (2002) used a 360° feedback approach in their book, *The Extraordinary Leader: Turning Good Managers into Great Leaders* (McGraw-Hill). Zenger and Folkman studied about 20,000 managers from whom they received 360° feedback on different tools. They were estimated to have been assessed by around 2,00,000 managers who constituted their peers, bosses, juniors and themselves. They presented the following insights on leadership from their study of the managers who became leaders:

- Great leaders make a huge difference;
- One organization can have many great leaders;
- Great leadership is about possessing several building blocks;
- The building blocks include character, personal capabilities, ability to focus on results, interpersonal skills and the ability to lead organizational change

Drucker (2004) identified eight practices that make an executive effective. He maintained that effective executives need not be leaders. Peter Drucker wrote on leadership (Cohen, 2020): 'Leadership is the lifting of a man's vision to higher sights, the raising of a man's performance to a higher standard, the building of a man's personality beyond its normal limitations.' To accomplish this, the purpose of an organization must be to enable ordinary people to do extraordinary things. Thus, while others talked of the need for organizations and their people to be properly managed, Drucker emphasized that they must be properly led. While others called integrity and social responsibility desirable characteristics of a good leader, Drucker maintained that they were mandatory characteristics to achieve the leadership that he envisioned (Cohen, 2020). Cohen said that practising social responsibility was as important as practising integrity and equally essential. One needs to be ethical and socially responsible to be a good leader (Cohen, 2020 on Peter Drucker).

Baking and growing leaders

On the basis of her research and studies at the Centre for Creative Leadership across the last three decades, Cynthia McCauley (Baker, 2014) suggests the following five types of assignments for developing leaders on the job:

- Cross-functional opportunities are critical for gaining the broader experience that all top executives need;
- Assignments that require them to lead a change initiative;
- Situations with higher stakes, where the executive has to make critical decisions under tight deadlines, with the situation providing him or her with higher visibility within the organization;
- Assignments that require them to work across organizational or geographical boundaries and situations in which executives have to use their influence rather than the authority of their position to get things done; and
- Assignments that require them to deal with diverse people, from different nationalities and cultures, or gender or from different professional and occupational backgrounds

Crucible of leadership

Bennis and Thomas (2002), in their quest for discovering how leaders are developed, came up with the seminal 'crucible of leadership' concept. In their life's journey, people go through some defining experiences that make for personal metamorphosis. Extraordinary leaders literally get baked through these intense experiences and emerge stronger and transformed. Bennis and Thomas called such events 'crucibles', after the vessels that medieval alchemists used in their attempts to turn base metal into gold. Crucibles could be violent and sometimes even life-threatening. They could also be positive yet profoundly challenging under demanding bosses. Leaders learn from both of these experiences.

In our study of HR Leaders, we have attempted to understand the crucible of experiences that they went through in their journeys, the lessons they learnt and how such experiences baked them to become who they became.

Changing Role of HRD and HR Leaders (HRLs)

The status of the HR function has been formally elevated across the world, particularly so in India. The enhancement of the top HR position to the director level in companies and the incorporation of the function into the board, with HR directors on corporate boards, provide ample testimony to the corporate recognition of 'people', not just as a resource but partners in business as well. This is what was explicitly envisaged in some ways when the first HRD department was designed in Larsen & Toubro in the mid-seventies. Elsewhere, the HR function also got expanded with some new initiatives.

Effective HR leaders

We hold that an HR professional should qualify on one or more of a dozen criteria to be considered an effective HR leader:

1. Position: should have occupied or be occupying a leadership position as Chief Executive Officer (CEO), Chairman and Managing Director (CMD), Managing Director (MD), director HR, Chief Human Resource Officer (CHRO), president HR, executive president or equivalent;

2. Recognition: should be recognized by the peer group as an HR Leader and be invited to talks, webinars, lectures;

3. Awards: should have received honours and awards from professional bodies like the NHRDN, NIPM, CII, AIMA or institutions like XLRI, TISS, IIMs, IITs and such others;

4. Thought leadership: should have contributed as a thought leader to new concepts, theories, practices, frameworks and approaches to HRD or any other people-related function;

5. Media presence: should be active on social media

6. Authorships: should have written books and have published articles;

7. Mentorships: should have mentored and coached others and be acknowledged as a mentor and coach;

8. Impactful: should be acknowledged for having made a difference in the professional or personal lives of a group of people, organizations, society and such others;

9. Leading initiatives: should have been invited by the government and other agencies to lead teams, groups, projects, reforms and such other initiatives;

10. Transformational role: should have created a role for oneself and transformed an organization, a department or a business unit and be acknowledged for such an accomplishment;

11. Leadership of professional bodies: should have led professional bodies and task forces and contributed to the development of the profession; and

12. Much quoted: one should be a figure of authority on innovative thinking, a point of reference, the go-to person for the profession, be oft-quoted by other professionals and sought after for sharing one's wisdom and perspectives in areas of interest to the profession

The HRLs covered in our study, by and large, meet most of these criteria.

Methodology and Approach

This project, initiated by Arvind Agrawal (first author), was essentially to trace the process whereby such exceptional HR Leaders were groomed.

The authors were influenced by the 'crucible' experiences outlined by Warren Bennis and Robert Thomas (Bennis and Thomas, 2002) and sought to grasp the crucible experiences that these HRLs went through while transforming themselves into leaders. Our questions were simple yet deeply penetrating:

- What was the nature of these crucible experiences that our HR leaders had from early childhood—at home, in schools, in the colleges that they attended—at their first jobs, the many lessons picked up from their bosses and the various functions that they handled by virtue of being in the HR profession?
- How did these HR leaders find meaning and substance in—and learn from—the most significant positive or negative events in their life journey?
- How did they deal with these experiences, or internalize lessons from them, and emerge from adversity stronger, more confident about themselves and their purpose, more committed to their work and more innovative as they went about making a difference to the function and other people around?

Over the past four or five decades, we have been working, through our association with the NHRDN, shoulder to shoulder with several very impressive senior HR leaders in a variety of roles. They have been passionate, impactful and constantly stretching to contribute toward the development of the HR profession. They have also been well-regarded in their own organizations, making meaningful contributions in addressing the 'people' agenda while helping the business grow over the years. Some of them have graduated from leading management institutes like the IIMs, XLRI and TISS and rose to be world-class HR professionals, and others have even risen to become CEOs of large businesses.

Yet others have moved from business roles to be very successful HR leaders in eminent enterprises, both in the private and public sectors. We saw some home-grown HR professionals thriving internationally and making a mark globally. We are honoured to have been privy to some of their early childhood stories; they are fascinating in their variety and invariably impressive. We have anecdotal accounts of their struggles and the excitement around the vibrant growth journeys that many of them have successfully undertaken. We have been awestruck by the resilience many of them have demonstrated and sought to delve into the secret sauces that propelled them to come up trumps.

It was clear that often spectacular growth would not have been possible without the sustaining support of the families that they were born into; the teachers who moulded their minds in their formative years of education in schools, colleges and professional institutions; and their bosses and peers who have been partners, mentors and coaches during their careers. These influencers touched their lives and shaped their mindsets. Often, their spouses have provided a silently salubrious home environment that helped them retain their value systems as they evolved over their working careers. This entire body of influence over their careers makes for richly inspiring stories that these remarkable HR leaders acknowledge, as they retraced their steps with us. These are accounts that should fire the imagination of young professionals, who can evolve into next-generation HR leaders, committed to nation-building while making a huge difference in the organizations that they serve and to society at large.

These stories hold equally important lessons for the families, teachers, academic institutions and practising managers seeking to make such worthwhile contributions in baking and producing the next-generation of HR leaders. To our surprise, we realized that while much has been researched and written about how CEOs were made, there is a curious dearth of literature on how HR leaders have been baked over the years. What role did their families play in moulding the characters of their young, to empower them to evolve into great HR leaders? What about teachers who touched their lives and did wonders in shaping the thinking of their students to help them grow into such responsible professionals? How do organizations and bosses nurture talent to bake them further, sustaining their evolution into impactful HR leaders?

The denouement of the HR story that we envisaged wrote itself out, as we undertook a systematic study of successful HR leaders whom we have known over the years. We wanted to know their unique stories and then see if there was a pattern to this baking process. We were curious to discover the methods that worked and to draw lessons that could guide the families, teachers and managers on what they can do to bake effective HRLs in the future.

Framework

For the purpose of this study, we came up with a framework as shown in Figure 1.

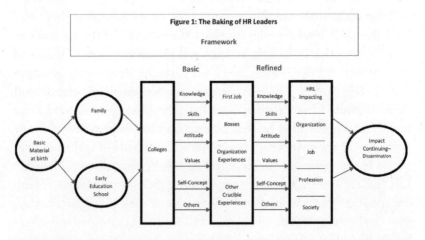

Figure 1: The Baking of HR Leaders

This framework shows a person's journey from birth. One is born with one's genes, the basic natural, god-given 'material', which in many ways account for one's natural orientations.

One's basic DNA is impacted upon by experiences within the family as well as in school. The twin tracks run parallel. The beliefs, values and behaviour of parents and others in the family have a deep impact on the child. The stories the child hears, the way it gets treated or experiences others being treated by the family, the family's lifestyle, conversations at the dinner table and even with the neighbours; everything impacts the pliable mental model—the dough—in specific ways. Alongside, the teachers' handling of the young minds in the school, the teaching style, subjects that are taught, focus on extracurricular activities, the behaviour of the peer groups and such other experiences have an equally lasting impact on the child.

To go by our framework, after the family and school comes the college that the youth goes to for professional education or higher studies in the general stream. Here too, teachers and professors impact and inspire the youth with their distinctive styles of pedagogy. The student graduates from college with some basic knowledge, skills as well as attitudes, values and self-awareness. This is 'basic' because it is the outcome of the baking done by the family, school and college as the individual attains late adolescence.

Thus armed, the person enters the 'workplace', where the next level of baking takes place. This happens courtesy the nature of work, the initial assignments in the first job and over the subsequent roles, which is further tempered by the way the bosses treat the young recruit and how the recruit receives and responds to the assignments and instructions. These then form the crucible of experiences that the individual has over the journey through the work life. This crucible refines the basic knowledge, skills, attitude and aptitude, the value system and the concept or awareness about the self that the individual holds vis-à-vis others in the work-sphere and, often, about the world in general.

Our systematic study of the creative process making HR leaders follows this framework. To accomplish this, we brainstormed to arrive at a list of highly accomplished HR leaders whom we had come across during our own professional work. This list ran rather long; almost sixty-plus. We then filtered the list using Rao's criteria for 'effective leaders'. This helped us identify thirty-two HR leaders whom we were keen to study in depth. We reached out to all of them and secured their buy-in into this project essentially because it would create a body of work to record the massive—and little documented—advances made by the profession. Only two did not agree to participate in this study.

One declined because she was planning her own autobiography and felt that this study would pretty much cover the same ground. Regrettably, the other person actually gave us all the time we needed for the interviews but backed out when he went over the output and realized that he was not comfortable with putting out such detailed private information in the public domain. He withdrew, leaving us with thirty HRLs, covering all segments of the economy, from manufacturing to services in both the public and private sectors. Regrettably again, on the gender front, the sample is somewhat askew with only two women HR leaders. This is one limitation of this study. There is perhaps a case for studying the unique aspects around the moulding of women HRLs, if any, by covering a larger number of women leaders in the profession.

Further, this study only focuses on seasoned HR leaders who have been CHROs and have more than thirty years of corporate experience. It has not covered the younger HR professionals, even though we are conscious of the large number of high-calibre young HR professionals in corporate India today. They bear testimony to the steady growth of the HR profession in the country. This study misses out on these outstanding professionals. There are also several seasoned HR professionals holding very senior HR positions in global organizations, located overseas. Our study covers only one such HRL. The study also does not cover the specialists, consultants, learning and development (L&D) professionals and coaches of outstanding calibre because it consciously focused on the baking of those professionals who have been CHROs.

It bears emphasizing that while our HRLs have been trailblazers in their contributions to their organizations, the profession as well as society at large, we are not suggesting that they are the only HRLs who have done so. There are many more who have been highly impactful as HRLs and we could have reached out to them. This is not, however, a quantitative research and we chose to limit our study to thirty exceptional HRLs, without implying that they have been the top thirty HRLs in the country. Our collection most definitely includes some of the best, but we reiterate that there are many more outside our universe. The accounts of the participating HRLs speak for themselves as incredibly successful professionals who have been highly effective, in terms earlier defined by Rao.

Our study involved in-depth conversations with each of the HRLs, traversing their life journeys from infancy to school and college, capturing sensitive moments and defining experiences before moving on to their corporate careers. We meticulously probed for their crucible of experiences because that understanding would hold the key to our research. What were those experiences? What were the inflexion points? What choices did they make to become who they became? We did have a set of questions (Appendix 1) to guide us and ensure that we captured everything that was essential for this study over the interactions. However, we needed freewheeling conversations that ran into several hours, ranging from three to ten hours, spanning several meetings to catch the sensitive points; the nuances.

These were largely in-person meetings with at least one of us. Sometimes both of us joined in the conversations. These were supplemented by Zoom calls whenever more detailed probing was required. With the outbreak of the pandemic, the meetings were held over Zoom. We made copious notes and also recorded the conversations. We also looked at papers and articles written by the HRLs and, occasionally, even attended webinars to listen to their position on different aspects of the profession for supplementary insights. We allowed for rambling to get to little nuggets of information on the moulding process that the HRLs went through but have not necessarily narrated every detail in the case studies. The idea was to suss out the moral in the stories, the lessons in the experiences.

These conversations quite often turned very emotional; they were soulful, heartfelt and deeply moving moments for us because, though we believed that we knew most of these HRLs well, having worked closely with them in many professional forums for several years, the details were eye-opening. Not till the HRLs began to tell us their stories did we realize the gaps in our understanding. How little we knew them, having taken their accomplishments at face value and never really having delved beneath the surface! Our notions were at best shallow, having known nothing of their struggles. For some, revisiting their past systematically, deeply reflecting on their voyage through life, sharing the high and low points, often for the first time, with anyone in such detail, was at times cathartic, at others joyous, occasionally poignant and always deeply steeped in value-driven learnings.

These were shared with the utmost confidence because of their faith in our professionalism and the knowledge that they would have the right to review their revelations and edit anything that could unwittingly embarrass someone or tread on someone's toes, which was not the purpose of the exercise. Our intent was to discover the internal processes in the recesses of their minds, the baking process and not to sensationalize through corporate exposure. We remained mindful of this as we drew them out into sharing stories that were theirs and theirs alone to tell, even as we ensured that no material learning was missed out in the process.

The voluminous information gathered through the recordings, supplemented by our handwritten notes—each transcribed material running into about 100 pages and more for some—presented the next big challenge. We had to decide what to keep and what to eliminate;

keep the meat and let go of the minutiae; sieve out the substance for our use, as it were. These case studies were not intended to be exhaustive accounts of the invigorating life journeys of the HRLs. They were intended to garner insights, through glimpses into such slices of their lives that would provide us with an understanding of the crucible of experiences that they went through to reach the pinnacles that they did.

Methodology Used in Analysis and Drawing Lessons

It was then necessary to proceed step by step for developing the case studies and then analysing them for 'crucible experiences', identifying patterns, if any, and drawing out the essential:

- Consolidating the case studies and preparing shortened versions; capturing the essential points by following our framework: early socialization and parentage, childhood experiences, school and college experiences, first job, first boss and later experiences. With the help of professional editors, we prepared our draft case histories.
- Mailing our case histories and crucible experiences to the respective HRLs for factual corrections and approval. Since the material was based on detailed interviews with the HRLs, it stood to reason that they would be the best resource for vetting and approving them. Every HRL took pains to go through the case histories that we presented to them, made amendments, ensured that the content and the nuances were right and sent their approval. In a couple of cases, there were further deliberations, when the HRL was keen to delete some incidents and we had to persuade them to let them remain for the sheer 'baking value' that they contained. The HRLs were kind enough to oblige.
- Converting texts into draft case studies was the next step we took and gave ourselves a body of thirty worthwhile stories to fine-tune. The draft case studies in place—and even as the HRLs were going over the final texts—we started analysing the cases by listing: (i) the crucible moments experienced by the individual, (ii) competencies indicated by the experiences narrated, (iii) values or value indicators, and (iv) timeless lessons from the HRL's case study. The box below

illustrates the process followed for the analysis, using one HRL as an illustration. For this process, both of us conducted independent analyses for a few HRLs and then exchanged notes. We repeated this process for ten HRLs to establish inter-rater consistency. That done, both of us examined the rest independently. Once our findings were merged, the final analysis of the crucible experiences was ready and the competency indicators, value indicators and lessons were listed out.

Box 1: Illustrative list of crucible moments, competency indicators, value indicators and lessons for one of the HRLs

Crucible Moments

Birth: Born in a farmer's family, deeply engaged in the freedom movement.

Parentage: Father in civil service. Highly patriotic family.

Schooling: Schooled at St Columbus; topper like his father, captain of sports, excellent in dramatics.

Derailer: Constant headache and burning eyes. Made him opt out of pursuing academics any further. Turned to spiritualism.

MBA: Tier 1 global university.

Learning: Saw the connection between good business and connecting with people.

General Manager: Dealing with external stakeholders/goondas/ hostile mobs, who were often armed, constant threat to life.

MD of XXXX :   Serious setback.

Tough assignment: 'Get us out of the hole' as the mandate for managing a company in the soup with huge losses.

Action: Involved closing down units, job losses for workers as well as top management.

Friction: Differences of views with chairman of the board, leading to separation from the company.

Values

Socialist views
Spiritual
Creating economic wealth in an ethical way for making India better
Creating happiness in the lives of people and serving mankind while
creating wealth
Sympathies for the underdog
Give 100 per cent of oneself—mind-body-soul—for the cause
Humility
Sensitivity
Truthfulness
Inclusive

Competencies

Very good in people connect
Avid reader
Deep interest in the theatre
Creative
Disciplined
Courageous to take tough decisions
Dealing with law and order in managing township

Timeless Lessons

Relevance of spirituality.

There are many factors that control the outcome. It is not the result of just what you do. So if things don't happen, don't blame yourself. There are five factors that produce results—your effort is one of them.

One failure does not define you forever. Equanimity to take success and failure in one's stride.

You don't have to be right all the time.

Do not lose your basic values just because of one adverse experience with one individual.

Give in return for all that you have received.

- We then revisited the case studies to elaborate on the crucibles, competencies, values and lessons. It was at this stage that we decided to present our analysis in four chapters: The crucible that baked the leaders, competencies that were developed or demonstrated in the process of their life (including those from the manner in which they handled crucible and other experiences), values and lessons. We further classified crucibles and lessons into stages of the HRL's journey, based on our framework (early socialization, schools and colleges, first job and such others).

- Remaining flexible was crucial and we used categories other than those that were included in the framework, as they emerged. For example, we did not expect that dealing with industrial relations would emerge as a significant crucible that baked many of our leaders. The chapter on crucible experiences presents the final classification.

- Focusing on the insights became important as we started writing the chapter on crucible experiences and we realized that a mere description of the crucible moments, without some insights and lessons, was providing a very limited understanding of the HRL. We decided to combine the crucible moments with the lessons and wrote what emerged as the main chapter of our analysis, presented in the second part of this book. This chapter on crucible moments and experiences is the core of this book and presents several insights into the baking of the HRLs. This was followed by a chapter presenting an analysis of the competencies. When we completed our analysis of this process, we identified 586 competency indicators for the thirty HRLs.

- Classifying these indicators was the next thing to do and they were given different labels as we visited them, classified them and reclassified them. After several iterations, we finalized a list of twenty common competencies, occurring and recurring for the thirty HRLs or most of them. This excludes a few other competency indicators that we could not classify under these twenty. Chapter 4 in part II presents these competencies and their indicators. The chapter also validates competency frameworks done by other agencies in India and globally.

- Arriving at values meant using a similar process to list out various values and value indicators. We came up with a list of 242 values and value indicators. We further grouped these indicators and finally came up with a list of nineteen recurring values. This is presented in chapter 5 of part II.

The book concludes with significant lessons thrown up by the baking of the thirty HRLs. The last chapter summarizes our findings for use by various groups.

In the Appendices section, this book provides tools for self-assessment of competencies and values. Further, there is a 'crucible experience planner' that can be used by HR professionals to actively seek out and immerse in the meaningful experiences for self-development.

2

Case Studies

Anand Nayak

Humane institution-builder

Creating social capital by creating wealth in the organization

Anand Nayak serves as a non-executive, independent director at ITC. A postgraduate in personnel management and industrial relations from XLRI, Jamshedpur, Anand passed out in 1973 and joined ITC in the same year. He served the company without a break for more than forty-two years until his retirement in December 2015. During his impactful tenure, Nayak held various portfolios and worked across several businesses as well as at the corporate headquarters, where he headed the human resources function from 1996 to 2015. He also served on the Corporate Management Committee of ITC for more than eighteen years, from 1997 to 2015. Anand was responsible for the overall superintendence of the social sector initiatives under ITC's corporate social responsibility (CSR) agenda and mentored the Mission Sunehra Kal team in crafting enduring sustainability solutions for rural India.

'Teachers make a man; exemplary parents make a man and eventually man makes himself.'

Son of a bureaucrat, an IAS officer in Karnataka, Anand Nayak enjoyed the advantage of growing up in an environment in which human values and service were accorded high priority. The focus of the family was on making a difference in the lives of others, thanks to an inspirational father, who served with integrity and commitment; and a mother, who devoted a lot of her time to community service. She managed both her home and community welfare work with equal élan.

This family influence apart, the Jesuit priests who ran the educational institutions that Anand studied in throughout his academic career were an immense source of inspiration right through his school and college days at St Joseph's Boys High School, Bangalore, St Joseph's College, Bangalore and the Xavier Labour Relations Institute (XLRI), Jamshedpur. The education imparted in these Jesuit institutions focused equally on academics and community service; on working with the poor in urban slums and rural areas, and spending a couple of weeks during every school and college vacation at rural work camps under the watchful eyes of Jesuit priests. Such experiences, supplemented by the 'service to others' concept instilled at home, became a core value proposition in Anand's life.

In the late 1960s, it was not uncommon for young graduates to consider emigrating to countries offering easier options for making a comfortable living. Many of his contemporaries packed their bags and moved overseas for a better future. Anand, however, was determined to stay on in the country of his birth, struck by a patriotic fervour that had by then been ingrained in him and strengthened by the galvanizing association with a Father Peter Ceyrac, SJ, whom he thought the world of. Father Ceyrac was a Frenchman who had made India his home for more than forty years. Anand vividly recalls listening to Father Ceyrac sometime in 1968, addressing the students in his quaint French accent and with tears in his eyes, exhorting them to 'Stay on and work for the people of your country. Only rats desert a sinking ship.'

After completing his bachelor's studies at St Joseph's College in Bangalore, Anand took a year off to volunteer with a students' organization, working full-time, organizing leadership and work camps for youth from all over India. It was at this time that Anand started to interact with leftist thinkers and activists, who added a whole new dimension to his world view. At that impressionable age, fighting against injustice and working to build a just and equitable social order became a priority.

Anand's sister, Nalini, a couple of years his senior, was just as strongly influenced by the spirit of service and has been a community worker and social activist in Kerala. Fresh out of college, she started with the protest movement over the rehabilitation of the villagers displaced by the construction of the Thumba Rocket Launching Station in the early 1960s, on the outskirts of Trivandrum. Imbued with the conviction that economic development must ensure that every citizen lives a life of social and economic dignity, she has devoted the past fifty years of her life to working for the benefit of the disadvantaged sections of society and fighting for their rights. Visiting Nalini at Thumba, Anand witnessed the protests developing into a movement by the affected fishing community. Nalini, now seventy-three, continues in the same spirit and is a constant source of inspiration for Anand.

Life was setting him up for a career focused on people as Anand travelled to XLRI, where every engaging encounter steeled his early intentions. The course was not just academically rewarding, the personal interactions with the priests, faculty and students were everything that a young man could have hoped for. Although Father Ed McGrath did not take regular classes, his very presence on campus and the nature of his work that he informally shared with the students, created an environment of self-discovery and self-learning. Father Joe Kennedy, the director, was a visionary and Professors Jitu Singh, T.K. Karunakaran, C.G.K. Nair, Sudas Roy and Nilima Acharji were down-to-earth members of the faculty, whose deep intellect and personal humility inculcated in the students the values of respecting and caring for people, irrespective of their stations in life.

There was a deeper purpose to learning here. The faculty involved themselves with every aspect of the students' lives, nurturing and supporting them, even while giving them their personal space to grow and discover themselves through the many activities that the institute initiated. Gaining institutional salience was also important to both the faculty and students, as they recognized that if the graduates from XLRI had to compete with students from the IIMs for opportunities in the corporate sector, brand XLRI would need to be positioned more aggressively. Anand was among those who became committed partners to the act of institution-building. The lessons learned in this entire process would stand the students in good stead when applied in their professional lives.

Towards end-1972, the students decided to host a Management Meet, inviting senior members of the corporate world to share their world view with them. This was the first-ever pan-India event involving all the premier management schools. The initiative was driven entirely by the students with background support from the faculty. Students toiled 24/7, without bothering about personal recognition because they were working to significantly enhance the positioning of XLRI in the corporate world. Industry stalwarts of the time like Russi Mody, R.S. Pandey, S.B. Aibara, T.S. Nagarajan among others, addressed the students, making deep impressions on the young minds. Anand recalls that this one event had a huge bearing on his own understanding of the corporate world.

The Management Meet also provided students with invaluable exposure as it positively altered public perception of the institute. XLRI quickly established its reputation as a frontline centre for learning. The two years that Anand spent there empowered him to become more proactive, enhanced his bandwidth considerably and strengthened his interpersonal effectiveness. It also enabled the 'leader' within to emerge and helped him to evolve into a more well-rounded individual, who could contribute meaningfully to the human resource management profession. During the campus interviews in 1973 and ITC visited XLRI, picking up the twenty-two-year-old Anand Nayak for the role of a lifetime.

The criticality of the deep HR–business connect had not yet dawned even in a progressive company like ITC. Within four years, Anand found himself as HR Manager of ITC's packaging and printing factory in Tiruvottiyur, Tamil Nadu, where he gathered meaningful insights into the employer–employee relationship. The most telling of these was the clearly adversarial positions that managements and unions adopted. By virtue of being the union, it had to be anti-management. Managements, too, considered unions as adversaries without even considering that there could be anything collaborative in this relationship; nothing by way of a shared commitment to organizational goals!

Over time—and after making serious errors when managing the complex arena of industrial relations—Anand embarked on a process of reimagining HR, whereby it would shift from a policy-driven approach to a strategy-driven one. HR policies and systems in this evolving paradigm would be geared to enhancing not just employee well-being but customer value as well, with a telling impact on the bottom line. He also realized that antagonistic positions were bred by management mindsets, with managers not 'valuing' the worker nor treating even those much senior to them in age, with respect. They were, at best, patronizing in their approach.

Anand picked up quick cues: the ability to listen and provide 'psychological air' to people—be it a colleague, direct report, union leader or shop floor worker—was of primary importance. Alongside, every engagement had to be informed by humility and a keenness to learn from others, irrespective of their position in the hierarchy. These were character-building qualities that empowered him to stand up and take responsibility and establish himself as a person with credibility. When chairman Ajit Narain Haksar came on a plant visit in 1980, Anand, along with three young colleagues, made a presentation to him on a fresh approach to HR.

Anand underscored the need to be fairer and more generous and treat employees in a spirit of genuine interdependence. In typical Haksar style, the chairman said that the company was a 'commercial, not a charitable' organization; that generosity could only follow the generation of a surplus. Anand admits that he was disappointed with the chairman's response, as it appeared to come from a 'capitalist' and exploitative perspective. However, on reflection, this dialogue with the chairman must have struck a chord, because in it lay the genesis of Anand's own mental linkage between HR and business. He realized that he ought to look at business differently; that business per se did not have to be exploitative and that businesses could be managed successfully, keeping the interests of all stakeholders in mind.

This dialogue was played back later in his frequent interactions with the ITC chairman Y.C. Deveshwar, with whom Anand worked closely for nearly twenty-five years. It underscored the need for deepening employee engagement in order to focus on enhancing competitiveness and generating a surplus for the benefit of all stakeholders. The seeds of this thought were actually sown much earlier, when the HR team at ITC's factory at Tiruvottiyur negotiated a long-term agreement (LTA) with the union, encompassing not just robust wage hikes but work practices as well. The management team and union leadership sat together for the first time, simultaneously discussing both the Union's Charter of Demands and Management's Proposals for Increased Productivity.

The idea was to align union demands with management expectations and Anand headed a six-member pan-ITC task force on the approach to the LTA, covering various dimensions such as merging basic wages, dearness allowance neutralization, retirement benefits, technology upgradation, rightsizing, incentive payments and productivity enhancements. This approach is common practice today but in the mid-to-late 1970s, it was pioneering. The outcome was a framework for future dialogue between the management and the unions. The 'Long Term Agreements in ITC: Principles and Policies' was prepared as a comprehensive document for managing employee relations across the company.

Very soon, a new generation workforce was at hand with changed expectations vis-à-vis their relations with management. With a new crop of younger union leaders, a serious disconnect re-emerged between the company and its unions. The psychologically relational contract, built in the late 1970s and in the 1980s, was no longer acceptable to a younger leadership that believed more in a transactional interface with little faith in such values as mutual trust and interdependence as then existed. The process of rebuilding the spirit of partnership and mutuality had to start all over again but this time with a difference. The needs, aspirations and priorities of a younger workforce had to be first understood and then channelized appropriately. This was a new challenge that the HR team of ITC had to address.

The HR team realized that this challenge could be addressed only if there was a paradigm shift in mindsets across the organization, whereby unions would be considered partners and stakeholders in the enterprise; not as adversaries. The successful transition to the new mindset brought about a drastic change in the manner in which management related to the union leadership. There was greater willingness to share the gains of productivity more equitably with employees, be transparent in administering rewards, and be more open to discussing the need for and implications of changes in technology and work practices with the unions. This tectonic shift from an adversarial relationship to one of commonality of purpose and alignment with a shared vision took place in the late 1980s, completely changing the nature of employer-employee relations in the company.

In the process, it achieved quantum leaps in productivity and enhanced competitiveness, with employees enjoying a larger share of the surpluses generated. Indeed, this new way of looking at things prepared the grounds for ITC to start on its next phase of transformation in the mid-1990s, catalysed by revisiting mindsets in every aspect of the company's operations. Another marked shift in perspectives followed. From a late 1970s' position of domestic competition being the only competitive concern, ITC changed its outlook by the early eighties and positioned itself in the global competitive landscape. This meant another paradigm shift vis-à-vis quality benchmarks and a radical change in cigarette-manufacturing technology, packaging and brand-building. The dramatic transformation over two years made its own demands on ITC's human resources, which was driving the change. On the one hand, the company aspired to be among the world's best and, on the other, it wanted to seize a larger share of the tobacco—not just the cigarette—market.

This led to expansive thinking within the company that now wanted a larger shelf space with a vastly varied fare, leveraging its current competencies to create a new engine of growth. Progressively, ITC built a substantial presence in hotels and the Indian fast moving consumer goods (FMCG) space. Anand believes that changing mindsets and revisiting paradigms can make transformational change possible and that HR managers must look at this as an important dimension of their role. How does HR build a culture of inquiry and inquisitiveness, and constantly reflect to question existing ways of looking at challenges and continuously explore how challenges can be turned into opportunities for the business?

An incident in the late 1990s powerfully influenced Anand's thinking. Deveshwar and he were driving to the office one morning when, at a traffic intersection near Tata Centre, a physically challenged person came up to the car, begging for money. Anand reached out to him with a Rs 10 note, but Deveshwar came up with a unique response. He mentioned with sadness that 'there are millions of people in our country like this person. Giving them a few rupees when they approach us is one way of salving our conscience; but if we can grow our businesses exponentially, create surpluses and invest these surpluses to build infrastructure for new businesses—more hotels and more factories—and create more new engines of growth, we would be able to create sustainable livelihoods for millions of these people. The more value ITC creates, the more we can do to enable the disadvantaged sections of our society to live better and more wholesome lives.'

Deveshwar argued, 'If Indian companies do not create value and invest their surpluses to create new engines of growth, who really would? Only companies with an Indian soul can genuinely address the problems of our country.' This powerful insight induced a dramatic change in Anand's thinking, driving the realization that the role of HR must extend far beyond the enterprise. The questions that he posed to himself were: What does HR need to do to look beyond the shareholder; to look to making growth inclusive? How would it establish a congruence between creating shareholder value while simultaneously creating livelihoods and making a social impact? His answer was: by looking to create innovative business models that meaningfully establish this congruence.

Over the next five years, ITC introduced two business models to drive this congruence. It focused on domestic feedstock and on tribals and marginal farmers to consolidate their fragmented holdings and create pulpwood plantations. The other model was the e-Choupal that dispensed information to its constituency of farmers through online kiosks across villages on weather patterns, best farming practices and price trends to empower farmers to better address the vagaries of Indian agriculture. The HR team was sure that ITC's commitment to India and Indian society was a very powerful purpose that had huge meaning for all employees. This is the inherent strength of the work culture that ITC successfully built over the years and over several generations of employees.

What made Anand focus on the inextricable linkage of HR strategy with business strategy? Anand speaks of the great influence that Dave Ulrich and Wayne Brockbank had on his thinking when he attended a human resource strategy programme at the Michigan School of Business, Ann Arbor in 1995. It was then that he realized that HR is 'good HR' only if it impacts value creation, enhances customer value and generates surpluses; else it has limited value. This prompted him to ask himself a fundamental question: In what way am I contributing to delivering superior customer value and in what way can I impact the performance and profitability of my company? He also realized that each enterprise being unique, HR practices would have to be in sync with every unique context. Upon returning from Michigan, Anand was elevated as HR head of ITC, a position he held until his retirement in December 2015, with tremendous support from the chairman over the twenty years that he reported to him. Anand acknowledges how privileged he was to learn several unique dimensions of HR strategy and management from the chairman himself, although he was the HR leader of the company!

What were the aspects of his role that gave him a sense of deep fulfillment? Anand unhesitatingly points to his involvement as mentor of Mission Sunehra Kal (MSK) from its inception in the year 2000 until his retirement in 2015. With Deveshwar's total backing, Anand initiated a comprehensive intervention to take the company's CSR agenda forward. This was long before CSR was mandated by law and incorporated in the Indian Companies Act. Deveshwar agreed to Anand's request to bring on board a younger former HR colleague, who had left ITC several years earlier to pursue his doctoral studies in developmental economics at The Hague. While Ashesh Ambasta conceptualized, articulated and implemented the MSK strategy, Anand, as MSK mentor, was always at hand, lending him support and guiding him towards directions in which the agenda could have the greatest impact.

MSK has grown from strength to strength over the years and has made significant contributions in the areas of social and farm forestry, livelihoods, women's empowerment, watershed management, wasteland development, value-added agriculture, drinking water and sanitation, health and hygiene, supplementary education and skill development. The objective of this initiative was to ensure that, in each of these communities, every woman would have an independent source of income, there would not be a single out-of-school child, all young men would be employable, having acquired a relevant skill, there would be no open defecation and every home would have access to potable drinking water. The team made this possible and realized this dream within a few years.

Establishing a culturally supportive space for innovative interventions in the linkage between HR strategies and practices and business performance required care and sensitivity. Anand confesses to getting lost in trivia during the learning process but life was all about new learnings. Developing competencies of HR professionals, creating linkages between HR practices and business strategies, establishing processes for engendering a competitive corporate culture, information dissemination and responsiveness to turbulence in the business environment, accelerating the pace of change through institutional practices and leveraging organizational capabilities for competitive advantage were all part of this new ball game.

The entire process was driven by the HR team and other business leaders. HR changed organically to be helpful to people at all times; giving its constituency the conviction that it only had to ask for help and the help would be forthcoming. On the flip side, HR actions were a source of emotional stress at personal and professional levels, especially when it came to managing redundancies. These had to be addressed by HR's helping hand, which was to be the key differentiator for HR under Anand. Nevertheless, it was a severe emotional challenge for him given the deep personal equations that he had with some of those whose exit from the organization he was to facilitate. To him, they were not just names on the company's rolls. Traumatizing though such experiences were, Anand accepted that they had to be done and handled the partings with as much sensitivity as possible, without the person facing any loss of dignity. He guided them to different options that would eventually help them reposition themselves meaningfully.

Other experiences were edifying, with some great influences in his journey up the ITC rungs; some came from his peers. Robin Sengupta, Anand's senior in ITC by six years, held that it did not matter if he inducted someone into a position senior to himself in the hierarchy if that served his quest for nurturing talent. His philosophy was that if the organization needed talent superior to oneself, one should have no hang-ups about who was being hired. For Sengupta, the joy lay in hiring bright people and giving them the opportunity to grow; providing them with all the support in their professional journey; making it pleasant for them to settle in; ensuring that comforts around family were taken care of through good housing, help with children's admission in good schools, among others. The operating style was very 'inclusive' because everyone was included in what evolved as collaborative learning; reinventing the art of delivering HR solutions and working on mindset changes when needed.

While Anand's first and abiding love has been ITC, he interacted widely with the HR fraternity across the country. He believed there was much to learn from fellow HR professionals just as it was crucial to share learnings from his ITC experience with the profession. Anand took an active role in supporting the NHRDN, where his key message was that HR could play a far more crucial role than what was commonly expected. He felt that it was important for HR to dive deep in search of a new identity in this expansive and inclusive world. In 2004, Anand conceived of an exhaustive programme for the NHRDN. He had the best HR minds in the country interacting with HR managers to enlarge their understanding of strategic frameworks, models, the logic and process of linking HR strategy to organizational vision, competitive strategy and goals, and thereby enhance enterprise value. The objective was to develop senior professionals as strategic CHROs, learning the art of providing leadership in a competitive and customer-centric world. This programme continues to be organized even to this day and is arguably the most exhaustive HR development programme in the country.

In all of this, Anand saw himself as an enabler, developer and facilitator, never claiming ownership of the idea or its execution. Between 2005 and 2007, he served as the regional president (Eastern Region) of the NHRDN, helping local chapters in the region to provide value-added offerings to their members, in order to equip themselves better to enhance the quality and impact of their contributions. Over the four decades and more at ITC, Anand's world view shifted from being anti-capitalist and pro-socialist to a more pragmatic one based on the realization that if a society values democracy and democratic values, it must believe in the market economy. Only in a market economy was it possible to engineer a congruence between creating surpluses and creating and enhancing social and environmental capital, prompted by the understanding that economic activity is necessary to generate livelihoods and enable people to live with economic and social dignity.

In December 2015, having risen to the position of executive vice president and head of human resources and member of the corporate management committee, on which he served for nearly two decades, Anand retired. Not for long though. In July 2019, he was invited to join the ITC board as an independent director. There are very few examples of an individual pursuing the cause of institution-building throughout his career, remaining devoted to one organization, contributing to making it a frontrunner in the market while also making it humane and fair and among the most coveted companies that people wish to serve with. To go back to the basics, the values that he learnt in his youth—compassion and humility, respect for all irrespective of their social status, the dignity of labour, a truly secular outlook, standing up against exploitation, integrity and transparency—raised the bar to a formidable height but Anand has tried his best to reach it. He carried on in the same spirit at Samraksha, a non-governmental organization (NGO) that he has been associated with since 2006. Here too, he is making a difference to vulnerable lives, helping the process of empowering them to take charge of their own lives.

At some point in the past, Anand had said, 'Industrial relations is all about engaging with people, wanting to make a difference, staying the course and being prepared to run the marathon, having a passionate desire to leave a legacy of value and taking pride in the outcome.'

Clearly, Anand Nayak has walked the talk.

* * *

Anil Khandelwal

Chess master and transformational leadership

Using HRD interventions as a lever of change to engage employees and build leadership across the organization

Throughout his career, Anil K. Khandelwal has used human resource development as a lever of change in various jobs and situations. This included the seminal act of neutralizing the impact of militant trade unionism through people processes. He used HR interventions to engage with employees and build leadership across the organization. Anil documented his analysis, the 'tough love' philosophy and experiences, in three of his books: Dare to Lead, CEO: Chess Master or Gardener? *and* Transformational Leadership in Banking: Challenges of Governance, Leadership and HR in a Digital and Disruptive World.

A thought leader, author, speaker on leadership and governance, and an acclaimed authority on HR and leadership in the banking sector, Anil is a rare transformation leader who moved from an HR specialization to the CEO position in two large public sector banks (PSBs). He was featured among the 100 most powerful CEOs in India by the Economic Times consecutively for three years, between 2005 and 2008. Transforming the Bank of Baroda (2005–08) in particular, from a staid Indian public sector bank to a valuable international bank, has won him many awards, including the Asian Banker Singapore's Lifetime Achievement Award. His brand of HR leadership and its application in business turnaround also won him the Lifetime Achievement Award from the National HRD Network.

Anil Khandelwal chaired the government-appointed committee on HR in PSBs and was a member of the first Banks Board Bureau (BBB) appointed by the government for selecting whole-time directors in PSBs. He has been a United Nations Development Programme (UNDP) consultant to Tanzania's banking reform commission and also a short-term visiting professor at the Asian Institute of Management, Manila. Adviser to several corporates with positions on several company boards, Anil is also an acclaimed international keynote speaker. Besides, he has trained over 5000 leaders in India and abroad. Peter Cappelli (Wharton) calls him an HR Hero; Dave Ulrich (Michigan) describes him as an exceptional CEO and Tom Peters (author, In Search of Excellence*) rates him as a 'very wise leader'. He has been an adviser to such international consulting firms as Accenture, Booz and Company, Hewitt and KPMG.*

An ace HR leader turned ace banker, Anil Khandelwal exemplifies how excellence in human resource management can serve as the foundation for corporate leadership at its highest echelons. As chairman of two Indian PSBs, Anil presents himself as a remarkable ambassador for HR and its power to equip one with effective and strategic tools to manage even a large organization like a national bank. Anil establishes the route for leveraging HR to propel one to an organizational leadership role. His impactful leadership of two large banks prompted the government to appoint him chairman of a committee on human resources for the PSBs (popularly known as Khandelwal Committee 2010). As a member of the first Banks Board Bureau that was tasked to appoint full-time directors and part-time chairmen in PSBs, Anil drove reforms in the HR and leadership domain. As he confesses: 'I want to tell you right in the beginning that I did not choose to be in the HR profession.' Fortunately for the profession, it chose him.

Anil grew up in a home comprising barely 500 square feet of living space with his parents, three brothers and a sister. It was in a ramshackle building with a common bathroom, catering to about twenty people. He went to a Hindi-medium municipal school in an uninspiring environment with no peer pressure to do well, nor any aspirational influences except, possibly, the magnificent Taj Mahal visible from the family home terrace. The Taj lit up a bleak landscape. His father, an accountant with a timber company, raised his five children on a modest monthly salary. The children were encouraged to pursue studies even in those difficult times. Even more, Anil's parents consciously inspired him to fight against all odds in life. His father, a great disciplinarian with boundless energy, inculcated the spirit of hard work in Anil. His mother, the real backbone of the family, kept the morale high and did not allow anyone to succumb to despair.

It was only in class VI that he first learnt the English alphabet. Later, when pursuing graduation, Anil and a close friend in Agra College often studied in parks. It was his elder brother, Krishan Gopal, who broke through this indigency trap with a masters in sociology and Anil had a genuine role model. He inspired Anil to get a first division in his BSc. Krishan Gopal found an opening at New Delhi's Institute of Economic Growth from where he migrated to London in 1964 and continued to mentor Anil through extensive correspondence. His long letters taught Anil about world affairs as well. Equally instrumental in guiding Anil was his maternal uncle, Kailash Rawal, an unusually broad-minded, warm-hearted and a self-made man.

After graduation, Anil secured admission at the Harcourt Butler Technological Institute (HBTI), Kanpur, to study chemical engineering, financially supported by Rawal and Krishna Gopal. Anil learnt the criticality of timely help in shaping one's life. After completing engineering in 1970, Anil returned to Jaipur, staying with Kailash Rawal as he joined an MBA course at the University of Rajasthan.

While doing his MBA, Anil received and accepted an officers' cadre job offer from the Bank of Baroda. He needed to financially support his parents. It was while doing his MBA that Anil was fascinated by HR and marketing. He wanted to pursue one of the two disciplines.

Anil joined the Bank of Baroda, Johari Bazaar Branch, Jaipur, in January 1971 and felt like a square peg in a round hole in a chaotic work environment in the branch. Intense unionism, restrictive practices and lack of punctuality defined the workplace ethics of the branch. Even though a greenhorn, Anil was assigned a regular desk from day one, without any formal training or an induction programme. He found the job dull, the working environment disincentivizing and was on the verge of resigning, when he picked up the courage to write to the head of the personnel department at the corporate level, L.B. Bhide. He had little expectation of any response but, to his joy, Bhide responded positively and deputed him to a four-week induction-cum-branch banking programme at the staff college, Ahmedabad.

The unexpected and positive response taught Anil the importance of responding to all communications, which then became a hallmark of his leadership style. He quickly appreciated the value of empathy, responsiveness and a positive approach in dealing with employees' problems and acknowledged that his interest in HRD and leadership came from experiences like these. The Johari Bazar branch was the epicentre of an all-India staff agitation and was facing intense staff problems with a breakdown of customer service. During a militant agitation, the branch manager, A.A. Raval, was gheraoed for seven hours and even though he was the juniormost officer, Anil went to the police station to lodge an FIR against the union officials. The first demonstration of initiative and courage was there for all to see.

Raval was a brave manager. When officers of the branch suggested that he leave that evening by a side entrance because of the union slogan-shouting at the front door, Raval declined. He refused to display cowardice in a manager and Anil quickly learnt about leading from the front. The induction into a difficult environment also gave him insights into the dynamics of industrial relations (IR) problems. Anil developed an interest in IR and personnel management and realized that there was much that the management could do to better employee relations. Fortuitously, the bank advertised for a personnel officer. Anil applied and got selected for the Rajasthan zone itself. However, as the zone needed the services of the existing experienced personnel officer, given the ongoing staff agitation in Rajasthan, Anil was temporarily deputed to Lucknow in Uttar Pradesh (UP).

UP had many more branches than Rajasthan and the environment was much more complex with multiple unions. Anil was sent on an ad-hoc deputation for a few weeks till a regular senior personnel functionary was posted. His services were largely utilized to douse the IR fire in various branches, giving him hands-on experience of solving industrial relations problems in the branches. In the early seventies, both UP and Rajasthan were on an expansion spree and there were challenges galore in recruitment, rural postings and grievances on account of poor infrastructure and other shortcomings, exacerbating the IR issues. Anil soon learnt his first lessons in handling industrial relations.

Anil was deputed for a day to investigate and report on a case of manhandling of the manager of the main branch of Varanasi by the subordinate staff. An agitated Anil met the district magistrate (DM) to initiate appropriate actions to maintain law and order as the bank was a nationalized institution. Happy with what he had done, he reported his action to the regional manager (RM), who admonished him for this extreme step that could lead to a grave industrial relations problem. Anil visited the DM again, requesting him to refrain from any drastic action. It was now the DM's turn to admonish him for reversing his stand. Unfortunately, even the unions came to know about Anil approaching the DM and he became the target of the trade unions of all the banks in Varanasi. Matters got so out of hand that Anil had to seek police protection for himself and the branch manager and stay with him for twenty-five days while the employee agitation at the branch was addressed.

Anil learnt quickly and UP provided many such IR incidents over which his baking process had begun. He developed insights about the dynamics of union-management relations, the negotiation process and facing and handling crisis situations. More importantly, he learnt the value of authentic behaviour in dealing with problems and gradually established himself as a young and transparent officer whom even the unions had become fond of. All through his career, the union leaders from UP remained in touch with him. After about nine months, Anil was transferred back to Rajasthan, a little upset that he had received no feedback about his performance from his immediate boss, the RM, UP.

Anil shared his concern with his colleagues in the personnel department at the regional level. One of them allayed his worries by showing him a copy of a confidential letter written by the RM to the corporate office about Anil's performance. He pleaded with the corporate office to retain Anil's services in Lucknow in view of his excellent performance and hands-on problem-solving skills. Anil was left wondering about the RM's parsimony in communicating his appreciation to the person concerned. This was another lesson learnt about the value of timely appreciation and motivation, which he used extensively during his career.

Anil worked in the regional office, Rajasthan between 1974 and 1976 and rose swiftly. Only three years back, he was a junior officer in a branch struggling to adjust to the trying circumstances and now he was spearheading the personnel function for the entire region. Fresh from his Johari Bazar branch and UP experience, Anil made significant initiatives in officers' training and the industrial relations support system to branches. Based on his reputation as a hands-on personnel functionary, a local private bank, Bank of Rajasthan, made him a job offer to come aboard as a deputy personnel manager. It meant a big jump, both financially and in terms of position, and Anil moved to the Bank of Rajasthan (BOR) in 1976.

Anil quickly restructured the HR function of the bank in line with its aspiration of becoming big and expanding its wings to major macro towns in India. He handled both the IR and training function and introduced many innovative initiatives in reframing HR policies. The initial BOR experience was very satisfying but, with a change of CEOs, the emphasis for transformation got diluted. Thus, when he got an offer in 1980 to revert to his first bank, Bank of Baroda, as senior core faculty in HR, he accepted with alacrity. This was an opportunity to deepen his academic foundations in HR and also pursue his PhD in the salubrious surroundings of Ahmedabad Staff College. Small wonder that he eventually became the principal of the institution in 1993.

Anil's thirteen-year stint at the staff college was significant in many ways. Armed with his operational experience at the branch level, regional level and the corporate level at the Bank of Rajasthan, Anil had probing knowledge of the industrial relations problems plaguing the banking industry of the time. He lamented the plight of the branch manager who was sandwiched between the business expectations of the higher-ups and the ground level constraints on account of the intense IR problem. At the staff college, Anil launched an important programme on IR for the branch managers that was very well received. The feedback was just as telling. Groups of managers pointed out that the policy framework and mollycoddling of trade unions by the senior management had actually complicated the workplace environment.

Anil, who was diagnostic in his approach, wanted to study the phenomena of IR in the bank and registered for a PhD under N.R. Sheth, a leading authority on IR and later director, IIM Ahmedabad. He also completed his three-year law degree in the meantime. Ahmedabad gave him the space to think and write and Anil took to writing extensively on training, HRD, IR and organization development (OD) in leading journals as well as daily newspapers like the *Economic Times*. Besides, Anil came in contact with the redoubtable Udai Pareek and T.V. Rao, both professors at IIM Ahmedabad, who pioneered the concept of HRD based on their work in Larsen and Toubro (L&T). While Anil was fascinated by the HRD concept, he strongly felt that a trustful IR environment is a prerequisite for embarking on HRD interventions.

Both Pareek and Rao encouraged Anil to explore the symbiotic IR–HRD relationship that Anil felt would help create a trusting climate in the organization. He wrote about IR and HRD relationships. Pareek also encouraged Anil to complete his professional membership with the Indian Society of Applied Behavioural Science (ISABS). This helped Anil learn process intervention, so useful in organizational transformation work. Alongside, Pareek and Rao taught him the value of experimenting with alternate viewpoints and pursuing the search for some workable models of change. Anil's PhD under N.R. Sheth was quite challenging in terms of learning the rigour of research work. Sheth once told him that he was as much a co-researcher on this project and Sheth's humility taught Anil that humility in the top leader can encourage a positive work environment and culture.

Ahmedabad also opened up the world of professional networking and Anil became actively involved in setting up the Ahmedabad chapter of the National HRD Network. Prolific as a writer by now,

Anil authored and co-authored four books on personnel, IR and HRD, enhancing his professional standing, especially in HR in the banking and financial sectors. Anil was, by now, establishing himself as a thought leader in his domain and found himself invited as a UNDP consultant on HRD by the banking reforms commission, government of Tanzania. The dozen and one years at Ahmedabad made for a perfect baking process in the fields of training, industrial relations and HRD. Anil's strong articulation of his thought process, his penchant for writing and his acknowledged positions of significance in matters of banking meant being noticed by the top management. They could not but select him for a senior executive position in the corporate personnel function. Anil moved from Ahmedabad little knowing that his deep insight into people-related functions could catapult him to the CEO's position one day.

As Anil took over as assistant general manager (Personnel) in Mumbai, the bank's officers' association did not take kindly to it. Their plea was that Anil's original letter of appointment mentioned that his career path would remain confined to training. An embarrassed management, the CEO S.P. Talwar included, redesignated him as AGM Training to circumvent the objection. For the initial six months, Anil was virtually without any job as the training function operated from the staff college, Ahmedabad. Anil knew that the CEO intended to place him firmly in the mainstream personnel function and he used this lull to prepare himself for the mainstream role. He went through files and learnt about various policies on union–management issues, various settlements and court rulings. He also mastered executive profiles, their seniority levels, track record and appraisal ratings. Occasionally, Talwar involved him in executive placement decisions, appreciating Anil's prompt inputs. Slowly Talwar was developing a liking for him, sympathy apart for what happened to him.

During this period, the CEO and the GM (HR) slowly involved him in mainstream personnel decision-making. Within a year, Anil was promoted as deputy general manager, human resource management (HRM) and administration and was firmly brought into the mainstream HR function. Anil's period of isolation thus made for as perfect an induction process as one could ask for in a busy environment. However, even Talwar was destined for higher positions and soon took over as deputy governor of the Reserve Bank of India, but Anil had learnt the art of hands-on management with a human approach from him. He put it to good use in managing his future jobs. With Talwar's departure, Anil's future became uncertain at the corporate level as the new CEO, an old Bank of Baroda hand, found it difficult to resist the collective pressure of trade unions to move Anil from the mainstream personnel function. Anil was considered a kind of heretic by the trade unions for he showed no intention of being part of the status-quo culture in IR. He was thus suspected to be a reformer, who could be detrimental to union interests.

Against his wishes, Anil was sent to banking operations to head the western zone, in Meerut, UP. Yet, quickly learning the ropes, accepting coaching from his junior officers on key aspects of banking, Anil not only succeeded but thrived in his very first operational posting. He firmly believed that his success lay in empowering the 200 branch managers who reported to him. His diagnostic sessions with branch managers, several town hall sessions with all the employees at various locations and frequent visits to branches gave him insights into the prevailing work culture and quality of administrative supervision. On a visit to a medium-sized branch, he found the manager abstaining from work without authorization for over three months and was aghast to learn that he was working at a customer's firm in a neighbouring state. Even more frustrating was that the concerned RM and the personnel manager were aware of this misdemeanour but had not disclosed this to Anil. Such was the influence of the officers' association in personnel and administrative matters!

Visits to other branches exposed even more curious facets. Anil learnt that many key decisions about business were stuck either in the regional office or even in Anil's own office. The officers in the administrative offices ruled the roost over the hapless smaller branches. He identified that the delays in decision-making and in front-line service were the key problems inhibiting the business growth. Anil took the bull by the horns. He took some tough measures to deal with recalcitrant staff and made several changes in the placement of managers. He found that branches had stagnated due to lack of effort by some managers, who managed to get prime postings with the influence of the officers' association. Anil's firm belief in putting the right men in the right jobs helped him to adopt unconventional measures like interviewing a group of middle and senior managers for placement as branch managers in some key branches. They had been selected on the basis of their track record and talent, irrespective of their seniority.

Anil also put in the personal touch by listening to their individual problems and making adjustments for them. The message went right through that performance and merit would henceforth matter and not the pulls and pressures of the officers' association. Though this approach was resisted by the association that expected to be consulted as per the earlier practice, Anil succeeded and motivated the general rung of officers. This sent the right signals in creating a performance culture. To further enhance the facilitative climate for business growth, Anil solved the key industrial relations problems in some critical business centres by his hands-on approach. Actions would vary from context to context.

Essentially, Anil was innovating with ways to motivate the staff to get their commitment for business growth. He acceded to the staff request for a change in premises in Agra that was in a bad shape and also signed a MOU with the entire staff for improvement in business. What brought him success in his maiden operational job was Anil's open and transparent style of working, accessibility and hands-on problem-solving style. His efforts led to a turnaround of the zonal business with the zone standing first among the fourteen zones on some important parameters and setting itself on a growth trajectory. Anil had learnt that agility and speed in decision-making, empowerment of operating managers and removing the roadblocks in the business growth were key factors in improving operational excellence. He was recognized for his performance in this maiden operational role and was promoted as general manager.

Promotion as general manager found Anil posted in Kolkata, as it was then called, to head the troubled eastern zone. Its abysmal IR track record was in keeping with Kolkata's history of IR problems and banking was no exception. The Bank of Baroda's eastern zone ranked at the bottom of the twelve zones with overstaffing, restrictive practices, stagnancy of business and abysmal customer service. Everything that could discourage any executive from staying there and completing his tenure was there for the asking. A culture of protest and agitation engulfed the atmosphere, making it difficult to conduct business. Branch managers felt they were under the union's siege and morale was low. The corporate management, too, treated Calcutta as an amputated leg of the corporate body and hardly engaged with the zonal problems. Anil knew that he had a tough task but his hands-on style in dealing with IR problems early in his career in UP and Rajasthan had taught him a trick or two. One was that trust-building is at the core in the problem-solving process. Anil had a reputation of walking on fire while addressing tough problems.

Peter Drucker's position that the bottleneck is always at the neck of the bottle was inspirational for him and Anil began with the much-neglected, long-pending issues of the Calcutta employees who were denied any forum for union–management interaction for rapprochement. He appreciated that it was unfair to blame only trade unions for the Calcutta cauldron. Never one to shy away from accepting challenges, Anil willingly accepted the posting, surprising even the top management. His only condition was that he should be given at least three years because the average tenure of a zonal manager in Kolkata was less than one year. Anil also knew that his would be a solo journey and no support would be forthcoming from the higher ups. He chose to find his support from the troubled waters of the trade unions instead, putting his fine art of engagement to excellent use.

Relentless interactions with the multiple trade unions using innovative tactics based on seeking engagement of people helped Anil break down barriers over time. He largely succeeded in changing a culture of obstruction and restrictive practices to a business-friendly culture and undertook confidence-building measures to reduce the trust deficit. In a forum for business development that he started, he had the committee involving the trade unions discuss the business growth and development issues. Over time, he was able to rotate jobs, computerize branches and open new branches that had remained stuck for over a decade and substantially improved staff morale. For Anil, his Calcutta tenure was another instance of being baked in fire and coming unscathed from a very challenging situation.

Anil's deep engagement with people and his never-say-die spirit resolved many complicated issues. As the general manager, he demonstrated that even in a hierarchical organization like a large bank, individual initiatives in reformatting people processes can turn around the most difficult situations. Meerut and Calcutta helped Anil rediscover his talents as he stayed in Calcutta for three years, building a trustful environment. It was his performance and turnaround record that brought him into the limelight in the government circles as well. Anil was richly rewarded with a promotion as executive director and member of the Bank of Baroda board.

Both the operational assignments provided Anil with the space to adopt his unconventional leadership style based on people engagement, removing bottlenecks and confronting the reality with conviction and courage. Anil's lack of operational experience was more than compensated by his OD approach that drove results and convinced him that a tenure and exposure in business roles was indispensable for being successful in the HR function. Besides, he realized that HR functionaries could make a great difference in business outcomes with their special talent in focusing on people processes.

Anil's elevation as executive director meant addressing numerous complex banking issues that he was not formally groomed for, nor trained to deal with. It was his innate capacity to manage the handicap by trusting his colleagues and subordinates and learning from them that helped him to deliver with panache. He had his brush with trade union interference in administration; in particular, the might of the officer's association and Anil was determined to change the collusive, collaborative culture in union–management relations. He sought to banish its baneful influence and streamline the processes in the context of the major technology-driven business transformation programme that the bank aspired to at that time. The CEO of the bank had been won over by the officers' association and seemed to oblige them, but Anil had figured out the strategy of these associations early in his career. They would barter cooperation in return for increasing interference in placement and transfers of senior executives.

The operating managers felt constrained in this environment with their own powers to put the right man in the right job compromised.

This culture would have to change if technology was to be implemented across the board. Anil introduced HR audits in the bank that revealed serious violations in personnel administration at the operating level. Anil recovered around Rs 3 crore from the employees for misuse of facilities and credit cards. This rattled the trade unions as it demonstrated the collapse of personnel administration at the operating level essentially due to the unions' pressures and failure of local management. The association struck back by organizing a united forum of trade unions to oppose Anil's initiatives and started a vilification campaign against him. His tenure as executive director was the most difficult and humiliating because Anil faced a barrage of circulars by the officers' association against him, including those to the president, National HRD Network, to withdraw a coveted award that it had given Anil for his contribution to HRD functions.

Anil stuck to his guns, hung on as he systematically streamlined the IR culture, stopped restrictive practices and interference from trade unions and achieved the transformation that he wanted. A culture of union interference in management that prevailed for over four decades (with some gaps) was almost single-handedly reversed by Anil. The pain and humiliation were the motivating triggers for this remarkable feat, which opened new gates for his career progression. Indeed, Anil was considered ready to take over independent charge of a relatively small bank, Dena Bank in Mumbai. It was not a perfect match for his experience and profile but Anil was always game for a challenge.

Dena Bank was in a shambles and the seriousness of the problems fascinated Anil. During his short stay of a year as chairman and managing director of Dena Bank, Anil initiated measures to revive it. This included having a successful public issue, completing the Dena Corporate Centre, inducting experienced bankers and other specialists at the top and a series of initiatives in technology and retail banking. One of his key initiatives was to hire a brand ambassador for the bank. For Anil, the length of the tenure was not a constraint because he drove change with a passion. The success was so remarkable that the government brought him back to Bank of Baroda as the chairman and managing director.

This prized assignment too fell short on many counts. Anil quickly realized that the bank had dropped to number four in its ranking, essentially due to poor credit growth. The industrial relations crises over the last few years had also delayed the process of technology induction and staff morale was at its lowest. Anil plunged into resuscitating the bank. His top priorities included kick-starting the core banking project, reviving credit growth and reconnecting with customers. His intense belief in people processes made him travel around the country and address a dozen town halls that were diagnostic sessions. The objective was to understand the problems ailing the bank at the ground level and use these inputs for strategic management. He encouraged the staff at all levels to tell him what would make them work with zeal and enthusiasm.

Anil also set up a system of daily morning meetings to discuss issues upfront with the top management group. The morning meetings helped him to bust the internal bureaucracy, create better level coordination and a provide a forum for speedy problem resolution. Besides, he engaged the board to develop a five-year vision plan for the bank. In order to activate the decision-making system and help everyone raise themselves to their higher potential, he unleashed an ambitious 100-day agenda, which included starting 500 ATMs, 550 branches and many other new initiatives. His focus on motivating the front line and reaching out to them through a variety of initiatives helped the bank achieve extraordinary business results.

Anil was a hard taskmaster and a no-nonsense leader, but this was balanced by his empathy and compassion, which helped him maintain a high-performance culture. Anil activated the board committee on HR to constantly prioritize HR processes and build future leadership. Innovative programmes like a direct helpline for employees and customers to the chairman, professional counselling services and talent-identification programmes instilled confidence and enthusiasm across the organization. New mechanisms for fast-track promotions, building the base for leadership, got the adrenalin flowing again as Anil launched a major programme to groom 300 leaders for the future. Through multiple strategies in business, technology, HR and governance, Anil restored the bank to its prime position in its 100th year. It was time for celebration.

The performance graph was quite exceptional. On the business front, the bank doubled its business (107 per cent), credit growth

(145 per cent), net profit (112 per cent), new customer addition (8 million) along with all-round improvement in employee productivity ratios. Anil's transformational strategy focused on building intangibles such as rebranding, technology initiatives and human processes such as leadership and governance. It was never a cakewalk but Anil's resilience, authenticity and personal credibility helped him to remove the obstacles and move ahead to achieve results. Anil received several awards for his rapid-fire transformation of Bank of Baroda, including the prestigious Lifetime Achievement Award of the Asian Banker, Singapore, for banking leadership. Among his many achievements, Anil is particularly proud that twelve of his direct reports (who were part of the transformation programme) came to occupy positions of chairmen, managing directors and executive directors with one direct report also becoming deputy governor, Reserve Bank of India.

This was the baking of an HRL at its shining best. The baking took place over a crucible-filled career that transformed a meritorious human resources person into a successful CEO. The journey was marked by constant learnings and application of learning, experimentation, demonstrable ability to rock the boat and confront the legacy attitudes, courage to dismiss attempted humiliation without ever losing faith in people and remaining focused on people-processes for business turnarounds. Such accomplishments are rare but Anil has always been a class act; the outstanding HR warrior, learning on every job, experimenting with innovative methodologies, busting bureaucracies, confronting challenges with the courage of his convictions. Anil Khandelwal vindicated his philosophy of leading change over a broad canvas, even in a short tenure, using HRD/OD processes with grit and gumption.

* * *

Anil Sachdev

Spiritual and Inspiring Thought Leader

Building institutions that contribute towards India's economic development

Anil Sachdev (Anil) is a thought leader and an institution builder. Founder and CEO of Grow Talent Company Limited and the School of Inspired Leadership (SOIL), Anil created Grow Talent in July 2000. By 2006, it had become a leader in the strategic HR consulting industry. SOIL enabled a large number of global and local firms to achieve breakthrough performance by realizing their people potential and creating a talent advantage. In October 2008, Anil and the other co-founders of Grow Talent entered the field of education by creating SOIL. He has been on the frontlines of leadership development and organizational transformation and has done pioneering work with leading global and local firms.

Anil began his career with Tata Motors in 1975 after completing his MBA from the University of Pune. He joined Eicher in 1978, where he worked in HR, operations and TQM. He founded Eicher Consultancy Services and was its CEO till 2001. Anil is active in management circles and has held several public offices, such as chairman of national committees on leadership development, human resources and industrial relations of the Confederation of Indian Industry. Anil is also a member of the Academic Committee and a faculty member of CEDEP, the leading leadership institute of Europe, at INSEAD campus, Fontainebleau. He is a member of the World Compassion Council, based in Seattle and a trustee of the Chinmaya Mission. Besides, Anil serves on the global board of the Shizenkan University in Tokyo. He was president of the National HRD Network Delhi and awarded for his outstanding contributions to HRD.

1962; Anil, a young army child, was going through a kaleidoscope of experiences, adjusting to new environments with every new posting of his father. Alongside, he was soaking up the inspirational impact of Swami Chinmayananda, the spiritual teacher, and internalizing the telling images of a war that India lost to China. India's valiant sons were returning home to their weeping widows, in coffins wrapped in the tricolour. The Army Wives Welfare Association (AWWA) was reaching out for help for the widows, in a street procession. Ordinary women took off the jewellery they were wearing and donated the items in an act of wondrous patriotism, amidst songs resonant with national fervour renting the air, somewhat dispelling the depression caused by the defeat at war. Stoking the patriotic embers was the late Lata Mangeshkar, singing 'Ae Mere Watan Ke Logon' on Army Day. These were abiding impressions shaping the bright young mind.

No more than five, Anil had fathomed domestic dynamics; the complex relationship between his strictly vegetarian, spiritual mother and smoking, whisky-drinking, meat-eating father, Yograj Sachdev. Notwithstanding her disapproval of her husband's ways, Anil's mother cared enough to have her husband's food cooked separately and allowed the hired help, the faithful Rikhi Ram, to get his liquor and Capstan cigarettes by the tin. The sublingual message was clear. It was possible for different opinions to coexist; to be supportive of another even when not seeing eye to eye; to live and let live; or, have faith that with time one can win over the other person to one's own world view.

Anil was witness to the transformation of his father. He stubbed out his cigarette and quit liquor and masala chicken one evening after an engaging dialogue with Swami Chinmayananda. The child may not have realized it then, but his father was undergoing his 'spiritual birth'. As Yograj, a masters in English, adept at Farsi and Urdu too, became a disciple, spending days with his teacher in Uttarkashi, he learnt Sanskrit to understand the slokas. In the process, he taught his son exemplary lessons on the art of the possibilities.

School was a happy experience for the academically bright, multitalented boy. So were the Bal Vihar classes under the aegis of the Chinmaya Mission, run by his parents, where Anil learnt tales from the Puranas, got his first lessons in meditation and was sent in as a volunteer for community service projects. Thanks to the influence of Chinmayananda and his father, Anil learnt to look inwards for answers to dilemmas that life would present to him, allowing his core values to guide him to answers that were fair. Juxtaposed with the soothing touch of spiritualism was the brutalizing impact of war and death.

If the image of his vocalist older sister, Neelam, a National Cadet Corps (NCC) cadet to boot, serving tea to an emotional Prime Minister, Jawaharlal Nehru listening to Lata Mangeshkar singing the moving number, was an intense experience for the eight-year-old, it was heart-wrenching for Anil to march as a bugler in Nehru's funeral procession. Due to the wars fought by India in 1965 and 1971, war became a recurrent theme in Anil's life and created an opportunity for Anil to collect funds for Army Wives Welfare Association (AWWA). At 17, Anil wrote a Hindi play and persuaded students of Pune's Film

Institute to enact it at the Dehu Road Officers' Club. Selling tickets for Rs 5, they managed to collect Rs 5000 for the AWWA!

Such experiences became entrenched in the psyche of the Sachdev family, who sat around the dinner table and sang patriotic songs. Anil also found himself going to great lengths to spend time with the Swami who clarified his thinking. So did his siblings in their own ways. Very soon, young Anil acquired a vision for an economically-developing India, founded on strong values of service. Anil went on to do his MBA, though that was not his first choice. His heart lay in medicine but his aversion for bloodshed meant that he could never dissect living creatures.

Thus an admission to the Christian Medical College, Vellore, went abegging. Instead, Anil did a three-year bachelor's degree in chemistry at the Nowrosjee Wadia College, graduating with first-class honours. That was when he developed a curiosity for a career in management and industry and joined the University of Pune MBA programme. A good student, Anil had the opportunity to intern at Tata Engineering and Locomotive Company (Telco). He was quick to realize that Swamiji's teachings and the study of Indian scriptures and philosophy went far deeper into understanding the human mind and behaviour than western books on management. Anil wondered: At what cost material wealth? He spent a lifetime addressing the allure of lucre.

The MBA done, Anil was in two minds about going for human resources in Telco (now Tata Motors) or marketing in an FMCG company. He was sure about the other life choice though. He was dating his future wife, Neera, then doing her final year at Fergusson College and had laid the foundations of a relationship that was to provide him lifelong strength and friendship. As far as HR was concerned, his supervisor at the Telco internship, Mahesh, took matters into his own hands. He believed that someone as sensitized to human values as Anil was would be far better suited to building people in a company that was trying to build the best automobiles. There was an air of finality in the order: 'Tomorrow you are coming for your medical test and you are joining Telco.' That settled it.

The Telco experience was more than an eye-opener to values and technologies and a sense of responsibility that resonated well with his

natural proclivities. As a twenty-and-a-half-year-old, Anil travelled
to IIT Madras and interviewed IIT students for placements in the
company, delivering the pre-placement talk and wowing the students.
One of them remarked: 'When we heard you speak, we thought you
actually owned Telco.' In his heart and mind, Anil had already 'owned'
his job, which was the key to enjoying his work. Matters were made
easier with the independence given to him as the HR person for the
Engineering Research Centre and the Machine Tool Division. Director,
R&D, Gurudutt was an encouraging boss and Anil's innate sagacity got
him to serve on the interview panel for the senior deputy director's role!
Gurudutt said that he liked Anil's way of asking questions.

Though this bright group, including the charismatic Arun Maira,
was bringing in a new narrative, Anil contemplated his prospects at
Telco. It was a large company and he would have to wait several years
before he got a role where he could make a difference. Meanwhile,
he got an offer from Vikram Lal at Eicher. Anil had not met a better
listener in his life. Lal asked perceptive questions with great humility;
revealing wonderful values, a genuineness of interest. More importantly,
he chose Anil, only twenty three and a half then, with three and a half
years of experience, over far more senior people to be manager, group
corporate HR, Eicher.

Their conversation was so remarkable that Anil joined Eicher at
a lower salary. The attraction was that he would report to Lal. Eicher
was a smaller company, with just 1000 people and a small turnover but,
as head of HR, Anil would be building the department virtually from
scratch. It was for him to ask searching questions at work and look
within for answers, carefully weighing his thoughts as he launched into
transformational changes. Shortly after joining, Anil had an attack of
typhoid and was laid up for forty days. He was totally floored by Lal
visiting his house ten times in forty days, with fruits and flowers and
spending time with him and his extended family.

Meanwhile, Subodh Bhargav, director of projects, was anxious for
new hires and, upset by Anil's absence, questioned his commitment
in front of Lal in no uncertain terms. Lal waited for a couple of days
for Anil to rejoin and address Bhargav's concern to his satisfaction.
There was nothing to be worried about as Anil had lined up the
interviews from his sickbed. Lal's underlying message was that one

should sort out misperceptions openly and with each other. This approach to relationship-building was like a breath of fresh air for Anil. Meanwhile, his first task was to harmonize many aspects of work, including the somewhat contradictory set of business values among units. For this, he created an HR Council, comprising HR heads of all units.

The council began by holding an HR conference, followed by monthly meets, with their minutes circulated. Business heads asking if they were to adhere to them were told that the council was only sharing its collective guidance. Thus, with no permission and no authority to start itself, the council had earned the right to guide and, indeed, decision rights. When times were tough and Eicher needed a major restructuring, instinctively the group management committee turned to the HR council for guidance. Anil had made the first mark with thought leadership in the group.

This led to the second aspect of his thought leadership around a common approach to talent selection. Eicher would look for professional and technical competence along with personal qualities and people skills. One CEO ridiculed the emphasis on people values and even issued his own appointment letters, without the authority to do so. The council members had to confront such dysfunctional behaviour of people even senior to them in the hierarchy. Thankfully, the company backed them. Two misfits had to leave for not accepting the Eicher value sets. Anil wanted to get people to change through dialogue, explaining why Eicher did things in a certain way; why it believed in co-creation. If people did not change, they were called out.

As the CHRO, Anil had to take other unpleasant decisions too. Eicher's new recruits, MBAs and engineers from good schools, IIMs, XLRI and IITs, were sent for product training to the tractor-testing station in Budhni near Bhopal, Madhya Pradesh. The trainees collectively fudged their travel bill and got caught.

Asked for his advice by the management committee, Anil pointed out that fraudsters had been asked to leave in the past. He questioned the current dilemma and found the answer equally compelling: Eicher needed this crop of talent. Yet, the management team and Anil decided that group values should prevail over business needs and all thirty-five were asked to leave. The young recruits were counselled by their business heads and Anil that this was not a lifelong condemnation for them. The point was that Eicher never condoned fraud and one did not sacrifice values for competence. This was the third element of thought leadership that Anil helped embed in Eicher.

Given his people skills, Anil was sent to Eicher's Faridabad factory as the works manager. There were 1000 people here, including a production manager many years his senior. It was a humbling experience working with the unions and richly rewarding too. Once, the tractor industry was in a slump, leading to stockpiling at the factory. A system, geared to increase production, had to reverse gears and cut production. Prior to that, Eicher had an incentive programme to drive productivity; the extra earnings had the workers buying televisions and mopeds on credit. Instalments were due and payroll paring was not the answer. Anil and the Eicher management team decided that there would be no pink-slipping. Instead, dramatically different solutions would be found to overcome the crisis.

Anil launched a trail-blazing process of changing the entire plant into a training company. Classes were held for all categories and the shop floor became a training workshop with union buy-in. Some were out for mischief; one was trying to get external politicians involved in his game plan. Anil and his colleagues strongly believed in an internal union and tended to trust the worker representatives. It paid off generally but Anil learnt some hard lessons too and his naïveté got exposed. The agreement was that the production would be cut, but when the market changed and the pent-up demand increased, the factory would produce and the workers would be given a gift. Later, the gift became a subject of intense negotiations. The newly elected union began to raise unreasonable demands. This went back and forth; after achieving record production one month, the output would plummet. People criticized Anil Sachdev; the greenhorn being taken for a ride by the union.

One evening, they organized a gherao and stopped employees from leaving the factory till late in the night in a clear act of indiscipline. Anil and his team issued charge sheets to the union leaders and 'suspended' them from work. This had a salutary impact as no one had expected the management to make such a bold move. Thankfully, the more positive workers and former union leaders intervened; the union leaders gave written apologies and the conflict was resolved. At other times, the reality was different from Anil's assessment and he found himself being teased about his gullibility; about trusting people too much, especially when he allowed himself to be taken in by a demand for housing for workmen.

Having secured the land, he realized that the union leader was really toying with him; the workers were not keen on getting the houses. Meanwhile, Anil had expended funds and energy on the aborted project. At other times, he and his team came out on top. Threatened by a gate meeting by the union, Anil countered it by addressing all employees in a public meeting. The union leaders did not expect that and Anil won that round and some hearts too. Extremely rewarding experiences with the unions followed, especially when the HR team miscalculated an incentive scheme for the workers, 'Cola' (cost of living, dearness allowance). It was an overly generous error; wages would go up by four times in ten years. The union leaders were quick to spot it, asking Anil with a smirk if he was sure about the formula. Not until the workers broke into a song and dance did the HR team realize that something was fishy. 'Sir, *koi daal mein kaala hai* (there is something fishy).'

Anil rechecked and detected the error in the formula and the buck stopped with him. He had to engage in damage control, for the signed agreement could not be implemented. Anil called the union back and addressed a couple of positive leaders using his most endearing voice, admitting that he had erred. He appealed to their sense of loyalty to the Eicher family; the agreement would be bad for the company. Anil must have melted their hearts because they started laughing and forgave the young works manager, agreeing to go back to the gates to announce the withdrawal in a show of overwhelming magnanimity.

Earlier, when he was in the corporate HR team, Anil had witnessed a life-changing scene during a strike in Faridabad. Every factory, save Eicher's, downed shutters. Eicher had to produce because there was a tractor shortage and the union agreed not to join the strike. An angry mob of 5000 people from other factories came to burn the plant. The Hitkari factory next door was ablaze. The union leaders took up the cudgels, asking the managers to stay in. Then they looked the mob in the eye and said: 'Kill us first before you enter the factory.' Such unprecedented defence of their plant, Anil realized, was owed to the remarkable work that Lal had earlier done on the shop floor with the workers. The leaders told the mob: 'This is not Vikram Lal's company. It is our company.'

Anil's three-and-a-half-year stint at the plant ended on a high note. He had remoulded the spirit of such agreements by placing a charter of demands on what the unions would be required to do for the well-being of the workers. How would the unions improve the quality of worker lives? How would they enhance the worker capability post superannuation? Anil offered solutions that were refreshing in the usually cloyed worker-management ecosystem. Eicher would give retiring workers time off to prepare for a post-retirement career two years ahead of time! It was not just about being an HR professional but driving quality of thought and driving quality itself. Upon his return, Anil headed all of HR and facilitated the TQM implementation at Eicher.

HR revolves around identifying talent and grooming them after identifying what they were best suited for. Anil nurtured Abha Nanda, a shy but sensitive girl from Solan, by giving her outstanding opportunities. Abha went on to become senior VP of HR for a global company. Her first major break was when Anil invited her to write a paper with him and present it at the HRD network conference without telling a soul that she was his secretary. His other secretary, Vivika, went on to become the head of corporate communications for Lehman Brothers. He noticed her talent for communication, written and otherwise, and nurtured her for a bigger role. So it was for every one of his colleagues who began as his assistants.

Devraj Sharma, a machine operator, was identified as a potential supervisor through a Development Centre conducted at the Parwanoo plant and sponsored to study at Symbiosis. He was later promoted as HR manager and went on to become VP, HR with PepsiCo and is currently working with Mondelez. People can rise to great heights if made conscious of their abilities. Anil believed in providing the opportunity to help the talented confront their freedom to choose to develop themselves. Some needed to be challenged, others needed compassion. The important thing was to make them believe in themselves.

Once, Lal was appointing a person from Yale, who was thought to be an idealist, keen to serve the poor. Anil learnt from the candidate's friend at Yale, however, that the man was a flamboyant person with expensive drinking tastes. Anil spoke his mind to Lal, questioning the qualities of the shortlisted person, only to have Lal lose his cool over Anil investigating a senior leader without the authority and reporting back on the basis of hearsay. Lal taught him never to share hearsay, which amounted to a penchant for loose talk. Biases could not be the basis of judgement; one should do one's homework and research before sharing information with the CEO. Anil realized his error. He was trying to impress his boss, showing extra initiative, providing extra information and got rapped on the knuckles.

Meanwhile, the Eicher Motors facility was coming up in Pithampur and Anil started working with the Japanese. He also went on several learning programmes on productivity as life became a continuous chain of learning. In his last years as CHRO, as the business landscape was dramatically transformed, Anil made his fourth impact on thought leadership. Multinationals were entering the country and manufacturing companies were losing the talent race to them. Eicher had to come across as a strong employer brand to counter them. Anil launched special initiatives to create a buzz in leading management institutes about Eicher's great learning initiatives. Lo and behold, almost the entire class of IIM Bangalore opted for Eicher, which was recruiting people till three in the morning. Well-crafted and targeted messaging enabled Eicher to withstand the onslaught of those offering twice the salary. Anil wanted Eicher employees to be inspired by what they had co-created and not quit. Eicher raised salaries too but only after Anil worked on changing management mindsets around salaries.

The fifth element of thought leadership was around resolving the emerging conflicts between unit-level autonomy and group values. Anil saw the early signs of Eicher business heads becoming individually powerful and unwilling to share their resources and top talent with other businesses. Allocating cash and talent was becoming difficult, as was transferring people from one business to another. Anil engaged with them to make them appreciate the company in its entirety and why talent transfer was necessary. It was for the business leaders to develop great talent and happily share them with other businesses for the larger good.

Impacting mindsets in a non-work setting became Anil's sixth major contribution to thought leadership as he engaged across hierarchies to establish the community spirit in the workplace, always with his ear to the ground and to his great advantage. When working with clients on large factory transformations as a consultant, Anil hung around with people at the grassroots and learnt their misgivings in advance. He then addressed them appropriately. He often used sports and culture routes to maintain the connect. Inter-business unit sports with management and workers playing together, with families joining in to watch the games, in a picnic spirit, made for easing tensions and building bonds.

Even the spouses were charmed by the warmth that the community spirit induced in their lives, away from the workplace, through cultural programmes and sports. It transformed the cultural relationships at Eicher and deepened the fraternal milieu. This was embedded in the management psyche and later, when the market was down and Anil had moved to Eicher Consultancy Services (ECS), the Eicher board approached him to co-create that culture. Asked to lead the movement that would celebrate Eicher, Anil organized a wonderful mélange of programmes with schoolgoing children of employees writing poetry, every unit putting up a skit, a dance, musical performance and singing the Eicher song, based on Eicher values.

Having spent a decade with Eicher, Anil informed Lal that he was done with operations and his heart lay in consulting. In his 1978 job interview, he had told Lal and Bhargava that after ten years of serving Eicher, he would create a think tank and consulting company to help transform Indian companies to produce world-class products and services, based on the right values. Lal offered him a consulting platform within the aegis of Eicher because he believed in enabling every employee to realize his dream. On offer were some Eicher talent and capital and ECS took off with the vision of India's economic development without spiritual impoverishment. It created several practice areas around its core values aimed at creating a workplace community that enabled self-discovery; taught people to do more with less to benefit more (waste elimination and just-in-time practices); to advance and win in the market without selling their souls; to develop an approach and strategy that is co-owned by everybody, based on the right values; creating a movement as it were.

Building ECS was not a cakewalk though. It could not afford the exorbitant salaries offered by the global consultants; nor the five-day week. With the cream of talent, trained in 6 Sigma, TQM and such other skills, ECS became a sitting duck for talent poachers, who were wooing its people with 70-80 per cent higher salaries. Anil called Gauri Sarin, who sourced talent for GE, and explained his vision and his plight to her. He managed to persuade her not to poach ECS talent for a couple of years. To her credit, Sarin kept her word and gave Anil the breathing space that he needed. Anil dealt with a threat by appealing to the human side of the source. The frugal salary structure proved to be a blessing when the consultancy business in India went through a downturn, along with the economy.

Even so, ECS had a substantial payroll and not enough business to pay salaries, when an interesting proposition came its way. A top corporate—its values at sharp variance with ECS's—offered a big contract involving a lot of money. Anil did not grab the offer but consulted his team on whether it wished to work with that company. The decision was not to take up this contract. Money was never the criteria for Anil, not even when AT Kearney wanted to acquire ECS and made Anil a dazzling offer; in multiples of what he was earning in Eicher. Anil told Kearney that he could not sell his dream of being the Indian company that would serve Mother India. Later, ECS did become a joint venture with the Palo Alto-based SDG, a values-driven company that found the spiritual impoverishment plank story guiding the ECS vision quite inspirational.

Tapan Mitra, managing director of Indian Aluminium, discovered the depths of Anil's relationship with his colleagues when he and his team visited the Eicher plant, prior to hiring ECS for a major TQM initiative. Anil was showing them around, when a worker from the assembly area came running and hugged Anil like they were old friends: '*Arrey*, Anil, *itne dino se aap aaye nahi* (you have not visited for so long).' That evening, over dinner, Mitra remarked about a sweaty, blue-collar worker in his uniform, embracing one of the managing directors and getting embraced back like a long-lost friend. Anil explained that when he ran the factory, he had spent many special moments with the workers; visited their homes in times of joy and sorrow. His age and position were never a factor because he was always deferential and eager to learn from people, just as he had no qualms about calling them out for poor behaviour.

When it came to downsizing, early in his career in Eicher, Anil and his team had taken a novel route without payroll-paring, instituting the seventh aspect of thought leadership. He launched a manpower optimization process, creating a personal database and plan for everyone, identifying individual needs and securing union buy-in to facilitate the transfers of even blue-collar workers across businesses. Many were retrained as workers resigned from Eicher tractors and were appointed by Eicher Motors in Pithampur. Security guards, for instance, were retrained to work in the accounts department; the incentive scheme at Faridabad was converted into fixed salaries as the new businesses absorbed the redundant manpower in the older units. This large-scale retraining, rescaling and redeployment became a case study for IIM Ahmedabad and was awarded by the National HRD Network and the CII too.

Anil had invested the organization with fine values and was ready to move out of Eicher, having spent ten years, in line with what he had told the ECS board at the time of its foundation. Anil quit to created his own consulting company, Grow Talent, after obviating potential conflict of interest between his former and future commitments. He informed all ECS clients that he would not compete with ECS. The angel investment in Grow Talent came from some ECS clients though, with Anil supplementing it with his provident fund and superannuation money.

Anil had been training himself for this role; as a teacher. While serving at both ECS and Eicher, he offered courses at the General Motors Institute in Flint, Michigan, Ohio University, Antioch University and Indiana University in Bloomington during the summers and occasionally delivered talks at B-schools such as IIM Ahmedabad. He loved going to the classroom and interacting with students. He sold Grow Talent because he did not have the capital needed to take it to a global level. This was a blessing, for once he let go of consulting in 2008, he became a full-time teacher with SOIL, his School of Inspired Leadership, co-created with the help of friends from the industry.

Anil's journey through life has been about reinventing himself, just as he helped others reinvent themselves. He had prepared himself for the role of founder of a school, which he currently serves as chairman. He visited unusual places—such as Cranfield in the UK, Ashridge, Harvard, Stanford, Carlson in Minnesota—without any fixed agenda but met some of their leaders and managed to hang around with them and their informal groups. He learnt what was going on to ensure that he was relevant to the times. Today, he is a mentor at SOIL, an active devotee of the Chinmaya mission and also creates new content, teaches and works with students, stimulating new minds and serving other institutions. At any given time, Anil is coaching several business leaders both in India as well as abroad and also learning with them. These make for a really full and enjoyable life.

As he grooms himself, so does Anil groom his successors for any space that he is vacating; he passes on his acquired wisdom in his own inimitable way, with time at hand. His game plan for possible successors was to give them disproportionate exposure and importance and push them into the open. He allowed them to take charge, let them build their brand, presented them with opportunities to represent the organization in different forums and gradually get used to the limelight, as he removed himself. He believed in pushing people into discovering themselves even when they were hesitant to do so.

The other abiding interest for Anil has been to advance the HR profession. He is always available for the HRD network. His life's original mission statement, which was instrumental in securing for him his first job, is still inspiring and guiding him; as he has guided the network. Today, he urges the network to serve smaller companies affected by the pandemic and for larger Indian companies to join hands to look after the weaker ones.

As always, Anil Sachdev has stayed relevant.

* * *

Anuranjita Kumar

Soaring high; scoring across the canvas

Claiming her space and relentlessly reinventing herself; trusting her instincts

Former chief human resources officer, Citi South Asia, Anuranjita Kumar (Anu), began her career with Procter & Gamble in 1994 and joined Citibank in 1995. An alumnus of XLRI, she worked across geographies and in multiple roles and became the first South Asian woman to be appointed as head of HR, global banking, the Europe, Middle East and Africa (EMEA) region, in 2007. She is on the board of various organizations and professional bodies and was recognized among the 'Most Powerful Woman Leaders' by Fortune *in 2013. An accredited executive coach and a senior trainer for the Senior Leadership Development at Citibank, Anu has always focused on the strategic capabilities of HR, talent management and cultivating a shared and vibrant corporate culture. Known for her challenging, candid and confident work style, Anu has continually endeavoured to groom young leaders by fostering a creative, entrepreneurial and business-orientated work environment. From Citi, she moved over to RBS International as managing director of human resources and thereafter started the Women in Technology (WiT) forum to help increase the number of women professionals in science, technology, engineering and management (STEM), by offering them the right training, skills and education.*

For Anuranjita Kumar, daughter of a doctor mother and father with a PhD in science, working for a leading pharmaceuticals company, the natural career would have been in medicine or the sciences. Her family put her on the beaten track of good education, sending her and her sister to the premium Dehradun boarding school, Welham Girls School, something the family could almost not afford. It taught her great values, especially the value of networking with peers from her school. From her mother, Anu also learnt to be resilient and such virtues as not taking no for an answer. She did well in academics and got admission in a medical school. After a few months in Lucknow's King George's Medical University, Anu decided that the life of a doctor was not for her and moved out of medical college.

Instead, Anu joined Indraprastha College in Delhi, to study psychology because she enjoyed exploring the mind and connecting with people. It was an unusual step and her mother was aghast, but Anu dug her heels in. Her parents finally agreed to let her change streams only if she could secure mid-term admission to a college. Even as she went from college to college in Delhi begging for a seat, she operated from a secure place in her mind that allowed her to push aside

experience had Anu being asked to rush to a branch one day as the administration manager was about to get arrested. A labour contractor had used a minor to clean the ATM and someone had complained. The Labour Commissioner's men had landed up and Anu used all her persuasive skills to dissuade them from arresting the bank employee for what was the contractor's fault.

These diverse experiences and her boss's calmness on the face of it, taught Anu how to face adversity. Meanwhile, she got the transfer orders to Mumbai so she could be in the same city as her husband. Anu was at first reluctant, but Gupta convinced her to move to Mumbai though it was a transfer for personal reasons. The way Gupta handled it became a lifelong lesson for her, especially when she faced similar requests from colleagues seeking transfers. Citibank was then a relatively small bank in India and, after her employee relations experience in Delhi, she was put in charge of recruiting and then in technology, giving her a bird's eye view of the entire HR function. This sustained her interest in the job as she was exposed to new experiences every other day.

Anu was perceived as a youngster who could get things done and she was allowed to dabble in many areas. One key learning was how to build relationships with bankers, very senior people, who earned money for the organization. Working with investment bankers was an experience on a different level, but Anu also learned to establish boundaries and figure out how to get things done, especially when a banker of stature opposed what she had to do as a member of the HR team. If she had a point of view, she would respectfully debate it with the senior. Her message was clear; the other person's seniority and client-facing role did not mean that the person was right.

Given that bankers are very intelligent people who could easily figure out what liberties they could take, Anu developed the art of pushing the system, testing her limits. She was particular about establishing what 'liberties' one could take with her. 'How much are you worth? That had to be established early.' The system also supported her enormously, on occasion. A project into which $150,000 had been invested went horribly wrong and Anu was prepared to take responsibility and resign. However, her bosses examined the details and realized that the fault lay with the supplier and asked her to execute the project afresh. Another $150,000 was sanctioned!

The next phase of her career with Citibank took her across the world. Anu and Sandeep tried to be posted at the same location and largely succeeded. Sometimes Sandeep moved first and Anu followed; sometimes it was the other way around. Meanwhile, Anu was passing defining career milestones, serving the bank in Singapore and then in New York, before landing a stint in London. She lived her philosophy: 'It's my career and I need to take charge of it.' She had consciously learnt the art from another crucial stint in Delhi. She picked up the nuts and bolts of a business from equity accounting to tax accounting, prior to her two-year Singapore sojourn. By the time Citibank announced the merger with Salomon Smith Barney, Anu was working for the bank in New York. She believes everyone should do a stint at the company headquarters. She would often see the CEO, Sandy Weill, in consultation with Chuck Prince, who later succeeded Weill. It was a heady feeling to work in their company and made for terrific learnings as well.

Talent management, Anu realized, was more an art than a science. She got a first-hand view of what really matters from discussions in top forums at an MNC; how processes are built around them and how the senior management think. As the merger—more of a takeover—played out, Anu, a relatively junior employee, was absorbing more and contributing less. The power dynamics encompassed all the players and as an Indian woman of 'colour', going to Singapore and New York meant having to exert herself and make her own space; nudge elbows where needed. 'You're not from a local environment. You're not of the same colour of skin. You speak in a different accent. All of this stands out. Why should they believe you?' Anu was realistic in her assessment of the evolving situation and appropriate in her response.

New York provided excellent training and prepared her to face the global tides. While working at the headquarters, she understood how small India was in Citibank's global scheme of things and how insignificant the issues that she dealt with back in India were. In 2004, Anu moved to London in what was her best professional move. Coincidently, her husband had moved to London too. Initially fuzzy about her strategy role in London, she ended up heading corporate and commercial bank HR there. When her boss left, she was asked to take on a larger role though she was yet to be noticed by the big guns;

the investment bankers and the dealmakers who raked in the moolah. Even as a director, Anu felt unnoticed while sitting in a room with the biggies. It was her New York stint that helped as she started researching investment banking systematically. Veteran dealmaker, Tom King, was heading Citibank out of London at the time and had his doubts about her. He would have preferred someone with a European background and Anu set about changing perceptions.

Anu made the most of her little meetings with King and even engaged in small talk about deals that were being discussed in the market at the time. She could engage intelligently if the conversations went on a little longer. Once she noticed King's bright blue eyes almost twinkle when she responded to his comments, guessing correctly whether Citibank was the buy-side adviser or the sell-side adviser. These moments, when her homework and diligence paid off, got her respect from the likes of King, and the bankers who ran Citibank in London at the time. Never hesitant to push the envelope, she requested another banking CEO, Richard Blackford, to send out an email about her taking over, so she could go and meet members of his organization on different floors. Blackford said he would not send a mail but walk with Anu to every floor and introduce her personally. This went a long way in getting her accepted and signalled that she was a part of the leader's camp.

The global meltdown of 2008–09 followed soon after and working on bonus awards—the bank was giving out equity, not cash—for bankers with King, Anu pointed out that it might not be acceptable for the bankers. King told her that the financial winter was there to stay, possibly for a decade and what was being given out was good. Anu had worked closely with King and gained his trust. He headed Europe, the Middle East and Asia and Anu helped him with such tough moves as building a new leadership team for Turkey, post-merger. These decisions often meant giving up on people or a part of the operations, which needed to be done while containing the damage to the bank.

In the middle of all this, Anu developed pneumonia and had to be hospitalized. She told King that Citibank should replace her as the doctors could give no assurance about when she would be back at work. King responded that Citibank would wait for her to get well: 'Just come back in time for comps (compensation).' Her bout of pneumonia was followed by a relapse, changing Anu as a person. The treatment was painful and frustrating as her fever refused to subside and her doctors were afraid that they might lose the battle. Her children were very young and occasionally visited her at the hospital. Those were gut-wrenching moments, as Anu was aware that she may not make it. Her husband was on a trip to Singapore when she fell ill and among the many things that she is grateful for is her children's nanny, who stepped in to tide over the crisis.

Anu parents came over to support her. There would be occasions where she broke down, unable to bear the uncertainty as the illness dragged on for months. Remarkably, as her resolve was breaking down, her family found and brought in a doctor who was not involved in her treatment. He started a new line of treatment and, as if by a miracle, there was marked improvement within a day. Slowly, Anu healed and managed to return home. After adequate rest, she was able to join work. The illness made her health-conscious as she constantly monitored herself for signs of malaise. It also made her more aware of the needs of her family with whom she spent more quality time. Citibank's gesture of holding her place till she got better told her how well-regarded she was and this made her more determined to live up to their expectations.

Yet, things did not always go her way. In another career-defining incident in London, she was passed over for a promotion. The entire office was expecting her to be promoted alongside some of her peers. While the others got their promotions, Anu's was deferred. This shocked her to the point that she offered to resign and was not sure that she would go back to work the next day. She did go in to work though and, after discussions at home and office, Anu decided to seek the counsel of a career coach. The feedback from her office, as well as the coach, was that while she did well in her work, Anu had not been able to manage the office atmosphere or ecosystem. There were also some surprising comments about her in a 360° review that she could not relate to.

Anu recognized the importance of managing the office environment for career advancement and, guided by her coach, she went about identifying friends and allies at work and also created new alliances and friendships. The coaching succeeded and soon the deferred promotion came through. Anu had started enjoying the altered equations of the workplace and the new relationships she had built and the promotion itself did not seem such a big deal any more. In any event, Anu was keen to return to India because her family had moved to Delhi and for eighteen months she had been travelling Delhi–London to manage both fronts. Being separated from her children meant emotional upheavals and she remembers how sad her son would become when she left the Delhi home for London. While in London, she learnt that her son was seriously ill and flew down immediately. Anu moved to Delhi as soon as a position opened up in 2012 and eventually became chief human resources officer for Citibank's south Asian cluster.

Staying back in London despite personal hardships was yet another learning experience that helped her in her career. She had learnt to take in the broader picture and a longer-term perspective, which helped her to 'zoom in and out of a situation, connect the dots and deal with the problems'. After Anu moved to Delhi, the position of the chief human resources officer for India at Citibank opened up and she applied for it. There was a hilarious first meeting with the India chief, Pramit Jhaveri, for this position that was based in Mumbai. Anu was keen on a Delhi posting or else would have to settle for a Delhi–Mumbai life because her children were going to school in Delhi. Jhaveri warned her that he was known to be a tough boss and Anu countered with: 'How tough, on a scale of one to five?' Jhaveri saw the humour in the question that was an obvious reference to her having worked for King and Manuel Falco and gone through a Delhi–London phase before returning to India. He started laughing and Anu got the India position. Humour is a great quality to work with when dealing with tricky situations.

The banking role had taught Anu how to penetrate deeply into an issue. The CHRO role taught her how to look at the big picture. She figured out that it was important to observe the interplay between different elements and then plug in the strategic elements around them. The India position also offered Anu her first board experience. Governance was a big issue in this role and there were multiple crises that Anu grappled with from day one, such as a Gurugram case featuring a bank employee defrauding a high-profile corporate and a sexual harassment-related FIR that forced Anu to cut short a trip to London and return within a day. It meant spending a lot of time at the police stations and the police commissioner's office. The role was more external-facing and Anu was often the public face of the organization. At some level, the role was akin to 'babysitting' the CEO, who had come in from an investment banking role to become CEO of the bank.

The other key issue with the CHRO role was that Anu had around ten colleagues, all her seniors and many from the Tata Institute of Social Sciences, an institute considered equivalent to XLRI as far as HR management education was concerned. Anu had to work hard to gain the support of this group; something that she had seen Manuel Falco do in London. She took them out individually for a meal or a drink for one-on-one chats, appealing to each one to continue to stay because all that she was looking to do was to forge a partnership with them. She was not looking to be the boss. Anu also made a couple of smart hires, one for employee relations and one for rewards and felt secure with these two in place. She trusted them to handle the routine work and free up her time for more strategic engagements. She was happy to have her team handle queries directly and not get involved unless there was an escalation.

It was important to cast one's net of touchpoints widely as Jhaveri had the habit of sending midnight messages asking for updates. Anu could keep a tab on every subject without being involved in everything. Two decades of vibrant experience and enormous learnings later, Anu decided to move to the Royal Bank of Scotland (RBS) in 2017, where she served as head of HR for international hubs. RBS's three-year stint was interesting and also gave her the mental space to get set for the next phase in her life—teaching, coaching, passing on her own learning and writing books.

Anu's life today is all about sharing her wisdom through mentoring. Her London colleagues are still in touch with her and she is happy to counsel them on what had worked for her in the past. Meanwhile, she has written two books, *Can I Have It All* and *Colour Matters*, in which she has shared her experience for the benefit of future generations. She has also been a board member of the National HRD Network since 2019 and does active coaching on a pro bono basis. As the Citi CHRO, Anu was invited to HR forums in the country, which gave her the opportunity to build networks. In many instances, it was about reinforcing what she was doing at Citibank. She reached out to senior leaders in the industry to deepen relationships with them and to seek their views on the areas that she wanted to work in. She was 'impressed with the breadth and depth of feedback' that she received through these interactions and got pulled into working with business chambers like the CII, FICCI, ASSOCHAM as well the National HRD Network. Anu said that this 'strengthened our position as an employer'.

Anu's prime concern now is to share knowledge; even as she learns, she teaches. As a board member, she often had to walk the extra mile to stay in touch with employees at the lower rungs. Equally important has been staying connected with younger colleagues, getting reverse mentored in the process. Spending time with younger people gives her a glimpse of the future. She believes that people who are more futuristic can probably look into the crystal ball and guess what can happen next. This is why she finds the younger generation quite exciting and derives a lot of energy from these engagements. With a new batch in HR, Anu would just sit with them or invite them for a glass of wine. Here, she would find some of them coming up with whacky ideas because they thought differently, and the engagement involved some informal reverse mentoring. The youngsters would also walk into her room quite fearlessly. Outside the HR function, Anu tried to stay connected by occasionally joining the morning huddle in different functional groups.

In big corporations or MNCs, there are structured interventions, such as town halls, skip levels, connects. Anu would do all of that but a lot more informal stuff too, because that is typically her style. Such informal outreach becomes crucial in organizations like RBS that are very hierarchical. RBS offered her a great deal in terms of formal structures but, as an informal person, Anu took every opportunity to socialize. As she lived in Delhi and often on visits to Mumbai with relatively free evenings, she would mingle a little more with her colleagues; maybe over a glass of wine. Also, even though she sat on the executive floor with Jhaveri at Citibank, she would drop by at the HR floor twice a day, sometimes unannounced. Not that she wanted to startle them but she would just go and chit-chat, sit in the board members' area with people and get to know them and ask about their families. The conversations would not be work-related. Anu did not 'operate in boundaries' and was not very hierarchical; she sometimes established 'one-on-one connects'.

Exposure to such diverse views has moulded Anu, showing her how a different opinion is not wrong. It has often helped her push back against management decisions. At Citibank, she recalls how Jhaveri would have to personally overrule her as she refused to change her position. There was an incident at RBS where there was a consensus that a leader in Poland would have to leave the bank. She looked closely at the situation and found that the man was a highly-respected leader in his market and the decision to get rid of him was a result of internal politics. She decided to disagree with the decision and pushed back hard.

Having served as the managing director, human resources, for international hubs in RBS for three years, she turned into an entrepreneur and started a forum, Wit-ACE, for women in science, technology, engineering and management (STEM). Wit-ACE is committed to helping women through skill upgradation to accelerate their careers. This is a large-scale transformational initiative leading to the empowerment of women who are quite at the bottom of the pyramid. Through this, Anu is leveraging her personal experience of building a stellar career to help other women build their careers, training them to jump in and survive deep ends.

* * *

Aquil Busrai

Crusading HR leader: learning, teaching and a 'tiger' for his team

Disseminating his wisdom passionately within the profession and the community at large

Aquil Busrai (Aquil) is a thought leader and has been a perseverant institution-builder over his forty-six-plus years in industry. A much-published writer, he is well-networked and influences not just professionals across the world but the youth through his webinars and coaching sessions. Currently CEO of Aquil Busrai Consulting, he is a gold medallist from XLRI with a post-graduate degree in law, an advanced diploma in training and development and a PhD. A university rank holder, he is the recipient of the J.M. Kumarappa and Bharucha Gold Medals for academic excellence. His penchant for learning is indicated by his pursuit of a second PhD in recent times.

Dr Busrai has worked in various HR roles with Unilever in Kenya and India, Motorola in Asia–Pacific countries, Shell in Malaysia and IBM in India. He is a fellow of the All India Management Association, a former national president of the National HRD Network and is associated with other professional bodies like the Indian Society for Training and Development (ISTD) and CII. A keen student of non-verbal communication, he is writing a book on body language. He is also an ardent wildlife enthusiast and a serious wildlife photographer.

Jeera roti and chai . . . Bilquish, Aquil's mother, would occasionally, 'treat' him for something that he had done well. What Aquil did not realize at that time, was that his mother would make jeera-roti with tea on days when she did not have enough money to buy even vegetables. Always dignified despite the humble means, Bilquish and this phase of life left a deep impression on Aquil's psyche. He imbibed great self-respect and poverty gave him one big advantage. 'My wants were always less than my needs,' he says. Strangely, this brought him a lot of happiness. His father, Fakhroodin, who died when Aquil was only eleven, worked in Mauritius and Aden and was mostly away during Aquil's early childhood. For her only child, Bilquish became the sole pillar, the main source of inspiration, shaping Aquil's tender mind and moulding him for life.

Upon Fakhroodin's death, Bilquish and Aquil moved from Surat to Kolkata, her maternal home, living in a 10x8 ft room with a balcony that served as a kitchen. Though not formally educated, Bilquish could read and write a bit, making ends meet by selling papad, some Unilever consumer products and giving tailoring and embroidery lessons. Finances were not easy but Bilquish managed to protect Aquil from the challenges of penury. He had one school uniform that was washed clean for the next day and got a new pair of shoes every Eid. The pair had to last a year, with repairs if necessary. Going to a movie was a big treat reserved for the end of every final examination in school.

Aquil noticed how respectful Bilquish was of people. She would even offer dates to neighbourhood servants if they came home while she was midway through a meal. If it annoyed Aquil, she would admonish him with: 'Respect everyone as a person irrespective of their status and truly empathize with them.' Aquil imbibed this and he would feel equally at home having lunch with a chairman or playing chess with a driver in the company recreation room. His hallmark empathy had its roots in this phase of his life.

Moving from a purely Gujarati-medium school in Surat to the English-medium Bharucha Day School in Kolkata was not easy. Aquil failed in every subject in class VI, save for geometry and arithmetic in which he topped the class. He knew his lessons but could not answer because he could not understand the questions in English. The principal, Miss Bharucha, understood the situation and promoted Aquil to the next class. School fees were waived but paying for private tuition was out of the question, so Aquil depended on Bilquish to teach him English, using a Gujarati-to-English dictionary. There were some sympathetic teachers at school as well, who occasionally helped after classes and Aquil was a smart learner.

By class VII, Aquil had managed to improve his English so much that he stood eleventh in class. In the next class, Aquil improved to the third position. He remembers the red-letter day with a joyous Bilquish making suji-ka-halwa after his results were announced. Neighbours were promptly treated to halwa and dates. From there on, it was a matter of habit for Aquil to top the class, whether it was in the pre-university examinations, the bachelor's degree or even at XLRI, from where he obtained his MBA. Bilquish had ingrained sheer grit in him and made Aquil self-reliant; values that he cherished. He also got spontaneously involved with emerging issues that must have been commonplace in his indigent childhood and was never hesitant to show vulnerability. These are the life lessons that Aquil learnt from Bilquish.

Aquil also took to books and reading. He joined the USIS, a free library set up by the American Embassy. While his friends played cricket, he spent hours in the library reading extensively on space travel—a fad in the early 1960s—and astronomy. As a very curious youngster, he always wanted to know things beyond his textbooks and read everything that he could lay his hands on; even 'thonga' (a packet made out of recycled newspaper, used by shopkeepers) or second-hand books from College Street—Kolkata's famous book bazar—pavement vendors. This constant thirst for knowledge prompted him to pursue a post-graduate degree in law even though his university class hours were from 6.15 a.m. to 8.30 a.m. This meant having to rush to work at 9 a.m. and complete his childhood dream of PhD at age sixty.

In school itself, his teachers noticed his unique ability to understand human nature as he wrote elaborate character sketches in his English literature class that showed great empathy. In class VIII, the English literature teacher had asked them to analyse the characters in the story 'The Bishop's Candlesticks'. This was a tale of a convict who had stolen silver candlesticks from a bishop's house. When caught, he was saved by the bishop, who said he had gifted them to the convict. The assignment was to analyse each character in the story in half a page. Aquil submitted more than four foolscap pages, analysing all the main characters, using his imagination, almost visualizing himself in each role and surprising his teacher with his ability to empathize. She encouraged him by giving him interesting assignments like analysing characters in other stories and his work was passed on to other students. The foundation for a career in understanding people's minds and managing people was being laid, even though Aquil was still an introvert and generally an anxious child.

Phoenix Scout Troop provided him a platform to develop confidence under the mentorship of his scoutmaster, Dr Kotwal. He learnt to express his talent and competence. He effortlessly learnt to respect diversity and inclusiveness. His peers came from various communities but each one genuinely connected with respect and camaraderie. Aquil soaked it all in and the lessons learnt were deeply entrenched in his psyche. They became his strengths as he championed diversity and inclusiveness later in life. The persona of Dr Kotwal, an ophthalmologist, affectionately called Koti da (a suffix meaning older brother, used to respectfully address men senior to one), had an immense influence on Aquil. Koti da's quiet yet powerful presence, his style of instilling a sense of excellence, his deep involvement with every individual and sharp observation skills appealed to the young Aquil.

Aquil observed and emulated the role model behaviour of individuals, but he did not idolize them. His deepening interest in scouting soon saw him leading a patrol of seven boys and doing his utmost to make his team the best, winning the President's Scout Badge, amidst other memorable incidents. At a scouts' camp near Darjeeling, there was a terrified shriek late one night. It was Mrs Kotwal, who had found a dead snake under her pillow. Dr Kotwal summoned the troop on that chilly night and asked who was responsible. Almost immediately the miscreant raised his hand and apologized. The scoutmaster dismissed the assembly without any remonstration. Another lesson learnt; Dr Kotwal had silently applauded the innate honesty of the boy and his courage in owning up. His career is replete with instances of Aquil backing his team members when they had erred. Many have acknowledged how he 'stood behind them like a rock'.

The commitment to the scouts was rewarded with Aquil getting selected to represent India at an international meet for boy scouts in Saudi Arabia. He got jaundice and almost did not make the trip. It was a seven-day voyage by ship from Bombay to Jeddah. Fortunately, his medical test results improved just in time for him to board the SS *Akbar*. Aquil was the youngest among the Rovers (senior scouts) from 147 countries. This was his first overseas trip and Aquil was excited to be invited for an audience with King Faisal of Saudi Arabia. To his good fortune, the Rovers meet preceded the holy Haj pilgrimage and Aquil combined the pilgrimage with the international meet. Being selected to represent India and his improved health served as a sign of a benevolent superior power guiding him.

Aquil went on to study BCom at Kolkata's St Xavier's College, but the scouting spirit stayed on as he was asked to take over as scout master of the Burhani Scout Troop, known as 'bandwala scouts' because it had a fantastic band. Aquil worked passionately for all-round excellence. With Dr Kotwal's inspirational style to guide him, within two years Burhani Scouts had become one of the best in Kolkata and Aquil had developed a mental frame for driving turnarounds. The success formula was put to excellent use when he headed the HR teams in Motorola. Drawing inspiration from people he admired served him well throughout his career. He pursued inspirational initiatives such as raising funds for uplifting the lives of slum dwellers along with the sisters of Mother Teresa's Missionaries of Charity. He visited the slums almost every Sunday, sometimes along with Mother Teresa. There could have been no better way to learn humility and servant-leadership than this.

Early in life, Aquil had learnt to take charge of his destiny, be it in school, college or with the boy scouts. In college, he gave tuitions, earning Rs 50 per month. He paid Rs 20 for colleges fees, gave his mother Rs 20 and kept Rs 10 for himself. The days of penury were over and Aquil opened an account with Citibank, Brabourne Road branch, with a princely Rs 100. It was an unusual decision but it had its own allure because Citibank would issue personalized cheque books and Aquil paid his college fees with a cheque that had his name printed on it. It gave him a sense of dignity and, though the college cashier was not amused, pride in his self and self-sufficiency had taken root in this young man who was among the very few students with a personalized chequebook.

Aquil's ambitions were humble to begin with, for he wanted to become a geography teacher after doing a bachelor of education course at St Xavier's College. However, destiny had other plans for him. He cracked admissions to both the prestigious IIM Calcutta and XLRI, Jamshedpur. Those were turbulent times for labour relations in Kolkata, with militant trade unionism at its peak. Yet, the prospect of dealing with people attracted Aquil and he opted for XLRI, never to look back, eventually graduating with a gold medal.

At XLRI, Aquil fully immersed himself in what was then known as personnel management, doing sociology and fieldwork under the much-admired Prof. Nilima Acharji. A tough teacher with her heart in the right place, she taught Aquil the practical aspects of employee engagement, guiding him on a project with the Tinplate Workers' Colony. He persuaded worker families to save each month and helped them open bank accounts. To get their buy-in, Aquil taught the families how to improve their kitchen garden, taking tips from the XLRI gardeners. In doing so, Aquil imbued the fine art of learning from anyone who had something to teach him. These experiences reinforced his virtues of humility and respect for other people.

Aquil had decided to go in for a PhD after completing his XLRI course but was helping as the placement coordinator for his batch. He visited many companies with the curriculum vitae (CV) of his classmates and during his visit to Blue Star, he met B.T. Advani, chairman, and Shyam Makhija, the regional director. They convinced him to join the company and set up their personnel department. Aquil joined as an officer trainee, less than half the age of other managers in the leadership team. He was conscious of his diminutive frame and boyish looks and decided to grow a moustache, wear a tie to work and even carry an impressive Echolac briefcase that was usually empty. Three weeks into the job, Blue Star was celebrating the Vishwakarma festival when the employees' families came for a customary feast at the workshop. Aquil jumped into the act, serving them lunch and joined the organizers for

other activities. His humility and ability to relate with people of all
walks of life got noticed.

The early 1970s were the tumultuous period of industrial unrest
in West Bengal with frequent strikes and gheraos. Aquil faced his first
gherao of over five hours when he was barely twenty-three and a half. He
instinctively knew that he would not be harmed physically and braved
the gherao with visible composure. His ability to connect with the
employees at the grassroots gradually earned him wide acceptance and
respect. For him, 'IR was the best way to learn real OD'. The regional
director to whom Aquil reported also became his mentor, giving
him for his first assignment the tedious job of filling the 'Kalamazoo'
employee record cards. Those were pre-computer days and Aquil hated
making the manual entries that carried on for a few months, wondering
if that was what an MBA should be doing. He realized what a smart
move it was when he started interacting with employees. He was au
fait with the backgrounds of everyone he met, which gave him a head
start. His exposure to IR continued and his skill of staying connected
with the employees was honed. He initiated a town hall-like gathering
with the regional director and the union president sharing the podium
and responding to employee queries. This innovative move in the then
confrontational environment of West Bengal taught him great lessons
as did some others.

During a long and heated meeting in the labour commissioner's
office to resolve a strike, the firebrand union secretary, Budhu Ghosh,
was at his deriding best. Midway through the discussions, he asked one
of his colleagues to unobtrusively pass two samosas and jalebis to Aquil
and then asked the commissioner to break for a few minutes. It was the
month of Ramadan and time for iftar (the evening meal with which
Muslims end their daily Ramadan fast at sunset) and Budhu knew that
Aquil was fasting. Not all the animosity could wring out the kindness of
his opponent's heart. Aquil cherished the strange love-hate relationship
and expressed his gratitude to many union leaders for teaching him in
their own manner.

He was particularly fond of Tapan da, union president and also a
member of the politburo (the principal policy-making committee of
the communist party, then in power in West Bengal). Despite the age
gap, the two related well and kept their differences to the issues at hand.

After heated meetings with the union, Aquil would often be seen at a chai dukan (tea shop) across the road, having tea and muri (puffed rice) with the same union leaders. The message was clear; the confrontation was between the two adversarial positions; there was nothing personal. The mutual respect was there for all to see.

Among the most meaningful lessons that Aquil learnt was around handling terminations. Barely three or four months into his career, he was asked to handle the termination of an office helper, Abdul Gafoor, on charges of frequent absenteeism. Blue Star's legal adviser, T.K. Jagadeesh, a highly respected labour lawyer (later Aquil's mentor), asked if he had personally examined the case or was simply carrying out the message from Gafoor's manager. An embarrassed Aquil admitted that he had cursorily looked at the file and relied on the manager's evaluation. Jagadeesh admonished him for not applying his mind on an important matter like a termination. This unnerved Aquil, but he got the message and resolved to never let such incidents happen again.

The next day, he called Gafoor for a chat and learnt that his wife was suffering from a terminal disease. His three children needed looking after and without any support at home and his brother (who also worked with Blue Star) not of much help, he was constrained to absent himself frequently. Aquil talked to both Gafoor's brother and manager and worked out a practical solution. The termination was withdrawn. Jagadeesh was ecstatic when he heard about how Aquil had handled the matter and complimented him. This encouragement after a stern reprimand was necessary for the young trainee, for later, Aquil never signed on any termination unless he was convinced that all approaches had been examined. Terminating someone was an anxious experience and no food would go down Aquil's throat after he had pink-slipped someone. Traumatic though the loss of the job was for a bread-earner in a family, if it had to be done, Aquil did not shirk his responsibility. His remorse was caused by the underlying empathy.

In 1979, Aquil left Blue Star to join Unilever (Hindustan Lever in India at that time) and served in India and Kenya. His initial IR postings in the sensitive Dalda factory at Shamnagar and the crime-infested Etah Dairy had earned him a reputation that preceded him when he moved to the head office. He performed several HR roles during his stint, including a secondment to Kenya as the training adviser. The company's emphasis on developing talent was its unique feature. For Aquil, it meant opportunities to work with and learn from some of the brightest people. The fourteen-plus years with Unilever form the most significant period of his career, particularly given the level of integrity in the group, which makes him proud to have worked for this great company.

The varied early-life experience and others in difficult environments had prepared Aquil well for what was to become an illustrious career that took him across the globe and to some of the best multinational companies. Moving from Unilever, which was 'home' to him, to Motorola, little-known in India in 1994, was not an easy decision. It was the excitement of setting up a business that attracted Aquil along with the challenge of plunging into the unfamiliar technology sector. Motorola had a small software centre in Bangalore and a handful of people in a makeshift office in Hotel Meridien in Delhi. Initially, Aquil was mandated to look after HR for the South Asian Association for Regional Cooperation (SAARC) countries. Within a year, he was looking after HR for the software business in the Asia–Pacific; some sixteen countries including Japan, Korea, China, all ASEAN countries and Australia, apart from India, Sri Lanka and Bangladesh. Rapid growth in fast-growing markets, cross-cultural teams, varied culture and customs, not to forget the varied cuisine, made for exciting times.

Motorola was Aquil's first experience as CHRO for multiple countries and he carefully selected his team, emphasizing gender, thought and background diversities. In India, for instance, he had built what he later called 'the best team he had worked with'. There was also a major shift in his approach because Aquil had begun to think more from the business head's perspective rather than as an HR leader. This earned him ready acceptance with the business leaders and he directly impacted on shaping the business rather than providing only HR support. His team members, though reporting straight-line to him, were encouraged to align strongly with the goals of their business leaders.

Straight-line reporting of HR made the CHRO more accountable for business performance and Aquil empowered the team and also held it fully accountable for agreed results. Team members had freedom and ownership for their own businesses. The approach won the businesses' respect and Motorola became a beacon for high-quality talent. Yet, he intensely maintained the independence of HR, while driving the team to deliver beyond expectations, earning himself the sobriquet of 'Tiger' within his team. Having thus set the foundation, Aquil began experimenting with stretching his team, focusing on building openness and trust within the team.

So successful was Aquil that the trust level got translated into an open feedback system at team meetings, which became the norm. Aquil had tossed away the bookish wisdom of 'praise in public, criticize in private' amidst growing team maturity and trust between the members, which encouraged them to share their views and feedback candidly, without any hesitation. Aquil then launched a mandatory 'quarterly dialogue' for all his direct reports in each country. He met each one for 90–120 minutes to understand what he could do to support them to succeed (not to discuss the progress of work that was done at review meetings). Aquil made notes about what he would have to do; a sort of reverse process. This became such a successful practice that the annual appraisal became merely the 'fourth quarterly' dialogue. There were no surprises and the team felt fully supported throughout the year. Aquil took this effective process to Shell and IBM when he moved there, with equally effective results.

There were some outstanding examples of HR shaping businesses under him. The semiconductor business was expanding and needed specialized and niche skill sets. A small organization with about 465 employees in Noida had the expertise and Motorola's compensation, pitched at above the seventy-fifth percentile, would enable it to 'poach' talent effortlessly. The impasse was that Motorola's ethical standards would not permit hiring a few employees from that company and asking them to share the end-to-end process. After an extensive discussion, Aquil proposed that Motorola buy the company. There was a brief silence, followed by an animated discussion and it was decided to acquire the company.

Aquil and one of his bright team members strategized on the integration approach. The business leaders had indicated ten to twelve months for knowledge transfer. Any special retention bonus was ruled out as it would adversely impact the other parts of the business. Finally, a comprehensive plan for employee engagement and career enhancement was designed for the new employees with amazing results; the first attrition occurred only after fourteen months of acquisition. That HR can actually shape a business was established beyond doubt.

However, with the advent of mobile phones in India, Motorola's pager business had to be shut down. It was for Aquil to strongly take up employee advocacy and ensure that the separation compensation was not only liberal but the separating employees were also provided re-skilling training at the company's cost. All separations are painful but this was handled with dignity and empathy, leaving intact the goodwill generated over four years. It was then time for Aquil to move as HR director for Shell Malaysia and Brunei, with the additional role of managing director of a full-fledged independent shared-service company; Shell People Services Sdn Bhd.

The prospect of running a profit centre with no directive for businesses to use the services was a challenge that Aquil embraced. His intention was to stretch to earn rather than spend as he had done so far in HR. Malaysia was his favourite country since the mid-1990s. He loved the people, the culture and, of course, the food. Living in Kuala Lumpur (KL) had been his dream and, work apart, he enjoyed the social life that the city had to offer. 'Teh tarik' (a drink of sweet tea with milk in Malaysia) and fish head curry sessions with his team were the bonding moments. He aligned with senior Bumiputera (Malay) leaders and took their counsel frequently. This collaborative behaviour earned him respect and acceptance. Setting up shared services called for financial acumen as he scouted for locations in Vietnam, Cambodia and the Philippines. He finally settled for Cyberjaya in a building adjoining the Shell head office in KL. After the initially anxious months to earn enough to meet the payroll cost, there was the joy of counting profits as business picked up quickly.

IBM then approached him for an HR head position for its global delivery business in India and Aquil was attracted by the company's plans for massive growth. It also gave him an opportunity to get back to his roots, to be close to his mother and in-laws. He accepted the challenge of growing the 14,500 highly specialized headcount to 40,000 over four years. In his characteristic approach, Aquil focused first on meeting a cross-section of business leaders and understanding the business needs. He soon developed sufficient insights into how HR could make a significant difference and shifted his focus to the HR team that he had inherited. It was a mix of seasoned, experienced and some relatively less experienced but bright youngsters. IBM, being reputed for its state-of-the-art HR processes and systems, Aquil knew better than to introduce 'new' HR processes.

Thinking outside the box, Aquil broke some well-established processes and developed improved recreations. The HR team was engaged in thinking through this strategy and key business leaders were taken into confidence. Having received a positive response, he formed six task forces. Each task force was mandated to plan and execute one initiative. His faith in the youngsters showed when he chose task force leaders not based on their tenure but on their ability to deliver. A lady HR manager with four years of experience was the leader of a task force with a senior professional with twenty years' experience as a member. By selecting team leads in an age and experience-agnostic manner, Aquil had breathed new life and energy into the HR team and made history. Global Business Services' headcount touched 52,300 before four years were up. The HR team had played its role well and the business leaders graciously acknowledged their contribution.

After retiring from IBM, Aquil set up an eponymous boutique firm, Aquil Busrai Consulting, offering executive coaching, HR strategy and leadership development, adding Indian entrepreneurs to his portfolio. It was a very different world from that of the multinationals and Aquil learnt the new nuances quickly to become a sought-after sounding board for many CEOs. Aquil coached C-suite executives with notable results. He had learnt to respect local customs in his global assignments; never to call for any meeting after 4 p.m. on Fridays in Australia or one at 12 noon on a Friday in Malaysia, when all the male employees left work first for makan (food) and then went to a mosque for Friday prayers. Aquil readapted to Indian cultural nuances and, after initial hiccups, he was on the ball.

Passion marked Aquil's illustrious journey as he got thoroughly involved in everything that he set his heart on, bringing to bear his enormous energy to the task. That was an immense asset and ensured that he was never short of time to pursue his varied interests. Little surprise that he spends two to three weeks every summer in the jungle photographing wildlife. The varied fare of interest is fascinating as is his yen for new learning, from chocolate-making to playing the saxophone or 3D printing. The many awards that he has won have only made him humbler and better grounded. Much of this he attributes to his daughter, his greatest fan and critic rolled into one. Most significantly, he has remained accessible, especially to young professionals even as he engages with higher learning. A decade after retiring from IBM, he is pursuing his second PhD and a master's degree in anthropology. Aquil loves to teach and is invited as a resource person to several major Indian and international educational institutions.

The other quality that marks him out is his fierce loyalty to his team. He has literally 'chewed up' line managers taking liberties with his HR team members. He is just as particular about keeping commitments, which has enhanced his credibility. Aquil does not take kindly to those who do not honour their commitments and there is evidence of frayed tempers that he reserved for offenders. These qualities he has inspired others to imbibe as he has built and nurtured a wide and expanding network of connections. Aquil's generosity extends to the national councils or advisory boards of major industry representative bodies or professional institutions that he serves on. It is equally reflected in his pro bono services to several institutions. He supports NGOs engaged in educating the girl child and an orphanage and, more importantly, his Bohra community for which he conducts leadership training. This is a throwback to his childhood and to the community that sheltered and nurtured him when times were adverse.

Aquil never forgets generosity; what he learnt from his mother or, for that matter, from Ghosh, the union leader and many more such impactful influences that have made him the man that he is.

* * *

Aroon Joshi

Breaking barriers; setting new paradigms

Distinguished OD professional with successful interventions promoting industrial harmony and raising productivity

With over fifty years of active service in the field of HR and OD, Aroon Joshi is one of the most experienced HR professionals in the country. Aroon has worked in companies in both the public and private sectors as well as in academics and the development sector. He has been group HR head of the RPG Group and director and board member of Cadbury India Ltd. A thought leader in HR and OD, Aroon has distinguished himself with the successful application of OD interventions to develop industrial harmony and raise productivity at the grassroots. Aroon has been a visiting professor at IIM Ahmedabad and Bangalore and is a founding member of the Indian Society for Applied Behavioural Sciences, to which he continues to contribute. A CEO coach and consultant in leadership development, OD and organization restructuring today, Aroon also finds time for a game of golf in Pune, where he lives.

Grandson of a Konkan teacher, who rose to the position of inspector of municipal schools in Bombay, Aroon had enterprise in his DNA. The Joshi joint family of some thirty-five members, including fourteen children, lived in a Gamdevi flat in Central Bombay. Five rooms for the five brothers and a large living space made for a typical middle-class family, with its unique value system. Its main breadwinner, Aroon's father, Dattatraya, served with the Imperial Bank and had great expectations of his son, who was sent to the Christian convent, St Teresa's High School, in Girgaon. Aroon's mind was thus trained to think in English, which set him apart from his sister and cousins, who treated him like a *saab* (master), making him something of a loner.

Aroon's early realizations were that money was not for squandering; one needed to start earning quickly, instead of sponging off the family, and that to be in debt was a shame. He hated to see his indebted uncle being abused by his lenders. Aroon never owed anyone a penny, going to the extent of returning a 20 paise coin that he owed a telephone call operator, who looked at him askance: Who returns 20 paise? Another emerging trait that worried Dattatraya was that his son was becoming anglicized and he switched schools to the more Marathi-oriented but excellent missionary school, Wilson High. Aroon, who was in standard V, welcomed the change and was outstanding here,

being the only student who responded in English. Principal Duncan
Fraser, a Scotsman, influenced Aroon with his talks on working with
nature while the Indianization process involved studying Sanskrit, in
which he did well.

Aroon also excelled in cricket and started playing for the school.
That did not sit well with his father's friend, a teacher in that school,
who was apprehensive that he would end up becoming a cricketer. His
father put an end to cricket by advising Aroon to focus on his studies.
Nudged by Dattatraya (as his mother Lila later told Aroon), even the
principal asked him to do so, though Aroon was within the top ten
in his class. Aroon took to swimming instead, excelling at it and was
also outstanding in NCC at Elphinstone College, Bombay University,
which he joined after school to study economics. He was keen on doing
law but also fancied the armed forces. It was as a swimmer that he made
a mark though, helping the college win the collegiate swimming title.
He also won the inter-university swimming title for his university and
eventually swam at the national level with some distinction.

As luck would have it, Burmah Shell Refineries came for campus
selections to Elphinstone College and picked Aroon. Dattatraya
would have preferred him to go in for the IAS but kept his aspirations
to himself, though not without putting Aroon through the Hindu
Gymkhana for lessons in tennis and equestrianism. This was when
Aroon's NCC instructor asked him to join the army. He jumped at
the offer but his shocked parents would not have their only son going
off to the army. Aroon thought otherwise and ran away to stay with
a friend at Chowpatty and sit for the army exams. He had prawns
for dinner the night before the exams and a leaky tummy the next
day put paid to his plans for taking the examinations. Determined,
Aroon applied for the Short Service Commission and was found to be
colour blind. This limited his options to the Corps of Signals, Service
Corps and other units that he did not fancy. He wanted the Gurkhas
or Marathas. Then came the Burmah Shell offer. It would have been
foolish not to accept an offer from one of the most prized companies
of the time.

Industrial relations was about law and Aroon was placed with
personnel and IR, though trainees were moved through all the
departments. He got acclimatized over the year, while he completed

the studies and was posted at the Chembur refinery, in the staff and IR department. The job afforded Aroon the opportunity to move out of the joint family and rent an apartment in Colaba. Refinery recruitment had just started for workers and upper supervisory staff at Burmah Shell and most management staff had been selected and sent to England for training. For Aroon, it was one hectic recruitment spree, selecting 1500 people in two or three months without any sophisticated interview techniques. Aroon and a colleague from the technical department checked the CVs for experience and the accompanying write-ups for both the technical and administrative supervisory interviews. If both agreed on a candidate, he was in. Aroon hit the deck running only to have things heating up further.

A strike in the refinery taught Aroon some interesting lessons about the negotiation drama in the petroleum space, the perils of overqualification for jobs and needless stratification on the shop floor. Some sahib had stipulated that an intermediate science would be the minimum qualification for a purely mechanical plant operator's job. Identification badges worn by the employees were coloured green for staff, red for labour and orange for the management staff. There were separate canteens to boot. Plant operators legitimately asked how a supervisor, also a BSc, was superior to them and why they were barred from entering the supervisors' canteen. The answer, that one was a labourer and daily-rated while the supervisory staff was monthly-rated, was unacceptable and prompted a two-day strike. Plant operators, whom Aroon was friendly with, said it was nonsensical and refused to be ordered around by those academically at par. Besides, they were bored.

This resonated with Aroon who realized that the operator's job did not need a bachelor's degree. He also picked up many skills during the next eighteen-day industry-wide strike. Managers were cooking, driving trucks, filling gas cylinders and measuring the levels in a tank. A training programme under Pratap (Bundle) Sen thereafter taught Aroon the importance of matching jobs to qualifications. His new boss, Jack Trigg, supported his position and under the new specifications, the qualification for the operators was dropped to Senior Cambridge or matriculate, with a week's training. This worked well. Sen's lessons had hit home for overqualified people are usually trouble; not a virtue.

Aroon had completed six years in the refinery when he went to Calcutta to see his father, then secretary and treasurer of the State Bank there.

Their neighbour, Ishwar Dayal, met him over dinner and told a shocked Aroon that he was wasting his time at Burmah Shell. No one talked of Burmah Shell with anything but reverence. To Aroon's further discomfiture, Dayal asked if he understood the drivers for the strikes in the refineries and Aroon had no convincing answer. On evaluating his work, he realized that Dayal was right; and that he was bored. Dayal asked him to see the personnel manager of Metal Box, Bombay, for an interview. He met Nariman Khory and the two hit it off. Dayal also set up interviews with Union Carbide and ICI, which had a vacancy, and asked him to consider his options. Burmah Shell was a very old British company and ICI and Metal Box were 'English' too. He opted for Metal Box since it was based in Bombay, to work as the industrial relations officer at the Bombay factory at Worli under Khory.

Aroon's halcyon days of comfort were gone; the early days were sheer trauma with a culture shock to boot. From the plush Burma Shell office, he was sitting on a table and chair outside Khory's room, with the canteen boy plonking his teacup on his table. Aroon found himself interested in what was happening nevertheless. The encouraging Khory got him to mingle with the people and Aroon realized that the personnel department was powerful but not popular. Aroon proceeded to make a few friends; Dilip Bhatt and Srinivas Rao taught him what IR was all about. He also made friends with the workers and some union leaders over chats and arguments. Then, at a three-day HR conference, when all the branch personnel managers met in Calcutta, he made a presentation on working with work committees.

It was then Dayal's turn to wow Aroon with his philosophy for HR. Dayal's opening sentence was that HR's role was to assist management to obtain the spontaneous cooperation of workers for achieving the organizational goals. HR was not about doing *mara-mari* (fighting). Thinking deeply about this was quite a moving experience for Aroon. Dayal asked Aroon to read *Glacier Metal, The Human Side of Enterprise*, and *People at Work*, which he would discuss with Aroon on his next trip to Bombay. Aroon's mind went from the minutiae to the big picture. *Glacier Metal* explained it beautifully and Aroon decided that he would have to educate the management on its role and that of HR. Aroon was ready for his second job in Metal Box as HR manager at the newly established Deonar factory where three major departments from the Worli factory were shifted.

Aroon used the opportunity to initiate a different way of working while retaining some practices. The responsibility of sanctioning leave to workers, hitherto with HR because it occasionally involved a union contact, was transferred to the shop floor, where it really belonged. No one took him seriously and the old practice continued. To send his message across, Aroon sanctioned leave to everyone who applied in May, and work in one section almost came to a halt one day. The factory manager was upset but Aroon had struck home. He also stopped needless charge sheets and insisted that they be raised on convincing grounds and after observing procedures, in which he would train them. As matters sank in, Aroon organized lectures from the Tata Institute of Social Sciences (TISS) to promote a better understanding. Soon he was promoted as the chief training officer, with a Calcutta posting, reporting to Kuldeep Puri, the HR head.

Puri had taken over from Dayal, who had joined IIM Calcutta. Metal Box was running a three-week programme at Aldeen, ITC's training centre. Aroon seized the opportunity to change the format and introduce IIM-C faculty, including stalwarts such as Yogendra Alagh, Suresh Srivastava, Ishwar Dayal and Nitesh De. People looked forward to them. Those (1966–71) were bad days for Calcutta and Aroon could run no more than four programmes a year. IR was time-consuming with constant gheraoes (fifty-four days on one occasion), even though IR was not his job. Puja bonus was a contentious affair and while he did not face the workers, he had to take care of habeas corpus, fetching the police or going to the court for orders to get the gheraoed managers released. The police released them only for them to be gheraoed the next day. These were perspective-building shenanigans and Aroon even went to meet Kanu Sanyal, the notorious Naxalite, with his friend, the union leader Chittaranjan Dasgupta, a Naxalite himself.

To his question why the gheraoes, Sanyal said: 'You management types . . . unless I close your nose, your mouth does not open.' Yet, the worker–management relationship was cordial per se and no one was physically harmed at Metal Box though Naxalism pervaded the Calcutta air. Things were in short supply and while Aroon's family lived in the posh Alipore area, times were stressful. Aroon moved to Lord Sinha Road, closer to the office but the growing hostility in the air with occasional bloodshed on the streets was disconcerting. After six years and a massive dose of learning on how to run effective programmes, Aroon returned to Bombay as personnel manager of the region, taking over from a retiring Khory. It was during this stint that P. Gopalan, the factory manager of Deonar passed away and Aroon was asked to temporarily hold the fort. Aroon doubled up as a factory manager and impressed the management. He was offered a position in line management but wanted to stick to HR.

As factory manager, Aroon was fed up with sending daily reports and realized how tiresome it was for all the managers, who dreaded the daily calls on production, daily scrap, percentage of this to that and such details. Realizing that a good HR manager would have to view the role from the management's perspective, he was in touch with people across the board, keeping an eye on grievances, production and such issues on a daily basis. He knew how HR could smoothen the process and, with a greater knowledge of line functions, drove remarkable productivity improvements. The can-making plants comprised a press and a body-maker and any change from large to small cans meant a twelve-hour wait, while the operators wiled away their time. Aroon suggested that the operators set the process themselves and make it efficient. The manager thought that the unions would not allow it. After much persuasion, ITI pass-outs were placed on three presses, trained and, during the changeover, they put the new die and started it again. The canteen break had been obviated.

This was successfully extended to the entire press shop including the body-maker, the core of can-making. With his shift in-charge friend, K.K. Thomas, Aroon got two people who understood the body-maker and let them set the process. They did it in ten hours, then improved it to eight hours and further to six hours, convincing the manager about the new approach. Productivity of the department improved by around 60 per cent. This became the standard and was adopted by the other plants and even the British were impressed with the innovation. Metal Box, Bombay, now had two can factories, one paper factory and one plastics factory, with 3500 jobs under one union. As line managers started managing people, IR improved with the management staff chipping in with relationship-building. Bombay never had a strike. There were three changes of union leaders and one was jailed during the Emergency where Aroon met him as a goodwill gesture. The next union leader, Dina Bama Patil, was a person of some notoriety but Aroon successfully engaged with him too.

Aroon had learnt a great deal about workers and had persuaded the management to shed its antipathy towards unions and learn to live with them. The Bombay branch was under Douglas Alger, who understood Aroon's position and insisted that the management engage with the union too. They fell in line and Aroon had another role model to emulate after Dayal. Alger, an elegant Oxford man, changed mindsets in Bombay. Aroon had spent some nineteen years in Metal Box and was deputy chief personnel manager when Puri got posted as managing director, Nigeria. Aroon was asked to return to Kolkata to replace him but he wanted to function out of Bombay. The MD did not agree and C.D. Menon got the position. Aroon was happy working with him, for Metal Box had become a great place for experimentation and trend-setting. The bonding with the union was close. His greatest learning was that relationships are everything. That was deepened with his engagement with the ISABS.

It was then that a close friend, Dipendro Sengupta from Ferguson's, told him about the position with Cadbury's. This led to a thirteen-year tenure with totally different experiences in an English company with an English boss, Ian Campbell. Cadbury's was then facing an eight-month strike and Bombay was in the throes of aggressive unionism. Aroon believed that only a third-party intervention could break the impasse because union–management dialogue had all but stopped. The workers had stoned management cars and even threatened managers personally. An appeal to the Maharashtra Chief Minister, A.R. Antulay, got him to order an end to the strike.

Antulay was upset with the bad name that Maharashtra was getting because of the rampant unionism. He told the unions to be satisfied with the 20 per cent bonus that the law allowed. He also told the management that they could not sack the suspended employees without proper inquiries. The directive was that the strike must be called off. Antulay angrily told the union that it was unreasonable and the management that it was harsh. That was that. Aroon could apply his wealth of experience, theoretical and experiential, at Cadbury's because he was well and truly in charge. Campbell reposed total faith in him. The unions had checked him out with the Metal Box workers and received fair feedback.

Aroon realized that Cadbury's scandalous master–servant relationship needed changing. The annual crisis in Bombay was over the Diwali bonus demand with the unions insisting on more than what the law stipulated. This led to the eight-month strike, when a large number of workers were suspended. Aroon took stock of the situation and realized that the managers had been ill-advised from the director downwards. He told Campbell that the worker misdemeanours did not warrant sacking, the case would not stand in court, and Cadbury's may have to take the sacked people back, making them heroes. His task was to change the management mindsets and worker perceptions. The solution was to tell the workers that they were wrong but the management was taking a soft stance because it did not want their families to suffer. The management created a halo around itself. The suspended workers were taken back, despite trepidation that the management raj would end, but Campbell stood by Aroon.

The upshot was that the credibility of both HR and the managing director, in terms of being fair to people, was established. The management had won a strategic battle and there was great jubilation among workers in the factory. Regular dialogues with the union committee thereafter saw problems discussed threadbare amidst arguments but things were settling down. A three-week training programme for managers reinforced correct notions of their role, managing and motivating people, and other HR issues. Alongside, a well-received management trainee scheme was started with recruits from IIMs and IITs. It was just as important to give the workers an understanding of the business.

Workers, sceptical that their strike could affect Cadbury's bottom line ('We're Cadbury's; how can our chocolates suffer?'), were put through a programme, specially designed by Aroon and conducted by Vasantrao Karnik, the HR head of the Times of India group. Karnik, a former member of the violence-espousing M.N. Roy group, had risen from the ranks of a union leader to head HR for the Times of India group. An IT expert helped Aroon to create a business game around a *chanawala* (peddler of gram) who bought gram, processed it at home and sold it at Chowpatty to create a thriving business. The game had the business expanding, the son joining the father, starting a shop to sell murmura, chana, bhel, sev and such savouries. The entrepreneur then started a small factory to process the gram into different food items; business flourished and he hired workers.

The game then had the workers going on a strike, insisting that payments were poor. As a consequence, business suffered. A part of the business was shut down before a negotiated settlement was reached. The moral of the story was conveyed to the worker over the game played on the computer and conducted in a day. Karnik explained what running a business and running a union were about in the run of the play, underscoring what the union's role should be. The union leader, Dastur, was suspicious but was convinced that this was no anti-union exercise after he attended a three-day programme. He only insisted that the union committee first attend the programme and decide who would attend it thereafter. The programme did thirty to forty rounds, covering all employees. Dastur admitted that with a better understanding of the business, worker demands on him had got moderated. More importantly, a relationship had been established between the workers and the management.

Next, Aroon organized groups of workers to visit marketplaces to check out the shops selling Cadbury's products' and ask questions. Amul had entered the market as had Caco from the south. Nestlé was also starting its chocolate business and many shopkeepers asked the visiting workers why they should stock the expensive Cadbury's. The penny dropped as the workers realized that Cadbury's market share was down from 96 per cent to 54 per cent; Bournvita's had dropped from 82 per cent to 22 per cent. The market share had to be reclaimed and Aroon counselled that it would need the workers to work with the management. This initiative was kicked off with a thanksgiving programme, a Satyanarayan puja. The workers collected the funds and Aroon raised a matching contribution from the company for a beautiful puja with the most recently married worker couple performing the rituals. A play was enacted too, whereafter the internal union leader,

Vishwas Ghatge, gave a speech. He picked up some soil from the ground and swore that there would be no more strikes. There has never been a strike at the Cadbury's Thane factory since. The transformation was complete.

Aroon had erred at times. In Madhya Pradesh, unaware of the importance of the Teej festival, the management had not declared a holiday at the Malanpur factory. Had the union committee been formed on time, the catastrophe of no worker turning up for three days would not have occurred. Aroon held it to be his fault. The absence without leave was forgiven and Aroon started participative management. There was consternation within the management about losing its rights and Aroon thought that the Japanese system of Quality Circles could help change mindsets. He got C.Y. Pal and T.V.G. Krishnamurthy, Cadbury's managing director and technical director, respectively, to attend a Japanese Union of Scientists and Engineers (JUSE) programme in Japan. They returned to start quality circles with help from a consultant. Participative management became a success and Aroon was happy to have the erstwhile critical Krishnamurthy visit his room to compliment him on his understanding of the process. Krishnamurthy later recounted how their disagreement led to learnings for him.

While Aroon could not implement everything that he had learnt, never having quite pulled off Dayal's philosophy of spontaneous cooperation, he moved in that direction and what he did achieve inspired other corporates. They constantly solicited his advice; Hindustan Lever looked for strategies to counter Datta Samant (the fiery trade union leader) as did Bharat Forge and Kirloskar from Pune. Aroon delivered lectures on how to do things differently and persevered with his pursuit of spontaneous cooperation. Training being critical to the developments at Cadbury's, Aroon also created a subsidiary company for consulting and training other companies as well with the revenues accruing to Cadbury's. When he first talked about spontaneous cooperation at Cadbury, he was dismissed for trying to achieve Utopia in Cuckooland. He did achieve greater camaraderie and his enhanced stature got him the honour of depute for the MD who had gone on long leave.

After retiring from Cadbury's in 1993, Aroon joined the RPG Group as president, HR. He quickly observed that RPG was importing top talent to meet its needs, overlooking resident talent. There were also enormous disparities in grades, salaries and scales, and transfers from one organization to another were difficult. Aroon restored order by first creating standards to assess people through an assessment centre for competencies for management jobs, followed by a unified grading structure and he took it forward with internal training. The building blocks to HR got constructed. Harsh Goenka gave him a long rope and Aroon organized a conference for the personnel departments of all group companies. He brought in Manohar Nadkarni to talk about competencies and assessment centres; he took them through these techniques and presented one at a meeting where the senior management, including Harsh Goenka, was present. Next, Aroon attended a Saville & Holdsworth programme to understand the technology to create the assessment centres, especially for the twenty-nine to thirty-nine age group.

Aroon also continued his work with the ISABS. What began with Puri of Metal Box sending him to attend the train-the-trainer programme at IIM Ahmedabad spearheaded by Tarun Sheth to give him his first encounter with T-group went on to three phases of ISABS internship. He became a T-group trainer and organized practice training sessions every weekend; he also ran a programme at ISABS every summer. This continued till recent times with the last programme in Jaipur a couple of years ago. T-group led to organization development and Aroon did an internship at National Training Laboratories (NTL) for two months learning from Richard Beckhard and others to see how OD interventions were done. He also spent an evening at Portland (Maine) and heard Carl Rogers. After a seven-year stint with RPG, Aroon retired in 2000 to settle down in Pune, where he got independent training assignments from friends and former colleagues. This phase took him across the world doing consulting and delivering training programmes to international clients, including Pepsi, Datacraft, Mahindra British Telecom and some local companies such as Asian Paints and the Anand Group among others.

In all this, Aroon encouraged people to think for themselves and take decisions, backing them up wherever necessary. He had learnt well from Dayal, Puri and Alger and had received infinite support from Khory, when he was a greenhorn. When Niraj Goyal, manager, and Chella Ganesh, HR manager at Malanpur wanted to try different things, they had his complete support. To enforce cleanliness at the food factory, they wanted workers to shower before starting work and provided bathrooms, towels and soap so that they entered the factory with clean hands and nails cut, having attended to all other hygiene issues. Encouraging such innovative thinking and sharing knowledge have been integral to his HR practice. While sharing his experiences with managing situations, Aroon often asked people to apply these learnings in their workspaces. That is how he developed leadership around work-related issues and even personal issues.

Alcoholism, another major problem at the Cadbury's factory resulting in absenteeism, was addressed by inviting Alcoholics Anonymous who held classes in the factory for alcoholics. Backed by Aroon, Pratik Roy, the training and development manager, ensured that it was a success, helping many alcoholics recover. On the lighter side, Aroon recalls a drunk emerging from his habitual stupor and taking charge of a kabaddi match at Cadbury's (they had an excellent kabaddi team and the man was interested in playing). He came to work sober, harangued his fellow workers to play a spirited match and they did his bidding. Cometh the hour, cometh the man, as Aroon experienced again when there was a bomb blast outside the RPG office. The street corner cobbler took charge of the ensuing melee; commanding Aroon to call the police and another to call the fire brigade and generally restored order. Everyone listened to him and Aroon witnessed this amazing leadership in action.

Leadership often came crawling out of the woodwork. To Aroon, the first aspect of genuine leadership lay in inspiring people with a purpose and then getting them to do things willingly.

HR professionals should understand the deeper substance of their role to deliver greater value as specialists in understanding people, he believes, though it is a low priority in modern-day HR thinking, especially with remote delivery of HR services. Human relations without the human touch seems to be anathema to Aroon. While he understands that younger fellow professionals are delivering value under trying circumstances, it is an issue that he struggles with. Digital HR seems to be depriving HR of the humaneness that only proximity can provide. As always, Aroon spends time contemplating a solution under these circumstances.

* * *

Ashok K. Balyan

HR alchemist striking right chemistry

A business leader who raised the bar of HR practices by transforming public sector mindsets

Ashok Kumar Balyan (Ashok) held many senior leadership positions in the public and private sectors. He was director HR, Oil and Natural Gas Corporation; managing director and CEO, Petronet LNG Ltd; and CEO (Oil and Gas), Reliance Group. Taking over as chief of Petronet in July 2010, he steered the company through a phase of rapid expansion to a leadership position in the liquefied natural gas (LNG) business. A.K. Balyan did his MTech from the Indian Institute of Technology, Delhi and his PhD from Germany. His major contributions include preparing the first twenty-five-year Perspective Plan of Oil and Natural Gas Corporation Limited (ONGC), 1990–2015; establishing and demonstrating the production of coal bed methane (CBM) for the first time in the country; establishing ONGC's first 51 MW wind power plant; and constructing and commissioning a C2+ extraction plant that was unique in the world.

A.K. Balyan was a director on the board of many other companies, including ONGC Videsh Ltd, Mangalore Refinery and Petrochemicals, Petronet LNG Ltd, Dahej SEZ Ltd, Mangalore SEZ Ltd, ONGC Tripura Power Company, ONGC Petro-additions Ltd (OPaL) and L&T Hydrocarbons Ltd. He has held many professional positions such as president of the Delhi Management Association and was national president of the National Institute of Personnel Management. His many recognitions included Business Today's *Best CEOs award in 2014.*

Ashok Kumar Balyan was born into the family of Chaudhary Bhupal Singh, the shahar kotwal (town police head) of Kanpur. It was an interesting childhood with stature, which came from his father's position, alongside humble living conditions courtesy the kotwal's emoluments, but it pegged his ethical values rather high. The memory of a father, with over 100 police personnel under him, refusing a Rs 50,000 reward for having rescued an industrialist's daughter was embedded in the psyche of the child.

Ashok's modest school had him sitting on a floor mat through junior classes I–II and then trudging four kilometres to reach the Chaharwati Intermediate School, Akola, for classes III and IV. It had one teacher for everyone. The fun lay in the loads of extracurricular activities because sports ran in his veins. His father, a sportsman and a family man, believed in the joint family in which he was the chacha (uncle). The home provided Ashok with all the joys that extended families, cousins, et al., afforded. Sharing was a part of this milieu and money mattered little.

The other abiding memory from his youth was of his father turning down a marriage proposal for him from a wealthy family with cars and bungalows. The Balyans 'lived in a rented home and had only a cycle', he told them. There could be no better example of living within one's means and staying within one's financial comfort zone. It was a discipline instilled from childhood and his father's spirit made several telling differences to Ashok's life. Little was he to know that being the son of a policeman would be an amazing strength when his career would take him to terrorist-infested terrains and the world of bullying unions. Or that his father's love for sports would make him pursue sports throughout his academic career and institute sports in the company that he would lead way in the distant future.

Teaching standards improved as Ashok moved to Agra though the medium was Hindi right up to class X. At any given point in time, sports took precedence over studies for the bright and reasonably attentive boy who ranked between tenth and fifteenth in class. Then came the big shift to Agra's St John's College—modern, Cambridge board, English medium. Class XI meant struggling to adjust to new circumstances but it was made interesting by Prof. P.I. Ittyerah, a PhD from India and Cambridge. He kept up with his classmates by observing their manners and emulating them while picking up a foreign language. Ashok had a lot of catching up to do. This struggle notwithstanding, he enjoyed sports in which he excelled and got hooked on chemistry, thanks to Prof. Ittyerah's engaging, storytelling style, graduating with a high first class in BSc.

Prof. Ittyerah soon became principal and persuaded Ashok to go in for a master's in chemistry. Thus, between representing his college in cricket and playing hockey, he did his masters, ranking fourth in the university. He wanted to teach but was underage for a lecturer's post. Disappointed, Ashok joined the MTech at IIT Delhi where he topped the batch. Then, he joined the R&D department at Delhi's Shri Ram Institute for Industrial Research in 1972. Hard work for long hours on polymers and plastics at the laboratory was rewarded by two patents to his credit; ABS plastics and polycarbonate. These fetched him some royalties as well. However, the company refused to forward his application for a commonwealth scholarship for a PhD in the UK, which triggered the urge to quit the Shri Ram Group. It also embedded a commitment to ensure that he would facilitate higher education and self-improvement, whenever he had the opportunity.

The next stop was ONGC, Dehradun, which he joined in October 1976. The office began at 9.30 a.m., but even the cleaners came at 10 and the bosses at 11. There was little time for any technical discussion because it was quickly time for lunch, followed by siesta up to 3 p.m. and it was time to leave between 4.30 and 5 p.m. The contrast from Shri Ram's was stark. There, Ashok worked from 9.30 to 5 but often came earlier and left later. Of his twenty-five batchmates, Ashok got seniority based on merit. Getting accepted in a sarkari work environment was a challenge, but he found solace in his brilliant bosses, learning a lot from S.N. Talukdar, director, who was a brilliant geologist and a super exploration man. Kuldeep Chandra, head of chemistry, was another outstanding support for Ashok as he plunged into the job of unpacking and commissioning new equipment lying unused. Chandra would visit the laboratory at 5 p.m. and spend an hour and a half with Ashok, encouraging him to modernize the laboratory so that it could actually support exploration.

A supercharged Ashok made an elaborate plan for 'change', driven by the vision to explore oil in India. He also applied for an Indo-German (government of India–Germany) scholarship for doing his PhD but was turned down by the junior personnel officer, who found him ineligible. Ashok wrote to the director, personnel, D.N. Awasthi, for leave to pursue his PhD and was given extraordinary leave in 1978, becoming the first person in ONGC to be given leave within one and a half years of joining. Ashok completed his PhD in 1982 and returned to ONGC. When the junior personnel officers said that he would lose seniority, Ashok escalated the matter to his seniors to have his seniority restored; yet another first for ONGC. It was time for Ashok to put his experiences to use. He was transferred to Ankleshwar, Baroda and then to Assam, for the mandatory three years and received exposure over a wide canvas. During his posting at Baroda, he prepared ONGC's twenty-five-year perspective plan under a group general manager of the exploration department.

Assam was a difficult, even dangerous, terrain. As DGM and project head in Jorhat, Ashok learnt that his predecessor had been shot at. The son of the kotwal was undeterred as he braved Nagaland and Assam, enhancing production and reducing cycle time. Overcoming such challenges was empowering and gave him the confidence to serve even under terrorist threats. The underground Naga Council demanded Rs 1 crore, or else! Ashok went to meet the senior rebel leaders without any security, networked with them and negotiated such that work could proceed. Each job entailed new learnings and instilled in him the love of sharing what was learnt. Ashok was keen to learn new technical things and start new initiatives, and encouraged others to take an interest in them.

Meanwhile, the ONGC chairman, B.C. Bora, transferred him to head management services in his office and also head corporate communications in a three-year assignment in Delhi. Ashok learnt the art of talking to the media and tried to tell the correct story, even if it meant talking about an offshore drilling rig blowout or some other crisis in operations elsewhere. He learnt to field difficult questions on camera. The next posting was as basin manager in Kolkata to head the exploration work from Tripura to the Andamans. Kolkata came with its package of union-led indiscipline and, over a five-year stint, Ashok dealt with them firmly, lodging several police complaints and getting the troublemakers arrested. When a group of 300 contingent workers threatened to go on strike in a seismic exploration survey, Ashok handled them within forty-eight hours and put an end to the trouble.

Ashok was the first exploration chemist to become a basin manager; 99 per cent of his colleagues were geologists. He established good gas reserves in the difficult areas of Tripura and demonstrated that Indian coal could produce methane gas commercially. Kolkata had nearly 100 excellent technical people. Ashok embarked on a process of retraining and redeploying them, including even drivers and telephone operators, shaking some from the complacence with their underperforming lives. He knew that performance picks up if the right chords are pulled and he did so.

Unknown to himself, Ashok was developing qualities of excellence in human resource management. He also realized that managers across the board had a major HR role to perform vis-à-vis people working under them. He had superseded some of them, but Ashok worked well within their comfort zones. He stayed friends with them at a personal level, never trying to be controlling or coming off as threatening or coercing. Eventually, the trick to getting good performance out of people lay in giving them the freedom to contribute. Assam and Kolkata were the real crucibles that baked him.

At this time, the redoubtable Subir Raha of Indian Oil took over as ONGC chairman. A workaholic, he brought in a disciplined style, visiting the Kolkata office five times in the first year and wanting to visit prospective sites like Bokaro after the fourth visit. On Raha's fifth visit, Ashok accompanied him to Bokaro. After returning, Raha wanted Ashok to move to human resources. Unhappy, Ashok thought he was being penalized for a job poorly done but Raha opened his eyes to the demands of organizational growth over drinks one evening. 'Transformation for organizations to change and grow had to be driven by HR' and Raha was looking for people who could lead this change. 'You have the widest acceptability and respect—cutting across all disciplines—and you will be the right person to drive the change. Competitiveness and change will emerge from HR.' Raha convinced Ashok over a two-hour conversation and conceded to Ashok's condition that, if he failed, he would be reverted to his current position. Ashok became the chief HRD officer, a new position, based in Dehradun.

Looking back, Ashok believes that his success was engineered by his love for meeting new people, to learn and share with them, as he had done right from the start, even as a research chemist in a Dehradun laboratory. There he had proposed that the team write a paper and share it at a conference. Knowledge, he believed, should be shared and people should network to get to know each other not just in the external world but within the workspace as well. Ashok moved to Dehradun as chief of HRD in 2001 and found that most HR peers were senior to him. They were bureaucratic in style, sitting on hierarchy. By contrast, Ashok unhesitatingly went down to the dealing level, meeting his colleagues, introducing himself and giving due respect to their seniority. He was not sure about how he would establish the HR ecosystem, to begin with. Nevertheless, he prioritized some key issues: transfer and promotion policy, performance management, and training and development. His peers were not on the same page, so he turned to Raha who gave them clear directions.

Ashok found that promotions, due on 1 January every year, were delayed by more than three years. This had to be set right. There would be no retrospective promotions, no interviews, but Ashok instituted an alternative mechanism, based on the last three years' performance rating for the corporate positions. The earlier rating used to be A/A+ with some qualitative comments. There were 500 senior employees involved and Ashok collected their last five years' rating, found a pattern and proposed the scale. He assessed people as good for leadership positions or promotion, executive workers and good for the current role. He defined scales and rating parameters. From the following year, the ratings were more quantitative; people going to Assam (mandatory posting) were given extra points. For promotions, the previous rating would account for 90 per cent and other personality traits—on eight to ten defined parameters—would be judged by the respective directors for the remaining 10 per cent.

To make the plan work, Ashok had to secure the buy-in of the officers' association in which there were many career politicians. He discussed everything threadbare with them, from the transfer policy, grooming strategy and the right to rotate. Anyone who had evaded an Assam transfer for ten years would have to accept a three-year Assam posting. Alongside, Ashok started refresher courses, had the intranet installed for communications and sought feedback/suggestions on policies through the intranet. He put out positive stories on the intranet that also had Raha participating. The other big change was to put 'transfer considerations' duly ranked on the net, injecting complete transparency into the system. Even the carping critics were turned around and shown respect.

Personally, Ashok was available to meet anyone from any rank. He travelled to work centres, held open houses that were very well attended with 300 to 400 people at a time. He used the platform to share company performance and HR policies, and engage with people on work and personal well-being issues. The sportsman in him introduced physical fitness for offshore postings. As far as dialogues went, he began his presentations to unions or officers' associations with an account of the company's performance to bring perspective to the deliberations. Ashok then introduced welfare schemes and training for all. Deployment policies, including role–roster–responsibility (R3), were worked out and there was a shift from levels to roles.

Ashok's operational experience helped him establish manning norms. There was a clear 20 per cent overmanning in the ONGC-owned-and-operated drilling rigs. Additionally, there were contract workers as well; a total of 15,000 to 20,000 contract workers in addition to regular employees at different sites. These were presented to the association using data, scientific studies and international practices, and no one could counter him with bogus talk. Ashok believed in seeking consensus, approaching the issue from a problem-solving perspective, not a bargaining one. Collaboration and consultation being the twin pillars of Ashok's approach to HR, he could conclude his discussions with the association. ONGC's multiple expertise had to be made collaborative and multidisciplinary for successful exploration. Within each basin, there was a disciplined team and Ashok introduced a specialist cadre for research work, distinct from the general management cadre, with separate policies for compensation, placement plan and promotion.

Ashok got Infosys to create a 'knowledge base', an IT platform for knowledge-sharing. He successfully introduced performance-linked variable pay after changing the performance rating from confidential to 'online', with rating by at least two persons (boss plus one other person working closely with the employee and of equal rank as the boss). People could check their rating 'online'. Over workshops, he got the acceptance of the staff union because the focus was on objectivity. He also introduced insurance-based higher benefit schemes for the employees that were posted on the operational site. Contributory social security schemes were introduced after discussions on the ratio of contribution. He could equally win over his peers through dialogue, engaging them to convince others: it was their case that Ashok was taking forward.

Regional dialogues were introduced too and people were persuaded to ask how they could become more effective and serve ONGC better.

In his open dialogues, Ashok engaged in role-playing and asked people to speak out on how they would approach the HR director's role and make recommendations for changes. Ashok got them involved in the process of change. That extended to upgrading skills and enhancing educational qualifications. ONGC needed academically qualified persons for specific roles and many technical staff did not have the right qualification. With the new educational enhancement scheme, ITI-trained people could obtain diplomas and the diploma holders could go for BTech degrees. Ashok tied up with the Punjab Technology University for a full-time two-and-a-half-year programme, with an open admission test. There was also a tie-up with a local engineering college for each batch comprising seventy to eighty people to facilitate practical work.

There were four to five batches and the convocations were held at the ONGC Academy in Dehradun. Full salaries were paid over the entire period as people were motivated to advance from Q3 (ITI) to Q2 (diploma holders) to Q1 (engineers). Ashok removed the earlier limitation that a Q2 could not go beyond the E4 (executive level 4 or middle management level) and ensured that upward mobility in the company could be earned right from the grassroots. People were also given leave to do their PhD in a wholesome initiative to promote growth and have a better-qualified payroll with greater exposure to their fields of activity.

To prepare GMs and higher levels for leadership roles Ashok developed a programme comprising three weeks in IIM Lucknow and two weeks overseas. He also signed MoUs with the Indian Institute of Foreign Trade (IIFT) and the Management Development Institute for chief managers (E5 level). Individuals went through the admission process via an open test in a batch of twenty-five in each institute for full-time residential MBAs. They were taken off the normal working roster but asked to do ONGC-related assignments for project work. The performance standard was defined and, after completion, the pass-outs were given challenging roles. There were three such batches with 75–80 per cent of the course in the standard course structure and the rest customized for ONGC.

To prepare the top rung for board positions, Ashok tied up with the Indian School of Business (ISB), Hyderabad, for a one-year special course with a two-and-a-half-month residential programme. The rest was done through programmes on ONGC-specific issues while being live on the regular job. Between three and five people were identified as likely candidates for each director-level position. General manager and executive director positions were all 'role-based'. For example, the chief of HRD could be a general manager, group general manager or executive director. These were identified and defined across the company and their growth was monitored by an executive committee of internal directors (EC) and an HRM committee of the board that was headed by the renowned Prof. Bakul Dholakia (former IIM Ahmedabad director) and independent directors on the ONGC board.

The process Ashok followed was to have the young people in the team make a draft policy paper that would be taken up for discussion with the union or association. Thereafter, it would be discussed in the EC and HRM committee, headed by Prof. Dholakia, to build consensus at each level. Sometimes this took several months. Prof. Dholakia was very proactive and always championed company autonomy and people-focused policies. When the 'incentive scheme' came up for discussion, everyone wanted distribution on an equal basis with no differentiation, but Ashok championed differentiation on the basis of the hardship of work involved and place of posting. His innumerable innovations made him the suitable choice for the post of director HR in 2003. Ashok had the added responsibility for business development, information technology and logistics (offshore).

Ashok not only became an accomplished HR man but kept in close touch with fellow HR professionals and contributed to the development of the HR profession in the country by actively involving himself with the National HRD Network. He also served as the national president of the National Institute of Personnel Management from 2006 to 2010 and on the board of the National HRD Network between 2013 and 2015, having left ONGC in July 2010, when he had another one and a half years to go. More than a decade after he left, Ashok gets calls from union leaders and members of the officers' association. They remember the tough HR chief with respect for his sense of discipline, the respect that he showed seniors and insisted that his colleagues show as well.

The honourable policeman's son showed his mettle when all company associations went on strike for compensation-related matters and Ashok warned them and then suspended more than fifty officers, lodging an FIR against three for disrupting activities. The strike was called off unconditionally, apologies were made and suspensions were revoked. The legal cases continued though and two were penalized. These remarkable changes were instituted at a public sector undertaking and brought him into the limelight. In 2010, Ashok moved to Petronet LNG Limited as CEO and managing director. Petronet was promoted by four public sector undertakings—ONGC, Indian Oil Corporation (IOC), Gas Authority of India Limited (GAIL) and Bharat Petroleum—with the petroleum secretary as chairman.

The board comprised three CMDs of the investing companies. He brought in his own core values to the HR functions over the promotion policy, SAP and transparency in the company's operations. The business did well and was recognized as the best Oil and Gas Company by *Business Today*, while he was recognized as among the top five CEOs of the year in July 2014, becoming the perfect 'Oil Man' in the process. Petronet share prices moved from Rs 62 in 2010 to Rs 200+ in 2015. A public-sector man almost throughout his career, he was coveted by the private sector after the Petronet accomplishment. Ashok joined the Anil Ambani-led Reliance Group as CEO of its oil and gas business. He led the group's efforts towards setting up the LNG terminal and LNG procurement for the Bangladesh power project being implemented by Reliance Power as well as other opportunities in the oil and gas space.

Life has been a mosaic of human and humane experiences, with Ashok striking the right chemistry with people. Every success was underpinned by hard work. The single most motivational force for him was never to say no to the work assigned. Having done his best, he moved on, without looking back.

* * *

Chandrasekhar Sripada

Leadership in execution and academics excellence

Self-reinvented leader; exemplary transformation guide

Chandrasekhar Sripada (Chandra), currently professor of organizational behaviour (practice), Indian School of Business, was a C-suite executive with large public, private and MNC firms and held the role of CHRO for more than twenty-five years. He has wide cross-border experience of leading people and building human capital strategies across continents, nationalities and cultures. He is also a certified executive coach and sits on the boards of both for-profit companies and NGOs. His recent publications include Leading Human Capital in the 2020s *(SAGE) and working papers on talent strategies in unicorns and global development centres. Over his career, starting with Steel Authority of India (SAIL), Chandra progressed to the position of CHRO in Dr Reddy's Laboratories, IBM, Cap Gemini, Reliance Infocomm and NIIT. He has been associated with the National HRD Network on its board and has received awards for his contributions to HRD.*

A Telugu boy, raised in rural Odisha, barely able to tuck his shirt into his trousers, standing with some thirty classmates, all educated in the English medium, seemed a trifle incongruous. That was Chandrasekhar, son of Sripada Narasimha Murty and Narasamamba, surviving Central University in Hyderabad on Rs 250 a month during the late seventies. Chandra had two pairs of slippers, three or four sets of clothes and took a public transport bus to college from his hostel. The only thing going for him was the Central Institute of English and Foreign Languages (CIEFL) to which his university provided access; his innate love for poetry and his appreciation of Odisha's rich literary heritage.

The dream in rural Odisha in those days was for boys to join the IAS. This meant going to Delhi, where one received the right exposure and, means permitting, one joined Rao's Academy. On a hot summer day, Chandra boarded a third-class compartment in a train to Delhi, where someone had found him accommodation in the servants' quarters of an MP. Chandra was fifth on the merit list for a master's in English literature at the Delhi University entrance exam. Yet, St Stephen's College refused him admission because they could not accept anyone who had not studied in the English medium!

Imagine his heartbreak. Then, picture the resolve, as Chandra boarded an unreserved compartment of the AP Express the next day and left for Central University in Hyderabad. He had heard about its excellent literature faculty. He sat for the second entrance exam, stood second and got a seat, no questions asked this time.

Life told Chandra never to succumb to adversities but to fight back through optional routes. Central University was worth the wait and influenced his thinking through poetry and its rich library. The CIEFL—now the English and Foreign Languages University (EFLU)—with its phonetics lab had the fantastic Mangesh Vital Nadkarni, professor of linguistics and phonetics, who helped him to speak English without the accent. Saying 'father' instead of 'phadaar' was another gratifying experience. That marked the beginning of endless practising in front of a mirror, to manipulate the lips and tongue so that the words came out right. 'Do not say car—as a Telugu-speaking person, you will emphasize the r—so stop at caa.' Chandra dreamt of speaking English like an Englishman or his convent-educated friends. He improved, even transformed and felt inspired because something was fundamentally changing within. Other awe-inspiring professors opened his mind to the power of interdisciplinary studies. They were immensely insightful when it came to interpreting poems as Chandra was compelled to read some forty books to appreciate the essence of one poem. He realized that the truth did not reside in any one discipline but in the intersection of disciplines: another invaluable learning.

Connecting disciplines and developing an overarching understanding of varied issues helped Chandra cut through layers of confusion and gain clarity, helping the village boy to reinvent himself; though Chandra did not know it then. There was so much to learn from the world outside, from the different nationalities, and Chandra seized every opportunity. Upon his graduation from Central University with flying colours, his teachers thought that he should apply for a Rhodes Scholarship and go to Oxford to do his PhD in English literature. Then came a three-line postcard from his father reminding him of his impending retirement the next year and his inability to fund further studies. Since Chandra was completing his MA, he was advised to find a job. In a life-changing moment, Chandra's visions of an Oxford education were replaced by thoughts of an office job; there was no time even to be disappointed.

Then came the challenging interview, when Chandra, a candidate for a management trainee position in SAIL, got stumped by the first question: 'What would a student of English literature do in the steel plant?' Fortunately, another panellist came to his rescue and asked what he had learnt from English literature. Chandra was in his element, talking about the great interdisciplinary connect through the course of history and the impact of poets and thinkers on their times, of the great Shakespearean dilemma in *Hamlet*, which was akin to human dilemmas in everyday life: 'To be or not to be.' Indeed, every experience from his childhood rusticity, from his immediate family, from his environs of mud walls, thatched roofs and areas without electricity and potable water . . . had prepared him for life's challenges through a constant flow of learning.

Chandra's house had lanterns. Under their lights, his father, a small-time magistrate and a walking legal encyclopaedia, read till 2 a.m. because he would have to give judgments the next day, which ran into several hundreds of pages. Chandra heard him meticulously dictating them to his stenographer, who came home between 8 a.m. and 10 a.m., referring to case laws that he had studied the previous night. The intense work, scholarship and passion with which his father approached his job made deep impressions on the boy. So did his mother's simple pragmatism. A class-III fail who could barely read, she advised him in Telugu, when he was barely fifteen or sixteen, '*Parigetti paalu tagakura, nilabadi neelu taagu* (it is advisable to drink water leisurely than to drink rich milk while running).' It meant, do not be too ambitious or run around; savour the moment and seek an unhurried life. Chandra is still striving to practise this deep philosophy.

There were equally strong influences from the teacher explaining Shelley's 'Ode to the West Wind', conveying the brilliant imagery of the west wind and inspiring his students to write poetry in Odia. They shaped his mind and contributed to his cracking the management trainee entrance at SAIL, setting him up for life and impelling him to zealously pursue knowledge. Chandra did his PhD from the Andhra University while working with SAIL and was deeply influenced and inspired by Prof. Venkatratnam. He got married and a year later, when the couple was expecting their first baby, he received the confirmation of a scholarship to pursue an MBA at Leeds University. Chandra got a year's study leave and had to go off immediately because there was no provision for a postponement. His wife stayed back. Post Leeds, the couple travelled to Paris but his daughter has not quite forgiven him for not being around when she was born.

The international experience meant the second phase of self-reinvention to adapt to the multicultural milieu. Literature and philosophy continued to shape his intellectual outlook, determining the many frameworks through which he understands life, even as a CHRO. Using his scholarship of both Bertrand Russell's history of western philosophy and Radhakrishnan's Indian philosophy, Chandra found insights into interdisciplinary complexities at the workplace. Interestingly, Chandra never had anybody to mentor him, nor did he see the value of surrendering to gurus though, being curious as he was, he periodically checked out various gurus and institutions for their invigorating thoughts. From Osho to Sathya Sai Baba to Sadhguru; visiting Ajmer's Darga Sharif, Goa's churches, meeting maulanas and even getting a darshan of the Pope at Vatican City and the Dalai Lama . . . Chandra engaged with them to nourish his receptive mind. So did he with his professors, even long after he passed out of Central University.

After he joined SAIL, the famous Shakespeare scholar, a Tamil, lungi and banian-clad Prof. Sankalapuram Nagararajan of Hyderabad's Central University, pointed out to him that 'management lacked the exactitude of a science and the profundity of philosophy'. Chandra's eyes were opened to the fact that in the league of learning, management came relatively low down, given life's more transcendental issues. At the actual workplace though, Chandra found immensely supportive influences. His boss at Vizag, Sachidananda Pandey, spotted Chandra's potential and rewarded him with quick promotions. Through his role as executive assistant to the director, personnel, he learnt the tricks of the CHRO's trade. His first formal CHRO position was with the Pennar group, Hyderabad, followed by NIIT, Reliance, Capgemini, IBM and, finally, at Dr Reddy's. Every role afforded him opportunities to hone his skills. He also developed a balanced view of HR. It was an important cog in the corporate wheel but not the key, though many delude themselves into thinking that HR held the key to everything. Indeed, the key to the CHRO role was the ability to integrate diverse agendas of others into the CHRO's own.

Being the CHRO involved influencing skills, stakeholder management, appreciation of the business, role-modelling and, more than building professional expertise, building personal credibility by managing one's ambitions such that they did not blatantly come to the surface. It also involved going beyond the routine to deliver on a promise. Chandra recalls the redoubtable R.S. Pawar of NIIT once asking him for some information on a Friday that he needed by Sunday. Chandra had forgotten about it. By the time he remembered, his phone was dead and he did not send the information, seeking shelter behind the dead phone. Pawar pointed out that there was a public telephone booth under his house from where he should have called. Chandra received a major lesson in personal reliability.

Indeed, Chandra was going great guns at Vizag Steel when the rug was pulled from beneath him. He was transferred to IR and it felt like a punishment at that time. He decided to step out of his comfort zone and venture into the private sector. A few years later, Chandra joined Reliance, where he realized how different phases in corporate growth demanded different roles for CHROs. The HR person was the gardener at the developmental phases of companies. At critical phases, the company demanded optimization, increasing efficiency, saving costs and fixing people into roles. From a gardener, the CHRO may well have to become a hatchet man for the management. Accordingly, the competencies and mindsets would need dramatic overhauling with the changing nature of the challenge. Chandra found himself struggling at the resource-optimization phase of the same company where he had earlier delivered excellence. He realized that he was not 'good enough' under this phase of the business. The analogy from literature that helped him accept this reality was that one does not ask a fish to climb a tree and brand it as incompetent.

At this stage, Chandra was happy to quit Reliance and served with such multinational companies as Capgemini and IBM. At IBM, Chandra learnt about matrix management. This involved managing the core people around every function, each with influence but without anyone being fully accountable. Navigating through several mindsets, sometimes across the world and time zones, was no mean skill and represented amazing learnings for Chandra. He stayed clued-in to obviate anyone putting a spanner in the works. The person who emerged from these vibrant experiences was a social and loveable person, who connected easily with people, bosses or a friend. It had to do with one's disposition and being an extrovert was a great inner resource for Chandra. Coupled with the depth of his mind, he was empowered to connect not superficially but with empathy, helping people to evolve and talent to mature.

While nurturing talent, Chandra has respected the more inclusive European school of thought around talent management as opposed to the exclusive school espoused by American capitalist thinkers. They identify superior talent and nurture them through a differentiated system of reward and recognition. The largely European welfare state and socialist view holds that the difference in calibre is not the only criteria because every horse has a course and every human being has some talent. It is HR's responsibility to find a match between talent and the task. Since organizations, like society itself, fail to create level playing fields—his experience of being denied a seat in St Stephen's College was a telling one—Chandra frowns at creating greater elitism around talent and favours levelling the field, while recognizing that some people are more talented than others.

Chandra is creating his own model for talent development, taking a portfolio approach. Much like how while managing wealth, people balance various assets, so should companies create a talent portfolio. Companies should not discriminate between talent because everything has a return on investment. A portfolio view of talent makes for a more de-risked strategy while an exclusive approach focused on one asset class—the high-calibre talent—would be far less pragmatic. Picking up nuggets of wisdom from every experience, Chandra also realized how the perceived power of HR, if inappropriately used, becomes a weakness. Besides, HR and personnel management were different ball games and Chandra fought for independent HR departments.

He also differentiated between the trivial and the vital when it came to disagreements at work. The idea is to reduce trauma and enhance the joy of working. Chandra had pleasant and abusive bosses. Shouting, insulting and humiliating, the latter made for difficult interpersonal relations, which bordered on attempted humiliation and hurt his self-esteem. It was his inbuilt resilience, developed over his transformation from a rural and indigent background, through his journey into mind-liberating literature, that helped him handle such depredations. While some acquiesce that the salary at the month-end justifies suffering the abuse, Chandra reasoned within. Should the need to provide for his family be met at the cost of self-respect? He was not given to such heroics as carrying his letter of resignation in his pocket and is still not clear whether accepting abusive behaviour with equanimity, keeping the long-term perspective in mind, reveals cowardice or courage. Never impulsive, he rationalized things, tried to see the other person's perspective and learnt to cope with it. Aggressive retaliation did not fit in with his soft nature. If the abuse got repetitive, he ignored it because retaliation could become self-defeating over a long fight. Is there a case for judgement here—does bravado score over pragmatism, does strength lie in dealing with the challenge or in quitting in the face of challenge? The jury is still out on that for Chandra.

Chandra recalls a childhood encounter with a snake that slithered off when it saw him. Yet he ran home to his mother terrified and crying. His mother explained that snakes are afraid of people too and asked him to 'simply walk away when practical; there is no point in fighting the snake'. Brought up on such wisdom, Chandra reasons that if snakes appear in the form of CEOs and others, one does not beat them with a stick. One realizes that the other person is a bigger and more poisonous player and the best course is to protect oneself, instead of being a champion or hero. The collateral damage has been in terms of some sleepless nights, acidity and backaches for Chandra. There is a price to pay for tolerating abuse. Underpinning all of this is the ability to see the big picture, connect the dots, see the patterns, move away from small transactions into holistic appreciation. Chandra refers to a non-religious chanting, *Om poornamadah poornamidam poornaat poornamudachyate; Poornasya poornamaadaaya poornamevaavashishyate*; the whole (the force behind our existence) is such that even if emptied in its entirety, it would still remain the 'force'. There is nothing religious about this piece of wisdom but when one is exposed to such monumental ideas, one does not see things in fragments.

It helped Chandra become a pragmatist, to invest himself with the survival instinct, to allow himself the ambition of raising his lifestyle without taking risks; taking some hits and misses in his stride without making issues out of them. They enabled him to rise above the trivia as the CHRO and generously help others; counselling, sometimes moving them to jobs more up their alley, persuading managements to shift people so that they could fit into the job profiles, teaching colleagues how to prepare themselves to do better or even to change jobs. People, not all of them were high potential, remember him for his support over their career advances. From secretary to senior management, he has helped people deal with boss-related issues or even with domestic problems. He has also managed complex issues at work that would have unsettled lesser people because he could grasp the key points and not get lost in the labyrinth of details.

Zeroing in on the vitals, as he did at IBM during the taxi drivers' strike or even at Capgemini, handling an acquisition, Chandra made the road ahead easy for all. Capgemini, where he was HR head, had taken over a larger company and retained its HR head too, without announcing who the boss was. Chandra examined the dynamics and found the man who was his counterpart was not only senior in age and experience but was also an erstwhile promoter. Capgemini had an arm's length philosophy towards acquisitions and allowed an acquired entity to retain its own culture and independence. Chandra would have to live with and work together when the need arose, without one reporting to the other. It was a rattling experience but Chandra put it in the trivia category for, truth to tell, his counterpart was a powerful and wealthy man. Chandra had a candid conversation with him, explaining that there was no competition and if there was no disagreement with Chandra's moves, he would find support. While Chandra anticipated issues when it came to standardizing pay scales, he had sorted out the personality issues.

When dealing with a powerful person, one needs to address the main drivers and build win-win situations by rising above the trivia, a strength that Chandra naturally possessed. The art of confronting one's dilemma transparently, through making full self-disclosures, are the components of this approach rooted in the framework of OCTAPACE (O—Openness, C—Collaboration, T—Trust, A—Autonomy, P—Proactiveness, A—Authenticity, C—Confrontation and E—Experimentation), which he had learnt from Udai Pareek and T.V. Rao. Yet, there were incidents when he dropped the ball. Taking his wife for a Valentine's Day romantic dinner at a five-star restaurant with perfect food and ambience, he gave her a lecture on Valentine's Day history and customs. The romanticism of the evening went for a toss and his wife walked off, leaving him to struggle for days to get her to come around. Examining concepts from various angles is fine but imposing such thinking on another is not. One's strength as a good speaker or orator becomes a weakness if limits are crossed. Chandra often had his better half or bosses pointing out his errors. He learnt the hard way about how one's strengths can also become weaknesses.

At times, his set personal habits came in the way of the cosmopolitan corporate culture. He was caught slipping out of a major integration dinner for a multicultural-multinational team in a big hotel to have a quick curd rice and returning to his seat because he did not like the Thai food being served. His bosses gave him a dressing down for having insulted the host and demonstrating his inability to handle even a different menu. How could he manage an integration? he was asked. Chandra learnt that one should control habits and mindsets that irk others or give one an edgy personality, as he helped himself become a well-rounded personality, changing with the times.

In its essence, life was about adjusting to change, sometimes driving change and even having to manage change by influencing mindset change and not by diktat. Chandra had challenging experiences at both Reliance and Capgemini, where the change mandate was implemented patiently and carefully to make it endure. CHROs often need to deal with such difficult agendas as withdrawal of benefits for employees, removing hierarchical levels for flattening the organization, removing positions or not paying a performance bonus because the company did not do well. It would be futile to use authority to drive such change. Instead, one prepared the ground by first convincing oneself about one's action and then taking key influencers into confidence. The HR heads cannot admit in private moments that they do not believe in what they are implementing. That weakens the exercise and exposes the hypocrisy of the person driving it.

There were also unpleasant tasks such as pink-slipping people, which Chandra recognized had to be done as his dharma, his professional duty. Chandra would be fully sensitive about the dignity of the fired individual, explaining the work or business context in which the loss of job was taking place. He supported the fired persons through referrals to outplacement services and job opportunities, taught them how to reinvent themselves, sweetened the parting to the extent possible, using a basket of techniques to make payroll-paring a less abrasive process. Many of those he fired talk of him with respect even today.

Through all this, Chandra's vision has been to become a better person. This drove clarity of purpose and enabled him to perceive others in the game as resources that would enable the accomplishment of organizational goals. Bosses matter up to a point, but peers facilitate continuance and success. Loyalty should, therefore, lie more with one's peers than one's boss, for whom one is just another resource. Chandra realized that without acceptance from one's peers, the boss's support fails to sustain because bosses, too, expect peer approval for their subordinates. One cannot go through one's career as someone's protégé and peers need to be considered as partners, who help one succeed and not as intimidatingly competitive beings.

Chandra's relationship with his peers has been excellent because he has divested his relationships of his ego and found enduring friendships, some guiding him to good career openings.

He found his final job courtesy an old friend, Saumen Chakraborty, who was serendipitously moving out of HR, as if ready to vacate the seat for Chandra at Dr Reddy's. Chakraborty, to Chandra's mind, understood HR better than he did. When Chandra wanted to dispense with the Employee Trust Fund, which was yielding negligible returns, Chakraborty reminded him that the trust was built with employee contributions and dispensing with it would be anti-people, even if the returns were poor. Chandra also never allowed differences to blow up into fights, sorting things out respectfully, often building lifelong bonds with colleagues. He approached Dr Reddy's with the mental ease of a man who has accomplished much in life and is able to take a detached view of things, being true to himself. Comfortable in his own authenticity even when circumstances were difficult, he had by then come to grips with his insecurities with no desire to perpetuate authority. Authenticity is a prerequisite for a successful CHRO and overcoming the need to dominate is liberating. It gives people genuine freedom though it often comes towards the end of one's career.

The import of his learnings, buttressed by huge experiences and exchanging of opinions, has meant a multiplication of wisdom that

Chandra has shared continuously. He had begun doing so almost habitually and became quite popular for his solutions to different tight situations. People constantly approached him for counsel. By the time he joined Capgemini, midway through his career, his 'Chandra-isms' became rather sought after and his colleagues would organize impromptu events just to hear him speak. Often, many tactical issues were raised at these events, issues around frustration at work, fretting over problems or inability to navigate tough straits. Even at IBM, people sought his help to handle the environment and Chandra found counselling and coaching skills coming to him naturally. He fortified his natural ability with a certification as a coach and that has been an independent area of work after retirement.

Chandra coaches CEOs and people down the line, cherishing the opportunity to help others. It has been humbling to find himself unequal to the task and Chandra works harder to find customized solutions. He is now reinventing himself as a teacher, as he was probably meant to be. He derives strength from his belief system, which he learnt should be sacrosanct from people like Udai Pareek, who represented humility combined with a steadfast belief system, and Prof. Dharani Sinha and Mrityunjay Athreya, who deeply influenced his understanding of organizational processes and leading change to make it inclusive and sustainable.

It was at Dr Reddy's, where he was managing HR across continents, covering thirty-five countries, that Chandra imparted significant cross-cultural teachings to his colleagues when a factory in the US had to be closed down. The layoff plan by the local HR leader, Steve Prentiss, only covered legal protection for the company and cost management, entirely ignoring the human impact of the layoffs. Prentiss had never been required to consider this aspect in layoffs. Chandra insisted that the process carry Dr Reddy's cultural imprimatur, analysing the impact on every laid-off person, making special arrangements for those being seriously impacted, even though Prentiss—who later appreciated the process—thought it would mean opening a Pandora's box. Chandra had learnt about never losing one's cultural moorings from a French company boss, Marie-Laure Riviere. Responding to a media question on whether Capgemini considered itself a French company or an Indian one, she said that for her it was the Indian operation of a French company, but there was no contradiction with being a French or a global corporation because she would respect all local traditions. It wanted to bring its unique operational culture as a gift to India. Chandra had learnt a beautiful lesson and applied it in Dr Reddy's context in the US.

The evolution of the CHRO is about achieving a change within, sometimes as fundamental as going from arrogance to humility. While at Vizag Steel, Chandra attended a lab by the ISABS where Oriol Pujol, the facilitator, churned him inside out and exposed him to his own arrogance. That is when he understood the value of humility, which he made an intrinsic part of his journey, as every CHRO must. Currently professor of practice in the OB and human capital area at ISB, Chandra is excited by the opportunity of sharing his experiences with young professionals and influencing HR minds with elan and empathy.

* * *

D. Harish

Dream merchant

Dreamt big, innovated and helped others realize their dreams

A leadership coach and consultant, Harish primarily focuses on supporting the pursuit of excellence in organization performance and leadership effectiveness, while serving as an independent shareholder director on the board of Bank of India. A PGDHRM from XLRI, Jamshedpur and the recipient of the Nanjunda Rao Memorial Gold Medal for the Best All-round Student in 1983, Harish served with TVS Sundram Fasteners (SFL) and Unilever and went on to become president, National HRD Network, Bangalore and convener of the 15th NHRDN Conference, Bangalore. As vice president, HR Services, Unilever, he established the HR services framework and managed the effective delivery of services in forty countries across Asia, Australia and Africa, where Unilever operates. He handled both the insourced and outsourced models, managing the portfolio personally or with consultants. Over his tenure at SFL and Unilever, Harish covered design, review, development and launching of HR systems and organizational interventions that served to enhance business performance. He mentored and coached leaders and groomed young HR professionals as well.

31 August 1981; the Tamil Nadu Express to Delhi, passing through Andhra Pradesh, got derailed at night, with many horrific deaths and serious injuries. One group of twenty-one students from Chennai's Vivekananda College, travelling to IIT Delhi to participate in Rendezvous, a cultural festival, survived miraculously. Among them was D. Harish, barely twenty. The boys managed to crawl out of their overturned coach in pitch darkness to confront the total devastation outside, save for a valiant group of army men travelling by the same train, who had sprung into action to manage the aftermath. Their leader, a Captain Wilson, taught Harish a massive lesson in the art of organization. He had the makings of a great organizer and now learnt how to take up a job and get it done at all costs. The Vivekananda College team shrugged off the trauma, proceeded to Delhi, and did quite well at the festival.

Son of R. Devarajan who worked for Dunlop, initially in the production department and later in charge of employment, training and safety, Harish came from a middle-class family that laid a premium on education. At St Bede's, where he studied till class X, Harish valued every aspect of the school that had great extracurriculars. He participated in sports, dramatics and literary events, was a first-rate Scout, winning the President's Scout Award and even volunteered at the school library, often staying back in school till 6 p.m., with meal breaks for which he came home. Then came the move to Padma Seshadri School for higher secondary studies. Harish found the sports infrastructure shocking but went about energizing things. His daily commute now was more than an hour each way, but he spent extra time at school to participate in every extracurricular activity, joining the cricket and volleyball teams.

Harish organized the Scouts troop to participate in the VIIIth National Jamboree, personally managing all external formalities and felt honoured when he was selected to lead the Tamil Nadu contingent at the inaugural march-past. Along with a Scout friend from St Bede's, he also won the National Morse Code competition. His multifaceted leadership saw the Padma Seshadri School cricket team beat St Bede's to reach the finals of the Inter-School Cricket Championship. It was a stand-out moment for Harish, who became the sure winner in the contest for the school's head boy position in class XII. Notably, his campaign leaflets carried a message asking people not to litter. Expectedly, Harish won the Best All-Round Student Award in his final year.

Harish's super organizing skills were inherited from his father and honed by his school and college. He had seen Devarajan handling workers during labour unrests when they demonstrated in front of their house. Besides, Devarajan shared stories of union negotiations with the family. His excellent people skills were noticed and he turned to HR, leaving Dunlop to join Union Motors as HR director and later becoming the president of the National Institute of Personnel Management, Chennai. Devarajan led by example, never took shortcuts and always acknowledged his shortcomings and mistakes. His exceptional integrity and uncompromising honesty extended beyond work, into his daily life. He planned well to avoid having to bribe people for last-minute favours; nor would he accept even a box of sweets that could be misconstrued as a form of palm-greasing.

Devarajan also cared for the worker and a well-known trade union leader acknowledged to Harish that his father never humiliated workers. He managed to get them to reconsider their options by gaining their trust and appealing to their hearts. HR was thus in his blood though Harish showed promise in sales and marketing too, when he interned at JK Tyres during a summer vacation at Vivekananda College. The eight-week internship over eight different petrol pumps saw Harish sell eleven sets of the newly-launched radial tyres. Impressed, the company offered him a sales job. His options were open; sales, accounting—he was taking a course at the Institute of Cost and Works Accountants of India—or management, which he fancied. Having failed to clear the Indian Institutes of Management entrances, he opted for XLRI, Jamshedpur. His organizing abilities came to the fore again as the general secretary of the XLRI students' union and a member of multiple teams.

Harish's first XLRI summer internship was at Larsen & Toubro. Prof. T.V. Rao, the L&T chair professor of HRD, had selected eight students, Harish included, for a pan-India survey of HR practices in the country. He gave a ten-day crash course to the interns for the job that involved surveying some of India's top companies and preparing around fifty papers in quick time. This excellent exposure prompted Harish to choose HR as his specialization and he stood second in his batch. When it came to a career, there was a toss-up between offers from Eicher,

Levers and TVS Sundram Fasteners. Alok Kavan and Sambamurthy of SFL wrapped up the discussion first and Harish joined their HR department as SFL's first management trainee. The job allowed him to push boundaries and apply his knowledge to create new systems, spanning performance management and career planning, to developing a matrix for evaluating interviewees and talent development.

Sambamurthy was a great boss and a mentor–protégé relationship was soon formed. Harish also got involved with industry bodies such as the NHRDN, NIPM, ISTD and Madras Management Association. NIPM was not new to Harish because his father was once active there as president. He also got to collaborate with his teacher, T.V. Rao, as a part of the NHRDN. Harish was a core organizing committee member of NHRDN's National Conference at Madras, working with stalwarts like S. Chandrasekhar and P.V.R. Murthy. He revelled in these circumstances; mingling with such people boosted his confidence as did his paper on 'HRD: A Beacon Light', which was adjudged as a prize-winning entry by NIPM. Harish was invited to present it at the Srinagar National Conference in 1988. Along with his colleague Robinson, he also had a podium finish at the ISTD's Young Trainer competition in 1989.

A fondness for softer skills and creativity drew Harish to classical Indian dancing and he started to learn Bharatanatyam from Padma Subrahmanyam, when he was twenty-six. He picked up quickly and performed at different places with his teacher's troupe. He also got involved with the Youth Association of Classical Music (YACM) and helped them organize a seven-day music festival, and soon he became its president. Harish brought to bear his excellent organizing abilities to help promote YACM and was rewarded with meeting his future wife, Nandini.

In 1987, SFL led the southern region in a review of best HRD practices organized by the CII with Harish making the final presentation. Then came his move to the personnel department of the SFL manufacturing plant, where Harish was exposed to QC circles, Kaizen and other world-class people-engagement practices, apart from the nitty-gritty of the personnel function. A year and a half later, Harish got a call from Hindustan Unilever that had missed hiring him at the XLRI placements. Harish was reluctant to leave the bracing

SFL environment but a persistent Levers and a meeting with the
HR director, Keki Dadiseth, left him with no room for refusal. On
his flight for the final interview, he found Sambamurthy and received
the most comprehensive career counselling and coaching session from
his mentor. Suresh Krishna, the SFL boss, was equally gracious in his
encouragement to Harish to follow his heart, adding that he should
see himself as an ambassador of SFL at Unilever and would always be
welcome back.

No one grudged his joining the much-sought-after Unilever,
because SFL considered employee welfare its prime concern, embedding
this philosophy in Harish. When thirty SFL employees on a worker's
education tour visiting factories in north India were stuck in Jammu
& Kashmir due to a landslide, Suresh Krishna bowled him over by
permitting Harish to charter a flight from Srinagar to rescue them at
multiple times the budgeted cost so that their families did not have an
agonizing ten-day wait for road routes to clear. Harish's HR sets great
store by 'employee welfare', which he learnt in his first job.

Harish's first assignment at Unilever as the personnel manager
at the Brooke Bond factory in Hosur was a challenge: managing the
integration of the Brooke Bond-Lever integration. Levers had just
taken over Brooke Bond and the IR cultures of the two had to be
blended. Levers was tough and demanding, while Brooke Bond had a
relationship-based approach. K.K. Nayar, the new technical director at
Brooke Bond, told Harish to discontinue certain unauthorized benefits,
cut down on excessive overtime and initiate a general tightening of the
screws. Within six months, the twenty-seven-year-old Harish had a
workers' strike on his hands. In a bold move, the company decided to
run operations with the help of managerial staff, importing managers
from other factories along with eighteen apprentices, who stayed inside
the factory. Harish organized police protection with the Director
General (DG) of Police.

The apprentices would meet the workers every day at the factory
gate, till two of them got kidnapped and things turned messy. Harish
managed to get them released and the strike ended on the thirty-fifth
day on favourable terms for the management, but Harish chose to
convert the victory into a celebration of reconciliation, welcoming the
workers back to the factory with sweets and garlands. Harish's success

got noticed and he was transferred to the much larger Coimbatore factory, with four bickering unions and eighteen strikes in fourteen years. Harish decided to stop the multiunion negotiations and introduced the concept of a negotiating union with a salutary effect on the IR climate. He was then sent for further training at Lever's training and development centre in the UK, where he visited the super-efficient and mechanized Manchester tea factory, among other institutions.

Once the merger of Brooke Bond and Lipton was underway, that company would not need so many factories and closures would be inevitable. Harish used his knowledge from Manchester to push productivity and efficiency with the Coimbatore factory workers to ensure its survival. Harish's deep involvement and contribution across functional lines caught the management's eye and he was made factory manager at the Whitefield Coffee Factory with a mandate to improve Whitefield's ranking among the four instant coffee factories in three years. Harish took Whitefield to the number three position in a year with improvements in the production process and productivity, confident of moving it to number two soon. However, the top management wanted Whitefield closed to make way for the Unilever International Research Centre.

A distraught Harish argued with his seniors about the unfairness of the decision, especially when the employees had been so responsive and turned things around. The next six months were unpleasant as Harish convinced the employees about the inevitable closure, offering other jobs and transfers, but he found few takers. Around 100 workers decided to take the separation scheme. The management asked him to manage it without adverse publicity and along with P.B. Dave, Head IR, Harish devised a novel package: a lumpsum compensation plus a pension till they turned sixty, along with medical benefits. Harish met the employees and their families to secure their buy-in. Around this time, the Levers general manager for management development, Satish Pradhan, as well as the training manager, K. Ramkumar, resigned. The HR director, R.R. Nair, convinced Harish to join his team at the corporate office.

This was a great opportunity as Harish was in charge of management development as well as recruitment and could work closely with the senior management. There were 450 managers across different factories, regions and offices, and Harish listed them all, many of them twice, taking the HR function to their doorstep. Keki Dadiseth, the HR director who had hired Harish, was chairman, Hindustan Lever now. Post the merger, Harish impressed everyone with his contribution to the integration process, objectively presenting the capabilities of the Brooke Bond Lipton employees and was asked to manage the development of some 500 middle/senior Hindustan Lever managers in India, as part of Prem Kamath's management development team.

Harish coordinated the company's functional resource committees going through the annual review of the 'listers' (high-potential employees) and made a presentation to the Unilever top brass and senior business leaders like M.S. Banga, Harish Manwani, Sundaram and Sanjay Khosla. He also wrote a white paper in 1998 on why the attrition in the HR function was high. There was a glass ceiling for HR professionals in HUL and top and senior HR positions were occupied by talent from other functional streams, resulting in high-quality HR talent moving out to head HR in other companies. Harish suggested a new functional structure with a business–HR partner role for every category and the board loved the proposal. This was implemented in 1999.

By now, Harish had got exposure to the top honchos from Unilever and was being included in global task forces, sometimes running global programmes out of India. He even won the chairman's Award and Unilever was keen to move him to London. Harish swapped places with Krish Shankar who was in London as part of the corporate HR group and helped develop and cascade an enterprise culture across the multinational company. Prof. Wayne Brockbank, Michigan University, was the consultant for this strategic project and Harish the project manager, working with fifty CEOs from across Unilever. After crafting the 'enterprise culture,' team Harish creatively leveraged the year 2000 Olympics in Sydney, Australia, to generate a buzz around Levers' Enterprise Culture. Olympians from different regions were roped in to exemplify the cultural characteristics. A live e-mail contest was organized for employees across eighty-plus countries with a 24/7 chat forum coinciding with the Olympics.

At the height of his exciting international assignment, Harish met up with Gurdeep Singh, HLL's HR director, then considering senior technical leaders with good track records in running large factories to succeed Dave as head, employee relations. Harish volunteered to return to India, much ahead of the planned expatriation, if he were offered the role. This was an unusual choice as most upcoming HR professionals wanted to deal with managerial staff only. His early experience with industrial relations at Unilever had taught Harish what needed to be done and Gurdeep was delighted with the option. Harish came into his own in this role and left his imprint by moving away from a legalistic, confrontational role and creating a more consultative and relationship-based culture. Even at the factory level, the personnel managers were re-designated as HR managers. So, instead of just managing industrial relations, these people were now responsible for the entire gamut of HR functions in the factory. The reporting of the HR managers was also changed from the factory manager to the regional HR manager. In the new scheme of things, the HR department in factories would now develop the workmen, staff and officers in the same way that the management development focused on the managers.

Harish had attended a two-week global HR programme in Michigan along with forty HR managers from eight multinationals. The peer learning was stupendous and helped Harish develop a major shift in his conceptual framework, from industrial relations to employee relations, to employee development, to strategic HR. He set himself a benchmark of having 'no strikes'. If there was one, he would derive some value out of it. Factory/regional HR manager roles were treated at par with corporate HR roles and the best talent was rotated between them. Harish challenged the Hindustan Unilever culture in more ways than one. Although the company followed a five-day week, the norm was to work on Saturdays too and then be available on Sundays, if needed. In London, Harish would usually work from 9 a.m. to 5 p.m. and only five days a week. Inspired by his wife Nandini's reminder that as a leader he needed to set an example, Harish encouraged his team to stick to a five-day week and still meet all deliverables.

Gurdeep allowed Harish to operate from Bengaluru as Nandini preferred that city, even though this meant constant travel to all the sixty-eight establishments and spending two days a week in Mumbai. During his factory and field visits, Harish insisted on meeting the managers, officers and workers and staff who had the potential of becoming officers. He also organized a walk-through for the managing committee members on the HR floor of the head office, where twenty members of his team explained different policies, practices, processes and the changes being created by them. They were very impressed and this got Harish visibility. At forty-two, he was being talked of as the next CHRO after Gurdeep Singh. Harish was also well on his way to proving that a top-notch HR professional such as the CHRO would bring significantly higher professional value than an excellent general manager. More than a personal accomplishment, this meant recognizing that HR was as valuable a business function as other key functions at Unilever in India.

It upset him that the Levers HR managers or HRLs were not talked about as much as the sales and marketing leaders outside the company and discussed this with the team. Harish stressed that HRLs should become icons and each of them should aspire to succeed Harish someday. He brought in an element of healthy competition among his reportees and urged them to engage with the outside world, make presentations at seminars and other industry forums. Harish led HR for Levers for three years, constantly challenging himself on the value-add that he was bringing to the table. The closure of the Sewri factory was achieved under Harish's watch with a highly focused team. He made some more radical changes, initiating category-level OD interventions, bringing in expatriates with domain skills for emerging roles in India, reinforcing a culture of engaging leadership and seeking opportunities for several Indian HR managers in the larger Unilever world.

After three years as VP of HR for India and South Asia (2004–07), Unilever wanted Harish to take up a role either in Europe or the corporate centre. Harish wondered what 'value-addition' would come from this job that would be similar or more niche compared to his role in India. Harish and Nandini were also evaluating their family aspirations given that Nandini had been virtually single-parenting, considering Harish's work and travel schedules. Reprioritizing his life, Harish expressed his desire to quit, surprising Unilever, which was never happy to lose people at the top of the organization and Harish was a high-flyer! Unilever had great career plans for him.

In an attempt to hold him back, they offered him the role of leading the global HR transformation journey for Asia, Australia and Africa, while continuing the responsibility for South Asia HR. Harish saw this as a good segue into his future professional avatar and agreed to take it on for a couple of years but with the licence to operate from Bengaluru. Leena Nair took over as HUL's CHRO from Harish and, after a year, the South Asia responsibility as well. Harish had helped establish the value of professionally qualified and experienced HR professionals at the top of the organization. It was no surprise that three out of the eight members of Unilever's global HR leadership team in 2010 were former members of Harish's team.

Harish now took guard for a new innings away from a corporate job, doing what he wanted to do as a freelancer, to add value to whatever he did, balancing his varied interests and passion. He tried his hand at consulting with an assignment with the Tata Group, facilitated a few training programmes, empanelled with the Center for Creative Leadership (CCL) as a coach and his métier in coaching. He started his own firm, People Unlimited (www.peopleunlimited.in) and also ran a course on leadership at Mudra Institute of Communications, Ahmedabad (MICA) and on contemporary HR at XLRI. He experimented with the format by inviting business leaders to learn alongside students in his class. Professional work gradually was relegated to 35 per cent of his time while Harish gave back to society. He was active in NHRDN and president of the Bangalore Chapter between 2009 and 2011. For the rest of his time, he plays golf, travels with his family, is available for his children and joins them in their pursuits, organizes extended family events and energizes the alumni networks.

His new routine saw him at home a lot more and allowed Nandini to go back to studying and starting her own non-profit venture. In 2011, as convener of the annual NHRDN conference at Bengaluru, Harish knit together a band of enthusiastic and capable professionals, who co-created a very innovative conference that set new benchmarks. It leveraged video technology, featured telecom-aided spot surveys and held a parallel conference of HR students alongside the main event. 'HR Showcase' had a carnival-like infrastructure with fifty top organizations welcoming the 2000-plus open-house guests, making presentations on their best HR practices. It attracted 1600 delegates, grossed a revenue of Rs 5 crore and added Rs 2 crore to the NHRDN kitty.

He has gift-wrapped his experiences in a co-authored bestseller *HR Here and Now* and serves as an independent director on company boards. Achieving success early in his life due to his propensity to do things differently, staying true to his own value system and aspirations, reimagining himself and leveraging every opportunity to achieve excellence, Harish has also ensured that people who journeyed with him realized their potential.

He continues his dream journey now as a coach, focused on helping others to make their dreams come alive.

* * *

Dileep Ranjekar

Shaping the next generation

Transitioning from a stellar corporate career to the education sector, raising the bar for the quality of education

Dileep Ranjekar has been an integral part of the Azim Premji Foundation, right from its ideation in 2000. A small-town boy, Dileep gave studies a pass but made excellent use of his college library, otherwise whiling away his time outside classes, seeing movies and chatting in the canteen, fascinated by many things from Osho to the theatre. His lacklustre academic performance notwithstanding, he completed his MBA from the Tata Institute of Social Sciences (TISS) and was hired by Wipro from the campus in 1976. Dileep played an important role in transforming the vegetable oil maker to a global IT company. Starting as the head of factory personnel in Amalner, Dileep rose to become the CHRO. An upright and values-driven professional, he played a key role in creating the value-based cultural fabric there. However, in the prime of his corporate career, at forty-nine, he made a conscious choice to become the founding CEO of the Azim Premji Foundation started by Wipro, committing himself to significantly raising the quality of public education in India.

Circumstances forced Kamalakar Ranjekar, a man of culture with his heart in education, to quit college and take up a job in the administration section of the Maharashtra police department, then headquartered in Pune. He grabbed the first excuse to get out, taking an early retirement scheme when the police headquarters were shifted from Pune to Mumbai. He was forty then and Dileep was barely six.

Anyone else would have jumped at the offer to shift to Mumbai but Kamalakar had had enough. Tired of the caste politics in the department, Kamalakar chose to learn English stenography. He got by just teaching English and focusing on his children getting quality education.

Kamalakar's third child, Dileep, was delivered at his maternal uncle's home at Sangamner in Ahmednagar District, on 5 October 1950. The infant, with much older siblings—brother, nine years his senior and sister by five years—refused to lose sight of his mother and cried inconsolably when she tried to enrol him into a regular school at the late age of seven. He had to be strapped to the bench to stop him from running back home, till the teacher began with a story. Dileep stopped crying and happily returned to school after that. A bright child, Dileep could read and write even before going to Gopal High School where he stood first in all the exams and used his creativity to make a scrapbook of stories published on Sundays in the Marathi newspaper, *Sakal*.

In standard III, the family shifted to Ahmednagar and on completing junior classes, Dileep eventually went to the Ahmednagar Education Society (AES) from standard V, excelling academically till standard IX, winning a state scholarship in standards IV and VII. He was naughty but never got caught, managing to remain the teacher's favourite and the class monitor too. The boy would excel, was the general belief. Then came an inexplicable slide from standard X, when Dileep lost interest in studies, though he continued to fare well in English. In college, he found no connect between life and calculus or trigonometry but had a yen for electrical things, displaying a technical bent of mind, repairing fuses in the neighbourhood, playing with battery cells and doing minor engineering. It was in physics that he submitted a blank paper and when his shocked family and brother asked him to take a supplementary, he threatened to commit suicide, since supplementary examinations would not qualify him for the medical entrance that he was set on.

His doctor dreams were shattered given his 43 per cent in the exam that mattered for admission into medicine and Dileep found himself at Ahmednagar College. An excellent institution set up by the Barnabas family, it had a beautiful chapel and a large library with more than 1 lakh books and over fifty cubicles for individual studies and offered education right up to a PhD in biochemistry. Dileep enrolled himself for a BSc with zoology, botany and chemistry. Save for Prof. Bharat Seth's botany classes, he gave studies a pass. He spent a lot of his time in the library, reading Marathi magazines, novels and plays. The rest of the time was devoted to watching movies and chatting with friends on subjects ranging from the theatre to Osho.

The college had an excellent auditorium and gave him exposure to theatre personalities, including the famous Prof. Madhukar Toradmal (a faculty member at Ahmednagar College) and his classmate, Sadashiv Amrapurkar, who had acted in much-acclaimed Bollywood films such as *Ardh Satya*. His large friends' circle had many girlfriends, but Dileep managed a high second class in BSc and went in for management. Dileep, who learnt from life, realized the importance of management when he single-handedly organized his sister's wedding. He joined the Pune University post-graduate diploma in business management, taking marketing, materials and personnel management as electives. Between 1972 and 1974, Dileep completed his MBA with distinction and the third position in the university.

In his very first interview for a purchase officer's position with Kirloskar's, Dileep realized that his MBA had little brand value. When he saw a TISS advertisement for its MBA programme, he applied and sat for a group discussion and interview without telling his parents a word. Kamalakar accidentally heard that Dileep had cleared the admission to TISS, instantly agreeing that his son should go. Dileep's mother gave him Rs 300 and Kamalakar gave him Rs 700 and saw his son off at the bus stop. It was pitch dark and pouring when the father and son parted. Kamalakar must have prayed for the bleakness of the night to become a prelude to a brighter dawn.

Dileep felt the simultaneous tinges of apprehension and excitement with the new world unfolding before him, especially living in a hostel for the first time in his life! Bombay itself was a novelty, though muggy in July and Dileep gelled well with his roommates, an interesting group of four: Amitabh Sanyal, an alleged borderline Naxalite, bright and humorous; Thomas D'Souza, a former priest who became a social work administrator; and Vijay Narayanan, the deputy chief jailer of Coimbatore Jail. They helped him plunge into leading the hectic social life and politics of hostel life and performing brilliantly in every space, except for studies. Classes were done by 1 p.m. followed by lunch and table tennis from 2 to 8 p.m. The faculty and studies were unexciting, but Dileep was confident that a combination of fieldwork, TISS's core and unique learning initiative, and his earlier Post Graduate Diploma in Business Management (PGDBM), would help him sail through.

Traineeships at organizations such as Metal Box, Seksaria Cotton Mills, Siemens, Century Mills and Godrej Soaps Factory also gave him unique insights. A block placement at Guest Keen Williams (GKW) gave him excellent exposure to workers' participation in management, while the Janata Colony behind the TISS campus provided a fascinating exposure to the deep inequities in society. It inspired him to understand matters in greater depth. He also found the session with visiting Prof. M.S. Datta, the Pfizer personnel director, particularly interesting. Dileep did not excel scholastically but got a near first class and had four job offers. Dileep chose Wipro (then Western India Vegetable Products Ltd) because he would be heading the personnel department in the factory. He enjoyed the rigour and friendliness of the three-stage interview, finally meeting Nalin Thakore, adviser to Premji on HR issues and a director on the board, along with the then MD, Azim Premji.

Dileep joined on 15 May 1976, in a factory with around 900 people (permanent and non-permanent), in a taluka in Jalgaon District with a population of 1 lakh. It was Wipro's only establishment apart from the fifteen-member head office in Mumbai. The key agenda he received was to professionalize people processes and to position the organization as one with high integrity and values. He learnt everything earnestly and hands-on. Dileep also picked up the art of managing the government functionaries such as the factory inspector in those days of 'inspector raj' (where everything needs approval from government officers or inspectors).

Around the time Dileep joined, the union negotiations were in the final stage and with no earlier experience, Dileep was required to represent the management, signing a historical agreement on 28 May, with an average per employee monthly raise of Rs 60. A unique pioneering agreement was simultaneously signed with the non-permanent workmen in five categories. The factory had 150 contractual workers, 200 non-permanent workers, 450 permanent workers, 100 in supervisory positions and eight management employees, including Dileep. A fortnight later, Thakore visited the factory and asked for the checklist for implementing the settlement. Dileep had no clue what that meant but managed to put on an act of knowing all about it. Thakore had huge expectations of him; so had the management at Amalner, but TISS had not quite prepared him for it all. Also, his young age went against him, for the average at the plant was around fifty and the earlier factory manager had retired at seventy-five, a year before Dileep joined.

The factory was full of oil, waste and rubbish. The temperature in summer rose in excess of 45°C and the twenty-five-year-old Dileep poured water on the bedroom floor, switched on the fan and slept on the ground. The sixty-two-year-old labour officer whom Dileep asked for a summary of the implications of the Employees' State Insurance (ESI) Act amendment, refused to help. The labour officer returned the next day after being reprimanded by his wife for refusing to help his boss. Relations with him were smoother but there were innumerable other issues, including corruption and theft. The chief timekeeper was reportedly at the epicentre of this corruption, charging a bottle of alcohol or a packet of non-vegetarian food to include people in the pool of non-permanent workers. When hired, they had to shell out 25 paise per day from their wages. Dileep confronted some members of the time office and took over the management of the workers' pool. Some resigned but more corruption had to be rooted out. Dileep caught people in the act, including one timekeeper smuggling out a soapbox. The word got around that he meant business.

The other tough task on hand was manpower rationalization. Illustratively, after placing bright lights and a fence around the factory, the strength of security guards was reduced to twenty-seven from seventy-two. Dileep spent nights in the village nearby, where many of these watchmen resided, interacting with their families and explaining Wipro's genuine intentions. In 1977, new issues cropped up. After the national Emergency was lifted, the leader of the new Janata Dal union commenced a hunger strike in a tent outside the factory gate, over demands pertaining to casual workers. Dileep visited his tent outside the factory gate every day without any antagonism and convinced everyone about the fairness of the management. The leader withdrew his agitation without any gains. Dileep reorganized and professionalized multiple teams of contract labour, engaged in diverse work, ensuring full legal compliance with legislations such as payment of wages to the workmen, ESI and Provident Fund, so that workmen got their full statutory benefits.

Learnings came from every exposure. Working in the factory exposed him to deeper issues of human relationships while giving him an understanding of manufacturing technology. Later, moving around with salespeople taught him about the hardships that they faced in the field. So engrossed was he in his work in the four years at Amalner that he hardly took any leave. Marriage meant a day's casual leave as it involved overnight travel. Dileep's style was of no indulgences, no splurging, no raising of voices even when arguing, no fighting, only reasoning. This paid off in the long run and even impacted the thinking of the management and the unions alike.

Within a month of Dileep's joining, farmers in the nearby village protested about untreated factory effluents leaking into their farmlands. Dileep convinced both the community members and management to implement long-term solutions for effluent water treatment and managed the turbulence. In the meantime, the effluent water was stored in the open premises owned by the factory opposite the main factory. When a bull of one of the farmers fell into this stored water, instead of taking a technical stand as to why the bull entered the territory, Dileep decided to gift a pair of bulls to this farmer at a function. There was endless learning during his factory stint after which Dileep was transferred to the Bombay corporate office in 1981 to head the personnel function of the newly formed Wipro Consumer Products Business reporting to the president, P.S. Pai, who had joined from Union Carbide. This was Wipro's main business (infotech had just begun in 1979–80) and Dileep went on to become the vice president, HR, leading its people function, handling special launches, expansions, new businesses such as leather products exports, multiple brands of toilet soap among other things, and therefore huge recruitment for the sales force. He travelled nonstop between the four factories in Amalner, Chennai, Bhavnagar and Tumkur and to some thirty sales branch offices across India.

Pai, a warm, highly analytical, solution-oriented person and a great operations strategist, was cast in a different mould. Pai and Dileep built a high-integrity organization culture and a leadership style that was fair and firm. This manifested in several actions such as dismissing the union secretary for raising a false travel bill and dealing with a five-month strike that ensued. Pai's middle-class values had little space for unnecessary sophistication, reinforcing Dileep's own values.

In the initial years at the factory, when Dileep was waiting for a good price to sell factory scrap, Pai told him that the aim was not to make money from selling scrap but to have a clean factory. Dileep also learnt not to go to Pai with a crib but with solutions and only when he needed clarity on matters. Pai set high benchmarks because he believed that people achieved 70–80 per cent of targets, irrespective of what they were. Therefore, targets had to be high and one ought to not settle for 100 per cent of low targets. He involved Dileep in operational matters but in an organic way, getting him to camp in the factory for several days to fix such hardcore manufacturing problems like oil loss. Pai was ruthless on matters of integrity and Dileep ended up softening the fierce impact of some of his actions. But Pai liked Dileep's sense of ownership, work ethic and sensitivity to home-office balance. Like Pai, Dileep never disturbed people on weekends.

The seventy-six-year-old Himmatbhai Maniyar, a paan-chewing Gandhian specializing in labour matters, taught Dileep the philosophy of law as opposed to just the sections of the law while dealing with Bhavnagar factory industrial relations issues. Maniyar explained issues in great depth and in a simple manner. Illustratively, when young Dileep spoke of 'teaching a lesson to the obstinate workers', he simply said: 'If you attempt teaching a lesson to people, you end up learning a lesson.' He said that only if you put yourself in other people's shoes, would you know what their pains are and what is behind their demands.

Effective communication helped Dileep manage the trickiest of situations; so did his fluency with the local language at Amalner. He learnt a lot from his union leaders, who included intellectuals, street fighters, committed Marxists and such others. These were career and personality-shaping and his views were valued even for product launches. Dileep became a complete 'business leader', breaking several traditions.

Moving into the corporate role, Dileep and Premji set about understanding and adjusting to each other's workstyles. Premji's leadership style was different but accommodating. Upon realizing that Dileep was not a morning person, he chose not to upset Dileep's biological cycle. Over time, Dileep too learnt to give people the freedom to decide, just as he cherished his own freedom to build the organization culture, giving everyone an opportunity to grow horizontally and vertically, keeping people tightly engaged. This enhanced his credibility too. When one division wanted his approval for a wage settlement for the factory workers, he asked them to go ahead and decide because they were the ones running the business and Dileep wanted to break such bureaucratic and notional barriers. Wipro also gave him diverse responsibilities such as HR, training, quality, corporate communication and corporate facilities, which was probably why he never felt the need to look out of the organization.

Dileep walked the talk about the culture that he built in Wipro. When a school was to be established near the Amalner factory, he visited many convents and schools. On one such trip, he claimed Rs 2 for his train travel by second-class from Bombay V.T. to Kalyan. Asked why, he told Pai that the second-class compartment was empty and it made little sense to spend Rs 70 on a first-class ticket just because he was eligible. For him, eligibility was to deal with the crowd; not for status. Even as vice president, he travelled to Tumkur from Bangalore by bus till it became physically challenging. The story went down the rank and file and became a part of Wipro's folklore. He inspired his colleagues not to travel business class even on international travel and led from the front vis-à-vis optimizing the company's resources and his demonstrable sincerity of purpose.

Dileep was deeply involved in policy-making, practising and communicating organization values to institutionalize them and build a solid culture of fanatical adherence to these values. By 1987, Dileep was a general manager, the youngest in the company at that point. Since building the organization meant knowing everyone, Dileep spent a lot of time getting to know almost 700–800 people closely. Over his extensive travels, he visited their homes and got to know their families as well. In his corporate role from 1995, Dileep and his large team aimed to make the HR function in Wipro a leader in global people practices.

Dileep travelled to global organizations such as Microsoft, Intel, Cisco, Sun Microsystems, Tandem and Acer to learn innovative people practices. Illustratively, CISCO had operations people in charge of people processes and HR's role was to assist them by finding the best people practices and developing line leaders to practise them. Working closely with some of the global management gurus such as C.K. Prahalad and Sumantra Ghoshal added value to his professional understanding. If a policy came in the way of delivering solutions, Dileep challenged that policy with alternative solutions and made his position public. Many policy changes ensued with people coming up with alternative routes—car policy, tax-optimizing ideas and coverage of parents in medical insurance were a few among them. In a way, a culture got developed to challenge the status quo. For Dileep, it was equally important to be credible and prompt in responding to a need.

Dileep never wriggled out of a situation or resorted to the 'I am helpless because of company policy' excuse. He believed that essentially, people felt the need to do good and constructively contribute. It is the approach of the management to them that makes them better or worse. Dileep never took talent for granted; the opportunities and treatment that one receives and one's learnability quotient shape one's character. When an HR team member complained about being swamped with processing 300 confirmatory appraisals per month, Dileep questioned the utility of the process. The evaluation added little value and Dileep scrapped it.

Wipro got SHL Singapore to help certify the competencies for all roles that were mapped internally by the organization and Wipro HR became the first organization in the world to be assessed at PCMM level 5 in 2001. His team made stellar contributions to this achievement. Way ahead of others, in 1999, Wipro e-enabled most people transactional processes because the organization believed that HR should contribute to a higher value rather than being lost in inconvenient transactions. None of this, Dileep emphasizes, would have been possible without the stellar contributions of his very talented and committed team.

Moving to Bangalore in 1995, with Wipro's corporate headquarters, hitherto housed in Mumbai—while the family remained in Bombay for the children to complete their schooling—Dileep had a great opportunity to learn from Premji's prodigious strengths: critical things such as paying attention to detail, time management, planning for every meeting, retrieval of papers through organized filing, preparing oneself thoroughly before an employee interview and such others. Illustratively, he was often the first to complete the annual appraisal process (including discussions) for the people who directly worked with him and it was a joy to participate in the appraisal discussion process because of the way he conducted it. However, Dileep had no hesitation in expressing his differences of opinion with Premji, who not only welcomed such feedback but never held it against people for asking seemingly awkward questions.

Nobody feared a job loss for making a negative statement about the organization or systems and processes. Significantly, in the Wipro Leaders' Annual 360° Leadership Survey, it emerged that Premji's survey results had improved the most over the years, indicating that he took all feedback seriously and made conscious efforts to change himself as necessary. Meanwhile, as corporate executive vice president, Dileep was responsible for multiple functions such as HR, training and development, corporate communication, quality, facilities, administration and such others for the entire Wipro corporation. After zeroing in on the Six Sigma approach for quality across the board, quality function was assigned to a separate head.

In his responsibility as facilities head, the new corporate office was set up on a twenty-five-acre campus. Since many Mumbai HR employees chose not to shift to Bangalore, the corporate HR department had to be built from scratch. Dileep did not even have a secretary. He looked for clear-thinking, committed persons who were culturally aligned to Wipro values, whom he would empower to take responsibility. This principle allowed others the freedom to decide and act on their decisions while freeing up his time. Besides, there were matters of critical importance around integrating the expanding world of Wipro companies, at home and overseas, providing comfort zones to all business heads and setting up structures and frameworks for two new US-based Wipro organizations.

The Wipro brand and Wipro identity were repositioned through an elaborate exercise that lasted over three years in 1995–97 with the help of a Paris-based Indian consultant. Witnessing and resolving the conflicting perceptions about the strength of the organization between the consultant and business leaders was an experience of a lifetime. Once the new Wipro identity was finalized, the internally-orientated Wipro 'Beliefs' had to be externally-focused as Wipro 'Values'. This meant travelling both within the nation and across the world clarifying what the shift was about and how to practise these values, to Wipro team members.

Alongside, Dileep focused on senior and top management recruitment, retention and development and gauged employee satisfaction through surveys, supported by quarterly feedback analysis. Premji and Dileep focused on a list of 100 carefully identified people across the organization to take personal responsibility to tighten their engagement company, ensuring retention through sustained relationship-building. Dileep guided his team not to recruit 'just to achieve the numbers' but only when they had an 'aha' feeling about the candidate. Wipro had a clear approach of always preferring an internal candidate, even if they were ready only 60 per cent for the role. Wipro became an outstanding example of a highly effective people process of mapping succession, reviewing critical talent, providing a structured process for their development and retention, etc. Illustratively, the current president of one of the $1-billion organizations within Wipro was identified to become so, way back in 1995.

Then Azim Premji, with his deep desire to contribute to society, expressed his wish to do something to address issues such as inequity, injustice and conflicts in Indian society. During a conversation, he asked Dileep to help to create a framework for an organization that could carry out the work. After many rounds of discussions, the Azim Premji Foundation was established, choosing education as its overarching strategy to drive social change. Dileep spent a lot of time in the field with eminent NGOs engaged in improving education. He was fascinated by the scale, the pathetic status and the potential to impact through professional efforts. Asked by Premji to find the CEO, Dileep was stumped because no candidate quite matched up to the role at hand.

The sheer excitement of the role enthused Dileep, who was only forty-nine then, to offer himself for the position of the CEO of the new organization to Premji, who accepted the suggestion after some discussions. However, it took two years before Dileep's Wipro responsibilities could be devolved and he could quit Wipro to join as a full-time 'Founding CEO' of the Azim Premji Foundation. His family was taken aback, but Dileep ignored the resistance. Premji showed his customary faith in providing an opportunity to a person who might not have been fully ready but had the potential. More importantly, the person was a 'known devil'. He was also an evolved HR practitioner and was felicitated by NHRDN as the Most Respected HR Professional in October 2002, after he took over as CEO of the Foundation.

Dileep began reshaping the space that had three main players: the government, civil society and corporates. As he wrote the guidelines for the Azim Premji Foundation, he willed himself to create an organization that combined the strengths of all three, without their shortcomings. It was about infusing professionalism into an ideology-driven space, moulding mindsets, bringing together the scale and legitimacy of the government, the passion of civil society with the quality, result-orientation and talent development of the corporate sector. The only way to quickly understand the domain was to extensively travel in the field to experience the reality on the ground, meeting people, sharing their experiences and discussing with people who had been in the domain for long. One of the persons who Dileep learnt hugely from was Shri Sharad Chandra Behar—the former chief secretary of Madhya Pradesh—who is also a board member of the Azim Premji Foundation.

Dileep commissioned Hewitt to do a survey of people practices in the social sector to broadly guide such practices at the Foundation at the outset. He also addressed the initial suspicion of some NGOs about the Azim Premji Foundation's 'real' agenda, given that it was promoted by a person who was a reputed corporate leader. Dileep set about creating an enabling environment to help people, constantly reiterating that the Foundation existed to serve the external society and minimum time ought to be spent in resolving internal issues. As with his other solid, sustainable and transparent relationships—at work and in his personal life—he laid the new foundations for abiding success, never treating anything as a 'one-time job'!

Dileep's professional journey, from a lower-middle-class family to his incredible leadership in multiple disciplines in a global organization that became a role model for its integrity, culture and values, has been riveting. His distinguishing style was to treat work as an opportunity to learn and to invest everything with a sense of fun. Work was a joy even when it involved exploring the depths of

a problem in its fundamentals, without any superficialities. With joy
for inspiration, he was undisturbed by feelings of competition because
the challenge was to be happier within, driven by the satisfaction
of having given one's best. Neither elation nor gloom visited the
final outcome.

Every day was a new day!

* * *

Hema Ravichandar

A Columbus in Search of Balance

Perfect professional at home and office

*Hema Ravichandar (Hema) is a master business strategist. A role model and
influencer among HR professionals, she was the global senior vice president
and group head HRD, Infosys Technologies Ltd and the Infosys Group, till July
2005. Hema designed and drove the Infosys HR agenda as it scaled from 250
to 39,000 employees. From 2005, she has provided strategic HR advisories to
multinational and Indian corporations and governance at both the statutory
and advisory board levels, pan-industry. She spearheaded large-scale HR
interventions aimed at future-proofing the organization, broadbanding,
compensation restructures, and defining and institutionalizing HR business
processes. Her current board memberships include Marico Ltd, Bosch Ltd, the
Indian Hotels Company Ltd, Tata Consulting Engineers Ltd and Titan
Company Ltd.*

*As a chief executive, she set up and ran a successful HR consulting
organization. She was a member of the National HRD Network and on its
National Executive Board (2015–16) and was regional president, South
(2015–16); the HR council chair India for Conference Board, USA (2003–
05); the Confederation of India Industry co-chair, HR Council, Southern
Region (2005); and co-chair, HR and IR Forum, Southern Region (2011–
12). Her many awards and accolades include the HR Professional of the Year
Award; Outstanding HR Professional of the Year Award—National HRD
Network; and she featured in* Business Today's *25 Most Powerful Women in
India and* Dataquest's *Successful Women Professionals of the Year in 2005.*

If there is one term that showcases how far the information technology boom changed human resources practices in the country, it should be 'Petit Infoscion', Hema Ravichandar's coinage for every child of Infosys employees. Heading HR during Infosys's rapidly growing years, when retention was the critical need of the hour, Hema made every employee feel like a proud scion of the Infosys family; hence Infoscion. Hema wanted Infosys to embrace family members, especially the children, and build a connection between them and their parents' workplace. Infosys would often host special fun and games events for kids with much hoopla, with chairman N.R. Narayana Murthy himself in attendance sometimes; hence Petit Infoscion.

Every Infoscion was a cynosure of other IT companies' eyes, especially of multinationals who were looking to set up large coding shops in India. The bus ferrying Infosys employees to and from work was targeted by rival recruiters, who pushed copies of the *Times of India*'s Ascent into the bus at traffic signals. Infosys then had an attrition rate of 22 per cent and the average employee age was twenty-three, so focused retention events were critical. Many employees were unmarried and separate events were planned for them as well. Sunday morning breakfast events for the singletons, with dumb charades and quizzes that Murthy would attend too, sometimes with his daughter. Occasionally, Nandan Nilekani would come and conduct a round of quizzing. Special anniversary parties for married employees were another big hit. Hema had hit the bullseye.

The daughter of a police officer in the Kerala cadre, posted with the home ministry in Delhi, much of Hema's childhood was spent in Delhi's Safdarjung Enclave—a diverse neighbourhood where people from different parts of the country lived, including some who had moved due to Partition. She studied, partly in Mater Dei, Delhi and partly at Lawrence School, Lovedale in Ooty, a boarding school. These made her au fait with the significance of cross-cultural environments and the importance of home. The necessity of a good education was dinned into her by her mother, her role model. As children, Hema and her brother were encouraged to express their views, irrespective of the stage and were often given topics to read up on and make short presentations during dinner. Occasionally, it was poetry that her mother would later explain so that they understood the finer nuances. Hema was already an accomplished people's person and admission to IIM Ahmedabad was hardly a surprise. She was forever cognizant of the fact that her mother had given up her own career for her children.

Hema opted for personnel management and industrial relations as her specializations as she wanted to work in the people space. She enjoyed learning with Professors Pulin Garg, T.V. Rao, Arun Monappa, Indira Parikh, Udai Pareek and N.R. Sheth; all impactful teachers. By the third term, she was clear in her mind that she wanted to be a people manager and explore the HRD space. Rao, who taught organizational development, was her favourite and inspired her to get into people management or HR. Her batchmate, Raghu Krishnamurthy, also chose HR. The first internship at Gabriel was perspective setting. Gathering data for the ongoing wage negotiation season, she encountered a tense environment; the Gabriel personnel manager, living on the factory campus, had security deployed for the safety of his children. This was hardly the gender-neutral space where a woman would feel empowered to achieve her potential and this put her off industrial relations or dealing with blue-collar workers in a factory setting. Yet she chose the auto-components maker, Mico and its management trainee scheme because Vikas Deshmukh, its HR head, had just won a best HR manager award. Hema felt it would be a great experience to work with him and she wanted to be based in Bengaluru, where Mico was.

As her mother dropped her off for her first day, the seeds of her empathy for the worker-family connect were deeply implanted in her mind. Mico had a bit of traditional old-world charm. It had a tough IR situation at hand. To Hema's surprise, some of the brightest employees were the trade union leaders. Hema never lost an opportunity to learn over the one-and-a-half-year management trainee programme, with three months each on a different area of HR. It made her a tad restless but she found the dining room to be a great place to break gender stereotypes, breaking the sectional divide between workers, managers and women. Hema sat in the management trainee/manager section, an all-male domain till then.

Mico also gave her a grounding of the basics around time: error-free increment letters going out on time with the rationale explained to employees, eating lunch at the right time, and more. It grounded her career, taught her the importance of being perfect and imparted such knowledge as specific ways of filing and preparing service card summaries, navigating the office environment and enlisting the help of different colleagues as and when it was required to find the way ahead. Working on compensation benefits taught her that she needed to go deep in one area but also cultivate a broader understanding of the human resources landscape. More importantly, it taught her the value of the transactional as well as routine work.

Data mining, considered transactional, delivered diamonds of information as nuggets; documentation and detailing were channels for passing on knowledge to future generations; documentation removed the stress of having to remember and obviated the danger of key decisions getting written on water. For tribal knowledge and native wisdom, there was always mentorship. At a philosophical level, Hema understood that transactional interventions were just as important as the strategic, but she consciously worked on providing bandwidth and capacity to deliver on the transformational. Mico gave her something extra. She was assigned a mentor, a senior from IIMA, V. Ravichandar, which blossomed into romance and marriage. Hema cherishes her choice of her life partner and advises others about the need to choose well; someone to be an equal partner at work and in the home because her two children were born during her nine years at Mico.

Mico's recruitment culture was interesting. For apprentices, it selected the brightest school children after they finished class X and trained them as turners and lathe operators, at the lowest level of skill category. They would be barely nineteen years at recruitment and often have much older peers, some nearing retirement age, who would treat them as their children. It was in this ambience that Hema learnt how to build credibility and trust; her own team members were older than her. Things changed when she moved to Infosys in 1992: the average age at Mico was forty-eight compared to Infosys's twenty-three, and Hema was one of the oldest in the organization.

Other differences were just as striking. Mico was a large enterprise, Infosys had only 250 employees and revenues of around Rs 9 crore. Mico's attrition rate was 2 per cent, compared to Infosys's 22 per cent. Mico would hire the best students from school and train them to become the best mechanics while the best from top engineering colleges worked at Infosys.

A meeting with Murthy and Nilekani during the hiring process settled her choice. The IT services industry being gender-neutral also helped as she make a break with IR options and settled for addressing rate of churn.

It was a small office in Bengaluru's Koramangala, where Hema's Infosys journey of building a unique employee value proposition (EVP) based on three kinds of value addition that Infosys offered commenced. A learning value-add, a financial value-add and an emotional value-add; a three-pronged strategy that helped Infosys hold on to its employees even after a posting in the US. Most IT professionals chose to stay back after their US posting for financial reasons; the US provided the sheer ability to save. Infosys countered that with its remarkable employee stock option plan at this time, before its IPO, with a premium of only Rs 85. The multifaceted Infosys dream had begun, creating millionaires out of its own employees and sharing the wealth. The company had little debt and was generous with the staff.

Hema personally ran around arranging for visas for employees to travel for overseas assignments; sometimes completing the paperwork even before the employee had joined, to ensure that they were 'project ready' when they came on board. Some young engineers did not have passports and were hand-held through that process. Hema's rounds of the consulates to build relationships and network was important; so was meeting up with the HR heads of the top IT companies like Wipro, HP and Motorola to discuss common issues.

While nurturing these youngsters, Hema realized the need to nurture her own and, between 1996 and 1998, she took a break from Infosys. Murthy said that he would not hold her back if she wanted to leave to take care of her family. She continued to consult with Infosys while doing projects with other companies too. By 1998, Nilekani, unhappy with the state of HR at Infosys, persuaded her to return. For Hema, quitting Infosys briefly did not represent a career break but just a break from an executive role, while she set up and ran her consulting firm. She only walked a little stronger on the 'mommy path' while consulting with over thirteen organizations. It gave her the chance to attend PTAs, paediatrician appointments and participate in the children's projects; a good transition between the executive and the consulting paradigms, especially for someone wanting flexibility. Hema did not career hibernate but remained au courant (to be updated with one's domain and developments in the profession).

Returning from mommy path meant making adjustments, for Hema had left in 1995 with 1500 employees in Infosys and returned to 3500. It meant a reorientation of HR policies for an organization that had transitioned to becoming a big domestic brand from a big external brand.

When Hema had come back to Infosys in 1998, the internal brand of the company was bigger than the external brand, and it was a good problem to have. By 2003, Infosys started falling off the best employer lists (Dataquest, Business Today and Great Place To Work) though the employee strength had grown to 10,000. The company was hard-pressed to honour offer letters to freshers from colleges, taking seven to eight months to onboard everyone with offer letters. Both Nilekani, MD, and S.D. Shibulal, the chief delivery officer, got involved in taking drastic remedial action.

The first realization was that the Infosys leadership had not carried the next line of leaders with them; a policy council consisting of line managers and business partners from the HR function to work alongside respective business leaders. Internal communications were brought under HR and led by a top HR professional, and the HR team diversified with people inducted from logistics, sales and delivery functions to HR roles. Analytical ability was valued along with management degrees and some Kargil-war veterans, too, were in the HR team. Hema's focus was to ensure that all 150 members had the one important quality of empathy. Hema had learnt how to combine strategy with empathy and balance the micro issues with the macro picture.

Leadership at Infosys always tried to practice what they preach; beginning with being an organization with a difference and have the Infosys credo articulated and practised by its leaders as they set in place a strong organizational culture. Tenets like 'When in doubt disclose'; 'In god we trust, everybody else comes with data'; 'The softest pillow is a clear conscience' and 'You can disagree with me as long as you are not disagreeable' were not just articulated by the leaders but practiced by the managers. These built a robust culture and enhanced the collective wisdom of the firm, percolating through the organization and reflecting in policies and programmes alike. There was also the need to future-proof Infosys but not without slips.

Infosys's first-earn-then-pay mantra and the concept of a large performance-linked-variable pay ended up in a debacle as the company fared poorly that year and Hema had to rebuild the trust and credibility. The pay at Infosys was never in the top bracket but in the 60th to 75th percentile; the idea was to cut one's coat according to the cloth. There was just-in-time hiring of candidates who had gone through the recruitment process and were waiting in the wings with their visas in place; appointment letters being issued as the need arose. At one stage, 5000 applications were processed in five days and in the true spirit of business partnering, Shibulal, who was the biggest customer for the process, celebrated successes with the HR team.

Hema devoted 35 per cent of her time to people issues and another 35 per cent to external clients; the rest to media interactions and nearly 100 per cent engaging with people. Between the peak hours of 9.30 a.m. and 6.30 p.m., she met different stakeholders (employees, investors and external people) and handled communication outside these hours. To enable decision-making down the line, she embedded HR business partners in every team across the company who were empowered to take HR-related decisions, cutting down the bureaucracy. She also had an HR team at investor meets.

The comprehensive HR set-up emboldened Hema to establish a niche HR consulting team for external customers, who benefitted from Infosys's sophisticated HR. It also started formal training with global leaders. While HR handled leadership training, technical training, quality and domain-specific training stayed with the respective business verticals. The external faculty included Sumantra Ghoshal and Wayne Brockbank, for a programme focusing on the external customer. For Brockbank, the only real customer was the external one. Thomas DeLong from Harvard Business School did a programme on the circle of inclusiveness, explaining that, 'While you may think you are in the inner circle, the company puts you outside the inner circle', the gap leading to dissatisfaction and attrition. Companies often moved their high-calibre HR heads to mainline functions like sales or delivery, but Hema preferred the HR domain and working with HR policies.

At forty-four, leading a team of 300–400 HR professionals and seeing Infosys back in various lists of top companies to work for, Hema left Infosys for the second time in August 2005. Harvard Business School had just done a case study on HR at Infosys. Hema felt the ship was safe in the harbour as she handed over charge to Bikramjit Moitra, who came into HR from a delivery vertical. Post the Infosys experience, Hema did not want to work for another company, there being no 'follow-up institution', as Prof. Pulin Garg would say.

There was empathy galore in her style by then. She engaged with the parents of employees, inviting them into the offices and showing them company videos. HR, with its personal touch under her, often came off as a guardian angel for the young and Hema inspired her team to be available. Her message was, not to 'switch on and switch off phones; not even on a Sunday afternoon; to take unknown calls on their mobiles'. Not doing so would mean failing the acid test. There could be emergencies; seven Infosys employees visited Shiv Samudra and one girl passed away. A recently married employee had a kidney failure. Infosys was around to take care of such cases. When an employee committed suicide, Murthy travelled to Mumbai to visit the family.

Infosys had also become a must-visit for Indian and foreign dignitaries, from Prime Minister Atal Bihari Vajpayee and British Prime Minister Tony Blair to Pepsi chief, Indra Nooyi and Lee Kuan Yew from Singapore. Lee offered an 'entrepreneurial fund' for setting up Infosys in Singapore and Vajpayee called Infosys 'the meeting point of the goddess of wealth, Lakshmi, and the goddess of learning, Saraswati'.

Her fascinating growth at Infosys was facilitated by her husband, V. Ravichandar, who considered both their careers as joint careers and supported Hema to balance her career with motherhood and family, enabling her to return to work just two and a half months after delivering her first child. Both their parents were there to help out. That help was forever forthcoming, as she travelled internationally, though her children were always on her mind. Quitting Infosys the second time in 2005 meant adjusting to the slower pace of being at home, but Hema mastered these track changes. With her kids grown up, Hema has taken up the 'daughter track', working on making her parents as comfortable as possible in their senior years. There is also the need for personal space, as she realized when the seasoned facilitator at a personal growth lab programme at Infosys asked Hema who was there for her, while she had to be there for everyone. It was an 'aha' moment, as Hema understood that HR professionals also needed some space and resources to share their own aspirations, concerns, dilemmas and sometimes even just talk to clear minds.

Hema dealt with the dilemma of choosing between giving more time to her family and pursuing a successful career by excelling in both, achieving path-breaking success with Infosys. There were workplace dilemmas, too, around rolling back policies with the enormous rise in payrolls. Infosys's eighty or ninety flats in Bengaluru for employees returning from the US were inadequate and employees had to find their own accommodation as these flats were converted to transit residences. Many employees, accustomed to company accommodation, were asked to move on as Hema used fairness as the key criteria for making decisions in these situations.

Constant moral dilemmas are par for the course in HR, which is constantly challenged to balance business imperatives and passion for people. The battle gets lonely at times when one has to opt for the business or the human resource. Finesse and empathy at the moment of execution are critical, with the lowest common denominator determining the message.

An employee on a Personal Improvement Plan (PIP) or one who had suffered a personal bereavement or had a spouse who needed handholding or an employee facing harassment charges threw the HR person in a 'double hatting' situation; between empathy and organizational interests. Objectivity and distancing oneself from the situation often led to the best solution. For Hema, it is acceptance of the fact that life itself is all about balance and harmony and only empathy and honesty, effectively communicated, can apply salve to such situations. It is the same when one supersedes peers or is superseded by them. An effective message is that everyone is a partner here and seniority is a detail best underplayed.

Success opened up another dimension to work—engaging with professional forums, accepting speaking engagements; she sometimes was unsure about the additional responsibility. Such extracurriculars that seemed exciting in her college days, as president of Stella Maris in Chennai, seemed larger given her responsibilities at work and home. Taking charge as president of the south region for NHRDN in 2015, Hema realized that she would not be able to visit the regional chapters even once a year and quit after one year as she felt she would not be doing justice to the role. This challenge got compounded after her Infosys tenure when she did not have the supporting infrastructure either but managed the HR Council Chair for the Conference Board (an international body with top companies as members) between 2003 and 2005, with elan. She also co-chaired CII's HR Council for the South in 2005 and its HR and IR Forum in 2011–12.

From 2005, Hema has engaged in advisory and consulting work, and serves on company boards; ABC, as she calls it. Hema prefers only one or two meaningful consulting assignments. She did a great deal of consulting between 2005 and 2011, and is now focused on advisory work and coaching engagements. This has broadened her own perspective, and she works across industry sectors—manufacturing, banking, FMCG, retail, energy and media, apart from IT. She does pro bono work too, while Ravichandar has shifted his focus to pro bono work in addition to being chairman of Feedback, a firm that he has promoted.

For Hema today, a four-quadrant balance, between work, family, health (mental and physical) and passion gives her the elusive equilibrium. When one is active, one needs passion, which she sees in abundance in Nandan Nilekani and Ravichandar. Passion does not allow work to become routine. Intellectual and emotional quotient apart, Hema also works on the spiritual quotient, which allows one to do one's best, while letting others things go. That is what provides her with the balance for the long haul; something that Hema is enjoying.

* * *

Kishore K. Sinha

Bahrupian professional

Continuously taking new and meaningful roles, in the public as well as private sector, in India and overseas, and in the world of business as well as now in academia.

Dean, Executive Education, Birla Institute of Management and Technology, K.K. Sinha (Kishore) is a graduate with honours in economics and a postgraduate in personnel management/Licences Social Worker (LSW) (Gold Medallist, University of Patna). He has worked for forty-two years and held leadership positions in HR in Steel Authority of India (Sail), National Thermal Power Corporation (NTPC), Reliance Energy, Reliance Infocomm, Reliance Industries Limited (RIL) and Jindal Steel and Power. During his eight-year tenure in NTPC as director HR, he transformed the HR processes and the work culture, facilitating NTPC's recognition as the 'Best Employer' and one of the 'Great Places to Work' consecutively for three years. He received extensive HR training from Harvard Business School, Templeton (Oxford), Michigan Business School, Tata Management Centre, IIMA, IIMK and ASCI, Hyderabad.

Kishore has delivered talks in academic institutions in India and abroad, including Auckland University, Martin Hautus—The Pacific Peoples Panellists' Profiles Learning Institute and Cornell Institute of Business and Technology, New Zealand. A keen learner, HR thinker and innovator, he also tailored and executed changes in corporations, working with international level consultants like McKinsey, Aon Hewitt, Mercer, Ernst & Young, AT Kearney, among others. He has written four books, My Experiments with Unleashing People Power, *featured in* Business Standard's *'The Strategist Top Five';* Manthan: Art & Science of Developing Leaders *with co-authors, co-authored* Return of the Surya: The Ever-Rising and Transforming Human Resources *and* The Bahrupian Challenge: Inventing the New HR.

Nothing came easy for Kishore Kumar Sinha, who was born in Jharkhand's Dumka district, his mother's place; not in his formative years, nor in his career, despite his incredible accomplishments. Every obstacle became a source of learning and strengthened him on his journey from the flood-ravaged Bishunpur, in north Bihar's Sitamarhi District, near the Himalayan river Lakhandei, their ancestral village, to the corridors of corporate power. Kishore's father, an imposing man—tall, broad-shouldered, with a largish moustache—was a friend of the children of India's first President, Rajendra Prasad. Given his strong political leanings, it was difficult to find a job in British India and not till Independence did he land himself a bank job in Ranchi. However, as the well-regarded 'Billu Babu' in Bishunpur, his children were well taken care of. Kishore's childhood—enriched by his four brothers and three sisters—had many lessons to offer. Among them, communal amity between Hindu and Muslim families, standing by each other in times of distress and participating in each other's festivals.

Kishore's school in Bishunpur had a swadeshi flavour. Students often did a village parikrama with the tricolour, singing inspirational songs. Run on Gandhian lines, it had students learning various crafts during the second half of the school day. Other inspirational memories pertain to seeing Prime Minister Jawaharlal Nehru with the Panchet Lama at Nalanda. Kishore and a group of fifty boys between age twelve and fifteen, had marched almost thirty-five to forty miles, singing songs to offer their labour (*shram daan*). The Farakka Dam over River Ganga was under construction and these fifty boys were sent over along with thousands of children from all over India. It was all about giving the children a feeling for nation-building.

Kishore's father lived in Ranchi and once the older Sinha boys decided that they would not take to farming or look after the village property, the Bishunpur land was sold and a property acquired in Ranchi. The links with the village stayed strong though, with guests galore at the Sinha's home, including students living with them and studying in Ranchi. Kishore took his first train journey to Ranchi and joined St John's School. They first rejected him because he knew no English and a private tutor helped him cross that bridge. The improvement over one summer vacation changed the school's mind. The Bishunpur and Ranchi schools were studies in contrast and Kishore was a shy child, refusing to participate in outdoor activities and sports. He chose table tennis (TT) instead and excelled at it, representing his school in TT. The regimentation at St John's made him studious and anxious to do well. What did not sit well with him was that the missionary school did not permit the customary Saraswati Puja (worship of the Hindu goddess of learning) and when Kishore decided to have one, collecting funds for the puja, there was a strong message from the principal to desist.

The next stop was St Xavier's, Ranchi for his intermediate, where his results were not satisfactory. Kishore joined Patna College to study economics, where he fared well and was ranked among the top ten. More importantly, he qualified for XLRI, but the family had no resources to fund it and Kishore had to settle for Patna University's course in labour and social welfare, which charged Rs 11 a month. It was both a good and a disappointing experience, for while Kishore won the gold medal, the results were declared and the degree awarded in 1969, almost a year after the exams were conducted in 1968. Meanwhile, Kishore and many other students had got involved in student politics and then had to go into hiding in Dumka.

While studying in Patna, Kishore participated in an essay contest conducted by the National Institute of Personnel Management (NIPM), on the occasion of International Labour Organization Day and he won the ILO Day Award. The award programme was held at the XLRI campus in Jamshedpur and Russi Mody, the chairman of Tata Steel, gave away the prize. Kishore travelled to Jamshedpur first class, as a Tata Steel guest and Mody gave a memorable speech about his own travel to England to study and his mother's instructions on deportment and etiquette. She had cautioned him that even if he did everything correctly, much would depend on his luck. Kishore remembered this throughout his life, especially when Mody did not respond to his letters even after promising him a job.

The economy was in recession and Kishore had to wait for eight or nine months before landing his first job, which was a far cry from what he had imagined after experiencing life at Bokaro with his brother-in-law, Arun Kumar Lal, who had inspired him to join their human resources management. Lal was married to the youngest of Kishore's three sisters and Kishore visited them often in West Bokaro, where Lal worked at the Tata mine. He liked their lifestyle, the respect the job carried and how it seemed to make a difference in the lives of the people it touched. Kishore's first job as a personnel management trainee with Usha Martin Black in Ranchi saw him on a desk in the time office at the main gate with four other people, overseeing the timekeepers, the salary bill and doing some recruitment. He also worked on absenteeism trends, assessment of welfare activities in the neighbouring villages and reported to the promoter, Brij Kishore Jhawar.

The three-month stint was not without excitement though, with a lightning strike and disruption of activity at the plant. The police were called to evict all workers from the plant, a lockout notice was issued and 150 workers were terminated. The police opened fire after some were injured by arrows that were shot at them. A trade union leader died and the plant remained closed for three months, opening only after the government intervened. Recounting the incident in his book, *My Experiments with Unleashing People Power*, Kishore talks of how vulnerable they were in the time office. They stayed inside the plant campus for ninety days and Kishore was appointed as the local assistant to a Kolkata-based lawyer, advising the management in what was baptism by fire for him. He learnt at the deep end of industrial relations; its nuances and the relevant legal provisions.

Shortly after, Kishore received an offer from Hindustan Steel Ltd (HSL) that Lal advised him to accept. After a six-month training programme, he was posted at a coal washery in Dhanbad. He did not get a home posting at Ranchi but got the opportunity to do case studies at the HSL Management Training Centre at Ranchi with luminaries like K.T. Chandy (ICS), the then HSL chairman. A three-month stint in Durgapur exposed him to an interesting experiment amidst continuous agitation. The frustrated management appointed Bagaram Tulpule, a union leader as the general manager of the plant! With such innovative exposures, Kishore got his first posting in Dhanbad at a small unit of the central office of the Central Coal Washeries Organization (CCWO). He had end-to-end HR responsibilities and interacted with some of the top bosses like I.B. Pandey, T.N. Srivastava and U.K. Choubey, who all later became HR directors in various PSUs. Kishore was posted here because of his prior experience in Usha Martin. Dhanbad was also a hotbed of trade union problems and his two years there gave him an immersive experience before he was transferred to Santaldih on promotion as chief of personnel of a coal washery.

Santaldih, in West Bengal's Purulia District, was in a state of tumult too, but the state government did not believe in sending in the police to deal with labour unrest, for which it held the management responsible. Only the state's labour department got involved. Nevertheless, it was a stable job and, amidst all this, in 1971, Kishore married his childhood sweetheart, Chitra. His luck seemed to change; multiple promotions followed and Chitra has since remained a major influencer in his career choices throughout his professional life. She first counselled him not to accept a lucrative job offer from Bata with a Patna posting, advising him to wait for an offer in a bigger city. Soon after, HSL moved him to

Kolkata, where their first child, Suvira, was born. Culturally rich Kolkata also allowed him the opportunity to expand his own cultural horizons. Kishore and Chitra made the most of it, becoming connoisseurs of Bengali theatre and were frequent visitors to Viswa Bharati, the university set up by Rabindranath Tagore in Shantiniketan.

Coal India was being formed then and all the coal washeries were moved under it. Kishore got an opportunity to compete for a few open posts and move to the Kolkata headquarters with HSL. The trade union front continued to be very volatile, though. Kishore would sometimes go around incognito, wearing pyjamas and even staying back in the office to find white collared-unionized employees get up on the tables and do the protest dance. The central sales office of Kolkata had 2000 employees and Kishore learnt industrial relations the hard way. Then came the formation of the Steel Authority of India in 1975, with Wadhud Khan as chairman and legends like Hiten Bhaya and K.T. Chandy, who led the company subsequently, around.

M.R.R. Nair, who was his mentor to be and the chief personnel manager of Hindustan Steel Works Construction Ltd (HSCL), a SAIL subsidiary, got Kishore assigned to HSCL's Bokaro steel plant. In Bokaro, Kishore's immediate boss, Rama Krishnan, was almost twenty years his senior and like a teacher to him. Here too, the trade union movement was violent and Kishore was again confronted with police firing that killed some people. Political pressure from the unions did not allow the government to conduct an inquiry and Kishore started to get complete exposure to the pressures and pulls of industrial relations. Nair then brought Kishore back to Kolkata and they worked together till Nair's appointment as the HR director, SAIL.

Kishore had to visit HSCL operations in Libya and Baghdad occasionally. In 1980, he accepted an Iraq posting on a four-year contract, incentivized by the extra money. It was a consortium of two Indian and two foreign companies with many workers from the Punjab–Haryana region. They gave Kishore a good grounding in Punjabi as well as Arabic languages in Basra, Iraq. The first project of the joint venture was to build houses and plants around an Iraqi port. Kishore headed both HR and administration for a project being monitored by Saddam Hussein himself. Kishore wanted his family over but the Iran–Iraq war broke out just then. Three months later,

Kishore had to recruit 2000 workers and continue work at Basra in the war zone, daring to bring his family in for three months. Access to Iraq was through Kuwait and Kishore waited for his family, not knowing when they might arrive. The relief when he saw his wife and children descend from a bus that had come across the border was enormous. After a short stay in a hotel, he found a house but not many were as lucky. They lived in caravans. Trenches were dug in front of the houses and often there would be shelling during the day, making it unsafe for the family, who decided to return to India after about four months. Correspondence continued via diplomatic bags.

Another major issue was alcoholism among workers, especially in the evening, and Kishore had to address it. First, he quit drinking to lead by example and changed his working hours from 5 p.m. to 9 p.m. because the days were very hot. A couple of gurudwaras were constructed and langars (free community meals) were organized to engage workers. There was rampant corruption with wage payment too, and often half the wages would be withheld. Kishore refused to work under such circumstances and after coming back home for a vacation, he refused to return. In the middle of 1983, Kishore asked for repatriation and was back to his Kolkata office. Things had changed there, though. The new managing director had changed the workflow, leaving little for Kishore to do. On M.R.R. Nair's advice, he applied to NTPC and got posted at its Korba plant. His elder daughter continued at La Martiniere for Girls, Kolkata and his younger child moved to Korba.

Korba, peaceful at first, saw its peace shattered within a year, thanks to an article in the NTPC house magazine by someone connected with the Bhilai Steel Plant. It was alleged that there were derogatory remarks about women from the state. That prompted an agitation around the plant, supported by the unions, who demanded action against three members of the editorial board, which the officers' association opposed. Kishore asked for two days to resolve this issue, met local leaders, villagers and other important people, returning home past midnight where he found forty-odd officers anxiously waiting on the lawns outside. He may have got things under control, but the general manager of the plant succumbed to union and local leadership pressure and asked Kishore to suspend the three officers.

Kishore was aghast but devised suspension-cum-transfer letters and designed a process where they could choose their next posting where the suspension could be withdrawn. So upset was he that he also tendered his own resignation and proceeded to Delhi, to meet his bosses and former bosses. He got offers to go back to Iraq and a posting at SAIL's Bhilai Steel Plant, but M.R.R. Nair, his mentor, reprimanded him for this hasty action and asked him to withdraw his resignation. Finally, NTPC's General Manager, Personnel and Administration, R.V. Shahi, told Kishore that he would need someone like him at NTPC's Delhi headquarters and Kishore moved to Delhi. There he got a hero's welcome, especially from B.P. Thakur to whom he was to report, that reduced the impact of the upheaval. Renu Rajpal from the Power Management Institute wanted to write a case study on the Korba incident. All this made him feel that people at large were supportive of him.

However, M.L. Shishoo, who took over as NTPC chairman shortly after, had his own style, micro-managing based on inputs of his own coterie, while he remained aloof from the rest. Kishore welcomed the opportunity to train at Templeton College, Oxford, under the 'Colombo Plan' to attend a three-month advanced personnel management programme in 1987. In the UK, Kishore got to interact with world-class teachers and British trade union leaders and started to admire Margaret Thatcher's iron-fisted handling of the coal miners' strike in Britain. He wondered why governments in India lacked such gumption. He also watched the fierce debates on privatization in the House of Lords and others in the House of Commons of the British Parliament. Back home, things changed at NTPC too, with the highly approachable P.S. Bami taking over as CMD in 1988. He often sought Kishore's opinion on the escalating executive association agitations and accepted his advice to communicate directly with the executives. Bami addressed executives across the country and paved the way for a new relationship culture.

Tragedy struck Kishore again in 1992. His younger daughter passed away at age fourteen and Kishore could not forgive himself for not being there for her when she needed him. He blamed himself for neglecting his family while he focused on work and for not giving the child the attention that she needed. Kishore and Chitra were devastated and wanted to stay close to their older daughter, who was then studying at Baroda. NTPC agreed to send him to IPCL in Baroda on lien till his daughter moved back to Delhi. Kishore and Chitra too moved back to Delhi and Kishore rejoined NTPC. Once again, things had changed drastically in the office and there was no room for Kishore. It took him six months to slowly get back into the NTPC system and be appreciated for his ability to handle conflict and potentially volatile situations.

Things were changing outside as well, with government policy allowing private sector players and multinationals in the power sector. Quality people from NTPC now got poached, adding to HR worries, but the leadership was good. Rajendra Singh became chairman in mid-1992 and Prem Nath came from SAIL to become director (personnel) in 1995. Nath was an honest man, learning and development-oriented, and initiated several changes that Kishore admired. He was appreciated as well and was elevated to the position of executive director. When the vacancy for the top post in HR in NTPC opened up again, Kishore was eligible. Nervous about his prospects, Kishore got Sunil Trivedi, senior coach, to prepare him for the interview for director (personnel), burning the midnight oil with him, discussing the issues and finally nailing the interview. Kishore took over as director (personnel) of NTPC from Nath in 1997.

Kishore had a satisfying eight years leading the HR function at NTPC, working hard, starting new processes and introspecting on ways of making NTPC a transparent organization. He met NTPC HR heads and groomed them; invited the younger HR team members as observers and encouraged others to do the same. He also sent many senior HR personnel to study at leading management institutes. HR groups from NTPC went on study tours to other PSUs and private sector organizations such as Hindustan Unilever, Infosys, Maruti, BHEL and SAIL. Kishore sought trainee feedback and constantly tried to improve himself. He had a coach to teach him rapid reading as well as counselling.

Several strategic training programmes in leading B-schools at this stage helped Kishore. He learnt from masters such as Dave Ulrich, Wayne Brockbank and C.K. Prahalad. His rapid-reading abilities helped him to read many books, but Kishore was most impacted by Arie de Geus's *The Living Company* and *The Fifth Discipline* by Peter Senge.

Kishore was now thinking expansively and NTPC adopted the motto, 'People before PLF' (plant load factor, a key measure of performance of a thermal power producer). Even so, Kishore's tenure as HR director had many rough turns; contending with a central minister demanding a bribe, among others. Kishore resigned, but his seniors counselled him to stay on, which he did

In 2005, at age sixty, Kishore retired from NTPC two years before time. He could have continued because his official age was fifty-seven, based on his school records but he shunned dishonesty in any form. Kishore found the age issue convenient and quit, as he had done four times in his career, when asked to make compromises. In any event, his relationship with the new chairman soured by then and the age factor was a good excuse. Kishore also had the opportunity to throw his hat in the ring for the chairmanship of NTPC before he retired but thought the better of it when the finance director, C.P. Jain, whom he considered a better candidate, applied. He regretted this decision because he was unhappy with the direction that NTPC took thereafter. On his farewell trip around NTPC facilities, he received the warmest possible send-off and, even six months after retirement, his former colleagues took charge of the arrangements for his daughter's wedding at the Stellar Gymkhana in Greater Noida.

There was much more to accomplish though, as Kishore talked of a feeling of incompleteness; of being the 'half-golden mongoose of the Mahabharata, who kept hopping from yajna to yajna, with the insatiable desire to find something', in his book, *My Experiments with Unleashing People Power* (2014) The hope, as with the mongoose, was that the rest of the journey 'could change the other half of his body also into gold and indeed complete this ever incomplete journey'. Thus did Kishore's journey continue into the private sector with Anil Ambani's Reliance Energy as director (HR) for a brief while. He quit, giving three days' notice, having lost his stomach for late-night meetings that were the rule there. Team Anil was unhappy because the battle between the Ambani brothers was brewing and an IPO was imminent. Thus, even after a settlement and separation, senior members of the group tried to hold Kishore back but he did not relent.

Kishore accepted another offer from the Mukesh Ambani-led Reliance Industries as HR adviser, where he served for four years adding little value, according to him. His tenure with the Ambanis helped him financially and achieved little else, to go by Kishore's assessment. Mukesh Ambani asked him to carry on, splitting his time between Delhi and Mumbai, but Kishore was not keen because Chitra was not interested in Mumbai and had moved to Delhi. Kishore then signed up for a three-year stint with Naveen Jindal, to organize HR for the Jindal Group. Kishore completed the task in two years, having got McKinsey to prepare a study and felt satisfied with a job well done. He chose to leave, possibly to retire for good. However, an offer from the Birla Institute of Management and Technology (BIMTECH) as dean of executive education, bang opposite his residence in Noida was too interesting to resist. In the interim, Kishore wrote books on HR, contributing to the understanding of the subject among professionals and serving as a board member of the National HRD Network.

The road to HR leadership is never easy; for Kishore, it was strewn with thorns. He picked out every one of them, and cast them aside as he moved on with persevering honesty, little bravado and bringing every imaginative strategy to bear on changing the HR landscape in a difficult public sector undertaking. From recalcitrant unions to corrupt union ministers, Kishore has dealt with them all, sometimes by going against the grain. He was often advised, 'when facing a storm, bend your head', but Kishore raised his head instead and conquered the onrushing waters.

* * *

Marcel Parker

Complete professional

Contributing in dramatics, HR and now sharing his wisdom mentoring youth and women

Marcel Parker, currently chairman of IKYA, has more than thirty-eight years of experience in manpower management at the highest levels across HR functions in leading companies. An IIM Ahmedabad alumnus with a degree in economics honours from St Stephen's College Delhi, he has led HR in such eminent organizations as the Raymond Group of Companies, Voltas Ltd,

East India Hotels Ltd, Modi Xerox Ltd, Bharat Shell Limited and SAP India Pvt. Ltd. He chaired the board of IKYA Human Capital Solutions, India's fastest-growing HR solutions organization till 2013 and is an independent director and chief mentor for the Quess Corporation.

Marcel works closely with the National HRD Network, Employers Federation of India and CII, to enhance employability and advocacy for the HR profession and academics. He serves as a subject matter expert on coaching with SHRM India and is a member of the SHRM Advisory Board for India and South Asia. A leading mentor and an International Coaching Federation (ICF) Associate Certified Coach, he trains leadership teams and individuals in MNCs and Indian organizations.

The beginnings lay in the catastrophe in 1884, when Marcel's then fifteen-year-old paternal grandfather and his younger brother lost their parents in the melee of the Kumbh Mela in 1884. As destiny willed it, they were found by an American missionary, Mr Parker, who adopted them and gave them a fine education and whose name they took. The older boy grew up to be a schoolteacher in rural Madhya Pradesh. His academically bright eldest son, Paul, Marcel's father, won a government scholarship to study engineering. at the Robertson College in Jabalpur.

Paul became outstanding in every respect. He was a devout Christian, good son, excellent tennis player and was eloquent to boot. He got into government service, worked for the railways on deputation and rose up the ranks, taking care of his siblings and getting his sisters married. For himself, he chose the daughter of a Bengali Christian educationist from Surat. It was a multilingual family, with Paul adept in Hindi and English and his wife in English, Bengali and Gujarati. English became the lingua franca for the Parker home, into which Marcel was born.

Their first child, Cecil, studied at St Xavier's in Calcutta from where he joined the Air Force to have a very distinguished career, becoming air vice marshal and honoured with the Mahavir Chakra and Vayu Sena Medal for destroying Pakistani gas fields. Marcel idolized his dashing and independent brother, sixteen years his senior, whom he met only occasionally and wanted to emulate. His sister married early and went on to become a great teacher, though his father would have loved to see her joining the IAS. Marcel was a lonely but a bright child who grew up to be a voracious reader, particularly of travel fiction, black comedy, a crossword addict and a Scrabble-player. Truth to tell, Marcel was good at whatever he did and was the teacher's pet.

When Paul was appointed as the head of the supply mission to Japan, a non-family posting, Marcel, only eight, had to be sent to the renowned La Martiniere College, India's oldest boarding school in Lucknow, graduating in 1964. He blossomed there, meeting his parents only twice a year, but found school a wonderful experience, where he learnt survival techniques and to be independent. Though indifferent at sports, he compensated by excelling in academics and learnt to box and play rugby. His father, who remained a distant though dominant figure of authority, wanted Marcel to serve the country as an IAS officer and sent his youngest son to St Stephen's College in Delhi, where Marcel did economics honours.

As with school, Marcel found the rather eclectic college exhilarating and very egalitarian. The thirty-five students in his batch included the sons of the prime minister and the chief justice of India and there was an elitist pride in being a Stephanian. From his contemporaries like Kapil Sibal, Kabir Bedi and others, he learnt to love dramatics and Marcel joined a dramatics group called Yatrik, which exposed him to well-known thespians. The independent boy became self-confident too. Everyone at St Stephen's then seemed to be preparing for the IAS and Marcel's 58 per cent in economics was considered quite good. His father's friends in the IAS/ICS, however, did not inspire him; the prospect of being a collector somewhere was unalluring. He was in a quandary when he came across management as a career choice. He drifted into appearing for the entrance exams to the Indian Institute of Management in 1968 and cracked it.

As his father, reconciled to this son not joining the IAS, came to drop him off to the prestigious IIMA, he asked Marcel what management he would be studying. Marcel recalls telling him: 'I don't know, Dad, but when I find out what management is all about, I'll let you know!' Marcel was among the first few Stephanians to join IIMA and soon realized the competition he was up against, with the profusion of very bright young engineers from the IITs. His batch of 1968–70 recently completed its Golden Jubilee, affirming his belief that being part of that group was a great education in itself. Then there were the great influencers in his professors—Kamla Chowdhry, Ishwar Dayal and Sudhir Kakkar; all were founts of knowledge.

Six students, Marcel included, found themselves getting interested in organizational behaviour (OB) as the subjects opened his mind and the breadth of the learning was stimulating. The challenge came in the quantitative methods and he found Prof. Meenakshi Malya, supported by Jahar Saha, later director of IIMA, most valuable. Other professors whom he looked up to were Keshav Prasad, K.K. Anand—who also taught OB, N.R. Sheth, Tarun Sheth and J.G. Krishnayya, who loved solving jigsaw puzzles and drove a Volvo, with whom he connected well. Director Ravi Mathai discovered his talent for dramatics and stage theatre, and encouraged him to set up a dramatic society, giving him Rs 75 to hire the Atira auditorium. There Marcel found the encouraging support of Mrs Ishwar Dayal and Vijay and Rupande Padaki. Theatre allowed Marcel to hone his public-speaking skills. This interesting set of influencers contributed to developing his skills, but he was yet to find his métier.

Upon graduation, Marcel joined Voltas' Pharmaceuticals and Consumer Products division, in a sales and marketing position. The company was great but not the job. Marcel found himself selling Horlicks with a quota to meet and found it a drag. Disillusioned, he networked and connected well with Madan Kamra and Ashwin Barua, the factory personnel manager at Thane. Marcel thought personnel would suit him better. Barua promised to put him on the shop floor after a thorough grilling. For Marcel, who lived in south Bombay, it meant a forty-five-minute ride to reach the Thane factory. This stint exposed him to the world of IR.

Voltas was highly unionized and no one wanted a factory job. However, Barua, his role model, did not want him to sit in the office. He also wanted Marcel to do job classification and evaluation for him and sent him to National Institute of Industrial Engineering (NITIE) for a three-month training. These made for good experience and Marcel had a yen for the work, but travelling from south to north Bombay was taking a toll. He saw many batchmates doing well, living and working in south Bombay and wanted to be doing so too. He met Soli Parikh, head of a search firm and Keki Bugwadia, later head of HR, Ashok Leyland, who offered Marcel an assistant's job at Vazir Sultan Tobacco

(VST), Hyderabad, makers of Charminar cigarettes and a subsidiary of the then Imperial Tobacco Co. (ITC). Marcel joined VST as an assistant in the covenanted cadre.

Anand Mukerjee, the HR head at VST, was an excellent and shrewd IR man, who spotted Marcel's talents and guided him into developing HR skills. There was also Vidyasagar Bhalla, an old-time factory personnel manager, who would constantly egg him on to visit the shop floor. Marcel's responsibilities included welfare and canteen, apart from housing administration for which there was an army of contractors that Marcel had to manage. This meant considerable power for the twenty-two-year-old and Marcel enjoyed it. He was learning IR both on the shop floor and in the tobacco fields of Andhra.

The union leaders liked the young man who introduced a credit society and sports for the workers. Marcel connected well with Badri Vishal Pitti, an external union leader, who was an art collector to boot. The two warmed up to each other over books on art that Marcel shared with him. At work, he learnt the hard way about creating the compensation structure, wage negotiations, calculating productivity indices and he enjoyed all of this. Trips to the field honed his market knowledge and not sitting in an office meant he built bonds with people who interacted with customers.

Life looked good for the young IR person, who had excellent social skills, living in a chummery, a fabulous place at Banjara Hills, playing bridge in his leisure hours. Only the money could be better.

At work, he had to conduct five or six domestic inquiries every day, which stood him in good stead vis-à-vis practising principles of natural justice all his life. After a year, the learning and development (L&D) function was started and Ivan Mathias, ten years his senior, was brought in from Bombay. A smart person from TISS with an excellent mind and a great influencer, Mathias played a huge role in Marcel's evolution. He exposed the youngster to different things by throwing him in at the deep end and getting him to learn the nuances of L&D, IR and employee engagement. Under Mathias, Marcel organized training programmes for the union leaders and workers too, and things were good till Mathias moved on. Marcel felt a bit lost but the silver lining in the cloud was his life partner, Leila, a teacher and the only daughter of a railway officer.

They married and their son, Samir, was born, followed by Smita two years later. It was fulfilling in a way for they had even built their own house at a young age! However, Marcel felt the absence of a guiding influence and when Coromandel Fertilizers, an American multinational, offered him a position with responsibilities for corporate personnel, he took it up to become their first MBA. Here too, there was little by way of guidelines for IR because the real power resided in manufacturing. Marcel was looking for a greater challenge, in keeping with someone of his calibre. He found it when Y.R.K. Reddy joined Coromandel as L&D head. The horizons widened further when Coromandel diversified from fertilizers to cement. Marcel worked for the head of the cement project and had to hire people for a project being put up in a pocket of acute poverty near Cuddapah, Andhra Pradesh. The union leaders were medical doctors and Marcel lived there as the project got constructed, coming home only on Saturdays.

Marcel's IR skills were learnt apropos of tobacco; fertilizer was different but the people in the cement space were a different species altogether. Once the cement plant started, Marcel felt that he was yet to evolve better. Life at Hyderabad was rather laid back and comfortable, but Marcel reflected he would not know how much better things could get unless he took risks. The answer came from Mathias, his mentor, who was an important person with the Oberoi group. He advised Marcel to grow out of his comfort zone, offering him a job with the Oberois at the Oberoi School of Hotel Management in Delhi. Sophisticated and well-turned-out, Prithvi Raj Singh 'Biki' Oberoi was an exacting boss and very quality-conscious as he rebuilt the Oberoi brand. Mathias was comfortable engaging with him and the school that trained people in service orientation for all levels in the hospitality space. It gave him an excellent opportunity to mould people by changing attitudes and preparing them for leadership roles. Marcel enjoyed being a facilitator of change rather than remaining in a command and control space, as in factory IR.

The Oberois were a growing group with operations in the Middle East, where Mathias wanted a person of high integrity. Marcel managed the Middle East properties, focusing on talent acquisition and then placing them in different locations.

He also had the onerous task of taking senior people to Biki Oberoi for interviews, sometimes even at midnight. Many employees had personal connections with the boss that had to be handled sensitively. Elsewhere there were problems, as in the Oberoi Palace, Srinagar, seriously impacted in 1988, when unrest in Jammu and Kashmir erupted. Marcel handled the strong unions there and managed the locals suspicious of outsiders, achieving a long-term settlement in the Oberoi Palace. It made for tremendous learnings, for the process was riddled with politics, external and internal. Marcel realized that being transparent and firm was the best way to win their confidence.

The hotel industry has its own share of issues between the sexes and there were emerging issues around gender harassment that Marcel had to tackle discreetly. On one occasion, the ninety-two-year-old Rai Bahadur Oberoi advised him to sensitively handle a complaint against a lady manager. 'Be fair to this woman. I am told you are a fair man,' implying that she was being framed because she had not accepted the advances of the higher-ups. Marcel did so and earned the admiration of the local satraps! It was a whirl of activity, career-counselling, teaching, building relationships with powerful people and remaining professional without getting into confrontations. This required diplomacy, tact and patience, most of which Marcel learnt on the job. Not being from the inner echelons of the hotel fraternity meant networking and fortitude to survive, and learning the tricks of the trade in the culinary arts by speaking the same language, which helped tremendously.

Mathias left and Marcel legitimately felt that he could step into his shoes. He met Biki Oberoi to present his case, only to be told that he was too young for the CHRO position; that he had no 'gray hair' and would 'have to wait'. As someone else was appointed, Marcel reflected on how well he had performed and looked for outside validation. In 1991–92, Marcel met Arvind Agrawal from Xerox Corporation, which had a joint venture in India with the B.K. Modi group, to understand how Xerox measured employee satisfaction. Marcel must have impressed Agrawal for, soon after, he was invited to join Xerox, to take over as CHRO from Agrawal, who was taking over as head of marketing and business strategy. Agrawal had invested the HR function with great credibility and Marcel met tall personalities like Khurshid Bandopadhyay, Prakash Nanani, P.M. Pai and Dennis Oliver. Some were inspirational, others were dominating, but Marcel found his balance, though it was tough stepping into Agrawal's shoes.

The HR function had a great team, comprising Brij Chandiramani, Raghu Krishnamoorthy and R. Shekar. Finding ready acceptance from them was satisfying; so was learning from these very sharp people around him. Thoroughly professional, Oliver, to whom Marcel reported, was all about doing an honest day's work and Marcel connected well with him. Oliver was the Xerox Corporation man at the joint venture, assigned to ensure that the JV ran like any other global Xerox operation. R.S. Desikan and Pradeep Kapoor in finance were great challengers; O.P. Dani, the company secretary and legal head, and Ashok Goel in taxation were experts in their fields. Chandiramani, R.K. Mathur, Rajvanshi, Rajan Datta and Krishnamoorthy were exceptionally supportive as Marcel knit a competent core around him in his first CHRO role. He focused on the important, often delegating to others in the team.

Working with B.K. Modi, chairman, was very enjoyable too, though it was more a directive-based relationship and Marcel gained confidence working with a promoter. When Oliver completed his term in India and moved back to the parent company, Marcel had to professionally uphold the values and ethics of Xerox, as the conscience-keeper. Krishnamoorthy quit too for a better job and Chandiramani was in two minds about continuing with Xerox. On the home front, Marcel's fifteen-year-old daughter studied at a convent, but he was getting apprehensive about Delhi being an unsafe place for a young girl to grow up in. Marcel managed the worry and other personally emotional issues at an intellectual level without allowing them to affect his work. This was a sign of great maturity. He also firmed up on getting out of Delhi. Tarun Sheth was at that time looking for an HR head for Vikram Mehta, chairman of Royal Dutch/Shell in India and Marcel found a welcome opening. He joined the Shell joint venture with the public sector, Bharat Petroleum Corporation, a unique combination of a start-up with two gigantic partners.

Joining Shell meant transitioning everyone to the Shell culture. Marcel comfortably slipped into his new role in the company, which had a distinct brand identity—Bharat Shell Ltd, integrating the best of two worlds, with people from several countries. It was the brand that imposed a certain culture. As he handled all people issues, he found his footing, building the core team and finding acceptance at Shell House, London. Marcel was soon involved in HR issues across Asia and as

Shell grew in India, so did his responsibilities to include new businesses of Exploration and Production, renewables, chemicals and LNG, apart from building the lubricants plant in Taloja. The excellent relationships that Marcel built here remain solid even twenty years later.

Marcel was by now an established figure in HR in India, with strong affiliation with the NHRDN, of which he has been a long-standing member. He started off with the erstwhile IIPM in Hyderabad as its Branch Secretary and realized the value of shared learning through networking. He absorbed the wisdom of its leading members, strengthened those relationships, shared his learnings with them and empowered himself in the process. He was instrumental in developing and establishing the Code of Ethics for HR and redesigning the logo for NHRDN, among other things. Among his many satisfying associations was the Strategic Human Resources Leadership Journey (SHRLJ), a national initiative of the NHRDN, initiated by Anand Nayak, the HR chief of ITC.

Marcel partnered well with Nayak and played a pivotal role in sustaining it from 2004 to groom the next generation of HR leaders in the country. He helped run the programme in Mumbai for the next six years and served as regional president of the NHRDN, Western Region between 2002 and 2006. Working with prominent thought leaders in HR and NHRDN Presidents Arvind Agrawal, Santrupt Mishra, Aquil Busrai, P. Dwarakanath, T.V. Rao, Fr Abraham, among others, was greatly enriching. For his contribution to the HR profession in the country, Marcel was felicitated with the NHRDN's President's Award in 2010. He continued his work with the NHRDN, initiating a novel Womentoring programme for the Mumbai Chapter in 2012, which he ran for several years. It continues to be the only one of its kind in the country.

At age fifty, Marcel met what was arguably his biggest challenge in life. He knew little of the knowledge-worker space but was headhunted by SAP AG, where he found himself in turbulent weather—as if trying to build an aircraft while flying—as he dealt with a multinational culture whose leadership was ignorant of the complexities of working in India. On the one hand, he was dealing with Germans with a definitive working culture. On the other, he had to report to a boss who did not understand India and the company was not doing well.

The headquarters were shifted to Bangalore with the HR head having a three-way reporting that was frustrating. Yet, there were lessons galore.

At a personal level, Marcel had to reinvent himself to add value. At ease learning from people much junior to him, Marcel could park his ego while engaging with others in any capacity. Not being a great one for a formal structure for connecting with people, he was always approachable. This stood him in good stead as he branched out as a coach. In his numerous working roles, he focused on consensus-building, allowing debates over issues and options, while he remained a good listener. This won him the innate trust of people and, truth to tell, it has never been belied. The many career moves enriched his palette of skills, and also involved personally mastering the change agenda; carrying people along and driving change when needed.

Change could be multifaceted; changing the structure of the organization or simply changing an individual's competencies. Marcel excelled at both and could groom successors with elan. He would work closely with them and constantly empower them by taking them to meetings, placing them in the limelight, networking with them and creating opportunities for them to present. These skills were mastered over his many moves. Going from Xerox to Shell to SAP invested him with agility on the one hand and breadth of experience on the other, and he mastered different roles, always from a position of humility. He also scrupulously avoided talking down to people. Eventually these relationships and social interactions helped him to constantly reinvent himself. The SAP experience was thus richly rewarding though not entirely a fulfilling one. The charm of working in a multinational wore off and an offer from a professionally-run Indian company was a welcome change.

Gautam Singhania from Raymond invited him to join the company and, for the first time, Marcel was reporting to the promoter. Marcel ran a host of publicly acknowledged management development programmes here and focused on building capability, L&D and restructuring of compensation and benefits. He retired from the Raymond Group as president HR and was wondering how to build a legacy of development of leaders. Marcel has had an opportunity to add value and learn from MNCs, Indian transnationals and promoter-led companies. When Ajit Isaac, a young HR practitioner-turned-entrepreneur, invited him to be chairman of the board of his start-up company, IKYA, now Quess Corp., India's largest private sector employer, Marcel loved the idea.

He had little idea of what he was in for, but Isaac's vision was to build a billion-dollar organization in a decade and it was accomplished! The challenge was right up Marcel's street, even though it meant new learnings and extending his HR role to a business and governance role. He picked this up with reasonable ease, even making sales pitches. He has been with Quess for fourteen years, first as chairman, till it went public and then as chief mentor. He continues in this role, mentoring and coaching people, especially the young leadership team and the HR leaders, building programmes for younger people and cascading the culture of building capability through coaching.

In recent times, he works closely with developing next-gen leaders through a unique programme called 'The Crucible'. Marcel derives strength from the fact that he never gave up on people or himself. Yet, he is cautious in his approach to coachees and conscious about not breaching their personal space. This is particularly important when mentoring women, which Marcel has done a lot of, coaching for women's development programmes for Mahindra & Mahindra and at the S.P. Jain University programme for women MBAs.

As he continues to work with Quess as chief mentor, he has been entrusted with the trusteeship of the Careworks Foundation, the Quess CSR wing that supports child education in Karnataka and Tamil Nadu, through upgrading government schools. He has served on the boards of several Quess-owned subsidiaries, including serving on the iconic Quess East Bengal Football Club in Kolkata. Other unique programmes have included one with XLRI for Recruiter Certification with Quess. India's largest private-sector employer tied up with XLRI, India's leading HR-oriented business school, to create a unique programme that no business school in India teaches. Marcel enjoyed starting and sustaining an HRD mentoring programme for HR students at Welingkar Business School and is proud that his mentees still reach out to him. Besides, he serves on two school boards and does coaching and leadership development programmes at some Christian community schools, hospitals and with teachers, doctors, nurses and NGOs.

A string of meaningful work has come his way, post the coach certification, paving the way for him to make a difference in the lives of young, middle and senior-level executives across the board. He has served as the senior career adviser at the National Rail and Transportation Institute, Vadodara, coaching students at this unique railway university to make them employable, and he also serves on the advisory boards of two organizations involved in talent acquisition. He is a member of SHRM's Advisory Board for the Middle East and South-east Asia.

Marcel's second innings has been just as rewarding with the flowering of his entrepreneurial streak. So have the hours of leisure, allowing him to engage with his world of pursuits and pastimes. Gardening, travelling in the US, watching Broadway plays and playing bridge, not to mention reading, keep him alive and contributing. As Marcel believes, what one leaves behind is not what is engraved on stone monuments but what is woven into the lives of others. In nurturing talent, Marcel found the most wondrous way to do so.

* * *

Niddodi Subrao (N.S.) Rajan

Quote me if you can

Versatile professional sharing wisdom through quotes in his pursuit to 'give back'

Known for his quotations and social media presence, N.S. Rajan (Rajan) was group chief human resources officer, group chief marketing officer and chief executive officer of the IDFC Foundation from 2017 till recently. Earlier, he was group CHRO and member of the Tata Sons Group Executive Council and a nominee of Tata Sons on the boards of various group companies. Rajan achieved acclaim as the Global Leader of the People and Organization practice of Ernst & Young (E&Y), when he led HR consulting operations in more than thirty countries with a team of over 700 people.

A graduate in economics from Loyola College, Chennai; a postgraduate in business management from XLRI, Jamshedpur; with a doctorate from IIT Delhi, Rajan has more than three decades of experience spanning various line and staff functions. He was conferred the Distinguished Alumnus Award by XLRI, Jamshedpur and serves on its Board of Governors. A former national president of the NHRD Network, a visiting faculty member at IIMA and XLRI, Rajan also helps various educational institutions and has received many accolades, including the Outstanding HR Leadership award by Hindustan Times *in 2012.*

In a small town, Bapatla, off the coast of Andhra Pradesh, with a population of less than 40,000, at a modest school set up by a women's NGO, Sthree Hitaishini Mandal, with two thatched huts for classrooms, the headmaster called the parents of a student and said that their boy deserved a better school, encouraging them to shift him. They did; to a school in a bigger town nearby. It was déjà vu for here again the principal advised the parents after a few years that the child had the potential to excel and should be shifted to a bigger school. They admitted him to Loyola Public School, Guntur, Andhra Pradesh.

A good institution can unlock a child's potential and while Rajan's first day at Loyola was traumatic, given its exceptional teaching standards, compared to his earlier modest schools, the finished product was outstanding. He barely spoke English and struggled to understand the lessons. Crestfallen but hardly defeated, he had an epiphany: begin from the beginning. Over the next month, he collected second-hand textbooks from the first to the sixth grade and willed himself to learn on his own. Burning the midnight oil, starting from the alphabet and learning the curriculum year by year, he caught up in three tough years, transforming his approach to learning, opening new vistas.

Rajan stood second in his tenth grade exams and was fluent in English, thanks to the wonderful Jesuit priests, A.J. Thamby and Royce Macedo. A major hurdle, which has stymied the careers of many rural youths, was overcome! Over the years, Rajan learnt eight languages, writes poetry in three of them and is a public speaker. For Rajan, the important dimension of learning was starting from the alphabet of any science and gradually building on it to gain proficiency. There is a fundamental difference between knowing a formula and mastering how it has been arrived at. When the context changes, knowing how to derive can help find a solution where a set formula may fail. This belief stood Rajan in good stead throughout his career, especially when he made a mid-career shift to HR from business management.

Rajan's father, Niddodi Subrao, a Vedic scholar from Karnataka, learnt scriptures at a temple in Kateel, a stone's throw from Niddodi, a tiny village with a population of under a thousand, in Mangalore District, Karnataka. He would often remind his eldest son, Rajan, that a true brahmin was respected not because he was born one but through service and good deeds. Subrao had moved to Bombay with aspirations of going overseas. This did not materialize because his older brothers requested him to join the family business, an Udipi restaurant in Bapatla.

Rajan was born in Kurnool, the erstwhile capital of AP, in 1961. His mother, Janaki Rao, grew up there and became the head girl in her school. She had the privilege of meeting Rajendra Prasad, India's first President and interacting with Pandit Jawaharlal Nehru, the country's first prime minister. Her parents were freedom fighters and her mother, Radha Bai, was an accomplished singer and played the violin. Rajan recalls meeting his maternal great-grandmother, who lived till the age of 105 and has fond memories of being doted upon by four generations on his mother's side of the family. His mother moved to Bapatla after marriage, where Rajan grew up, his outlook in life much influenced by her.

On completing ICSE, Rajan joined Loyola College, Madras, a Jesuit institution par excellence, graduating in economics and completed his post-graduation in business management from XLRI in 1983. At fifty-four, three decades later, he earned his PhD in leadership from IIT Delhi. Investing in education makes latent talent blossom. Loyola's excellent teachers, especially the head of the economics department, Professor Felix, a double postgraduate and revered academician, had an abiding influence on Rajan's progress. Tough as a teacher and kind as a person, he guided Rajan as he developed a penchant to question any law, understand how it evolved and accepting it only when he could apply theory in practice.

Rajan also participated in the many extracurriculars on offer and became a member of the Students' Council, joined the fine arts and dramatics clubs, and was elected as the secretary of the Hindi Association, though he could barely speak the language. He ran the LOHO (Loyola Hostel) Stores, a departmental store for hostelites, as its student director, raising seed capital of Rs 10 each from student investors and managed to give a 50 per cent dividend. He understood how business worked and how to sell in the process. When Rajan invited Usha International to display their fans at LOHO Stores, they agreed, provided he sold at least three fans. Rajan went door to door in the hostel and in the faculty quarters too, selling twenty-two fans, and getting a job offer from Usha.

Besides, Rajan attended Bharatanatyam classes for a year at Rukmini Arundale's Kalakshetra before opting for MBA at XLRI in 1981. Before he left, he received a much-cherished testimonial from Fr Felix saying that Rajan was among the top 2 per cent of students he had taught over twenty-two years and commended his eagerness to 'test received knowledge in the light of experience . . . (his) critical mind, clear expression and an ability to feel at home with both facts and theory'. At twenty-one, after graduating from XLRI in 1983, Rajan joined Ranbaxy as a management trainee in the Sales and Marketing function. He was delighted to see his name in the annual report where executive compensation above a certain sum had to be declared, for the first and last time. Rajan jokes that his compensation did not keep pace with the declaration limit above which salaries were to be reported.

As FMCG area manager, North, Rajan experienced his first stint in sales and over three years in Ranbaxy, got a firm footing in both product management and sales, which became his forte. The ability to influence and ensure mutually beneficial relationships and long-lasting connections that went beyond the transactional became his abiding strength and paved the way to leadership. Rajan demonstrated this early. Asked for advice by his best salesman on how he should respond to an offer from another company, Rajan dealt with his dilemma around whether he would safeguard the company's interest or the colleagues'. He advised him to accept the much more lucrative offer and never regretted giving this honest advice.

Travelling with him by bus, another salesman asked Rajan when did one earn a promotion. Rajan confessed that, being new to the job, he was unsure, much to the disappointment of the colleague, who wondered how he would work on his career progression if even his boss had no idea. The penny dropped and Rajan conceptualized a role matrix and a model to isolate requisite quantitative and qualitative skills with the steps to prepare oneself for career progress. He explained the Professional and Personal Development Plan (PPDP) model to train his team on how to excel in sales. This competency-based approach served as the bedrock for the leadership development methodology that

he created a couple of decades later. That became a core offering of the
EY HR consulting arm that he started from scratch.

Rajan then joined Asian Paints (AP) for a five-year stint as an
executive in 1986. It was a period of priceless learning and growth,
working closely with Bharat Puri, Verghese Anthony and V.V.
Kannan. It had a remarkable pool of professional talent at all levels
who helped retain market leadership. Puri taught him the value of
believing in and empowering the team, the need to persuade and
influence all stakeholders through enabling mutual gain, and leading
people with care and concern, backed by one's own self-belief, to fuel
relentless execution. Anthony had the gift of identifying talent early
and investing in them. He emphasized the power of paying attention to
detail and analysis to take reasoned decisions, to maintain equanimity
through highs and lows and being a trusted mentor. Kannan's unique
ability was focusing on the team's strengths while filling up for their
weaknesses, developing deep relationships in the marketplace and
ensuring consistent outcomes.

Rajan evolved as a professional, honing his skills in leading teams
and serving the markets, learning not just to survive but to thrive in
some of the toughest units where AP's market share was abysmally low.
Soon, he was recognized for his innate ability to sell, transform the
team and markets, and achieve new benchmarks in every location he
was assigned to. His AP experiences taught him to emulate the best and
excel in assignments. He also learnt that good leaders are followers too,
imbibing key lessons by observing others at work and learning from their
beliefs and actions. Rajan encouraged his team to go beyond offering
monetary benefits and focus on building enduring relationships; not to
sell but to make the customer buy.

Posted in Vijayawada, Andhra Pradesh, Rajan visited a
Machilipatnam dealer, who was reluctant to place orders. When Rajan
sought an order, the dealer offered laddus, joking that for every laddu
Rajan ate, he would put in an order of Rs 5,000. Rajan literally ate
his way to success, walking away with a handsome order of Rs 1.5
lakh. Even better, he met Vidya (she is 'learning' itself, he jokes) at
Vijayawada. Their families knew each other and they married in 1989.
Their only child, Deepa (meaning light), who means the world to him,
was born here.

In Coimbatore, the biggest retailer was threatening to stop dealing with AP. Realizing that the usual persuasion would not work, Rajan found out that the dealer went for a daily morning jog. Rajan joined him on the daily run, never talking business, but soon, there was no more talk of quitting the dealership. They became friends for life. Rajan believed that rendering exceptional customer service and commitment delivers sustainable growth. Coimbatore became one of the fastest-growing units and Rajan got a promotion to Cochin, Kerala, a tough market with intense competition and deep discounting by competitors.

Apart from intractable dealers and unpredictable markets, Cochin was the home of three different unions and was a labour relations nightmare. Life was a daily challenge and Rajan was the first branch manager posted who was not a Kerala native and did not speak Malayalam, the local language. Dealing with the hostile market and unions was enervating but helped Rajan to grow as a person and a leader as he took to inimitably novel ways to change the rules of the game, beginning with stopping discounts and taking the system by surprise. He used the savings to build the brand locally, creating customer pull, opening rural and underserved pockets and focusing on enabling exceptional customer service. Cochin soon ranked among AP's best-performing units.

It was exemplified by salesmen like Gangadharan. In Cochin for his monthly review, he received an SOS from his dealer at Trivandrum, asking for a particular shade of paint to complete a house that had to be made ready for a family wedding. It was a stormy night but Gangadharan collected the paint cartons from the warehouse and biked through the torrential rain to Trivandrum at night and, reportedly, pitched in to paint some of the walls when the painters left for the night. Rajan believes that such exemplary commitment to customers earns their heart-share and augurs well for the enterprise.

Rajan left AP for Blowplast and moved to Kolkata as the regional sales manager, East, selling Leo Toys and Barbie dolls for three years prior to joining ABC Consultants, a pioneer and leader in executive search in India. He was based in Delhi and after two years in management consulting, he moved to the executive search space. It involved meeting accomplished professionals on his headhunting missions and Rajan picked up the art of consulting. After four years,

Rajan was posted to Singapore, as country manager, getting a passport for the first time in 1997. In Singapore, Informatics, a leading IT-education enterprise, asked him to head strategy, marketing and HR because it had started India operations. Two years later, he joined Asia Online, a US multinational providing IT services to the Small and Medium Enterprises space, as director of sales and marketing.

Serendipitously, a call from E&Y, offered him an opportunity to build an HR advisory services practice from scratch and Rajan entered the HR domain after eighteen years of sales and marketing. He quickly learnt on the job, given his yen for unravelling principles and their application at work. EY was a late entrant in the HR consulting space where pure-play firms were well established. Rajan looked at freshers from XLRI and TISS, based on academic excellence and IQ, recruiting those with the right attitude. Rajan planned to take a solution-oriented approach and not rely on existing products. In just the first fifteen months, Rajan met with over 500 companies to connect and convey how EY's HR offerings were unique, focusing on the underserved Indian promoter-led companies and government-owned undertakings and not on the MNCs that the others served.

He wrote for financial publications and spoke at HR forums to build equity. When EY acquired Arthur Andersen, it strengthened the consulting team and made a difference in the market, helping companies headquartered in India and envisioning their people strategy, rather than just implementing it. Once Indian Oil came on board, EY won some thirty significant contracts and became a forerunner in that segment. EY's deep relationships with Indian-led enterprises were leveraged to work in the HR space too and the practice gained significant client share.

Meritocracy and empowerment were to serve as the foundation as Rajan built a team of extraordinary young professionals for an excellent advisory practice. Rajan treated his team with immense care and respect and they carried it forward into their relationships with their clients because they shared a vision. He exposed them to every HR vertical to facilitate proficiencies across the board. He explained his approach in the EY house magazine, 'Connect', underscoring his endeavours for 'delivering tangible outcomes; effectively delegating while guiding his team; being non-judgemental; seeking to elicit the best from everyone and empowering them in the face of adversity'.

These principles were developed over his sales roles and helped the people practice build an enviable portfolio, serving over 200 clients in HR transformation, organization design, talent management and leadership development. A remarkable 65 per cent of EY's work came from past clients, reflecting the value of its solutions, and EY's HR in India won a special mention in the Kennedy Research Report on the global management consulting industry for earning the trust and respect of clients and stakeholders with its cutting-edge work. Rajan then proceeded to lead the Europe, Middle East, India and Africa (EMEIA) markets in an exciting and daunting phase, working with a cross-cultural team of colleagues heading their respective countries.

Rajan believed that leadership was sustained by service excellence and leveraged the diverse cultures to mine the knowledge and wisdom of his peers while leading them. He created a knowledge framework that captured the collective strengths of the region and structured methodologies and models to help the partners respond to clients with a pitch document in just a day, instead of the standard week. He was available to the EY partners for client meetings and helped them to win without charging them. This engendered cooperation with country partners, helping one another to fuel growth.

In less than a decade, Rajan became global head of the HR consulting practice, the first time any partner from India helmed a practice globally, leading diverse teams across multiple geographies and sharpening his global perspective in the process. Rajan travelled to over forty countries, learning from every visit and shares credit for this growth with his brilliant team and the unstinting support from the visionary Rajiv Memani, the country managing partner, India. Memani drove excellence across the firm at all levels, had the remarkable gift of enabling shared vision, reimagining the future and investing in people and infrastructure much ahead of time, thinking big and delivering.

After twelve years at EY, Rajan was invited to lead the human resources function at the Tata Group. In late 2012, Rajan received a call from Cyrus Mistry, who was taking over as chairman, Tata Sons, the holding company of the Tata Group, with over 6,00,000 employees across 100 companies. Over meetings and interviews by five senior directors, Rajan was appointed as a member of the Group Executive Council (GEC) and as the group CHRO at Tata Sons, arguably the most coveted CHRO role in the country. EY gave him a warm farewell in an event titled 'Jeena Isi Ka Naam Hai', with an outpouring of love and respect, and published a coffee table book titled 'Reminiscences' that captured his EY journey.

The Tata assignment involved HR leadership and support for all group companies with his sixty-five-member team, heading the Group Diversity Council and chairmanship of Group Affirmative Action, enhancing board effectiveness and creating a governance manual. The opportunity to make a real difference was exciting and challenging, and Rajan led key initiatives that had salience group-wide, including overseeing the Tata Management Training Centre and Tata Administrative Services (TAS), among India's best known in-house leadership programmes, designed to create future CEO/CXOs. In nine months, Rajan had met nearly 400 senior leaders, learning from those who collectively reflected what the group stood for. He worked towards refreshing the group-wide leadership competency model. Gender diversity was another area of special interest and Rajan demonstrated his commitment to inclusion, making seminal changes, including a group-wide, cross-company mentoring for future women leaders.

Rajan also facilitated the hiring of over 100 people at the leadership level and supported the chairman and nomination and remuneration committees of the various boards to add independent directors. Rajan was Tata Sons' nominee on the boards of Indian Hotels (Taj) and Tata Services. In recognition of his commitment to HR, Rajan was invited by the United Nations' Economic and Social Council to be part of a policymakers' panel, on achieving sustainable development through creating 500 million jobs across the world. He addressed the delegates at the UN headquarters in New York. In his role as the chair of Tata Group Affirmative Action, Rajan received a national award from the prime minister, for the group's service to the underserved and underprivileged.

For Rajan, it was a privilege to serve the Tatas and work closely with chairman Cyrus Mistry, a visionary leader with innate humility, unfailing grace and equanimity in handling the toughest situations. He was overwhelmed by Mistry's intellect, incisive decision-making, ability to hire the best, abiding compassion for people and unshakeable belief in ethics and governance. Nevertheless, the eventful change at the helm of Tata Sons meant that Rajan too had to bid adieu in October 2016.

He was promptly offered the CEO's position at the IDFC Foundation and as group CHRO and CMO of IDFC Bank, a banking start-up, where he served for two years, helping it through a merger transition. He also consolidated the foundation's activities to drive banking services to rural pockets, through micro-ATMs and supporting farmers in remote villages through specialized programmes.

After thirty-six years, he chose to step down from formal employment and has developed a personal and professional portfolio that keeps him busy. Amidst all this, Rajan made exemplary contributions to the HR profession through his active role at the NHRD Network, leading the Delhi Chapter and the North zone as president and becoming the national president; the first HR consultant in this position. He introduced the Governance, Engagement and Networking (GEN) Framework and other initiatives, creating a lasting impact. The NHRDN recognized him as 'HRD Professional of the Year' in 2008, for his contributions. Rajan has also been a member of the governing council of Consultancy Development Centre, an autonomous institution of the Department of Scientific and Industrial Research, Ministry of Science and Technology, and XLRI, his alma mater, conferred on him the coveted accolade of 'Distinguished Alumni' for his accomplishments. He now serves on the XLRI board of governors.

Family and friends have served as a great source of strength, anchoring him through stormy periods and sharing his joys at other times. His siblings and friends have stood by him, the oldest, M.V.S.N. Murthy, has been a friend for over fifty years. A man of many parts, Rajan is a keen photographer, philatelist, art and music aficionado, who attempted to learn classical dance and Carnatic music. He even served as a model for Informatics and has been an anchor investor, funding early start-ups in HR and technology, investing in and mentoring many early-stage entrepreneurs. Active on social media, he shares his reflections every day and wrote a book, *Quote Me If You Can*, published by Penguin Random House India, compiling his thoughts on life, business and happiness. A second book on happiness at work, a subject that he has pursued for long, is on the anvil.

Life for him is a matter of opportunities, used well, a lesson embedded in his mind by his father, when he was just fifteen at Bapatla.

His house help, Mohan, had forgotten to get him the newspaper that he had asked for and Rajan berated him. Overhearing this conversation, his father asked him what was the difference between him and Mohan. Rajan did not have the answer and his father pointed out that it was 'opportunity'. Rajan should have known better than to admonish a boy who was employed by his father. 'Be grateful and count your blessings. Take every opportunity you get and make the most of it, but never ever hurt those who have been less fortunate. Help others who haven't had their share, when you can and create opportunities for them to grow too.'

Rajan never forgot the message. Blessed with the opportunity in the HR space, he cherished his ability to serve and harness people's potential. He believes in the nobility of purpose that drives HR practitioners, seeing their role as alchemists, creating a platform for progress. The opening lines in EY's coffee table book on him sums up his contributions to HR: 'A salute to a leader whose passion towards his profession, compassion for his team, humility towards the people around him and a magical ability to build everlasting relationships has taken him to great heights.'

Rajan turned sixty in November 2021. The flame still burns bright, illuminating the road ahead.

* * *

P. Dwarakanath

Building people-centric organizational cultures

Experimenting with rules and processes, sometimes establishing them, and often going beyond them

P. Dwarakanath (Dwarka), chairman of GlaxoSmithKline (GSK) Consumer Healthcare Ltd and group HR head, Max Group till recently, has rich and varied experience of over four decades. As GSK's director, human resources and administration, India/South Asia, for four decades, he was a member of its international HR team. Among his numerous achievements is the progressive and people-centric culture that he championed in GSK, acknowledged as one of the best places to work in India and overseas for several years. Initiatives to drive the new corporate culture during times of integration, through concepts such as 'Simply Better Way', were benchmarks for the erstwhile SmithKline Beecham.

Dwarka has held several management positions in various professional bodies and was president, NHRDN, president of the Delhi Management Association (DMA), regional president, Northern Region, All India Management Association (AIMA) and its treasurer. Dwarka has won several awards for his invaluable contribution to HR, including the Pathfinders Award and Lifetime Achievement Award by the NHRDN, Career Achievement Award by GSK International and Chairman's Award by Max India.

To be mentored by a legendary business leader is a dream for any youngster; it came true for P. Dwarakanath when he began to intern with the DCM/Shriram Group (DCM), often directly under Lala Charat Ram. It was a fascinating learning opportunity for Dwarka as DCM was one of India's corporate giants of that era, and he worked across India with varying job profiles, including a stint as a part of Charat Ram's office. Not just professional exposure, DCM imparted training in soft skills, such as ballroom dancing and dining etiquette. More importantly, it taught him to be his own man for Dwarka quit DCM after seven years when he found robust processes not being uniformly followed across the company. A certain degree of arbitrariness is not unusual in promoter-driven Indian businesses, but Dwarka found it off-putting. So was the reprobation from the top that could be humiliating even for seniors. Occasionally, meetings with visiting teams got cancelled on whims and Dwarka was a man of discipline.

A lawyer by training, practising in the Andhra Pradesh High Court under a senior advocate before joining DCM, Dwarka had seen his father P.V. Ramana Rao, a member of the judicial services, being a stickler for rules as a judge. He once donned his black robes at 4.30 a.m. because a convict was to be hanged and he wanted to ensure that processes were followed and the last wishes of the convict were recorded. Doing the right thing while performing his duties was sacrosanct for his father, who would not even pronounce verdicts in two cases on the same day when the same lawyer was appearing, just in case both the cases went for or against the lawyer, conveying an impression of bias.

Dwarka's childhood, in south India, saw fluctuating fortunes upon the passing of his well-to-do grandfather, with business interests in mica mining and textiles. Dwarka was seven then and his father only twenty-one. His father and uncles could not hold on to the business and the family was in financial straits. His mother taught English and Dwarka had to shift from a private to a government school. Though an average student, Dwarka was an accomplished debater and enjoyed sports, especially tennis. He wanted to do political science in college but gave in to his father's desire and studied science at Loyola College in Vijayawada. He had been urged to apply to XLRI to study personnel management and labour relations after college but not having heard of the discipline nor about XLRI, he ignored the advice, studied law, followed in his father's footsteps and started practising. When his senior was elevated to the bench, Dwarka was contemplating his future. He saw a DCM advertisement seeking management trainees and applied. After a three-month-long selection process, ending with an hour-long interview with a ten-member panel that included Lala Charat Ram, he got the job.

DCM was being run by the two sons of Lala Shri Ram, Bharat Ram and Charat Ram. Bharat was the face of the organization and Charat the nuts and bolts man. Apart from textiles, the group's diverse interests included engineering and chemicals. Asked why he should be selected at the interview, Dwarka replied that while he did not have a great academic record, he was good at managing people and DCM should give him a chance. It did and Charat Ram himself was closely involved with the management trainee programme, doing quarterly reviews on the progress of the trainees. Dwarka was also a part of Charat Ram's office before his first assignment in Kolkata, at DCM's Jay Engineering Works, making Usha sewing machines. The factory had 10,000 employees with renowned trade union leaders—Bhupesh Gupta of the Communist Party of India (AITUC), Priya Ranjan Das Munshi (INTUC) while the CPI-M-affiliated CITU was led by Haridas Malakar, a confidante of the future chief minister, Jyoti Basu. West Bengal then had the United Front government.

Dwarka reported to the regional personnel manager, Chanchal Raj Singhvi, a remarkably clever man. When the trade union leaders approached Singhvi with a problem, he would respond in Hindi, though he knew Bengali perfectly well. This would slow down the conversation and buy him time, but he slipped into Bengali when talking to them

one-on-one to build rapport. Industrial relations here were trying and
the factory saw India's first gherao in 1969, though its workers were
among the highest paid and bonus was six months' wages. The striking
employees wanted eight months' wages as bonus. The United Front
government did not believe in the police intervening in any labour
protests, which were under the labour minister's purview.

On his part, Dwarka realized early in his career that appeasement
did not buy peace. The entire ecosystem had to be managed. Yet,
businesses followed a policy of appeasement till the younger generation
of promotors got assertive. The management decided to push back
and Dwarka was asked to put up a notice for a lockout. As industrial
relations officer, he also dealt with senior lawyers, attended tribunals,
met H.M. Ghosh, the joint commissioner of labour and other
government officials, and learnt a lot from Ghosh. A passionate officer,
he was navigating the tricky waters, balancing pressures from both the
super-aggressive union leaders and managements. Dwarka found the
DCM culture empowering as he was allowed to tackle tough situations
on his own. Such freedom Dwarka did not find in many other senior
roles later in life.

Working with Lala Charat Ram was an exceptional experience,
beginning with simple learnings like the importance of knowing
everyone's name or breaking norms when necessary. Asked to shortlist
applicants for a management trainee's post, Dwarka submitted a list
of fifty but was asked for the list of the rejected candidates too. Some
candidates from the rejected list were called for interviews and five of
them were selected. This experience taught him to break norms on
occasions. Dwarka's peers were outstanding: Ashok Taneja from IIT
Kanpur and Subbaratnam Ravi from IIT Kharagpur with Ashok Soota
and Shiv Nadar as management trainees at one point. Highly intelligent
people, their insights offered Dwarka tremendous learnings over many
invigorating discussions that continued even with later batches of
management trainees.

Three years into his DCM stint, with the Kolkata IR experience,
Dwarka was appointed as the organization, recruitment, training and
development (ORTD) officer, which roughly translates into an HR
officer's job profile today. Dwarka honed his analytical skills and ability
to look at issues with clinical objectivity and his horizons broadened.

His outlook, largely influenced by his upbringing in south India, was now influenced by the varied cultures of Delhi and Kolkata. Dwarka met people with different levels of affluence, intelligence, diversity of thoughts and lifestyles over his seven-year stint that saw him posted at Lucknow, Hyderabad, Agra and Delhi. DCM's open culture encouraged people to express views, debate an issue and challenge seniors, which made Dwarka a well-rounded and confident person. His problem was with decisions like laying off people due to redundancies, and he thought multinational corporations, where processes and rules were sacrosanct, would be a good option for a career move.

From DCM, Dwarka joined Hindustan Milkfood Manufacturers Ltd (later HMM Ltd, a subsidiary of Beecham) to head the personnel function at its Rajahmundry factory, which made Horlicks. This company later merged with GlaxoSmithKline (GSK) and Dwarka could immediately apply his learnings from DCM and joint commissioner Ghosh. This was a semi-urban posting but Dwarka was conversant with the local language, a great advantage in HR management at the plant employing 1000 people. At age thirty-one, he was the plant personnel manager and practised the 'art of tough love', picked up from his soft-spoken boss Shyam Duggal from Burmah Shell, who was also a shrewd and demanding man. Duggal taught Dwarka a lesson or two, especially the art of using the right people for the right job. Getting the marketing teams to help him pitch new HR policies to the staff was one. Marketing knew how to sell!

Duggal's lesson of 'tough love', taking hard decisions but communicating them in a soft, humane manner, resonated very well with Dwarka. It was about doing what is right without getting carried away by emotions. Duggal also managed a great relationship with the India MD/CEO Simon Scarfs, who later became Dwarka's manager and mentor for several years. A big strike instigated by a few disgruntled employees saw Dwarka bring to bear his Kolkata learnings in striking a balance between the management and union positions, but he never regarded himself as personnel manager. Dwarka tried to go beyond the role, though GSK was hardly as empowering as the owner-run DCM. Dwarka needed approvals that sometimes left him feeling drained out, but it also helped him develop social networking skills with colleagues and the government departments.

Over time, the shy Dwarka came out of his shell, interacting with groups large and small, including the 20,000 farmers, meeting them on visits to GSK's milk collection centres. The next move was from the factory to the corporate office where he eventually became the chief human resources officer. Dwarka felt grateful to DCM for having initiated him into the club culture that was most helpful as he adapted to the environment at the GSK corporate office. The HR director, M.N. Batra, was a tall retired army general and both he and Duggal were very pukka. Dwarka evolved over numerous visits to the UK and the US headquarters of GSK and by attending global training programmes. He learnt that humility was not a weakness as he made rewarding connections with people at the grassroots as well as his bosses. There were relatively rustic people from the factories too, and Dwarka was at ease with all.

Dwarka had also seriously started networking with professionals through the NHRDN and visiting management institutes for recruitment. His predecessor in the HMM corporate office was from IIM Calcutta who taught him about such HR tools as job evaluation and benchmarking methodology, but Dwarka had a tough time with the finance guys' audit and tax-related queries. With Duggal becoming director HR, Dwarka became the corporate personnel manager at thirty-four and learnt how to deal with finance, marketing and other corporate functions with his customary softness of speech and firmness of decisions.

Experiencing four rounds of mergers and acquisitions (M&A) was another great learning opportunity as multiple mergers meant adjusting to multiple cultures. So was mastering the MNC's way of doing things. Mergers became his forte as he understood how they would impact people across the board. There were job losses that had to be de-traumatized and culture clashes that had to be smoothened using sophisticated integration processes. Dwarka's first M&A experience was with Beecham acquiring Horlicks, in which he had little to do, save for handling one factory closure. The merger of SmithKline and Beecham was a marriage of equals and Dwarka had to be very candid and fair in his messaging across the organization. Factories in Bangalore and Hyderabad needed to be closed; some sales offices had to be shut. Dwarka also had to sensitize the top management about personnel 'hot spots'. For instance, the pharma and consumer businesses had to be kept separate because the pharma sales force was unionized while the consumer sales force was not. There were different cultures that were merging across countries, geographies and companies. Horlicks followed Beecham's culture in India, Pakistan, Bangladesh and the UK. The tricky SmithKline and Beecham integration is documented in *From Promise to Performance* by Robert Bauman, then CEO, Peter Jackson, then HR director and Joanne Lawrence, former corporate communications director.

In GSK, everyone was on first name terms; it favoured promoting team players over individualistic achievers, internal politics was frowned upon and junior executives were encouraged to express their disagreement. Dwarka respected this position and when a young woman from HR expressed her disagreement with Dwarka strongly in public, everyone, including the dissenter, thought her life would become difficult. Dwarka put her at ease and mentored her on the art of sensitively expressing disagreements. She did well later and went on to head HR at Microsoft Asia. Dwarka, too, never ceased to learn. On a Rotary scholarship to spend eight weeks in London, he had to stay with British families, moving to a new home every two or three days. Dwarka got 360° exposure to their lifestyles and culture and into British administration, legislature, hospitals and educational institutions. Discipline and timeliness were important in English homes and Dwarka had to adjust to dinner at six in the evening in broad daylight and drinking wine after dinner.

Dwarka also saw humility in important people, like the city mayor who was unassuming, showing visitors around. Tony Newton, trade and industry minister of the UK, bowled him over with his self-effacing ways. He was just as pleased to visit the House of Lords and sit in the 'distinguished strangers' gallery. GSK's was such a warm environment that Dwarka turned down a Hindustan Lever offer in 1983. Almost a decade later, in 1992, he became the GSK CHRO, pipping three other peers to the position. People his senior or peers were reporting to him, but Dwarka never threw his weight around and ensured that nothing changed at a personal level. When it came to making tough calls, especially with performance management and promotions, he was transparent, consistent and fair. There was much more to learn. When

GSK's UK-based HR director asked him about how had shepherded and developed those who worked with him, the penny dropped. Dwarka realized the need for a system to map the evolution of people and he created systems for developing people instead of doing it intuitively or relying on instinct for spotting talent. He also introduced reverse mentoring by younger people and benefitted from the process.

In 1998, Dwarka was elevated to the GSK board. He found two books of great help—*Good to Great* by Jim Collins on the importance of rigour and *First Break all the Rules* by Marcus Buckingham and Curt Coffman on the importance of not being a prisoner to processes but going beyond them. For all this, Dwarka felt challenged when conveying retrenchment decisions to colleagues, though using set processes was helpful. When necessary, he went beyond them. This included pink-slipping someone who had served alongside him for thirty years. Dwarka mustered all the grace at his disposal to handle the situation. When a colleague was to be laid off barely two months before his daughter's wedding, Dwarka found a way to postpone it till after the wedding, on his request. His philosophy was being consistent with policies but making changes within the overall framework, depending on the exigencies. 'At the point of execution, one has to apply one's mind in a manner that is humane and graceful. To be able to do this, one has to know the heart of the people, their circumstances, and their pulse.'

GSK had elaborate structures for everything, including how to reduce risks and develop talent. A 2+2+2 system envisaged assigning a person two functions, with responsibilities across two businesses and in two countries. He found leaders are those who asked the right questions. GSK also had interesting training modules and games. A husband and wife conducting a training session in the UK on not getting bogged down by routine activity, likened the burden of the routine work to the feeling of a monkey on one's back. One pushed it off. Dwarka loved the message and carried two toy monkeys with him. Asked to handle a problem that was not his to resolve, he would take out one of the toy monkeys and leave it on the table, saying: 'You are dropping some trouble (monkey) on my back, so I will leave a monkey for you too.'

GSK's system of coloured cards to moderate management committee meetings was interesting as well. If someone got too emotional and verbose, a green card was shown indicating 'caution'. A yellow card signalled that the speaker was exceeding the allotted time and a red card meant the speaker must stop. There was also the concept of 'Psychic Income'—that employees perceive more at the psychological level. GSK's Delhi office offered a taxi ride home to all female employees for two decades until the office shifted. This is contrary to the current practice of assigning a monetary value to all benefits that an employee might derive at a workplace.

Dwarka had the unique experience of being asked to travel to London with his wife even though no meetings were lined up there. On arrival, he found that it was a treat to celebrate his twenty-five years with GSK. The icing on the cake was an envelope with congratulatory messages along with two tickets to the Wimbledon tennis matches. Dwarka was passionate about tennis and the company remembered to honour him in this way. It may not have been of great monetary value but invaluable in terms of a morale booster. When he finally retired, GSK invited him to Philadelphia to watch the US Open and to stay on the GSK board as a non-executive and independent director.

As a member of a 'remuneration club' where colleagues from member companies shared information about remuneration practices, he built close bonds with the others and often compared notes, making for very satisfying industry-wide bonhomie. It also inspired him to work for the All India Management Association through which he networked with CEOs and entrepreneurs while building satisfying connections for the NHRDN, where he served as a board member and national president. Dwarka was also felicitated with the National Award by the NHRDN in 2004.

Post GSK, in 2007, Dwarka's golfing partner, Sanjiv Sachar, referred him to the Max Group led by serial entrepreneur, Analjit Singh, who was looking for an HR adviser. Dwarka met Analjit Singh at the Taj Chambers for a meeting that lasted three hours, after which Singh requested Dwarka to drop by at his home. Dwarka had mentioned that it was his birthday and found a gift-wrapped tie waiting for him. The gesture impressed Dwarka and he joined Max as director of group human capital, building the HR edifice with its own processes and rules and becoming the first person to start working out of the newly-created Max Corporate Group Human Capital Office. Singh's vision was to build HR as an enabling function and not a controlling one; to have verticals for quality, people, governance and strategy. Dwarka focused on hiring people for a culture that respected people, was benevolent in nature and honoured commitments.

In 2011, after Singh became chairman of the group, a professional head of operations was brought in. Dwarka supported the nomination and remuneration committee of the Max board. The board was packed with professionals, not with the promoter's family and friends. The Max and GSK boards were different; the Max board was marked by healthy debates. At GSK, the deliberations were very professional, structural and clinical. Dwarka's legal background came in handy for both and his negotiations skills were useful while dealing with different stakeholders. Max was, of course, more empowering than the largely process-driven GSK and Dwarka would issue appointment letters even to people at his own level, only needing the chairman's approval when it came to firing someone.

Taking advantage of the free hand that he got at Max, Dwarka created a dynamic process facilitating people to move across functions. People from HR were elevated as CEOs while strategy experts were moved to operations. For instance, Rajat Mehta joined as CHRO of Max Life in 2000 and rose to become managing director of the group.

Max's review process allowed people to move from one business to another and Dwarka put a premium on transparency and acceptance, instead of investing his position with greater authority. He also stayed in touch with the grassroots, attending sales conferences at times and remaining connected with people at the lower levels of the organization. Max's healthcare business was challenging, especially vis-à-vis corporatizing the business on the functional front with the introduction of goals and objectives and the performance appraisal system. These demanded elaborate training involving senior clinicians, doctors and specialists. Dwarka revelled in processes and norms, and was a stickler for rules, using them for business goals, going beyond processes and breaking with norms when necessary.

As a swansong to his illustrious career, Dwarka was invited for a new role that needed all his experience of setting boundaries, going beyond them and performing a balancing act. Brian McNamara, the global CEO of GSK Consumer Business, asked him to be the non-executive chairman of GSK's consumer business in India. He had been on the

GSK board for two decades and was now being trusted to safeguard the interests of both the minority shareholders and GSK's with its 72 per cent holding. For the first time ever, GSK was entrusting an HR person with this charge. After Dwarka had taken over, the company announced its merger with Unilever and Dwarka shepherded the board and the senior management through the merger process, ensuring that everyone understood the impact of the merger proposal and how it would play out.

The divestment of the GSK consumer business to Unilever was a worthwhile learning experience as he handled the tricky issues around the transition with union agreements and aligning the retirement benefits of employees, among others. The success of the merger depended upon such people issues and practices, and Dwarka brought to bear his learnings from Max to his GSK consumer chairmanship role. His role at GSK coming to an end with the merger and Max businesses getting consolidated—the health insurance business was wound up in June 2020 with some tail-end activities spilling over in July—Dwarka decided to call it a day, on 31 August 2020, just a month short of turning seventy-three.

It has been a richly rewarding career for self and the profession; establishing path-breaking norms to achieve excellence, bringing potential to fruition, enriching people and the organization because Dwarka is all about showing the Simply Better Way.

* * *

Pradeep Mukerjee

Black and white man

Challenging the system to get rid of ambiguity, seeing things in black and white and doing what he thought was right.

Pradeep Mukerjee (Pradeep) works on enhancing organizational and leadership effectiveness. As a consultant and certified executive coach, Pradeep has been bringing to the table his rich corporate experience in India and overseas as founder director, Confluence Coaching and Consulting since

2013. With twenty years of managing the human resources function in multinational organizations, Pradeep's proven competencies include strategy development, talent management, leadership assessment and other facets of HR. An alumnus of the Tata Institute of Social Sciences, IIT Kharagpur and Mayo College, Pradeep has been country lead and CEO, Mercer Consulting; director and vice president, Citigroup, between 1994 and 2007; and head HR at Citicorp Software and Citicorp Overseas Limited.

Given this remarkable business orientation, he helps to build organizational capabilities and supportive structures and systems for effective performance; define and implement people strategies that drive business success and develop leadership talent through coaching. Pradeep is accredited by the International Coaching Federation (ICF). An independent member on the board of two publicly listed Indian companies, Pradeep also serves on the Board of Trustees of the Society for Nutrition Education and Health Action (SNEHA).

Pradeep Mukerjee had always seen things in black and white. Over multiple instances as an HR professional with large iconic companies like TCS, Citibank and Mercer, he has challenged existing systems or his bosses to get rid of ambiguity, almost as an extension of this desire to find the truth and be true to it. This fascinating amalgam of a commitment to do what he believes is right, his inattention to building relationships and his strongly independent streak, was both empowering and obstructive, especially when he encountered leaders who he could not respect.

His first brush with leadership came early; at his first job at Bombay Dyeing. Pradeep saw the personnel manager leaving the office and asking Pradeep to go home even as the unions were going from floor to floor fomenting trouble, following a court order served on their union leader. Pradeep had personally delivered the order to the union office. His boss, a much-respected writer of articles on HRM in industry journals, with a formidable reputation, was not quite practising what he preached. A personnel manager was hardly expected to slip away with trouble brewing. More such incidents followed and Pradeep quit within three months.

This trait was seeded in school. He was made a prefect and having to deal with a physically bigger delinquent boy, who refused to abide by regulations, Pradeep beat him with his hockey stick to get him in line. Condoning indiscipline was not an option and the end occasionally justified the means. Cut to the Travelers–Citicorp merger to form Citigroup in the late nineties in New York with multiple changes leaving Pradeep unsure of where he would fit in. With certain decisions of the new management being diametrically opposite to Citicorp's values, Pradeep wanted to move out of headquarters and sought a 'job discontinuance' package or to be allowed to return to India, his 'home office'.

Notwithstanding the hiccups, Pradeep's career in human resources management has been a rewarding one, spanning the India CHRO's position with Citi and other complex HR assignments that helped him evolve as an independent consultant and coach, learning to appreciate his own flaws as he helps others overcome theirs. This suits his own penchant for seeking the truth and keeping things ethically simple.

Pradeep's family belonged to West Bengal, but he was raised in Mumbai where his father worked for Tata Power. His mother was a homemaker. After his early schooling at Our Lady of Perpetual Succour in Mumbai's Chembur, his parents felt that he needed to be toughened up and Pradeep was sent to Ajmer's Mayo College in class VII. The boarding school made him independent and Pradeep made important choices about his board examinations in class VIII, informing his parents only later. He was a house monitor in class VIII and a house captain in class IX. Traditionally, Mayo College pass-outs joined the National Defence Academy, St Stephen's or Hindu in Delhi. Pradeep's was the first batch in which many students cracked the IITs, while others went in for medicine. Pradeep joined IIT Kharagpur to study BSc in physics having rejected engineering, his father's profession. When asked to help his father, who loved fixing stuff and doing things with his hands, Pradeep tried to escape these sessions. His father, therefore, suggested that he study physics at IIT.

Pradeep liked physics but not the research-oriented approach to the subject at IIT Kharagpur. He preferred the other aspects of IIT, winning the prize for the 'volunteer fresher' in his hall, helping with organizing things and becoming secretary for hockey and football at his hostel in his second year. He realized that many seniors were questioning their commitments to an engineering career and contemplating management studies after IIT. He felt similarly but failed to crack the entrance exam for the top IIMs, considered chartered accountancy but was put off by the syllabus, when his father arranged for him to meet the HR head at Tata Power. He encouraged Pradeep to pursue a course at the Tata Institute of Social Sciences. Pradeep studied the TISS prospectus, concluded that the course could be a passport to a good job and joined TISS in 1979. Once again, he was disappointed with the institution but enjoyed the practicals, wherein students were placed in personnel departments of organizations for two days a week every semester, getting exposed to the realities of HR work in four different organizations during the two-year programme.

At the 1981 placements, Pradeep was impressed by the interview panel of well-known names from the industry. He did well and was selected as a management trainee by Bombay Dyeing. This was the first year that the company was hiring management trainees and Pradeep was the only one hired from TISS. Four others came from XLRI and the IIMs. After a short stint at Bombay Dyeing, Pradeep joined Tata Consultancy Services for a very fruitful tenure. He interacted with TCS leaders, including the legendary F.C. Kohli, who was the acknowledged 'father' of the Indian software industry. TCS had around 600–700 people and the personnel department did the hiring, but a committee of senior business leaders allocated people to projects. Pradeep was the secretary to the manpower allocation task committee, reporting to Nirmal Jain, an amazing boss.

All TCS software professionals were a part of a talent pool from which they were allocated specific roles and time frames, matching their skills with those required by the project. Jain asked Pradeep to prepare recommendations for the committee's consideration. This involved understanding the project requirements, the people capabilities within TCS, updating information about all facets of their lives, including their current commitments and understanding their aspirations and desires, among others, to make informed recommendations. Pradeep felt more than fulfilled by the charge, working on Saturdays just to get the information systems upgraded and updated to ensure accuracy of data to the committee for correct decisions. It also made him think about one's purpose in life.

The criticality of understanding the business and understanding people and getting both to deliver was clear to him and served as his mantra. He had experienced organizational needs conflicting with the employees' needs and desires because TCS won project bids by showcasing employees who had the kind of experience that the clients were seeking. However, some employees wanted to work on different hardware and software environments that would enrich their résumés with the diversity of experiences. Pradeep saw himself in a balancing role, made himself very approachable and interacted with many employees, some working overseas. He also got a taste of internal politics but stayed transparent, which endeared him to colleagues. Pradeep's second boss was the illustrious S. Ramadorai, who went on to head the company. Even so, Pradeep felt the lack of an industrial relations experience, which would be important for a career in HR and quit after three years. He declined an NIIT offer that included sales responsibilities and joined Asian Paints (AP) at its Ankleshwar plant as personnel officer, reporting to the plant's personnel manager. Kohli was present at his farewell and said that he had 'never seen anyone who held this portfolio become as popular as Pradeep'.

The young AP factory manager, Anurag Handa, had earlier headed all-India sales at the age of twenty-eight. A dynamic professional, he made this stint a defining one for Pradeep. The average age of workers was around twenty-four to twenty-five years with the union leaders stopping work on the smallest pretext, showing zero sense of obligation towards the plant. Handa, however, encouraged Pradeep and his boss to keep communicating with the 300 staff members and workmen, even when they struck work. IR was about effective communications; building worker–management understanding and credibility. The process gave Pradeep an insight into the power of credibility as the factory management, a closely-knit team, helped to turn around the IR situation. The norm of work stoppage at the drop of a hat changed to none for significant periods.

Pradeep also experienced innovative practices like taking union leaders on market visits to facilitate a first-hand understanding of what buyers looked for when buying paint. This exposure led to improvements on the shop floor. Teaching English to shop floor supervisors, who were graduates from local colleges and keen on improving their proficiency in English to raise their 'social quotient', was another popular initiative. Besides, plant visits for employee families were designed to invest them with both an understanding and pride in what the employee was doing.

With better credibility established, Ankleshwar union leaders spun off from the Bombay union and formed their own independent union. The momentum dissipated once Handa was transferred to Mumbai and Pradeep lost interest because he had seen it all. He quit and joined Nelco's computer and office products division as head of HR. Asked to sort out a problem with the union, Pradeep figured that it was only a question of a small amount of money and got it done. Nelco too bored him and he quit after six months.

A former TCS colleague, then with Citicorp Overseas Software Ltd (COSL) informed Pradeep about an opportunity there, also putting in a word with COSL. Pradeep moved on as COSL's chief human resources officer in 1988. This was Pradeep's first as HR head with only seven years of experience and was as professionally satisfying as his earlier TCS stint. In six years, COSL's payroll expanded from eighty-eight to 900 and an organization without a structure was professionalized. There was great camaraderie though everyone was hired on a one-year contract. However, at a Madh Island performance management workshop for the leadership team, when the external consultant had stepped out, there was a sudden and overwhelming outpouring of emotion by the participating managers. Huge issues around identity and involvement in decision-making with regard to organizational matters and questions on where the organization was headed, what it stood for and such others tumbled out in the open. Agitated, Pradeep told Ravi Apte, the CEO, about the negativity, encouraging him to get an independent view from the external consultant.

Apte agreed and Pradeep shared his own analysis of the situation. He recommended that the organization decide its mission, vision and values, institute mechanisms for greater involvement of the leadership team in organizational decision-making and greater management transparency and communication. Apte was a great techie and a very charismatic and sensitive leader. He initiated significant changes that included defining a vision, mission and values. Each leader took charge of communicating one value to the organization through a month-long effort, engaging all employees in defining the value, articulating behaviours that represent the value and ensuring a shared understanding of the value. Monthly open houses saw employees updated on key matters and encouraged to ask questions about the organization, business, policies and such other things with the concerned leader responding. Besides, certain bodies were set up for specific issues; a personnel policy-making body to determine policy and exceptions to policies where warranted and an allocation committee determined which software professional would go to which project.

On the softer side, a monthly newsletter updated people on organizational matters and showcased talents of employees and their families. The entire culture changed to an open and transparent one with a performance-driven but collegial environment. In early-nineties research among software professionals, COSL was rated as an employer of choice, based on employee feedback. The advertising agency then coined the COSL signature line: 'If you feel good, you work good.' That was the employee value proposition. Pradeep also moved employees from annual contracts as consultants to employees and introduced a grade structure and the cafeteria approach to compensation in the early nineties. This became so popular that other IT organizations followed suit. He studied income tax laws and secured the concurrence of senior income tax counsel to incorporate innovations, making corrections along the line. He collapsed the sixteen-grade structure to four a couple of years later. When the company split into two in 1993, employees were allowed to choose which company they wished to be part of!

Pradeep's contributions got noticed, especially his presentations to visiting HR leads, Citibank seniors from other markets and even to some prospects. Among them was Margaret Llamas, who offered him a position at Citi's Dubai office in 1994. His wife, Ronita, was happy with the prospect and Pradeep shifted to the HR department in Dubai. It was a slim operation, the incumbent Dubai HR head left within two months and Pradeep ran the department with four members and a secretary, who sent out offer letters. Taking charge, Pradeep changed HR policies, hired one professional and, in six to eight months, was in command of all basic HR activities, establishing credibility with the business departments. They started calling HR for advice. Citi kept its promise to move him to New York in twenty-four months. He hesitated because he was unsure about continuing with Citi but accepted when the offer was reiterated six months later.

Pradeep's New York role was in the executive resources group responsible for managing the senior-most leadership talent for

Citicorp globally, staffing and developing for the top 350 jobs, including the pipelines to these positions. It managed the talent inventory process and the expat programme that was seen as a developmental opportunity. Pradeep's job was providing users' inputs for the talent inventory system that was being upgraded, training HR professionals on the processes and systems and assessing the high-potential candidates for the top 350 future leadership roles. By now Pradeep had become organization-savvy but there was a rub. On the day their second daughter was born, Pradeep had to take his older daughter to office because there was no one to leave her with. She got a lot of attention and excellent care from Pradeep's colleagues but it made one think.

A year into his stint in New York, Citi was bought by the Travelers Group, followed by a flurry of changes at the top deck. Global HR head, Larry Philip, did not have the support of the new leadership and was the first to go. Llamas also quit in a surprise move and Pradeep's group was disbanded. The new boss, Mike D'Ambrose, took Pradeep out for lunch and suggested he take on both the leadership staffing development role for global operations of capital markets and be HR head for this operation. This was among the first groups to move under the new management but Pradeep, unhappy with Travelers' overall approach, worked out things so that he could quit New York and come back as CHRO for Citigroup, South Asia.

Back home, Citibank's consumer banking business was growing rapidly and Nanoo Pamnani was the India CEO, a tough boss who considered the CFO and the CHRO as the two arms of the CEO. As a doer, Pradeep pioneered new processes like a sales incentive scheme for bank employees and job evaluations too. He also emphasized that consumer banking did not need MBAs from first or second-tier institutes for sales positions, advising the management to save manpower costs here, though it took a couple of years to be implemented. He also got the local union to agree that the new branches would be outside their purview because the people required for the work did not aspire to belong to unions. This reflected original thinking and Pradeep hardly looked for industry benchmarks when faced with a fresh problem. Thanks to his science and maths background, he had the originality streak, enabling him to think ab initio.

The difficulty was with managing the constant demands to make exceptions to policies and these involved difficult discussions. Over time such requests decreased, thanks to the support he received from Pamnani. There was also the worrying culture of centralized decision-making and diktats, post Travelers' entry, which started impacting countries by 2004. More power was vested in the regional headquarters and New York and, in an environment when one was told to do things without asking questions, Pradeep was constantly asking questions and expressing his views that were often contrary to the corporate direction. This happened with a number of global roll-outs like a Human Resource Information Technology (HRIT) system, whose flaws Pradeep pointed out, being proved correct later; a stock scheme rolled out without being aligned with regulatory requirements; a performance appraisal system that required the country head to request access to complete appraisals for his directs from the regional product heads and such others.

Pradeep was increasingly being seen as a challenger to the corporate direction and the CEO and the regional HR head called Pradeep and suggested that he consider roles in New York. After spending thirteen years at Citibank, Pradeep decided to leave in March 2007. Pradeep was keen to stick around in Mumbai but headhunter friends told him that it would be tough to find as complex a role as he had at Citibank, so Pradeep started afresh as an independent professional. He did not eat into his savings nor did he take up recruitment and training work, focusing instead on organizational and leadership effectiveness. The other big change was having lunch at home, after years of having office lunches at Citi, giving him more family time.

Sanjay Reddy, group vice chairman, GVK Group, gave Pradeep his first assignment with the group's Mumbai airport. Though there was an HR team, Reddy wanted Pradeep to come in for four days in the week. Pradeep set three critical areas right. He observed that the expats managing the operations needed to understand the GVK vision for the airport and align themselves to it, and drove a vision exercise for the airport. He found multiple gaps in the organization structure and, with Reddy's consent, recruited for these positions, bringing senior people into the organization. He also created the vital job descriptions across the operations, which was done by Mercer, who were consultants for GVK. After around nine months, Pradeep felt that he had no more value to add. He helped hire a new HR head and completed the GVK stint.

By 2008, Pradeep was a certified corporate coach and got coaching assignments and HR consulting projects with leading companies till 2013, when Mercer appointed him as their India CEO. It was Pradeep's first experience at being a CEO but he found his hands tied. He was given an impossible profit margin target without any business reporting to him (they reported to the vertical heads outside India). All he could do was use his influence to drive change with multiple discussions with his superiors making no difference.

Nothing if not creative, Pradeep found areas to improve, cutting costs and building a strategy leveraging Mercer's strengths. He recommended a merger of two lines of businesses and either a divestiture or acquisition to gain scale for the third, which could never meet the management's profit expectations. He shared the strategy with his boss, who flew down from Dubai and announced the closure of the talent vertical, taking Pradeep by surprise even though this was in alignment with his strategy. Pradeep spent the evening 'consoling' the team and then handed in his resignation. He also recommended that the company did not really need a CEO, making his own position redundant and resigned from Mercer. The loyalty was to the job and not to himself.

The compulsion to see things in black and white accompanied by his lack of tact were not quite his strengths, but Pradeep served on his own terms. His learnings from independent coaching have been even more enriching than what he had with Citibank or Mercer. Among others, he has got to appreciate the art of being diplomatic, even when considering things in black and white. The trick lay in communicating sans extreme aggression, and not articulating things obnoxiously as he was capable of, especially when dealing with authority. Pradeep does not 'like those parts' about himself at all. There have been other sophisticated learnings too. Coaching involves training but the empathy is conveyed through listening. In fact, many of his coachees have struggled with similar problems.

In 2004, while still with Citibank, Pradeep went for the executive management programme at the Kellogg School of Management.

He stopped over at New York to see his former peers and bosses and met the senior who had recruited him into Citi from COSL and who Pradeep turned to for the job discontinuance in New York. He told Pradeep that he would have headed HR for Citibank with region-wise responsibility had he managed relationships, which is very crucial. People in senior positions need support from their bosses but if they intimidate the bosses, it is difficult to find that support. Pradeep realizes that this truth should have dawned on him and he should have taken corrective action on his own.

Though late in his career, Pradeep was thus nudged into building relationships and tried to do so from the Kellogg programme onwards. He wrote down the action points from the executive management programme on building relationships and practised it on a couple of key people at work. He failed because he neither liked nor respected either of them and could not overcome his dislike for them. Pradeep comes from a position that people in authority should uphold the values they profess, be authentic and walk the talk, and has struggled with dealing with deviations on this fundamental position from his school days. Helping his coachees with their career problems taught him the criticality of building relationships even with those that one did not admire.

Yet the black and white focus meant that he would consciously do things that were right, without realizing that perceptions on what was right could differ. On the plus side, this gave him the strength to challenge the status quo and experiment with pioneering initiatives. Two outstanding examples were introducing flexibility in COSL compensations whereby up to 55 per cent of the fixed compensation for the highest grade could be split by the individual as per own needs and sales incentives for officers in the sales and collection function in the banking industry.

For a person who does not consider himself as greatly creative, these seem pretty exceptional contributions. Also exceptional are his guts to swim against the tide if that is the route to the destination. That is a rare trait worth emulating.

* * *

Pratik Kumar

Bihar to Bangalore, the practical person

Trusting, relating, learning, developing people and growing the business

CEO of Wipro Infrastructure Engineering, Pratik Kumar (Pratik) is a member of the Wipro Group's Executive Council, closely associated with shaping Wipro into a leading global player over his more than two-and-a-half-decade association. He became CEO of Wipro Infrastructure in July 2010 and transformed the four-decade-old hydraulics business into a global leader in custom-built hydraulic systems and a frontrunner in the Indian industrial automation, aerospace and additive manufacturing spaces, while consolidating its leadership in the existing hydraulics and water sectors.

A postgraduate in management from XLRI, Jamshedpur, Pratik spent his initial years at Wipro's IT business before taking over its HR leadership in 2002. Under him, Wipro was recognized as the first company globally to be assessed at the PCMM Level 5, the highest maturity level on the Carnegie Mellon University's SEI framework. Pratik is also an active member of various industry bodies.

Working as a government official in Bihar meant frequent transfers for Maheshwari Prasad, till he retired as chief inspector of factories and settled in Ranchi. Pratik, his second son, loved the peripatetic life, from Dhanbad to Jamshedpur to Muzaffarpur and Bhagalpur, every couple of years, enchanted by new schools and new friends. He comfortably adapted to new circumstances; playing with children from all strata of society, with no questions asked about background, fending for himself, standing up for his friends and, of course, playing cricket. There were holidays too, one pan-India tour in 1972, when in class X. Pratik travelled from Muzaffarpur to Ludhiana, feeling empowered that his parents trusted him to undertake the solo trip that was as engaging as it was educative. Resilience was inbuilt into such a childhood and grounding came from holidays spent by the entire clan at the Prasad family home in Patna with grandfather, the paterfamilias.

Pratik's grandfather, a much-respected retired official in the Bihar government, was a widely-travelled man, overseas included, but it was his affection and erudition that held the family together. As the extended family of well-established uncles and cousins assembled, camaraderie and caring became part of the territory. At any point of time there were four or five cousins living and studying at the Patna home. Close family friends often joined the party.

Occasionally, they studied in Patna, where Pratik's cousin, a bright girl, introduced him to the world of books with P.G. Wodehouse and Erle Stanley Gardner becoming abiding influences. The kaleidoscope of diversity and the influence of a principled grandfather made for a fulsome environment. Homemaker mother was always around. After school, came the first rub at Bangalore's Bishop Cotton Boys' School with a new culture and environment but Pratik completed class XII with decent grades. He was considering an MBA in a liberalizing India when his father suggested having a crack at the civil services. This meant three years at Delhi University and the steepest learning curve for Pratik, away from the homogeneity of missionary education and into the vast Indian socio-linguistic diversity.

Matters became intense with no hostel accommodation and Pratik settled for a shared space with another older person from Bihar. A princely Rs 450 took care of his mess fees—one room, two mattresses, no cots—pocket expenses and college fees. This shocked his uncle who came visiting but helped Pratik shed the baggage of his sheltered upbringing. His roommate knew little English but could talk Leninism and, for the first time, Pratik was confronted with issues around casteism. Pratik got decent grades and started preparing for an MBA in his second year, forming his own study circle with a bunch of other MBA aspirants. The group worked on sharpening analytical skills, vocabulary and enjoyed quizzing each other. He did appear for the IAS preliminaries but did not pursue it, opting for personnel management and industrial relations (PMIR) at XLRI, where he met eighty very bright and accomplished classmates across PMIR and business management programme.

Pratik arrived at XLRI a week ahead to attend calculus classes recommended for all non-engineers and found calculus and quantitative techniques unnerving. The overall XLRI experience was a delight though. Life was one big experiment with Father McGrath announcing no rules: 'Come any time, go any time; come midway'; permitting smoking in classrooms and making it 'uncharted' freedom. Students were assigned mentors and were invited to their homes for occasional meals when the conversation would traverse from the syllabus to the wider world. These were expansive for the mind as were lessons on 'conducting' oneself. The director, Father D'Souza (Diro), was a stern man. Upset with students who were unruly at a gathering, he gave them a tongue-lashing and asked the students responsible to own up. A few of them did, including Pratik. They were summoned to his room only to be let off with a light reprimand and their 'honesty' acknowledged. Pratik has since valued the 'courage to own up' to one's mistakes. Had Diro dealt with it otherwise, Pratik may have become more careful about owning up.

There were T-group sessions too at the personal growth laboratory, where one talked about oneself and received feedback from others and Pratik secured a lot of personal validations. XLRI was a very secure space with people providing mutual emotional support. His personal values and beliefs had been firmed up in childhood and his professional values got seeded here under exceptional teachers. While the bright but mercurial Prof. T. Gangopadhyay was intimidating, Pratik's helpful IIT roommate, Mudit Saxena, made quantitative studies simpler; Fr Theo Mathias guided him into public-speaking, even on esoteric topics like 'the moustache'; Dean Kamla Mathur's lectures on personality management, Prof. Nilima Acharji's classes on industrial relations and the especially engaging Prof. C.G.K. Nair on organizational behaviour left their indelible marks. The communications course even involved designing advertisements! There were, besides, important lessons around basic respect for people; the kitchen and hostel staff were referred to respectfully by their names in this hierarchy-less, boundary-less experience that Pratik found uplifting.

The project work around adopting a community, observing it, assessing its needs with empathy and sensitivity about the environment was enriching. The session on power and politics was intriguing as Pratik learnt about the fine art of picking up signals, realizing that while one should shun playing games, it was important to understand the nuances. Politics, he began to appreciate, was not a dirty word but could be destructive if misused. He read Machiavelli, Rousseau and other philosophers in an immersive melting pot. Pratik's first summer

job, regrettably, was an underwhelming experience at Hindustan
Petroleum Corporation Limited (HPCL), Mumbai (then Bombay).
The purported 'manpower planning study' had nothing clearly defined
and Pratik put together a rough plan on his own since he would have
to discuss the project at the campus. Yet, HPCL was his first earning
experience. He also dined in style at the luxurious executive dining
room, served by liveried waiters!

Choosing a career meant a toss-up between organizational
development and hardcore IR. Pratik wanted to start with IR, finally
settling for Hindustan Machine Tools (HMT), then on a modernizing
mission. Bernard Martyris and HR director, H.R. Alva were present
for the recruitment since they wanted young MBAs as part of the
initiative. Pratik surprised his peers by choosing a public sector opening
but his family was supportive as he joined HMT, full of enthusiasm in
May 1988; only to rue his decision. The original project had not been
cleared and he was assigned to the corporate office with an unappealing
hierarchy. People considered the MBAs with bemusement because they
were a first for HMT. The saving grace was his boss, Moid Siddiqui,
who gave him a meaty project and personally looked after him, inviting
him over to his place on weekends and being a wonderful coach and
mentor. Pratik realized that HMT had exceptional managers, failed
by its bureaucracy, and got a ringside exposure to a large public sector
organization, especially the 'detail orientation' and planning at scale.

In the evenings, Pratik networked with his other MBA friends
from XLRI and IIMs. V. Kartikeyan, also from XLRI, suggested
that he consider TVS Electronics, where Chella Ganesh was bringing
in diversity in a traditionally south Indian organization. Pratik met
Ganesh, P.S. Srinivasan, P.V.R. Murthy and others and received an
attractive offer as HR manager for sales with independent charge in the
second half of 1989. His HMT bosses were disappointed but Pratik
parted with a happy handshake and stayed in touch with Siddiqui.
TVSE's brand new plant was inspired by Japanese work culture and
office design and had exceptionally bright engineers and MBAs from
the best institutes. There was palpable energy but the company, still
in its build-up phase, was overstaffed and overspending and decided
to downsize. Pratik had to pink-slip seventy to eighty people in a
700–people organization within days, agonizing over separating young

campus hires he had recruited just months ago. They had become friends and letting them down made him lose sleep. Some got angry while others sought help as they looked for alternatives. Some stayed with Pratik, others were accommodated in friends' homes.

Pratik understood how different reality could be from appearances and was deeply scarred by the experience, even though the learning was terrific. Life continued to be tough for Pratik, who travelled to Tumkur almost six days a week, leaving the house at 5.30–6 am, returning by 9 p.m. with very few weekends off. His parents wondered how long he could continue and there was Ruchi in Jamshedpur, who he was engaged to. When he got a call from Wipro's Divakar Kaza, whom he had met at an IT forum, Pratik overcame his initial hesitation about meeting a competitor but when Mani Subramaniam, the chief at Wipro Systems, talked about the mess that TVSE was in, he diplomatically dodged the questions but got the job that he joined on 4 November 1991. His father questioned his frivolity around changing jobs every year and Pratik promised not to leave Wipro before ensuring that he had qualified for gratuity!

Wipro Systems was a 400–500 people organization with revenue of under Rs 1100 crore and on a growth trajectory. He was waiting at the reception on 4 November, when he saw a flurry of activity. Kaza later told him that Wipro had lost one of its biggest accounts and a big chunk of its revenue. Everyone on the account had to be redeployed. Pratik wondered why such drama followed him everywhere; from HMT to TVSE and now Wipro. He met the new Wipro HR head, V.S. Mahesh, who had a formidable reputation. He was quite impressed with Mani and other top quality people at Wipro as he assisted Kaza in organization-building, campus recruiting and enjoyed the exposure to all aspects of the organization. Competition was ushering in dynamism and Wipro Systems sought to find its 'place in the sun'. Pratik learnt something new every day, taking more responsibility and loving HR that was a strong and well-regarded voice in the company. Mani reported to the Bombay-based Azim Premji (AHP), who kept a low profile but was very clued in. He knew who he was when Pratik accompanied Mani to meet AHP, saying that 'he is the new person who has joined Divakar'.

AHP's once-a-quarter value workshops were lucid and great learning experiences, typically attended by 200–250 people. He explained Wipro's values, their significance and why they made great business sense. Wipro helped to get the best of customers, suppliers and employees. AHP underscored that no cost was too high for preserving value. Values could make transaction time go up but would bring down transaction cost; integrity was not just fiduciary in nature but had to reside in every aspect of the company's engagement; every promise to a candidate or contract with a customer or supplier had to be viewed through the integrity lens. Wipro folklore had remarkable tales around them, making for very impressionable moments for any new hire. Employees, particularly the leaders, were made to appreciate the Wipro 'newspaper test': do nothing that will embarrass you, if printed.

Kaza moved on as HR chief at Wipro's lighting business and Pratik smoothly transitioned to his new boss, B.P. Rao, a very different personality. Pratik loved this variety that Wipro nurtured, allowing space for individuality and diversity of thinking. Once Mani moved on to his own entrepreneurial venture, V. Chandrasekhar (VC) led Wipro Systems with his engaging style that people loved. Pratik too was growing and started seeing more of AHP in Bangalore. Soon Wipro Infotech and Wipro Systems merged into Wipro IT business, under CEO Ashok Soota, a revered and astute leader while VC was business head for much of the IT business. HR leader Mahesh introduced novel OD and training initiatives, while AHP participated over free-flowing sessions with engaging questions and answers.

An incident in an AHP-employee session provided a massive learning. People were moving in and out and AHP asked them to either settle down or to leave, if they would not sit through the session. It was late in the evening and many left, making things awkward. It irked AHP, who asked Pratik in a leadership huddle if he had anticipated this. Pratik had not and AHP sensed a disconnect with the ground level. He emphasized that the leadership was expected to anticipate such reactions by staying connected. Notwithstanding the stern talk, AHP asked Pratik for a ride in his humble Maruti on his way out. It was pleasant driving to the MG Road office because it was AHP's way of separating the issue from the individual. There were more such telling moments as Pratik got more exposed to AHP's leadership and felt at home with Wipro's culture and ethos; conducting one's business the right way while being unrelenting on performance.

Wipro was a sustaining experience amidst constant change. Dileep Ranjekar had moved in as HR leader of the corporation and had asked Pratik what he thought of Ranjan Acharyya, who had two earlier stints with Wipro, joining HR, a role new to him. Pratik liked the much-evolved Acharyya instantly and assured him that they would work together. Acharyya, ever willing to learn, took himself and the function to an altogether different level and eventually became chief of CHRD. Pratik became the HR head reporting to VC, with frequent interactions with Ashok Soota and experienced a high point in his career, when pitching for the GE account. GE was pioneering the outsourcing model in India and Wipro wanted the prestigious account. The competition was intense. Accompanying Soota and other leaders to Delhi, Pratik was both thrilled and petrified when asked to go first for the interaction with the formidable GE team. He sat alone on a chair facing the team while his teammates sat at the back. Fear fled as he rose to the occasion to present a very persuasive and winning performance in a great moment for both Wipro and personally for Pratik. It was Pratik's aha moment and he would only move up from here.

More changes at the top followed when VC moved out in 1999 and the forty-year-old Vivek Paul took over with his new approach. He had led the Wipro-GE business earlier but was a relative outsider and perceived to be cast in the Jack Welch mould: if you don't fit, you quit. Eager to whip things into shape, he reorganized Wipro and asked Pratik to join as the HR leader for the IT business. Pratik was expecting the move but it was a great high when it happened. It also meant that former friends and peers were reporting to him and Pratik ensured that the new role did not sit tightly on him. He remained friends at a personal level, families included, even as he led the team. Working with Paul was enriching; a true global leader, full of ideas and very articulate, he impressed Pratik with his deft decision-making, even though he was based in Mountain View (USA), visiting India every forty-five to sixty days.

It was Pratik's first experience of working with a remote leader but Paul was strategic, sharp and energizing as he rolled up his sleeves to get into nuts and bolts if needed. He was strong-willed, yet balanced. Given that AHP himself had an eye for detail and often interacted directly with Pratik, there could have been misunderstandings with Paul but that was obviated by the complete openness and transparency between the trio. Paul moulded Pratik's thinking, made him decisive and helped him cut through the clutter, improved his responsiveness, and taught him to look at the business dimension. He always involved HR in key strategy decisions, be it M&As or organizational strategy.

The high point in Pratik's career was Wipro going for the PCMM assessment. The IT business became the first company globally to be assessed at level 5. This was a huge feather in HR's cap and a matter of pride for everyone. Pratik, closely involved with the PCMM journey, received accolades, though he acknowledges that much of the credit belonged to a very committed team that he had shaped. The team could speak out, carry bold ambitions, was unafraid to aim big and extremely hard-working. Paul next wanted to take Pratik's career forward and discussed a likely overseas position, possibly as the 'integration leader' as Wipro was on an acquisition spree. Pratik was not particularly enamoured of an overseas posting, though he appreciated the challenge. Around then, CHRO Dileep Ranjekar called him for a chat, taking him through Wipro's philanthropic mission through a newly-formed Azim Premji Foundation. The detailed context-setting was to inform him that Ranjekar would take over as its CEO and that AHP and he considered Pratik to be the right choice to take over as the CHRO. Pratik was only thirty-five then.

Pratik felt pleased with the offer but wondered if it was too early for him. AHP provided perspective and convinced him that spending time with corporate and returning to business later was a possible course of action. Paul was surprised that he had opted for the corporate role but considered how advantageous it would be for the IT business to have Pratik, with his strong exposure to IT, in the corporate role. While Pratik formally transitioned into the role in 2002, Ranjekar pulled him into various reviews and consultations to initiate him into the role though not even a year's preparation had quite readied him for the corporate office. From the high-decibel, high-energy environment, where days and nights blurred into one with plenty of travelling, to the rarefied surrounding of Block 'A', in a large room with a view, on a floor that housed Suresh Senapaty, the CFO, and Vineet Agarwal, head of Mission Quality, was some transition. Pratik now worked in a quiet, calm world but followed a 'door open' policy even here. Though unusual for a corporate office, it was Pratik's way to 'feel and remain' connected.

Even as he missed the vibrancy of his old job, he was impressed by the exceptional work done by HR leaders before him with deep rigour around talent and leadership planning, done years in advance. Pratik also ensured that his former connect with the IT business did not jeopardize the position of the new incumbent, as he politely refrained from entertaining appeals from former colleagues. Meanwhile, he plunged into understanding Wipro's diverse businesses and their challenges, identifying opportunities where HR could make a difference. Wipro's lighting, consumer products, engineering and other business demanded exclusive time but matters were helped by the enabling environment that AHP had created; allowing people to speak out. Pratik never saw a need to second-guess as all interactions were open, transparent and built on trust. Disagreements, if any, were usually on approach, not the objective. On his part, Pratik allowed questions to surface and sorted them out; never letting issues fester.

The learning curve got steeper now as Pratik got involved in strategic business discussions outside of HR, while coming to grips with the new ESOP valuation models, working on new instruments for employee wealth creation or simply redefining the executive compensation philosophy. Pratik leant on his informal network of industry colleagues, friends and even customers to bounce off or validate ideas. He meticulously touched base with them over formal and informal meets and found their counsel useful. When the IT business went through its first real slowdown, Wipro had to perforce defer the joining dates for candidates, who were assured placements a year ahead in campus interviews, but every offer was honoured. Across the industry, many reneged on their commitments. That was never an option for Wipro where faltering on a commitment amounted to a breach of integrity and even deferred delivery of a promise had to be done with grace and transparency in Wipro's book of values.

There was more turbulence when Paul quit in a dramatic development. Instead of finding an immediate replacement, AHP stepped in temporarily and IT business leaders directly reported to him. Pratik and Senapaty found themselves taking a more hands-on role, much to the discomfiture of some leaders who thought that corporate office was becoming a 'power-centre'. The new arrangement ran into too many hurdles and the board opted for a joint CEO model. A bold experiment, but it did not work with fault lines fast appearing. They were swiftly addressed by appointing T.K. Kurien as the CEO of Wipro's IT business. The speed of decision-making took Pratik aback but more organizational reshuffles were underway, with an interesting fallout for Pratik.

Anurag Behar of Wipro Infrastructure Engineering moved to the Foundation as co-CEO and Pratik took over his role. With AHP asking him to lead corporate HR as well for the next year or so, Pratik was double-hatting. At board meetings, he would present to the governance and compensation committee as the corporate HR chief and later attend it as the business head. Meticulous allocation of time to both was disrupted by unanticipated escalation of issues in both spheres. The dual role continued for three and a half years till the non-IT part of the business was demerged from Wipro Limited to form a separate legal entity, Wipro Enterprises Limited. Fantastic teams at both ends enabled Pratik to manage the two roles for this extended time. He also allowed himself be coached by them. The valuable lesson was that if one opened up to learning, people would go that extra mile to share.

Pratik's mandate was to scale up Wipro Infrastructure business globally as he led it over new lines with an expanded presence in Europe, China, Brazil, the US and the Middle East. It got into aerospace in Israel and the US, with a manufacturing presence. Wipro's water business was turned around and Wipro Infrastructure entered the nascent but exciting additive manufacturing (3D printing) space and then forayed into the automation business. Very quickly, Wipro's automation business led the space in India with a significant business presence overseas. Pratik's HR experience helped him pick the right people, deploy and trust them. He had also become a fine observer of people and behaviour, a great advantage when dealing with organizational issues. As a business head, he realized that HR needed to shed its self-restraint and develop muscles to talk straight to the leadership while retaining its ability to listen. It needed to be perfectly aware of the 'pulse' of the organization to be the genuine custodian of organizational value and culture. HR could not remain a bystander but had to be out there actively engaging with all stakeholders both internal and external.

Delegation was critical in organization-building but Pratik kept tabs and took periodic stock; delegating without abdicating. Empowering talent to take charge while holding it accountable was just as critical but was a function of trust that could only be earned over time. Grooming, testing and maintaining a telescopic view of the HR organization were all critical for Pratik to have a fair sense of the scalable talent that could be further groomed by giving it opportunities to engage in cross-functional teams. Pratik loved the opportunity to mentor his team across multiple HR initiatives as he believed that everyone brought something unique to the table.

Pratik bets on people. He gives them opportunities and second chances, effectively deploying his HR competence in his business role. Trust is the strong byline here. Pratik gets energized by the thought that Wipro trusted him and gave him the big breaks ahead of his expectations. It is the same trust that keeps him going even today, as he continues to deliver.

* * *

Raghu Krishnamoorthy

Global HR leader

Drove business outcomes as a human resource professional; now mastering new knowledge for delivering the future in human resource management.

With thirty-six-plus years of experience in driving business outcomes as a human resources professional, Raghu Krishnamoorthy (Raghu) is co-director of the PennCLO Executive Doctoral Programme, having recently got his PhD from the University of Pennsylvania, Graduate School of Education. He retired from General Electric (GE) in early 2019, after twenty-five years with the company, as the global CHRO, head of talent and chief learning officer. Trained initially as a finance professional, he switched to human resources when he discovered that dealing with people is far more complex, intriguing and fun.

Raghu's work spanned four continents, Asia, Europe and the Americas, several multi-billion-dollar lines of business and exciting corporate leadership roles. At Mentora, Raghu serves as an executive director and senior faculty, leveraging his expertise to drive pragmatic, application-oriented solutions in learning and transformational change. An expansive and creative thinker. Raghu leans into complex business challenges and garners trust through his authentic leadership style. He is often sought out to share his expertise at colleges and forums like Harvard, MIT, Yale and the Economist, the Milken Institute, among others. A Fulbright Scholar from the University of Minnesota, Raghu has a management degree from the Indian Institute of Management Ahmedabad. He was named as one of the top fifty Asian-Americans in the world of business in 2009 and has authored many articles for prestigious publications, including the Harvard Business Review. *Raghu lives in Chicago with his wife, Bala. Their daughters work in New York. In his spare time, Raghu reads, writes, teaches classical music and enjoys a good workout.*

Like a page right out of *Malgudi Days* featuring the son of a railway guard in the Bangalore-Mysore section, born into a family of eighteen children in a little town near Coimbatore, began V. Krishnamoorthy's pursuit of excellence. Straitened circumstances meant an unfinished class X for Krishnamoorthy and earning a living. He continued to train himself though, first by learning typing and shorthand, then sales and accounting while he worked at a multinational company, rising up the ranks, polishing up his English at work. Krishnamoorthy finally advanced to the position of regional accounts manager for Brooke Bond in Hyderabad. Marriage had to wait till he was thirty-two. Bhagyalakshmi, who came from a farming family and had studied up to class IX, and Krishnamoorthy had fifty-eight years of married bliss.

It was to parents who had broken the poverty trap by dint of discipline and hard work, that Raghu was born in 1960. Krishnamoorthy had husbanded his resources to have enough money to educate the children. Raghu, raised in Hyderabad till 1978, with two sisters, one five years younger and the other five years senior, initially gave studies a pass, managing to scrape through till he was in class VIII. He preferred playing table tennis in his father's office and that drove him to a world of achievement. A first-class TT player, Raghu represented his school and eventually played at the state level. The sport instilled in the aberrant student the need to compete, revelling in his parents' pride when the school won the TT championships. TT was also Raghu's ticket to Nizam College, Hyderabad, for a bachelor's degree in commerce. The college extracurriculars and his peers made him aspirational. Raghu actively participated in debates and quizzes, travelled with the college team, gaining social confidence, developing resilience and an ability to take winning and losing in his stride. He was becoming academically accomplished and ambitious.

Raghu did well in mathematics, topped in French and completed BCom in 1980 but failed to crack CAT for gaining admission to IIM Ahmedabad. Disappointed, Raghu relocated to Coimbatore, where he was articled with a CA firm but had another crack at IIMA and clearing it, much to his own disbelief. Raghu joined IIMA in 1981, the first person to go in for post-graduation from his family, keen to major in finance and do his CA thereafter. It was a tough first term with brilliant classmates, such as Ashish Nanda, who later became director, IIMA, who were miles ahead of him. Raghu gradually got used to rigour and pedagogy, settling down after two terms. An enjoyable internship at the public sector Electronics Corporation of India followed, but Raghu realized that a bureaucratic world was not for him.

The inflexion point came in his second year at the personal growth lab offered by professors Pulin Garg and Indira Parikh. A transformational experience, it gave Raghu the opportunity for deep reflection as an individual: who you are and who you want to be. As opposed to finance that was binary, humans comprised many shades of grey and Raghu's mind was awakened to a career in HR, as a journey into self. Intrigued by stories that he heard at the personal growth lab, he switched gears, taking several courses in organizational behaviour and HR. Matters were reinforced with courses with Prof. Ramadhar Singh and T.V. Rao. Raghu realized that his future lay in HR. Following campus interviews, Raghu had offers from BHEL, Enfield and Escorts, which offered him a position in Faridabad.

Several things clicked at Escorts; the recruiter was Vijay Kumar from Nizam College. Besides, Prof. Garg had told him about Arvind Agrawal, an IIMA alumnus, in Escorts HR, adding to his comfort levels. He found himself in the newly-created organization planning department, headed by Agrawal. Escorts was about the joy of learning about the organization as its people; cherishing being treated as an equal, though a trainee. It was motivating to see young professionals in senior positions. Rakesh Chopra was head of finance in the tractor business and Agrawal, thirty-three, was senior manager directly reporting to Rajan

Nanda, the joint managing director. Raghu visualized working for a few years and doing his PhD thereafter; a dream he successfully chased.

When Escorts launched Niki Tasha, Raghu was reassigned to it as assistant manager, HR, working with Rajan Nanda, who inspired him to dream big. Raghu wanted to become HR head at thirty-three. Niki Tasha was an invigorating assignment to transform traditional Indian kitchens to state-of-the-art ones, in line with the reimagined Indian woman. This meant getting into the minds of Indian homes in an otherwise operational role, which added a new dimension to Raghu's learning. He hired people, set HR processes, made policies and trained with a sense of urgency in his small but high-calibre team. It was making a difference and this made for a great learning experience between 1984 and 1986. The business did not take off though.

Raghu's next short-lived stint was with Ballarpur Industries Ltd (BILT) with its unionized workplace and a different HR ethos, which was not quite his cup of tea. In 1987, his former boss, Agrawal, then with Modi Xerox, a joint venture with the American multinational, Xerox Corporation, made him an offer. Things looked up as Raghu got married and experienced the most formative six years of his career at Xerox, benefiting from Agrawal's mentoring and having a blast. He even wrote on HR, getting published in the *Times of India* and making a name for himself in the external world. Raghu also connected with stalwarts like Khurshid Bandyopadhyay, V.K. Taneja, Karl Kumar and U.R. Saha. More importantly, he felt that he had a voice as he participated in the company-wide Hay job evaluation, contributed to HR policy-making; took part in every facet of HR and experienced a remarkable breadth of exposure.

A Rotary scholarship for a four-week study tour in the US was an added feather to his cap. He visited the Xerox headquarters at Stamford, Connecticut and met the chairman, David Kearns. There he got associated with the anti-smoking campaign in association with the Johns Hopkins-promoted National Cancer Foundation, which he continued even after returning to India. In 1992, Raghu won the Hubert Humphrey Fulbright Scholarship for a year's study at the University of Minnesota and received further academic orientation to HR as he studied organizational behaviour, leadership and HR by choice, along with a course in statistics. It felt good to have his family join him after around eight months and even better to be able to do his internship with the Malcolm Baldrige Award Institute, before returning to India.

Back home, Raghu found Agrawal heading the marketing function but to his joy, the new boss, Marcel Parker, made him the employee satisfaction manager. Raghu put his HR knowledge and statistics to good use. A call from Anil Sehgal, formerly with Modi Xerox and later the HR head of American Express Bank, introduced new options. Sehgal offered him the position of HR head of Amex. Raghu was thirty-three! The offer was his dream come true as Raghu joined Amex in Mumbai, was given a flat in the posh Prabhadevi area and a chauffeur-driven car. The regret was that his family stayed on in Delhi. Amex demanded a massive cultural adjustment for a largely transactional job in a hostile, unionized environment, with four unions pitched against the management. Raghu faced a gherao and severe animosity, learnt a lot from his boss and was enriched by these experiences, not intimidated by them. In 1994, he pulled off an agreement but resented the lack of autonomy, with strings being pulled from the regional office at Singapore and global HQ in the US.

A year later, Raghu got a call from GE Capital in Delhi. His first reaction was to say 'no' to the 'Neutron Jack' company, but the search firm persuaded him to take a meeting with an open mind. Raghu met the GE team en route from Hong Kong. What was to be a forty-five-minute meeting extended to three hours. Raghu came away impressed with GE's values and culture. In July 1994, Raghu came back to Delhi and to his family having switched to GE Cap as among the first employees with Manab Bose, the overall GE India HR chief. He did everything—hiring people, setting policies, conducting entry-level programmes, putting in place a performance management system and learning from GE's set practices and policies.

A significant act on day one was to fire a very senior manager, who had knowingly violated company policy and exchanged his business class ticket to the UK for two economy tickets, to be able to take his wife along on the trip. GE had zero tolerance for the violation of integrity that Raghu found reassuring. Meanwhile, business history was being made there. The pilot project for running GE Capital's back-office services evolved into one of the first large-scale captive companies in the world, GE Capital International Services (GECIS), with Raghu at the centre of things. Charged with the responsibility of starting GECIS, later Genpact, in 1996, he hired the likes of Raman Roy and sixty others. In 1997, Raghu moved to Hong Kong to the substantially bigger GE Capital with some 5000 employees across Asia. This was his first overseas posting and a major jump from GECIS India with its 760 people. However, the 1988 Asian financial meltdown meant paring down GE's Asian operations.

GE had to restructure twenty-four businesses to four and drop 1500 people from the payroll within three months. Raghu was in charge but had never done anything like this before. He had just announced the retrenchment of nearly 500 people in Bangkok when there was a shriek of the siren. One retrenched employee had attempted suicide by jumping off the sixth floor of the office. At the evening review, Raghu was told off by his boss for mismanaging the announcement. How would the incident read in the next morning's newspapers? Raghu learnt his lesson on cultural sensitivity and empathy without which institutions could be damaged and personal ratings as well. His performance rating for the year was sad and Raghu had to make restitution. The opportunity came from the crisis.

Companies were auctioning off non-performing assets and GE bid to take over auto loans of 1,00,000 cars. If it won, it would have to hire 1000 people in a month. If not, no hires would be needed. It was a challenge to locate and train 1000 people, ready to join in a month, if needed. Raghu was told that GE would bid only if he could guarantee the hires. He resorted to unconventional advertising, through radio channels with twenty-five interviewers to hire people in two weeks. He arranged for paid training for three days and gave provisional appointment letters. GE won the bid and all 1000 got hired as Raghu's coup was flashed across GE, giving him a celebratory moment. More importantly, GE decided to invest in him by giving him a global assignment as HR head of the $300-million Global Fleet Services, Minnesota.

Not overwhelmingly large though it was the world's largest fleet company, the global responsibility had Raghu truly assimilating GE's culture and processes. One of his first acts involved firing a poorly-performing compensation manager, who threatened to kill him and hurt his children. Police protection was organized to ensure Raghu's safety.

2001 brought a London posting as regional HR chief for Europe, the Middle East and Africa for GE Money. Raghu was in a quandary because it was a regional job though with 17,000 employees and a revenue of $1.6 billion. His boss explained that it would offer him in-depth exposure to Europe and Raghu found the 2001–06 experience phenomenal, especially with immense learnings from Dan O'Connor, his Irish boss. O'Connor had extraordinary emotional intelligence and a distinctive leadership style; sensitive, empathetic but tough enough to make difficult calls. He was an HR leader's dream because he did the right thing, the right way, while giving Raghu the freedom to be, leaning on his advice and making sure that he had Raghu's back on difficult calls. This support was critical because, over this period, Raghu had to handle forty-three acquisitions and divestments.

Raghu learnt about business integration and assimilation and got to understand Europe with all its cultural and regulatory diversity. Germany's works councils, for instance, were a worker–management bargaining forum, which tilted the scale in the workers' favour. He also built a leadership pipeline and championed Career Express to accelerate the development of high-potential talent. He was elevated to the senior executive band of the top 750 GE managers, considered as enterprise talent and loaned to various businesses. Its compensation and career plans were determined by the corporate headquarters and the 750 got invited to the annual corporate event in Florida!

In 2006, Raghu asked Bill Conaty, the legendary HR chief of GE, to give him a fixed tenure as his children were about to complete school. Conaty moved Raghu to the US as HR head of a global sales and marketing force of 45,000 people across the businesses. He now had a seven-member HR team and a helicopter view of all businesses; was a member of GE's commercial council, comprising twenty sales heads of all businesses, whose quarterly meets were personally attended by Chairman Jeff Immelt. Raghu now could learn from the senior-most leaders, while innovating himself. He developed an excellent capability development model for the sales force here, using GE's global training centre at Crotonville. It helped leaders shed their transactional mindsets and understand the big picture through an innovative programme design, assisted by visiting professors from top institutions. Externally too, Raghu was gaining visibility with his writing and was the core lead on the Asia-American Network, recognized as among the top fifty Asian-Americans in the US. His growing brand image got a boost when Immelt felicitated him as a 'hero of growth'.

In 2009, Raghu joined the GE aviation business as HR head, based in Cincinnati. An enormous business with revenues upwards of $16 billion and 35,000 employees, it used to be a money-spinner but needed restructuring and payroll-paring with the 2008 recession looming large. In line with GE's aviation policy, Raghu learnt to fly, getting a critical understanding of divisional culture. This was important because Raghu was a part of its strategic leadership team and kept getting added responsibilities as a member of the board in the joint venture in China and a member of the transition team in Italy. Aviation presented an intimidating scenario. It took ten to twelve years to develop engines in this long-cycle business that was in the doldrums. It had to be downsized, taking 3000 people from 35,000, all of whom had niche skills in this technology-rich space. The talent paring had to be very precise so as not to lose any critical skills, making it a pretty kettle of fish to manage.

Putting things on an even keel needed top-quality leadership and Raghu first focused on investing in high-calibre talent while reminding the larger audience that the tough times were a temporary phenomenon. He focused their attention on the deeper purpose of the business: manufacturing for the defence sector; saving lives; serving on the cutting-edge of science, which made them a distinguished workforce. The task at hand was restoring damaged pride, extricating people out of their sense of helplessness that was making them want to give up and wallow in self-doubt. It was equally about innovating with strategy around people, technologies, products and getting everything to coalesce into an ecosystem with a unique 'culture'. Raghu helped to define and create the culture, leaving nothing to chance, discovering opportunities and bringing back the mojo in the workspace while reshaping the business. Raghu positioned it as a re-creation and not a bailout as he addressed the greatest professional challenge that Immelt personally 'entrusted' him with.

Raghu launched a series of workshops over six months to help people come to the purpose of their existence as a business, involving a large cross-section of aviation employees. Over the journey, he shepherded the aviation business to a 'coherent, purposeful culture' and leadership. Alongside, Raghu focused on developing a leadership pipeline, bringing in diversity and boosting morale in the post-restructuring phase, when sentiments were bleak. Raghu invested the process with energy that brought back the magic through reinventing, with skyrocketing employee engagement scores. Raghu also conceptualized the purpose of the business through crowdsourcing innovation, which helped rally spirits and got motivation running down the system in an energized culture. People started believing that they were making a difference and business started coming back. Aviation was challenged to launch 'new engines' as airlines wanted oil-efficient engines with a 'guaranteed 13 per cent' engine economy to beat the oil price hike. Rehiring exceptional engineering talent and nurturing them to rebuild a talent bank over five years, Raghu had them coaching the new entrants through knowledge transfer, capturing the resident knowledge in the system and making it work.

In 2013, as he was contemplating eventual retirement in the aviation business, Immelt posted him as chief learning officer at the GE Training Centre, Crotonville. The company combined 'executive development and learning' there with courses on leadership development. Raghu drove succession planning all the way to the top; was the torchbearer externally and contemporized practices. He interacted closely with the board to arrive at a common understanding of what being a leader would mean in 2020 and how such leaders could be built as more entrepreneurial, agile, systems-thinking people, who could both connect and inspire. Raghu benchmarked Fortune 25 leaders as new age leaders and worked on unleashing people's creativity and resilience; dramatically shifting the paradigm from 'rein in' to 'let go' and getting GE recognized as the best company for leadership development by Fortune.

The earlier KRA-based appraisal system was replaced by performance development as the approach shifted from performance management to performance development. Feedback woven into the system provided insights. Performance would always be work-in-progress with strengths scaled up, weaknesses watered down and all feedback, by subordinates, peers and even outsiders, heeded. This was a radical cultural shift in GE from the draconian '9-blocker' that automatically ousted the bottom performers, to something more developmental, contemporary and positive. Armed with new insights and approaches to people power, Raghu created an internal digital platform, BrilliantU. He tied up with Skillsoft and McKinsey for sophisticated online opportunities for leadership training. Exploration of leadership meant an out-of-the-box approach; putting people in entirely new situations to gauge and develop their ability to learn and reflect. He took promising prospects to Antarctica, Normandy and even Cuba to have them confront the unknown and unexpected. Raghu personally spent a humbling two days with the homeless in Boston. Over the process of leading and experiencing, Raghu had evolved as a human being.

In September 2015, Immelt turned to Raghu again to infuse life into the healthcare business that had been struggling for a decade. Culturally a tough space to be in with entrenched despondency, it was not entirely bleak with around 90 per cent of insulin agents produced by GE. The equipment space was troubled though: CT scan equipment, ultrasound machines and such others did poorly while the competitor, Siemens, was doing well. Under a new CEO, John Flannery, Raghu figured that the problem lay in the remote leadership with the divisional headquarters in London. He shifted it to Chicago, travelling to and from London for eight months to facilitate the shift with very visible results. Operating profit rose to $3 billion with an 80 per cent change in leadership. Raghu helped turn cynicism into confidence and pessimism into pride in people who started believing that the situation was irredeemable. There were 55,000 people in the $17-billion business. For the first six months, Raghu asked every team leader what it was like when they were on top. He synthesized their experiences to arrive at 'the purpose' of the business: improving lives in moments that mattered.

Raghu hired afresh, changed the innovation-killing layered matrix and simplified the leadership structure, reducing the layers from twelve to eight using crowdsourced ideas. In the process, he invested the space with employee ownership. People voted for the best ideas; of the 700 ideas generated, 50 got selected as the purpose got refined. People felt happy to help to improve lives, enhancing their sense of purpose, which Raghu sought to recapture. To help people 'live the purpose', Raghu crowdsourced real-life stories to convince employees that 'doing good' would lead to 'doing well' and eventually turn the business around. Raghu personally felt this special sense of purpose because he was engaged in saving human lives, which was a privilege. Delivering improved technology that could save even a twenty-four-week old premature baby with advanced incubator technology was among them. Project Northstar, GE Healthcare's next-generation IT solution for ambulatory care, was another notable achievement.

Raghu empowered these by breaking the silos in which people worked, opening up the organization. Employee engagement scores soared and profits went northwards as the business was turned around in a year and a half, from the worst-performing to the best-performing. The pride was back in the workplace. Raghu's proudest moment came when he converted a culture handicap into an asset in the first year; converting it into an advantage with palpable hope and optimism all around, in the next. It was energizing to put his thoughts into practice. At fifty-six, Raghu thought that this would be his last assignment. However, fast-paced changes were overtaking GE by then. In 2017, Jeff Immelt quit GE. In June, the same year, John Flannery from GE Healthcare was appointed CEO. In November, GE's global CHRO Susan Peter, sixty-seven, chose to retire. Raghu went through the selection process and got the coveted position of global CHRO for GE.

In a cruel twist of fate, this also coincided with a slide in GE's fortunes. Immelt's $12-billion purchase of the Alstom power business turned sour, eating into GE's cash flow. Not even the other better-performing businesses could help as the adverse impact of the power business, compounded by the problems of the acquisition, took GE stock prices and employee morale down the tubes. Literally, as GE went into shock, its employees froze. With an aggressive activist now on board, the organization went through a churn in the board and reprioritized its focus. An adverse media blitz destroyed Flannery and, in September 2018, GE took a 'goodwill impairment' of $22 billion on its books, sending its stock plummeting further. Raghu was again on the back foot, reducing numbers from 2,10,000 to 1,80,000 to achieve a $5-billion cost saving. Salaries were frozen and the group HQ was reorganized to make it lighter by outsourcing everything. It sent everyone down a demotivating spiral.

If this was not enough, Raghu had to manage the new board's different expectations and gave himself no more than a B rating in his handling of the board, from whose vantage point GE was unfolding in a disastrous way. He had the difficult task of navigating employee sentiment and the board's need for urgency in driving changes. He was often in a no-win situation because sometimes what the board wanted went against what the employees wanted and vice versa. The cookie crumbled on the night of 29 September. Flannery was fired and Raghu failed to persuade the board to position the departure softly. It insisted on positioning it as a firing.

On 1 October, as Henry Lawrence 'Larry' Culp, Jr took over as executive chairman and CEO, Raghu realized that it was time to rethink his future. He informed Culp about his intention to retire. On 23 January, a new CHRO was appointed and Raghu parted ways with GE on 1 March 2019.

It was a well-earned break and time to introspect and plan how to put his lifetime's experience to best use. Though disillusioned with board dynamics in corporate America, a financially comfortable Raghu had the liberty, leisure and mental agility to reinvent himself at sixty, and he went ahead to achieve his dream of doing a cross-disciplinary doctoral programme in the University of Pennsylvania, at the Graduate School of Education, supported by Wharton and stepping into a new career as co-director of the PennCLO Executive Doctoral Programme.

Raghu Krishnamoorthy continues on his path, delivering the future in human resource management.

* * *

Rajeev Dubey

Mindful multiplier

Touching lives and making a difference in business as well as society at large, following principles of truth and compassion

Rajeev Dubey (Rajeev), till recently group president (HR and corporate services) and CEO (After-Market Sector) and a member of the Group Executive Board, Mahindra & Mahindra Ltd (M&M), has served over a wide canvas, from business leadership to driving human capital

initiatives for nearly five decades. He continues to serve the Mahindras as the chairman of Mahindra Insurance Brokers, Mahindra Steel Service Centres and Mahindra First Choice Services and on the boards of several group companies, including SsangYong Motors, Korea, Mahindra Intertrade and Mahindra First Choice Wheels. He is also chairman of the Group CSR Council and the Corporate Governance Cell, a member of the Governing Council of the Mahindra Institute of Quality and a member of the advisory board of Bristlecone, USA. His key contributions to the Mahindras, apart from the human capital space, have been in areas of group communications, government relations, CSR and infrastructure. Rajeev joined M&M in January 2004 after twenty-nine years in the Tata Group that he joined in 1975 as a member of the TAS, the central managerial cadre of the group, spending twenty-one years with Tata Steel, and seven years as managing director of Tata Metaliks and Rallis India.

Rajeev studied economics at St Stephen's College, getting a First Class (First) in Delhi University and a national scholarship. An MBA from the Yale School of Management, as a J.N. Tata scholar, he was selected as a distinguished alumnus of the school. Rajeev is also a member of the governing body of the International Labour Organization (ILO), Geneva and serves on the board of the International Organization of Employers, Geneva, where he is also the chairperson of the Future of Work Policy Group. Besides, he is a member of the National Executive Council and the Steering Committee of the Federation of the Indian Chambers of Commerce and Industry (FICCI) and chairman of its HR Committee. He also serves as a core member of the Council of Global Advisors of the Yale School of Management, USA, on the Advisory Board of Konecranes India and is a past-president of the National Human Resource Development Network (NHRDN) and the Employers' Federation of India.

It was not often that the child of a large land-owning farmer in eastern Uttar Pradesh, especially at the turn of the twentieth century, wanted to be a teacher. But Dhoop Narayan Dubey was exceptional. So was his son Bidyanand Dubey. A brilliant boy, he was active in the freedom movement, often chased by the British police. He won a scholarship to Banaras Hindu University in 1941, but the struggle for Independence became his overwhelming passion and he spent three years in British jails. He sat for his BA finals from prison, topped the university and after his record-breaking gold medal in MA (Philosophy) went on to become a lecturer in Allahabad University, pursuing his vision of transforming the newly independent nation.

Under pressure from senior Congress politicians, who were his jail-mates in the 1942 movement, he sat for the Indian Civil Services examination and stood fourth in the written exam. With the brown sahib culture dominating the steel frame, a candidate wearing a churidar pyjama with a sherwani and Gandhi topi at the interview, chaired by an ICS officer with a British wife, was asking for trouble. To the chairman's 'Good morning, Mr Dubey,' he responded with a 'Namaskar', setting a confrontational tone and getting demoted from the fourth to the forty-ninth position and a posting with the Indian Postal Service. Fortunately, he spent most of his career in different ministries in Delhi and retired from a UN posting in Africa. He married Savitry Sharma, a brilliant student from an ultra-revolutionary Arya Samaj family that had sacrificed almost everything it had in the freedom struggle. Rajeev, one of their three sons, was blessed with the best of educational opportunities, tremendous genes and inspirational forebears.

An elite education at St Columba's, Delhi and a background of care, compassion and truth provided the right grounding and imbued Rajiv with the spirit of wanting to make India a better place, especially for the have-nots. Rajeev was captain of sports, excellent in dramatics with top grades in science and stood first in India in the science stream of the Indian School Certificate Examination in 1969. He wanted to teach and study economics at St Stephen's, Delhi University. An unexplained headache and burning eyes made studies difficult but he was persuaded by his mother to take the exams, topping the university yet again! He went on to study at the Delhi School of Economics on a national scholarship but the headache obviated a career in academia. Rajeev joined the Tata Administrative Service (TAS) in 1975, among the nine selected from the forty shortlisted from all over the country. The redoubtable Freddie Mehta was alarmed by his 'deeply socialist' views and wondered if he had Naxalite sympathies. He later learnt from Dinshaw Malegamwala, member secretary of the high-powered TAS Committee, that he had pushed the comfort zone of the panel with his 'strident socialism'. Yet, they must have connected with Rajeev's dream of creating economic wealth in an ethical way.

Rajeev's natural sympathies for the underdog continued to be at deviance from the mindsets of many colleagues and peers; some considering him to be 'too good to be true'. This dissonance riddled him with self-doubt as he wondered if was in the wrong place, as one of only two people without an MBA degree in a TAS batch packed with IIM/IIT graduates. Rajeev read a great deal and sought to get accustomed to the term 'profit' (often equated with 'profiteering') but was troubled by his inner struggle with continuing with TAS. Life in Bombay too was far removed from the tree-lined avenues of Lutyens's Delhi and the left-leaning St Stephen's. Rajeev wanted to get away and try his chances with Russi Mody, then managing director of Tata Steel. For his two-month probationary assignments, he chose Tata Chemicals (Mithapur), Tata Exports (Delhi), Tata Oil Mills Company (Bombay) and Tisco and Telco in Jamshedpur, working on materials management, marketing, finance and accounts—nowhere near HR!

Rajeev finally met Mody, using his social connections in Jamshedpur for a 'do or die' interview. Mody, in his signature multicoloured shirt with a gold chain around his neck and a cigar in his mouth, went into a serious discussion on why Rajeev sported a beard, after preliminary courtesies. At the end of an hour-long conversation, Rajeev mustered the courage to say that he wanted to be Mody's executive assistant. Mody agreed to hire him for a couple of years and then move him to sales and marketing for an exciting two-year assignment with the legendary leader Russi Mody. Rajeev learnt a great deal about human behaviour. Mody was a tough boss, who did not encourage the fancy lifestyles of TAS officers and Rajeev had to walk down from his Kaiser Colony house in a Panama hat to ward off the fierce summer sun unless a kindly colleague gave him a ride. In this process, he made a large number of friends, from ordinary workers to assistant foremen to superintendents and even the general superintendent of the steel plant.

There was turbulence galore in his personal life though, but he was a picture of equanimity and composure, which led to Mody giving him the sobriquet 'Rajeev JC (Jesus Christ)'. Mody tried to advise him on how to handle his personal space, but Rajeev wanted to be left alone here. Mody took this response very sportingly, saying, 'You are an altruistic idiot, Rajeev. But you will soon realize the wisdom of what I have just told you.' Mody was right, of course, as Rajeev's innate trust in people and compassion were constantly taken advantage of, even as he believed in the power of unleashing the potential of people through Satya, Prem and Seva, the guiding principles of his life. Exploring his inner space, working through his torments, he sought to discover 'Who am I?' and later 'So now what?'

About five years after joining TAS, when he was posted at the Delhi sales branch, he took the advice of his elder brother, a professor of game theory at Yale University, to do his MBA from Yale. Mody, who believed 'Knowledge got is better than knowledge taught', was not keen, for he thought that it would be two years wasted. He suggested that Rajeev take two months off at the French Riviera at Mody's expense and return to India. Notwithstanding such pressures, Rajeev got himself a J.N. Tata scholarship and went on sabbatical from Tata for the Yale MBA, graduating as a distinguished alumnus of the school with a profoundly transformational experience. He understood that being good at business and relating well with people need not be in conflict. This helped him validate his basic instinct that economic wealth could be created and people treated well at the same time.

At the end of his first year of the MBA programme, Rajeev came for a scheduled two-month summer internship with Tata Steel and, after initial hiccups, got Mody to get him the internship in Delhi. That is when he met Padma, whom he married later. Like many other crucial decisions in life, this was an intuitive decision. He had met Padma only once when he decided to marry her. Fortunately, she felt the same way!

This happy turn of events restored his faith in three principles that formed a very powerful philosophical and psychological framework for him, especially when things were not going his way: What happens is the only thing that could have happened; What happens is the best thing that could have happened; and What has happened, has happened so one should not waste too much time in anger, guilt or regret, on repeatedly asking 'Why?' and whether it is good or bad; focus instead on 'What do I do now?'

Rajeev returned to rejoin Tata Steel in Kolkata and got reconnected to the Bihar School of Yoga. Yoga became an integral part of his life; so did the search for answers to how he could create happiness in the lives of people and serve mankind while creating economic wealth. At a personal level, he was careful never to be arrogant, especially if 'success' came his way but focused on giving 100 per cent of mind-body-soul to whatever work he did, getting happiness from the process of doing rather than from the outcome only. The search took Rajeev to the realms of Reiki, past-life regression, fire-walking and other things esoteric. For the rest, he sought solace in family and books and also loved being in communion with nature, especially the mountains. Equally life-sustaining was his deep interest in the theatre right from 1962.

Rajeev was eight when he started acting in numerous TV and radio plays, including the role of the child Shankaracharya on a national radio programme. This performance brought tears to the eyes of the then Shankaracharya of Puri, who met the child actor. He was intensely involved in school and college theatre, became secretary of the Dramatic Society, St Stephen's and was a founder-member of Theatre Action Group, for many years the leading theatre company in Delhi. He continues to identify closely with the stage, saying, 'Theatre brings out who I am. Creativity, interpersonal relations, spirituality, mysticism, all get played out in the "here and now" space. Theatre also involves a lot of hard work, discipline and working without any ego.' All of these suited Rajeev.

On the work front, Tata Steel assigned him to look after sales and marketing for the eastern states and then posted him in Delhi as chief resident executive. This involved dealing with the bureaucracy, political establishment, media and industry associations, which often meant kowtowing to government officials. It was also embarrassing, especially because his father-in-law, the late Vidya Charan (VC) Shukla was a senior cabinet minister. Some relatives and friends made snide comments about the *dalali* (commissioning) nature of the job, which were hurtful. Nevertheless, Rajeev earned his spurs with the Tatas over his Delhi stint, when he was also blessed with two children. Returning to Jamshedpur, where Jamshed J. Irani had taken over as the managing director, he was soon posted as general manager (town services). Irani convinced him that this assignment was a critical function for the company and could be the stepping stone for much bigger assignments, even though it was not a mainstream business assignment.

In retrospect, this was among his finest and most challenging assignments over his three-decade-long association with the Tatas. He had 5000 people working with him and was entirely responsible for the civic administration of Jamshedpur, including water and electricity supply, sewage and sanitation, roads and engineering, forty company schools; maintaining markets and parks, and ensuring security and regulatory compliance of company assets over 64 sq. km. He was like municipal commissioner and mayor rolled into one (Jamshedpur had neither) with massive challenges. Rajeev had to constantly deal with externalities on which he had no control; nor any judicial powers. He managed with support from the district administration and police. Rajeev reached the Town Office one morning to find an angry mob of women, children and elderly shouting slogans of 'Rajeev Dubey *murdabad* (down with Rajeev Dubey)' because the electricity supply to an unauthorized colony had been cut off. Issues like encroachment removal, occasional hostile mobs, local politicians/leaders with their AK-47-toting security men, all made for an enriching experience.

On another occasion, he was sitting in his office with the superintendent of police (SP), a good friend, when he heard of violence against the town division officers doing a market inspection. The SP volunteered to personally deal with the situation and returned in half an hour, to complete their chat and have the unfinished cup of coffee! Once, Rajeev was woken up at 4.30 a.m. by a frantic complaint over the attempted demolition of an unauthorized temple coming up on prime company land. The company's team was surrounded by a mob led by Dinanath Pandey, a firebrand local politician, and their lives were in danger. Such situations required quick decisions amidst the huge uncertainty and Rajeev learnt how lonely life could be for a leader. For wisdom, Rajeev turned to A. Jankinath, a former civil servant and an erstwhile GM Town, and heeded his advice to 'not try to change everything' but to 'pick his battles'.

Nevertheless, civic service delivery apart, he had to undertake measures like creating a new Transport Nagar that required land clearance and dismantling unauthorized constructions obstructing public places on a scale that had not been attempted for many years. He also maintained good relations with both the company and non-company stakeholders, Jamshedpur being a mixed township and not a 'company town'. His sense of purpose and mission, his humility and spirit of service to the town and its citizens and a strong sense of fairness and justice, without ever being influenced by vested interests, helped him to deliver. Rajeev remained very approachable and connected naturally with people from all walks of life. This earned him a good name with the citizens of Jamshedpur though there were rumours about threats to his personal safety, forcing him to change the route his car took for the 8 km from his house to the Town Office. There were rumours that 'Shukla ji (then union minister) had sent black cat commandos in mufti to protect his son-in-law'. This helped Rajeev in no small measure for it kept unwanted elements at bay!

Over the two and a half years of this intense experience, Rajeev's beliefs about leadership and human behaviour were deepened as was his faith in the principles of Satya, Prem and Seva. Irrespective of stature, Rajeev listened to people and believed in being fair and being seen to be fair, considering multiple perspectives for the longer run, sticking to strategic plans without sacrificing principles even when taking quick decisions, under extreme uncertainty, never losing sight of the truth. These empowered him to do well as the GM Town, which often served as the testing ground for future leaders. Rajeev became MD of Tata Metaliks in December 1996. The company was turned around and the foundation was laid for it to become one of the leading returns-on-equity and Tata Business Excellence companies of the group. Rajeev went on to Rallis India as MD in August 2000 after a well-contested selection for the challenging position. This shift marked an end to his active engagement with the stage that had meant participating in the theatre world of Delhi, Jamshedpur and Kolkata.

Rallis was Rajeev's toughest Tata assignment between August 2000 and August 2003, turning around the 1868 Greek company that had entered the Tata fold through a reverse merger with Tata Fison in the 1960s. It was Rajeev's first real working experience in Bombay. The board wanted him to 'get us out of the hole', but the erstwhile statutory auditors having been asked to leave, it was difficult to fathom the depth of the hole over Rallis's geographically widespread business verticals. These included agro-chemicals, fertilizers, engineering products, pharmaceuticals, fine chemicals, gelatin, sericulture, a huge R&D establishment in Bangalore and several joint ventures abroad, and a large number of subsidiaries. Turning things around meant drastic decisions, pink-slipping larger numbers and disposing of assets. After two years, Rallis had returned to cash profit but cracks had developed between Rajeev and the new chairman. Things came to a head in mid-2003 and Rajeev put in his papers.

That he had been acknowledged as a 'turn-around' man at the annual Tata Group CEO meet in 2002 meant nothing. While several directors, including his mentors, sympathized with him for being made a 'scapegoat' for past mistakes, they could not help as Rajeev awaited his next assignment. Ratan Tata heard him out for more than an hour and it was proposed that he be appointed adviser to the Tata Steel MD for the interim period, but Rajeev chose to quit after serving for twenty-nine years and without a farewell. A godsent offer from Anand Mahindra appointing him a member of the Group Management Board with responsibility for Group HR and Corporate Services along with the Spares Business Unit worked out wonderfully and some senior Tata leaders thought it was the right offer to take. His late younger brother and some friends told him that Anand Mahindra is 'your kind of man'—authentic, empowering, with strong values and driven by an overwhelming purpose to create a better future not only for his organization but for the country. Rajeev, inspired by Anand's vision, took a leap of faith and joined him without discussing terms and conditions. Ratan Tata 'respected' his decision and promised to welcome him 'with open arms', if he wanted to return. Rajeev had earned respect for the dignity with which he handled himself during this entire episode, which was enriching in many ways.

The three frenetic years at Rallis taught Rajeev a lot about business, people and himself, about payroll-paring and closing down plants and managing all this with sensitivity, allowing people to retain their dignity and being generous with the terms of severance. On the positive side, Rajeev enjoyed the growth and expansion, happiest when working with people to co-create solutions in complex situations. Nevertheless, the experience shook him to the core and it was his father who made him realize that outcomes in life were not only a result of what the individual did, and factors beyond one's control and knowledge played their part. Rajeev has a copy of the Bhagavad Gita with his father's inscription: 'There are five factors that produce results. Your effort is one of them.' He has the relevant pages marked out in the Gita. Rajeev's personal philosophy supported him to bounce back with resilience and a positive approach to life. The big learning for him was that he had not paid enough attention to the politics, nor spent enough time with board members and other relevant actors in the larger ecosystem. His wife helped him get closure with 'the Tatas did not deserve you; you should move on.'

Financially, Rajeev was vulnerable with a negative bank balance, having borrowed to pay for a small flat he had bought in the Tata Steel Officers Co-operative Housing Society in Greater Noida. His children were both young and the disruption in his family life due to the Rallis resignation was telling. The Mahindra job restored his self-respect and provided a meaningful seventeen-year experience, working with excellent people and helping to create the 'Rise' culture and the after-market business that Anand Mahindra added to his portfolio, cautioning him that the business would be tough and the chances of success remote. Rajeev happily accepted this challenge in addition to his HR role as he knew that his credibility would depend on the quantifiable difference that he made. The business role would give him that tangible measure of his contribution.

Rajeev was also serving on multiple boards associated with M&M, apart from being a member of the Governing Council of the Mahindra Institute of Quality and serving on the Advisory Board of Bristlecone, USA. Bringing humility, sensitivity, authenticity and an empowering approach to people, given the freedom that he enjoyed, he plunged passionately into the pursuit of achieving the M&M core purpose of driving positive change in the lives of its stakeholders and communities across the world to enable them to Rise. Rajeev looked forward to coming to work every day as CHRO, bringing to the function his core beliefs of listening to people, looking for genuine areas of pain and addressing them. He found redemption of his faith in the limitless potential of every person, which was at the core of the Rise movement.

Anand asked him to present at the annual Blue Chip Conference of the top 500 M&M leaders globally on how Rise could be better implemented, without even checking the presentation. It would be the first articulation of the five Rise leadership behaviours. Rajeev brought to life the Rise concept over a '3+5' framework defining 'who we are and is the mother font for all strategic business and human capital initiatives'. The '3' referred to the Rise pillars about attitudes and views of the world that had to come into play seamlessly and effortlessly in any situation: Accepting No Limits, Alternative Thinking and Driving Positive Change. These combined to lead to sustainable competitive advantage. The '5' referred to the behaviour to bring the three pillars to life and lead to sustained business outperformance and passion. These involved the whole mind, combining the left brain of logic, intellect and rationality with the right brain of emotion, connection and empathy.

Formulating this multiplier of energy, passion, engagement and a sense of ownership involved the ability to do deep listening, without the compulsive need to show 'I am the best and have all the answers', focusing instead on asking the right questions and co-creating the answers with one's teams. The joy comes from seeing a thousand flowers bloom and in admitting that others know more than one. It also involved managing fear and leveraging failure to develop leaders to experiment and take risks, casting aside the fear of the unknown and failure, leveraging the learnings from failure to create success. In management jargon, it was about rapid prototyping, early failure, quick feedback loop and trying again. Besides, it inculcated mindfulness to all possibilities in any situation, without being a prisoner of the past or viewing things through the prism of failures and successes and being unable to perceive the present reality. It empowered people to reside in the 'here and now'. Finally, it was all about creating trust through authenticity; continuously walking the talk, removing the mask and having the courage 'to be who I am, with my strengths and equally with my weaknesses'.

This was the transformational work culture Rajeev brought to bear to unleash the potential of all employees, including blue-collar workers. It was aligned to the entire ecosystem of HR levers, focusing on talent management, succession planning architecture and processes. The Mahindra Leadership University played a major role, while the Mahindra War Room caught the attention of MBA graduates in all the leading business schools of the country. These were not cut-paste initiatives but evolved over time, sans the management jargon and the flavours of the day. Rajeev focused on creating enabling leaders who would be led by purpose and vision and shape the right environment for learning and co-creating with their teams, to unleash their potential while creating sustained business outperformance.

Rajeev was equally clued in with the ground reality. Keshub Mahindra had told him that the measure of his success as the M&M

HR head would be feedback from across levels, from the lowest-paid workers to board members. Rajeev was always available to hear them out with empathy and an open mind and kept their trust and confidence. He believed that one needed to create multiple channels of dialogue and communication, including surveys, to relate to the grassroots. One such channel was M&M's unique engagement survey, MCares. He did ruffle feathers occasionally, even while being respectful but remembered Tata Sons' Ishaat Hussain telling him during his Rallis days that if he had no detractors, he should be worried. 'If you are doing something substantive, there will be detractors. The important thing is to have more supporters than detractors and avoid creating enemies as far as possible.'

Rajeev heeded that and also got succour from Anand Mahindra's advice that he did not have to be right all the time, as he blossomed into a fine HR man. Rajeev was honoured by the NHRDN with the Seasoned HR Professional award in 2010 and many other accolades in the HR arena. He acknowledges the profound role of the NHRDN ecosystem in his HR journey, facilitating meetings with great people, networking and developing a sense of brotherhood—a priceless gift and giving him a rewarding tenure as National President of the NHRDN from 2013 to 2015. He also served as president of the Employers Federation of India (EFI) from 2010 to 2012, where he worked with other employer associations to help create 'a competitive, fair and inclusive labour ecosystem'. His prime thesis was that labour was not a short-term cost to be minimized but treasured as an asset that appreciated over time with the benefits far outweighing the investment cost to develop it. Rajeev stayed true to his larger focus on developing the human potential and the socio-cultural and economic evolution of society.

M&M gave him the opportunity to mould minds at the top of the rung and he equipped himself by becoming a certified coach of the International Coaching Federation (ICF). In addition, he did a certification in Group Dynamics at the Board Level at the Tavistock Institute, London. Anand also encouraged him to take up positions beyond the formal M&M boundaries and Rajeev found great fulfilment as a member of the governing body of the International Labour Organization, Geneva, where he was elected for a second term of three years in June 2021. In addition, he serves on the board of the International Organization of Employers and is the chairperson of the Future of Work Policy Group. Besides, he serves as a core member of the Council of Global Advisors of the Yale School of Management, USA. At home, he is a member of the FICCI National Executive Council.

At the end of the day, business is about being led by purpose, being simultaneously competitive, fair and inclusive, exploring the limitless potential in people and ecosystems, and being committed to the interdependent triple bottom line of profit, people and planet. Investing in people is always worth the effort because people pay back many times over. It is also about making truth life's defining principle and backing it up with compassion, service and gratitude. When it came to balancing the book of life, it would be about 'What have I given in return to the universe for all that I have received from it?'

* * *

R.R. Nair

Going to the core

Coach and trainer par excellence; maximizing human potential

R.R. Nair is a doyen in the field of human resource management. More than three decades of experience with Unilever have seen 'RR', as he is affectionately called, serve on the boards of Unilever subsidiary companies in India and abroad. The corporate experience has been enriched by years of professional executive coaching. In 'recognition of his exemplary lifetime achievement in facilitating the growth of human potential as a coach and mentor, the Executive and Business Coaching Foundation India Ltd admitted him as an Honorary Fellow CFI'. RR serves as a master coach and leadership development facilitator for some leading Indian conglomerates and MNCs. He also contributes to executive education at the Indian School of Business and is a frequent speaker in professional forums.

RR currently serves on a few company boards as an independent director. He has graduate and postgraduate degrees and diplomas in applied psychology, industrial management and individual and group development.

He is an alumnus of IIT Kharagpur, and of Stanford and Michigan Universities through their management programmes. He was president of the Bangalore Chapter of the National HRD Network and has received its outstanding HRD Professional Award.

R.R. Nair was born in Kerala, the youngest son in the family. His father was a first-class district magistrate in Kottayam, who eventually moved to Trivandrum to become a secretary in the Kerala government. Childhood was a secure place, supplemented with all the core middle-class values and beliefs and the determination to grow and succeed, which typified such families, that he imbibed. While love and nurturing came with the territory of being the youngest son, so did the not-so-welcome dictates of a few of the older siblings that had to be followed. The introverted child found great sustaining affection in his eldest brother and father and was influenced by his disciplinarian mother. His father also taught him the virtue of being grateful for every good thing that came his way, as a matter of habit.

RR spent the most formative years of his life in Trivandrum. An intelligent lad, RR loved reading and he became diligent in his studies, getting a double promotion in primary school. At fourteen, he completed school and cleared his intermediate at sixteen. RR then had to perform Nirmalyam for forty-one days, which meant waking up at 2 a.m., bathing, wearing his wet dhoti and walking to offer prayers at the Lord Shiva temple. In between, he attended Swami Chinmayananda's lectures, which had him mesmerized and helped him to imbibe the goodness of all religions. Later, he studied economics, philosophy and psychology for his bachelor's degree.

Swami Chinmayananda apart, there were two important influences in RR's early life. The encouraging Nelson Sir taught him physics and the value of self-belief, giving his confidence a boost. Later, there was E.I. George, the psychology professor, a student of H.J. Eysenck who had him spellbound and influenced most of RR's early career choices, including going for a masters. RR graduated at eighteen and completed his master's at twenty; a First Class (First) in the university, much to his family's delight. Doing his master's involved group practicals in clinical psychology, including a deeply engaging study of factors that contributed to neuroticism at the city's mental health hospital. A darshan with Sri Satya Sai Baba in Trivandrum and his blessings made him a devotee for life.

RR got admission to the All-India Institute of Mental Health, Bangalore, to specialize in the clinical field and IIT Kharagpur for industrial psychology and industrial management. He chose the latter, upon Dr George's advice that he had the potential to pursue a career in industry. He also wanted RR to become more independent of his family. At IIT, the hugely impactful Durganand Sinha and Harish Ganguly stoked RR's scientific curiosity and taught him to dive into how human behaviour and psychology affected work and are affected by work. RR did a post-master's at Kharagpur before applying for openings in industry.

RR's first assignment was with an engineering company in Calcutta for a short while, followed by a position in the personnel function at DCM, Delhi. A.P. Paul, his boss, provided him with a deep understanding of business functions, which he absorbed and began developing his ability to take initiatives and risks. RR learnt to distinguish between three types of risks: at the feelings level, at the financial level and at the physical level, and figured out what was holding him back. A great mentor, Paul cast RR into the managerial leadership mould, encouraging him to understand and diagnose the human side of the enterprise. 'Close all the open item lists; if you don't, you will have oil on the floor and will slip and fall.' Administrative efficiency was ingrained into him early on, as was the need to keep an eye on the big picture and develop communication skills while receiving feedback in the right spirit.

Paul's training involved reading and internalizing concepts, and RR had to summarize articles and make lunchtime presentations of his key learnings. In the process, RR became a master presenter, developing an executive presence while learning the subject thoroughly. Closely observing how Paul handled the selection processes, RR learnt how to identify high-potential talent. The candidates for the Senior Management Trainee (SMT) scheme were fresh graduates from IITs, colleges of engineering or universities in various disciplines. RR quickly understood that group discussions enabled one to evaluate a variety of management qualities: communication skills, analytical orientation, critical thinking, problem-solving, teamwork and discussion leadership. His motto was 'recruit for attitude and train for skills', recognizing that interviewing is both an art and a science. RR wanted the selection process to be objective and impartial, such that even those who were not selected felt that the process was transparent.

RR was soon able to look beyond the marksheet and into the candidate's mind. He learnt how to ask insightful questions to understand both the depth and breadth of the candidate's capacity to think and reflect and was soon recognized as a talent spotter. This flair to spot the uncut diamonds, combined with his competence in transferring knowledge and insights during classroom sessions, endeared him to the learners and drew the attention of senior management. Entrusted with leading the SMT scheme, RR invited faculty from IIM Ahmedabad to take classroom sessions. He also encouraged senior managers with the capacity to conceptualize from their experiences to provide faculty support. Through a combination of classroom learning and on-the-job action learning projects, the SMT scheme attracted top talent from across India.

The achievement motivation laboratory, facilitated by David McClelland, emeritus professor of psychology at Harvard University, helped RR to discover his own motivation profile. The achievement and affiliation drive apart, McClelland was working on power motivation. He highlighted his research findings on the characteristics of people who are driven by 'personalized power' as distinct from 'socialized power'. RR had to deal with both types in his professional career and was well served by the insights gained from the laboratory and further explorations on the subject. He designed and incorporated a module on developing achievement drive in the general management course.

Another laboratory on OD by Kenneth Benne ingrained in him a deeper realization of the four strategies to bring about organizational change and later, he seized an opportunity to join a team for a change initiative in a textile mill in the company. At IIMA's Trainers in Organization, Prof. Ishwar Dayal, his T-group facilitator, helped him to become more reflective, boosted his courage to share vulnerabilities and encouraged him to be forthright in acknowledging his blind spots. RR realized the criticality of such crucible learnings for self-management and their application in live business situations, and in shaping an HR professional's growth journey.

While in DCM, RR actively engaged with the IIPM and Delhi Management Association, which offered opportunities to develop his professional network, and became IIPM's vice chairman. At the annual conference, a chance meeting with Ranjan Banerjee, personnel director of Hindustan Unilever led to his joining HUL eventually, as selection and training manager. Not only was HUL his dream company because it relied on meritocracy, but it gave him an opportunity to test his potential and build a long-term career. Thus, from 1973 to 2005, he served HUL/Unilever companies in about eleven roles, working with a similar number of bosses and delivering with panache.

RR strove to institutionalize the ability to look beyond academic records into potential attributes and unfailingly helped in identifying candidates with the right values of integrity, teamwork, drive and creativity. To strengthen his capability for attracting the right talent, he took the high standards established by his predecessor Tarun Sheth to new heights, introducing methods like assessment of achievement motivation profile and such others, to continuously infuse the organization with top quality talent.

As selection and training manager, RR became the custodian of Gulita, the management training centre at Worli. Taking over from Sheth, he designed and delivered innovative courses, giving the managers a broader picture of the company's operations and its environment, a deeper understanding of the values of meritocracy and business ethics, how to perform with a purpose, and an opportunity to sharpen their managerial skills. RR conceived competency-based courses like teamwork, leadership in action, finance for non-finance and sharpened a range of skills for managers on selection interviewing, appraisal interviewing, skip-level dialogues, performance feedback and such others. He developed the concept of 'tutor development', created a large base of senior managers who could nurture and develop management trainees and the next-gen leaders. These early steps were crucial for developing qualities that HUL managers are now famous for.

Recognizing the importance of a vibrant organization climate for excellence, RR introduced a systematic study through a 'climate questionnaire' for participants at every course at Gulita. After initial reservations about sharing their views on the company environment with a newbie, they trusted his intent. RR consolidated and analysed the responses and presented his diagnosis to Banerjee, explaining his initiative of doing a perception check of HUL's organizational climate;

what seemed to be working and what needed improvements. Banerjee shared the document with the chairman, T. Thomas, and, before the end of the week, RR was personally complimented by Thomas and Banerjee for sensitizing the top management about manager perceptions and the organizational environment. They asked him to further sensitize the board and senior management on the emergent issues. Thereafter, RR either led or was a key member of organizational culture study teams, helping the company to consolidate strengths and overcome shortcomings.

While he was handling the selection and training role, his services were requisitioned in the face of a complete IR breakdown at a particular sales branch. RR carried out a widespread sensing study involving the field force, staff members and managers. It helped identify some additional root causes; more importantly, it led to a shift towards building a constructive relationship.

RR benefited a lot from observing Banerjee's probing questions at interviews, as he explored the 'engineering of their minds' to ascertain how they would engineer the business, which were massive learnings. He watched his boss's subtle exploration of the interviewee's ability to analyse and judge, connect the dots, self-drive and, in that process, further sharpened his own interviewing skills. While Banerjee had great depth of thought, he left RR to fend for himself, often holding one-on-one debriefing meetings with RR. These were immensely valuable for the sheer quality of the insights Banerjee provided. At a personal level, RR needed the opportunity to have reflective conversations, in good times and challenging times. Sometimes one could err on a decision as judgements were made on people. Lessons learned were therefore equally important. RR came to grips with the three pillars of talent management too: early identification, development and retention. The idea was to pick up early warning signals of possible disengagement and address them proactively. There were also suboptimal performers who posed a different set of dilemmas and demanded tough decisions. These were taken in the interest of the organization but actioned in a humane manner.

RR's professional progress was further fortified by some high-impact Unilever learning events for which he was nominated to Four Acres, the global training centre in the UK; the international trainer conclave on innovative design and evaluating training effectiveness; the experience with Tavistock Institute faculty on group-development processes; and an international management seminar, an early GM course for high-potential young talent, to name a few. Not only did these prepare RR to review the linkages between competencies, performance and training, providing a deeper understanding of business strategy, but they helped him come to grips with an understanding of authority, influence, empowerment and networks as they manifested in organizational life. RR aspired to progress in the strategic HR domain and was challenged to contribute to the industrial relations function for the next six years. It was clear to him that no leader progressed without crucible experiences in factories. His first assignment was in Garden Reach, the company's second-largest factory in Kolkata.

Initial learnings from IR veterans were helpful but no substitute for real-time, on-the-job baptism. This was especially true for the eastern region, where emotions surfaced very fast, with many challenges like disputes and conflicts with the workforce, especially with the contract labour. RR's early exposure to IR included his experience with his initial boss, Prem Chadha, who helped him to transition into the IR arena through his coaching-style leadership. There were many veteran manufacturing managers, notably A.C. Chakravorty from whom he learnt the fine art of spotting weaknesses in union leaders, attitudes and mindsets of the diverse workforce, factors leading to employee disengagement and picking up early signals of poor morale. This was buttressed with learning how to be both 'tough and nice', apart from adroit handling of multiple union dynamics and addressing manning and productivity issues.

RR leveraged the support of the veteran labour law-oriented personnel managers to resolve long-pending disputes. The permanent workforce and the recognized union generally had the interest of the factory and believed in the collective-bargaining process that helped in arriving at a long-term wage settlement. RR was convinced that IR was a triangular concept featuring the management–employee axis, employee–union axis and union–management axis. Invariably, experience showed the management–employee axis to be the weakest link, while the employee–union axis was the strongest. At Garden Reach, RR observed the significance of the role that line supervisors and managers played to connect with employees at every level by keeping the communication channel open for strengthening the management–employee axis.

Many new initiatives were introduced like employee-engagement surveys. Periodic workshops on 'Our Business and Us' educated the employees on the economic imperatives of the business and how they affected the performance of the factory. Newsletters in the vernacular, involving spouses and children in different activities, case study-based education programmes for first-line supervisors and managers, and a revised productivity-linked incentive scheme were introduced. RR moved on to assume a larger responsibility as the area personnel manager, eastern region, covering the Garden Reach factory, the edibles factory in Shamnagar, the newly established chemicals factory in Haldia and the Calcutta sales branch. The first long-term wage settlement was signed amicably with the internal union at Haldia, despite its own unique challenges due to its local environment.

An equally challenging task was to bridge differences with the Calcutta branch union, which had a legacy of taking disputes to the labour court. The joint branch visit by the outgoing chairman, T. Thomas, and incoming chairman, A.S. Ganguly, provided an opportunity to encourage and influence a change in the attitude and mindset of the office and field staff. Through adroit, bilateral negotiations that followed, the union finally withdrew the cases, resolved all pending disputes and signed a long-term wage agreement. This ushered in a fundamental change in the quality of relationships with the field staff and office-based employees. Faith in the collective bargaining process was restored, whereby all issues could be resolved bilaterally and the three-member negotiating team, comprising M.K. Sharma, C.S. Basu, branch manager, and RR, had an early morning darshan at the Kalighat temple before going for the signing ceremony. The power of divine intervention could never be ignored!

RR now moved back to Mumbai to tackle his biggest IR challenge at the Bombay factory, accounting for 60 per cent of the company's production. Datta Samant, a militant trade union leader, was disrupting production and productivity in many Mumbai industries, HUL included. The challenge for RR and his team was to engage with the internal union leadership through a dialogue process during the go-slow phase thereby avoiding closure, as closure was not seen as the right option at that time. To the credit of the dedicated band of managers and senior departmental supervisors, together with a highly committed HR team, the company withstood several challenges that followed and arrived at a settlement with the union. Soon after, RR moved to the head office in the Corporate IR function for a short while. There he primarily helped in reviewing the IR policies, proposed many steps for creating a positive employee–employer environment, and assisted with manpower planning and staffing in new manufacturing units in Chindwara and Kandla.

M.K. Sharma, who became vice chairman, once remarked in a column on RR published in the house magazine, *Hamara*, that 'RR is a practising psychologist, who can distil every individual's uniqueness and respond accordingly'. It was this people-connect that helped him steer through the state of flux during his six-year hardcore stint in IR. Soon RR was chosen to be HUL's first HR professional for secondment to Unilever London, as a member of the HR team in the overseas committee. While in London, RR was trained as a consultant to do greenfield structure reviews. Following this, he joined the personnel division team and co-facilitated the organization review exercise at Lever Bros Pakistan and Lipton India. Alongside, he gave Unilever's operations in Africa and South Asia a key building block by training its local talent.

Communicating how much he valued and respected people with diversity, especially when new to a place, RR married tact and wit as he travelled from London to Unilever companies in Africa, South-east Asia and South Asia for management development planning reviews. A keen student of culture and how it played out in terms of values and styles, he appreciated what was going well to establish comfort zones, before proceeding to deal with sensitive human issues. The best indicator of this people-orientation was RR returning to India as personnel director in Unilever's foods company, Lipton India, and later for the combined Brooke Bond Lipton India Ltd (BBLIL).

To quote from the *Hamara* issue, 'There can be no better examples of how business success squarely depended on the management of human resources. When RR steered HR at Lipton, the HR strategy required a complete change. It entailed synchronizing HR needs with business needs, team-building, manpower productivity improvement, reduction of manpower cost and, above all, upgradation of the management cadre.' Lipton India's commercially savvy chairman, Bipin Shah, often exhorted his colleagues to be part of the solution, not the problem and, with a small team of high-potential leaders from the HUL stable, jointly turned around the business, RR acknowledges. 'Lipton walked into the eventual merger with Brooke Bond as an entity equal in performance and potential,' *Hamara* summed up.

The emergence of BBLIL posed an altogether different challenge under the astute stewardship of R. Gopalakrishnan, as MD and vice chairman. Gopal, the new management committee, RR and a highly versatile HR/IR team had the collective responsibility to weave mindsets, improve the morale and implement a human resource plan to support the business strategy. Simultaneously, new hires from Kissan, Cadbury's Dollops, Kwality and the Pepsi tomato-processing plant had to be integrated. It needed a tailored mix of open communication with employees at every level, leveraging and consolidating the trust built with unions and their leaders, team integration through a 'confluence process' for departmental managers, team-building, retraining, rightsizing and many other structured solutions. That the merger did not come unstuck was because this was achieved by managers and employees, and constructive unions and partners such as distributors and suppliers. HUL Chairman S.M. Datta, together with Sumantra Ghoshal, helped in facilitating the creation of a common vision for the merged entity. The HR/IR team together with operating managers at the branches and factories collectively showed the ability to think dynamically and creatively. Beginning with first principles, they proceeded to understand the context, analyse data and strategically develop purposeful solutions.

For RR there was no let-up on his self-directed learning, and he periodically took courses at Four Acres. Ram Charan, a visiting professor, taught case studies on what constitutes successful business strategies and approaches to diagnose change management issues. From Stanford University's Jeffrey Pfeffer, RR learnt the effects of work environments on well-being, power and leadership, the role of influencing styles in a matrix structure and the knowing-doing gap. Michigan's global management development stood out for its peer-learning opportunities as well as the presence of C.K. Prahalad and Dave Ulrich. Prahalad advocated that strategy was about making

choices and that effective leaders should know what to do and what
not to do. Power needed to be wielded effectively and with empathy,
like the surgeon's scalpel that saved lives. His motto, 'Eradicating
poverty through profits', was inspiring. Ulrich focused on HR
outcomes, governance and practices. His famed HR model that
helped corporations to succeed was very engaging. Ulrich also shared
early insights on future HR competencies.

Post the merger, RR moved to Unilever Arabia as personnel director
and addressed diverse cultural issues. His earlier board roles helped him
to quickly comprehend the HR imperatives to support the growing
Arabia business. It was here that RR met Sanjiv Mehta first and again
when he became CMD of Unilever Bangladesh. Mehta leveraged his
coaching skills to groom high-potential local talent. The Unilever
Arabia board spent five days with Arnaldo Hax, the strategy guru from
MIT at Boston, and finalized the long-range plan along with a strategic
HR plan. As the article in *Hamara* said: 'RR left his indelible stamp
on Unilever Arabia. Such was the achievement that Unilever Arabia
Chairman Tom Stephens told CAME (Central Asia Middle East)
Business Group President Jeff Fraser that RR had restored confidence
in the HR function in the company.' The article added: 'He has equally
made a decisive difference in the entire CAME region as Advisor for
organization development and head of business group training. No
wonder RR has been an indispensable member of the Unilever HR
teams on organization effectiveness and global learning network. One
of his key contributions has been in helping the development of the
PDP (Personal Development Plan) concept as part of a team set up by
the personnel division.'

Dadiseth, former HR director, with whom RR was closely
associated during his Lipton days, was another great inspiration. As
HUL chairman, Dadiseth reposed faith and involved him in Project
Millennium. Even after Dadiseth moved to London to join Unilever's
global board as a director, he continued to evince interest in RR's
professional pursuits. *Hamara* reported HUL's chairman Dadiseth's
tribute at RR's farewell function, 'Here is a manager who is not bound
by hierarchy and establishes links at all levels. Here is a mind, which
is not constricted by an already wide knowledge and is ever open to
new learning. Here is a teacher, adept at transferring knowledge with

felicity. Here is a man who is genuinely interested in people's growth and well-being, helping them to overcome hurdles than create new ones. RR symbolizes the profession in its truest sense.'

Vindi Banga, succeeding Dadiseth as chairman, who later went on to the board of Unilever, utilized RR's experience and insights when Wayne Brockbank of Michigan was invited to work with the detergents team and for many other OD initiatives in the company. Roger Harrison, Regional SVP-HR, also reposed trust and confidence in RR. Recognizing his potential as a leadership coach, Harrison offered him his first break, supported by Fraser and this took RR to many Unilever companies. Throughout his career, he leveraged the support of HUL's HR directors, notably Rajesh Bahadur, Anil Lahiri and Gurdeep Singh. Among other leaders whom RR admired were Harish Manwani, HUL chairman, who became the first Indian COO of Unilever and Nitin Paranjpe, who also became COO of Unilever, and is presently heading a combined role as Unilever's chief people officer and chief transformation officer.

In shaping himself as a professional, RR strongly believed in giving back to the profession by supporting human resource transformation endeavours in the country. He found the time to energize young professionals and contributed to the growth of HR professional bodies; from NIPM in his DCM days to ISTD when he joined HUL in Mumbai. He worked closely with Sharu Rangnekar, George Menezes, Homi Mehta and several others and was elected chairman of ISTD's Bombay chapter. Much later, he was president at NHRDN's Bangalore chapter. Together with a core team, including Kishore Rao, Subhas Devre, Rupande Padaki, D.R. Nagaraj, Vasanthi Srinivasan and others, he galvanized the chapter. They invited Udai Pareek and T.V. Rao to conceive and design a research-based, unique conference that was an unparalleled success.

RR always leveraged his passion for fresh learning and thinking because personal and professional growth provided meaning and purpose for the profession, especially the young professionals, to embark on next practices. He also strongly believed in challenging and supporting his HR colleagues on the path to personal renewal by sponsoring many of them to participate in global learning experiences. He recollects with pride D. Harish, who went on to become VP HR of HUL as one who not only blossomed as a professional but also hugely benefited from such opportunities. RR is equally proud of Sanjiv Mehta, who rose to become the CMD of HUL and president, Unilever South Asia, besides being a member of Unilever's Global Leadership Executive, and Leena Nair for becoming Unilever's first lady CHRO who recently took up the CEO role for Chanel.

By 2005, RR concluded his extended association with HUL and Unilever's regional business group and began a new journey in knowledge and experience-sharing in diverse industries. He is now a strategic HR consultant, leadership coach, independent director and coach at ISB programmes. His engagements in a wide range of industrial sectors provided the impetus to explore newer solutions and support leaders on various transformational agendas. Today, he serves as a trustee at ArtSparks Foundation, a non-profit organization envisioned by his daughter, Nisha. It is an educational non-profit that works to support primarily the development of twenty-first century learning and life skills in children through the medium of visual art and design.

Earlier in his career, RR was trained by Hay McBer as an executive coach. He also recalls John Whitmore's first session on coaching for development at the trainers' enclave at Four Acres. Whitmore laid great importance on meeting ethical and professional standards as a coach, for coaching is primarily about improving performance and helping people realize their potential. Over the years, RR has developed a 'coaching mindset' with skill sets that include active listening, explorations through powerful questioning, establishing coaching goals and facilitating new insights to achieve growth targets. These coaching skills are creative ways to uplift leaders in their efforts to realize potential while improving the quality of their lives.

RR attributes the making of a strategic HR professional to a deeper understanding of the business strategy, industry trends, societal trends, market forces, global competitive landscape, role of emerging technologies, apart from people and organizational capabilities. It was essential to keep an eye on the big picture. He watched the dance from the balcony, as it were, while focusing on the steps on the dance floor. Humility is a great virtue in all of this along with empathy and respect. The other important key is the communication strategy. RR learnt many lessons from his grassroots level exposure and experience in IR. There he discovered raw emotions in action, processes for prevention and resolution of conflicts, the importance of the community and the external environment, the power of networking with external stakeholders and obtained many other insights that HR textbooks do not always provide. RR is an ardent advocate for including IR/ER as an essential component of any career template for grooming a CHRO.

It is just as important to find time to reflect and review the intended and the unintended consequence of one's actions and learn from both successes and failures. RR noticed the emergence of a post-pandemic caring and nurturing leadership. Similarly, he acknowledged that learning agility and the adversity quotient should form part of emerging leadership competencies. A believer in reverse mentoring, he benefited from acquiring an appreciation of subjects like behavioural economics, data analytics, AI and process automation. While working with a few exemplary industry leaders and their value-driven companies, RR realized the importance of global aspiration, trust, quality, obsession with customer insights and community empowerment. The pandemic has also taught one not to underestimate the importance of one's accountability for the larger ecosystem, and the economic health and well-being of the extended enterprise partners, their employees, and communities. For RR, self-renewal or self-revitalization proved to be vitally important to remain relevant for now and be future-ready.

As with Unilever, the outside world too recognized that RR is cutting-edge in his chosen field. He received the NHRDN's award for his outstanding contribution to the HRD movement, followed by their Lifetime Achievement Award. CNBC–KPMG bestowed upon him their award for his significant contribution to harnessing human resources in an environment of rapid change. In recognition of his exemplary lifetime achievement in facilitating the growth of human potential as a coach and mentor, Coaching Foundation India admitted him as an Honorary Fellow CFI.

But RR's belief is that human resource development should not be the exclusive domain of the function alone. Managers at every level must play a people-leadership role. While developing one's own career, people tend to devote less time and space to the development of colleagues. But central to a growth strategy is how people around are identified and developed and realize their potential. Each manager or leader, therefore, needs to make a greater effort and demonstrate commitment to coaching and developing their teammates. RR believes that if he has been able to achieve anything at all, it is because he was fortunate to have been coached, challenged and supported by his well-wishers. More importantly, he acknowledged the phenomenal support that he has received from his wife, Vasanta, son, Rajesh, and daughter, Nisha.

According to RR, culture change is 90 per cent attitude and 10 per cent technique. When people start saying, 'I can do it and I believe in myself', we have achieved two-thirds of the distance. Therefore, those who ignore change, will lose; those who merely react to it, will just survive; only those who lead change for now and in the future, will succeed.

RR's personal mantra lies in going beyond the materialistic and becoming emotionally, intellectually and spiritually relevant; being relevant to the core. There is far more at the centre of the plate than on the periphery; the centre restores balance, connects the past and the future. RR tries to convey this locus of control to encourage people into taking a holistic view of life, to appreciate and contextualize, to understand their purpose in life. On his part, RR makes coaching an uplifting experience by becoming an enabler. It is agonizing when young people struggle to cope with pressure and succumb to stress, with the unpredictability of the ecosystem in which they operate. Sometimes, technology is a 'disabler' here, requiring responses in nanoseconds, in real-time, making life akin to a treadmill with increasing speed that people are unable to get off. Dr Banerjee had taught him to check with his heart before making lifestyle choices, to secure internal tranquility that provides the balance.

The medium that leads one to that path is not important; it could be a guru, but it is important to find the elusive peace within oneself to cope with the challenges of the future.

* * *

S.V. Nathan

Versatile and reflective articulator

Helping develop future leaders and high-performance teams

S.V. Nathan (Nathan), partner and chief talent officer for Deloitte in India, has over thirty years of experience in HR management across diverse industries, including manufacturing, services, telecom and information technology. An industry leader, mentor and advocate of ethical leadership, he has helped develop future leaders and high-performance teams in both multinational and Indian organizations such as ICI, Sterling Holidays, Philips Software and Reliance. Nathan, a behavioural specialist in sensitivity training, is a respected voice in HR in India and speaks regularly at national and global forums on contemporary HR subjects.

An XLRI alumnus, he received the 'distinguished alumnus' award in 2015 and was recognized among the top 25 Voices and as an influencer in the year 2020 by LinkedIn. Nathan is the recipient of several other awards and honours as well. He is currently president of the National HRD Network and has been past president of the Hyderabad chapter of National Association of Software and Services Companies (NASSCOM). Besides, Nathan serves as the chairman of Sumedhas, a not-for-profit professional body engaged in sensitivity training for individual growth.

After seating an interviewee, S.V. Nathan, HR head at Sterling Holidays, left the room to say a silent prayer. The candidate, a highly-rated marketing professional, had turned up two hours late, looking shabby, hair dishevelled, wearing slippers and a dhoti (traditional Indian 15-feet long sarong) draped around his waist. Not wanting the appearance to cloud his judgement, Nathan sought divine help. A ninety-minute engrossing discussion later, Nathan knew that he had found his man, never mind the attire. The man explained his condition; he had come straight from the crematorium, after performing the last rites of a close relative. He had tried to call Nathan earlier without success. Those were pre-mobile days. The incident ingrained in him the message of never judging people by their appearances and, on a broader plane, not to assess the abilities of a person through just one prism—appearance, academic qualifications or their present position in life.

Nathan's childhood had shaped him to look beyond the obvious, invested him with an open mind and the ability to constantly learn from his own experiences and from his peers—all of which helped to make him one of the best nurturers of talent in India. Flashback to child Nathan with his grandmother. 'Grandma, can I ever sit in a car?' 'Of course. When you sit in a car, the car must be yours.' Young

Nathan's eyes opened wide. 'Only if you work very hard for it from now, while you are in school.' It was as a child that Nathan understood that education was the best leveller; the means to a better life; a lesson entrenched his mind and repeatedly practised on self and others in life.

Nathan went to different schools across India thanks to his father's transferable job and was exposed to diverse experiences. These were consolidated courtesy the campus at the XLRI, Jamshedpur, where he mingled with people from various backgrounds. Early in his career, he saw his superiors backing their juniors during conflicts, treating them with care and respect, and pushing them on to do well. Nathan never lost an opportunity to identify professionals who may have been overlooked and support them, including personal assistants or secretaries who were guided into executive roles and then groomed as future leaders. Nathan promoted S. Venkatesh, a gym instructor, who went on to become an industry leader in HR, and Mahidhar Reddy, a payroll assistant who was diligently printing out salary slips late into the night. Reddy had studied management at a tier-3 B-school that had turned out just one batch of graduates before shutting down and had perforce done his college at an ill-reputed institution as a last resort. Nathan was looking for a regional manager, HR, in Mumbai and backed Reddy for the role at which he excelled, going on to lead HR at an MNC in India.

Nathan's beginnings were humble, the entire family living in a single room in Chennai. He attended the corporation school that had no benches and sat on the floor. In standard I, he had to make do with a couple of shorts and two shirts. His father moved to Kolkata for better prospects leaving Nathan with his uncle, a radical trade unionist who often wore a bicycle chain around his waist, for two years. However, he influenced a Chennai school to admit Nathan as a student. More importantly, he gave Nathan first-hand exposure to industrial relations, including some lessons of what-not-to-do. Nathan moved to Kolkata with his father and back to Chennai and then to Nagpur, picking up Marathi rather late in school life. He insisted on staying back at the St Francis de Sales School which had a hostel, when his father moved again.

Nathan inherited his father's athletic genes and became a long-distance runner. His father had been a sprinter at the university level, but the coach turned him down for sprinting at the local corporation sports ground at Marina, Chennai. His mother sent him back to ask the coach what he could be good at. The coach asked him to run a few rounds on the 400 metres track and confirmed that he could be a good middle-distance runner, for races like the 800 metres and 1500 metres. His mother taught him to ask the right questions, and Nathan went on to win many medals in middle- and long-distance races in Nagpur, while also winning academic plaudits. He also learnt that it was important to work on one's strengths.

Ritualistic as a child, Nathan chanted mantras before beginning his day in the morning and started going to church in Nagpur because the nearest temple was 10 km away. He sat in the pews and listened to the sermons and went by the name Steven Vincent Nathan when in church and felt comfortable. He would have been just as comfortable had it been a mosque and this syncretism helped him make friends across the board, with Niyaz Abdul Sattar Khan in middle school and Brian Rodrigues in high school. Their families welcomed him warmly and broadened his outlook on religions as he realized the universality of the messaging: be good, do good.

Nathan's commitment to inclusivity was also driven by his mother, Bhageerathi's experience. Though a school topper, she was not allowed to pursue studies because of straitened circumstances and the problems that a well-educated girl would have finding a suitable match. He found the same story playing out for his sister, Jayanthi, four years younger, who wanted to pursue management like her brothers, having cracked IIM and another management college. Nathan's father did not have the means and believed that finding a groom would be difficult for a highly qualified girl. To his eternal regret, Jayanthi, a Mensa member with an IQ above 125, ended up as a clerk in the State Bank of India. She wanted stability in life and did not opt for the probationary officer position that would mean frequent transfers. Had his mother and sister found support for education, their lives would have changed and they would have impacted others. Nathan was, thus, committed to looking out for women in his career, helping them in every possible way.

As the eldest of the three siblings, Nathan also had to look after his family, given his father's addiction to alcohol and his hapless mother having to deal with its consequences, often having to take him to hospitals to deal with drunken accidents. Nathan received such sad tidings over letters from his mother, which he dared not open till he had three of them. The overhang of the clouds at home prevented him from enjoying even the highs in life or laughing aloud in happiness. He also worried how happy tidings from him would affect his mother, little realizing that they were a source of succour. Even today, he is mentally prepared for bad news and checks emails immediately, lest he misses someone reaching out for help. The experiences facilitated close bonding with his siblings and he carried on the caring spirit to management school, where he was a topper and always ready to help others with studies, interviews and placements.

The road to XLRI was not a straight one and Nathan ended up there almost by destiny. He had studied mathematics for graduation from Vivekanand College in Chennai by default, as he was late for admission and it was the best the city could offer. He did well and was the 'best outgoing student' though his heart was not in mathematics. He wanted to get into a professional career and join a management school. The Common Admission Test for the IIMs was a disaster and Nathan left the hall in twenty minutes realizing that he was woefully unprepared. The XLRI entrance, XAT, was coming up in a fortnight and Nathan studied fourteen to fifteen hours a day for this; oblivious to everything else going on around him, as his mother later said. XLRI happened and opened new vistas for him.

Nathan opted for an HR degree with industrial relations, his trade unionist uncle saying that he had moved over to the other side. Indeed, Nathan tried to come to terms with two contradictory facets of his persona at XLRI. He was a bit of a loner, spending a lot of time in the library or going on long walks and runs, but he did not socialize or drink. With his best friend, Raja, he would dance to Baila music that came out of Sri Lanka. He would, however, be available for anyone before interviews and his friends could turn to him for last-minute preparation and as a sounding board. XLRI is not for yourself, it is for others, he believes, as he acknowledges how his batch taught him the power of networking, the power of an individual and the power of standing up for each other.

A casual challenge by a classmate egged him on to do well in his papers and he emerged as the topper in his batch. There were also contributions from outstanding professors who expanded his horizons.

Young Dr Gangopadhyay (nicknamed Gangs) talked of juggling with statistics. Father E.H. McGrath (one of XLRI's founders) and Father Oswald Mascarenhas left deep impressions, as did Nilima Acharji who taught industrial relations. Nathan carries one of her teachings like a talisman: an organization deserves the trade union it gets. Acharji urged her students to cultivate good relations with the trade unions at companies they worked in. He held as *ved vakyam* (gospel truth) her advice: 'You want a good trade union, be good yourself.'

Professionally Nathan started with ICI India Ltd (Akzo Nobel India Ltd and Astra Zeneca today), choosing this Kolkata-headquartered company over ITC Ltd and Hindustan Lever, and spent twelve years there. The company culture improved his outlook and reinforced his beliefs around standing up for others and doing 'good' as industrial relations personnel. He quit when he was asked to do something that went against ICI's own values and against his too. Upset with a just concluded (and a good) voluntary separation scheme for the ICI Ennore unit, Nathan found the act of throwing young men out of jobs disturbing. When the company wanted to pay him a bonus for handling this well, Nathan suggested that the company just let him go too and save the money they paid him as salary. It might save the careers of at least three young men.

Nevertheless, ICI had shown him the culturally enriching facets of top multinational companies—the integrity, a sense of humility in the top echelons with practices like standing up for one's subordinates, treating youngsters well and courteously; a culture where CEOs carried their own briefcases and did not expect help even when they were heavy. These stayed with Nathan who found reverential behaviour in offices revolting. Even during the ICI interview, a gentleman looked after the candidates, offering them tea and coffee and ushered them into rooms. Upon selection, Nathan learnt he was Ganesh Jejurikar, general manager, a super boss in the organization. The principled Jejurikar had many lessons to teach. When he wanted some changes in a piece of furniture (a bed) at his company residence, he asked for the invoice for the plywood and paid for it as changes were made for his personal comfort. Talk of integrity!

Nathan worked at the Gomia explosives factory, which hosted a mini-marathon every year with the legendary Vincent Lakra winning it for twenty-two years running. Nathan practised running every morning, often meeting the production manager, Daljit Singh, a shot-put champion, who was practising as well. The race had started and there were two kilometres to go to the finish line, and Lakra was about 400 metres ahead. Suddenly, someone on a scooter came up beside him even as he ran and used the choicest Punjabi expletives to egg him to speed up and catch up with Lakra. Daljit Singh had decided to inspire Nathan to win and he did. That was the camaraderie at Gomia.

After Gomia, Nathan moved to ICI in Chennai where Daljit was the general manager. Here Nathan put to test XLRI professor Nilima Acharji's message about a company deserving the trade union it gets. In Chennai, the trade union leaders would barge into the HR or industrial relations manager's room. On one occasion, they had entered his room when he was not in and were waiting. Nathan walked in, pulled up a chair and sat down alongside the trade union leaders. The men were not used to this. They needed someone across the table for a confrontation. Nathan at thirty-one, way too young a replacement for the just retired IR head, had sent a message that his relations with the union did not have to be confrontational. That went a long way to better relations at the factory. It was important to put people at ease and Nathan put away all his medals and trophies, once displayed in his cabin, because they had an overpowering effect. Nathan wanted to come across as a relatable person.

After ICI, Nathan had a long stint with Sterling Holidays, a shift from manufacturing to the services industry and with a major difference. ICI hired the best from the management schools. Here the talent target was pitched at a lower level. Also, people had to be convinced to work for a time-share company, timeshare being a new concept. Sterling made a salesperson of him as he convinced candidates about the job and then trained them to sell timeshare. Nathan chose to learn to sell timeshare himself and started doing it all the time, selling the timeshare concept to whoever he met, even those he sat beside on a train. It was also at Sterling that Nathan started backing people with unusual backgrounds for leadership HR roles.

Nathan credits many learnings to the Sterling experience. He was helping run Sterling's service management programme, run by V.S. Mahesh and Anand Kasturi for all employees across the company, in Kodaikanal. An inebriated guest drove his car to the edge of the Kodaikanal lake, and the vehicle was half-submerged in the water. It was 11 p.m. and the guest panicked and ran for help to the hotel front desk, being managed by Venkatesh, the gym instructor. He placated the panic-stricken guest, sent him to retire for the night, ensured that the car was retrieved and cleaned up, ready for the next morning. Nathan felicitated Venkatesh and presented him with a cheque in the presence of all the resort employees. Later, Venkatesh expressed the desire to work in HR but did not have the qualifications. Nathan told him that he had a quality that many in HR lacked; rendering service at the highest level. Mentored by Nathan, Venkatesh rose up the HR function and is vice president of HR with a large retail business.

Nathan had moved out of Sterling for a few short stints with a UK-based IT company, followed by Pradeep Kar's Microland and a year with Philips India. Among his many IR teachers in this phase was Zaki Hasan in ICI, who had his ear to the ground and asked Nathan to spend a morning in the canteen to report what was going on. Nathan told him later that people had not been eating and were hanging around in small groups engrossed in discussions. Within a couple of hours, Zaki Hasan had gathered the entire union and by the end of the day, he had called the management team and asked them to be on standby. The next day, Nathan learnt that his boss had averted what would have been one of the biggest industrial strikes. Nathan learnt to pay attention to people's actions and body language, to detect patterns and ensure that anything addressable was addressed. These have been of enormous help. Hasan also taught him to be politically aware, even if one was not political and have a feel of the undercurrents of office politics. A much-seasoned Nathan then joined Reliance Infocomm, Mukesh Ambani's first telecom venture after one aborted attempt. Nathan had come to Mumbai for his interview with Mukesh Ambani but had left before the interview after he heard the receptionist call, 'All rise.' The entire staff rose to their feet when Ambani entered. Nathan found it obsequious.

Later, he was persuaded to join Reliance Infocomm in Mumbai, while his family remained in Bengaluru. He caught Ambani's eye for his unconventional approach at a meeting and was asked to attend all meetings taken by Ambani. At one such meeting on technology, Nathan got bored and started doodling, and Ambani saw him doing that. He asked Nathan if he had any idea why he was being asked to attend these meetings and Nathan said he did not have a clue. Ambani explained that he wanted Nathan to know the complexities around hiring a top-technology leader for Reliance. It was a big learning on possible dual purposes for inviting someone for a meeting; either to contribute to the discussions or learn something. Thereafter, he took notes during meetings so as never to lose connect with the deliberations. He enjoyed the Reliance experience because people were expected to do their share of the work with no one being a star. He learnt a lot at Reliance but left as his family had remained in Bengaluru and the weekend Mumbai–Bengaluru travel was taking its toll.

Nathan moved out of Bengaluru again for Deloitte, the global big-four partnership firm, which reminded him of his early days in ICI. Seniors treated their juniors with care and respect; the focus was more on culture than on scale and about setting the right culture early on. The culture was about respecting people regardless of their pecking order in the organization; about expressing one's point of view without worrying that it would be held against one. These were outstanding practices and Nathan has spent sixteen years at Deloitte implementing much of the learnings from his long career and learning along the way. Deloitte felt like a multinational but with an Indian core and Nathan has worked on inclusivity, bringing more women into the workforce. More importantly, his perspective on recruiting changed.

Deloitte needed a team to build processes but all the twenty hired from the ISB campus quit within six months. When the last one was quitting at the end of the year, Nathan asked what went wrong and was told that the Deloitte experience was not what they expected in terms of career aspirations. Nathan realized that he had to re-tailor the campus recruitment process to be true to the aspirants and to the company. Even when the job is being correctly described, one needed to view it from the joinees' perspective to ensure that they stayed with the organization. Nathan adopts a systematic approach to talent scouting: Figuring out the person's strengths and playing to them, trusting the person, backing them up, making them share their learning from the assignment, enabling them to internalize their learnings and aid their own development.

Nathan also learnt a great deal about managing difficult interactions. During a heated argument with Tracey Edwards, who had recruited him at Deloitte, she used strong language and overrode his decision. Nathan went back to her later, apologized for his behaviour and explained the point. Tracey pointed out that he could have told her before they got into an argument. Two lessons were received: clarify positions at the outset and another that he wrote out in his notebook: 'To win an argument, lose your ego; to lose an argument, fuel your ego.' There was also Nathan's commitment to colleagues and to speaking out his mind. Alok Sarkar, an engineer, was sent by Deloitte to Canada and the US, where he contracted meningitis. The doctors there were giving up on him; however, it was known that India is better equipped to deal with meningitis. That would mean massive expenses to fly down Alok in an air ambulance because he could not take multiple landings. Nathan reasoned with his bosses that the company had sent him to the US; he had done his duty and it was for Deloitte to 'bring the soldier home'. The CEO agreed and Alok returned to India by an air ambulance, was treated at a leading hospital and was back to work in six months.

Nathan found the moment personally empowering because he had chosen to speak up. He felt that he should have spoken up on earlier occasions too and made a difference. He learnt that convictions within need to be given a voice for a personality to make a difference and Nathan used his voice. When he joined Deloitte India, it was an old firm that needed systems and processes to be set in place. One of the processes, which he helped introduce, was to build capability through systematic learning and development programmes. He was also able to influence the recruitment of more women and Deloitte has a full-fledged programme in place for this. Nathan feels pride in having contributed to building an inclusive culture at Deloitte.

Successfully harnessing his learnings over the years, Nathan has also engaged with several industry organizations, like NASSCOM, NHRDN and the Hyderabad Management Association. He learnt about the power of networking while working at these organizations, especially NHRDN, where he served as the national secretary and now as the national president. Nathan runs a reverse mentoring programme at Deloitte, where a younger person comes and teaches him something about the latest gadget or app. At the same time, he keeps going back to management books by Peter Drucker and Tom Peters, and shares special nuggets of learning that he has gathered down the years. What works in manufacturing does not work in the services sector. Skill sets needed to change with the specific needs of the industry sectors. A person who does not speak English well may not be good enough in certain organizations like ICI, for instance. However, the IT industry is English-agnostic and English language skills may not matter at all but temperament and IT skills do.

Nathan has also been focused on succession planning, with both the successor and others knowing well before time who the successor will be. Nathan equally believes that talent scouting involves spotting high-potential talents that are scalable and can be backed. He looks for two qualities: people who take initiative and never hesitate to come up with new ideas and the ability to drive the ideas to completion. Much depends on the energy level of a person; some are visibly energetic, talking fast and gesticulating while others can be quiet but are visible storehouses of energy. People who are scalable are those who are free, quintessential givers and problem-solvers interested in other people's success; committed to completing the work and not just the portion assigned to one. Nathan describes his administrative assistant as someone who fits the bill.

A bill from Singapore could not be processed by Nathan's L&D team because it had to be cleared by five agencies. She took it upon herself to approach the five agencies and figured out how to simplify the process. Nathan compares these people to magnets sought out by information seekers. These 'quintessential givers' organize things and share them to make things easy within an organization. They are the much-needed long-term players who can be relied on. Nathan's life is a message on ensuring that such people are trained so that their energies are not limited within a certain circle. Long-term players can be fine-tuned and chiselled over time. Nathan holds up his personal credo: 'Water cuts rock'. This is about patiently grooming talent and developing resilience. In all of this, Nathan describes himself as a 'pioneer driver'; pioneering ideas and driving them to their logical conclusion.

* * *

Santrupt Misra

Endless energy

Leading people and businesses globally, seeking complexity with constantly moving goalposts

Santrupt Misra (Santrupt), currently group director, carbon black; director, chemicals; and director, group human resources for the Aditya Birla Group has been an erudite HR and business leader for over thirty years. He has worked at the board level for close to two decades in several companies and non-profit organizations in India and overseas. Santrupt was president of NHRDN and has been a thought leader on change management at various forums, across the globe.

Santrupt has two PhDs in public administration and industrial relations, from India and the UK, respectively, and is a double master's in political science and in personnel management and industrial relations. He is a Fellow of the National Academy of Human Resources (NAHR), USA; an Honorary Fellow of the Coaching Federation of India; an Eisenhower Fellow; an Aston Business School Fellow; an AIMA Fellow and a Commonwealth Scholar. Besides, he serves as an independent director on the Oil and Natural Gas Corporation board, and is chairperson of the board of governors of the National Institute of Technology, Rourkela; member of the managing committee of the Aston Business School Advisory Board (UK) and board member of the Xavier's Institute of Management, Bhubaneswar. He was also a member of the SHRM Certification Commission, USA, for three years.

Santrupt Misra lived and breathed diversity from his childhood, growing up with his parents, grandparents and extended family of eleven uncles and aunts around. They made for a delightful potpourri of personalities, including a freedom fighter, a trucker and a Marxist poet in the mix. The talk at the dinner table was riveting, from international politics to the Cuban missile crisis, China's role, Stalin, United Nations, world history and wars. Such eclectic discourse shaped Santrupt's mind and personality, and helped him understand complex issues at an early age, so that he could manage human resources later in life.

His parents, Biswamohan Misra and Sarajubala had married for love, quite remarkable for the time and provided a liberal environment though not an ultra-modern one. Biswamohan, a professor with a grounding in social sciences and a liberal social crusader, held the Misras together while allowing them the freedom to tread their chosen paths. Santrupt's mother, a public servant, instilled in him respect for women, particularly working women. Biswamohan had a larger than life image and strong values, and taught Santrupt to enjoy achievements quietly without making a fuss. He never did things to please others, particularly those in positions of authority, and was both feared and respected.

His posting as principal of a private college in Nayagarh, Puri District of Odisha, meant that Santrupt and his sister were homeschooled till he was seven. A retired schoolmaster walked 2 km or more to come home to teach them, telling them stories that inspired them to read, from folk tales and the Indian epics to biographies of famous people. Santrupt's formal schooling began when his father moved to Angul and then to Sambalpur, whereafter he went to Cuttack's Secondary Board High School. As a child, Santrupt was fascinated by gadgets; his two prized possessions were an Isoly II Camera from grade 8 and a spool-type tape recorder.

It was in Sambalpur where he showed an acumen for organization and earned the sobriquet of 'safai mantri' (sanitation minister) as he was assigned the task of picking up straws on his way to school, making a makeshift broom and cleaning up the classrooms! Santrupt was forever trying to improve himself. When he failed at public speaking at a Rotary Club event, he trained himself to speak and won many prizes for debating in school and college. He also joined the National Cadet Corps, learnt to do manual work like polishing shoes and helped people carry their luggage during train journeys, among other things. His problem was with maths, flunking in class XI, though he scored 95 per cent in the other subjects. His maths teacher, Vishnu Prasad Jena, showed up at home on a bicycle at 4.30 a.m. to counsel him lest he lose confidence in himself the night before the board exams. That gesture taught Santrupt the meaning of going beyond the call of duty; a quality that has stayed with him.

Santrupt opted for humanities at Ravenshaw College in Cuttack and, at age seventeen, completed his BA with political science honours along with history and English with a First Class (First) and was adjudged the University's Best Arts Graduate. He repeated the feat for both his postgraduate degrees. A career in the administrative services may have been a natural choice for Santrupt but his father drew his attention to the Tata Institute of Social Sciences (TISS) in Mumbai. He cracked the entrance exam but was underage and joined the School of International Studies at Jawaharlal Nehru University (JNU), Delhi instead. Santrupt loved the infrastructure, but his discomfort with his drug-addict roommate made him come away. He pursued a master's degree at Utkal University in political science and when the TISS entrance came again, he appeared and stood first. Santrupt joined TISS but came back to appear for his master's final and topped again.

Post TISS, Santrupt was impatient to start working and opted for the JK Organization in 1986. It offered a higher salary and accommodation with even some direct reports. He chose not go for the typical management trainee position even with sought-after employers such as Hindustan Lever. JK provided him with critical experience in handling labour agitation and other IR issues. However, when he got a teaching position at TISS the next year, Santrupt grabbed it. He also started working for his PhD at Utkal University. In 1990, Santrupt did a second PhD from Aston Business School, Birmingham, UK, with leave from TISS. It took him three years; the rigour of the research process, the academic environment and the close industry–academia linkages impressing him. He returned to TISS as a reader but TISS was legally challenged by another candidate eyeing the same post. Santrupt did not have the stomach for such unpleasantness, choosing what he had hitherto considered a corporate rat race instead.

Santrupt's academic profile interested HUL and when he dropped in for lunch one day at the HUL cafeteria with his friend Aizaz Baig, head of HUL's management development arm, he was taken to meet the director personnel, Naren Nanda. A formal interview was fixed for the following week and the job was his after this. The confirmation letter was signed by Chairman S.M. Datta himself. Shortly after, a twenty-nine-year-old Santrupt made a presentation to the HUL board, seeking a 25 per cent hike in the training outlay. The approval was a big boost and rather high even by HUL standards. However, HUL's entrenched processes and the distinct MNC culture was not easy for an academic to navigate and Santrupt often found himself cut off from information flows. Much of that happened through informal networks that a lateral entrant like him could not tap into. Nor did he find the senior management seriously committed to training and development even though, as the training manager, Santrupt interacted with the entire hierarchy. While the senior management came in as trainers, occasionally they did not turn up on their scheduled days but sent their juniors instead.

On occasion, participants in a workshop would be called away for other work. Santrupt confronted a senior director for pulling out a training participant, questioning his commitment to training, and while the director praised Santrupt's action to his peers, he did not send the participant back. There were other unseemly occasions of senior managers getting into a slanging match in the middle of a training session on personal issues and Santrupt realized that things could easily get unstuck in even apparently well-knit, process-driven organizations. Even the caterer, who had failed to provide adequate food, dropped names when taken to task and Santrupt got a taste of failings common even in large and successful companies. Matters got trickier. When an expatriate arrived from the London office, Santrupt was asked to evacuate his own office immediately, even though the alternate room at the training and development centre was not ready. The new man arrived and just took away the keys. The entire episode was disrespectful and smacked of subservience to the expat. Lack of respect was something that Santrupt had been taught not to accept and he quit. An offer from the Aditya Birla Group (ABG) came in most handy at that point in time.

The group was looking for someone to take over from the retiring P.N. Singh, the HR head at Indian Rayon. A thirty-year-old Santrupt met twenty-eight-year old Chairman Kumar Mangalam Birla who was dividing his empire into traditional and new-age businesses and planned to hire two persons to helm HR in each part. Birla had taken over only six months back and was still building his team. After a few days, Birla called to ask if he had considered his offer of shared HR leadership. Santrupt's response was that he had read that one could have a team at the top but not a team as the top. The message was clear; he would accept the offer if he was allowed to head HR for the group and Kumar

Mangalam decided to bet on Santrupt. Members of the senior HUL management tried to hold him back but the prospect of leading HR at ABG was rather alluring. The two companies were like chalk and cheese. Santrupt's first office at Aditya Birla was a sofa in a corridor.

On his first day at ABG, Santrupt arrived at Industry House in Mumbai's Churchgate, to be greeted by his only direct report, K.H. Venkatachalam, an assistant manager who was serving out his notice period. His computer needed to be thumped to start and his first office was in the basement, beside a stinking toilet. Santrupt told himself that if he changed his job, he would check out his office before accepting an offer! He never did have to change his job again and managed to build a team that stayed on, even persuading Venkatachalam to withdraw his resignation. There were legacy issues galore, positions going to relatives, juniors touching seniors' feet and many such. The optics apart, merit was often superseded by nepotism in the process. Santrupt's first policy proposal, therefore, was that no relative could be hired in the same domain, the existing employee could not be part of the selection process and all such recruitments would need approval from the chairman's office. Such hires fell drastically.

Santrupt pitched the new policy at a group company meeting in Bangkok and reasoned that it lowered the intellectual heft of the management. The meritorious among the employees' children would not sign up for the group and instead, aspire to work for global MNCs like Arthur Andersen (now Accenture) or P&G. As luck would have it, the daughter of the director in charge of the Thai unit worked for Andersen and it was an awkward moment. None of his proposals found wide acceptance, though, and Santrupt found himself being lectured on the virtues of the legacy policies and the wisdom of those who had created them. Others suggested that employees were the customers of the HR department and, reading between the lines, Santrupt realized that he could hardly drive change by taking everyone along. He decided to bank on Birla's backing to push through changes and backtrack if things went wrong.

To make things smoother, Santrupt started a programme with the Management Development Institute, Gurgaon and took senior managers for three- or four-day sessions in groups of twenty or thirty, away from their familiar domains. He spent the entire time with the group seeking breakthroughs with people bonding over lunches, dinners and sharing living space. His bigger problem was with a presentation that he made to Kumar Mangalam along with the twelve senior-most directors. It was a somewhat homogenous group with almost all directors save one being chartered accountants with roots in Rajasthan. Very few questions were asked and Santrupt asked Kumar Mangalam if he was on the right track. Birla's response opened Santrupt's eyes. English was not the group's strong suit (and Santrupt's Hindi was suspect) but, more importantly, not even the senior leadership spoke out in the presence of the chairman. Santrupt had to get creative but even a request that everyone communicate through printed letters went unheeded because people preferred writing with a pencil on paper. Politically correct statements in favour of change would find no follow-up action.

Santrupt introduced innovation through the ABG Oscars, named after Aditya Vikram Birla, Kumar Mangalam's late father, featuring awards based on performance. While the group businesses were very competitive among themselves, there was hardly any external benchmarking on efficiency, cost or production parameters that Santrupt wanted to introduce. He created a show around the awards with industry veterans as jury members, people such as R.C. Bhargava, Gurcharan Das, N. Vaghul and M.R.R. Nair for the very first round of awards. An audience of around 600 senior managers saw the directors of the different businesses being questioned on performance by the jury. Santrupt also worked on a group logo and a group anthem with external consultants as the group communication function was yet to be formed. The idea was to create a sense of cohesiveness in a more modern business environment.

The other challenge was the lack of diversity in the workforce. Santrupt wanted to infuse quality, vibrancy and youth. ABG never went to the top campuses like IIMs or IITs to hire trainees and top young talent was not expected to join this group. To inject inducement into the process, Santrupt selected around a dozen overseas group companies and built in a one-month stint at a foreign location into the first year for management trainees. That was a big draw at the time. Santrupt also introduced Kumar Mangalam to the top management institutions. In the late nineties, for instance, Birla spent a day at IIM

Calcutta, interacting with students in a programme coordinated by management guru Sumantra Ghoshal. Top talent started taking notice of the company and though many early management trainees left quickly, the organization had begun to prepare itself as a cradle for such high-calibre talent. The alternative of preparing the organization first and then hiring might not have worked at all.

To hire for technology roles, he invited the eminent scientist R.A. Mashelkar to London to sit in at the interviews. This demonstrated that the group was serious about its technology hires and the candidates also took the opportunity to interact with Mashelkar as a big allure. To push mindsets to look outwards, the group invited industry stalwarts like B.M. Munjal and Anand Mahindra for landmark internal events. The lower rungs of the organization desired modernization, processes and transparency as well and Santrupt focused on them. As he built the HR regime, Santrupt sought help and tried other models and learnt from others' experiences. For the management trainee programme, he not only drew from HUL's processes but also from the Tata Administrative Services model, to create a uniquely distinct system for ABG. Similarly, while setting up Gyanodaya, a training and development institute in Navi Mumbai, Santrupt visited five similar management training institutes across the world, to learn from those models.

ABG also started hiring for the top deck from outside, for group functions like communications, legal and IT. Pragnya Ram came in from Ciba-Geigy, Chandu Mishra from ITC, Debu Bhattacharya from HUL and Prasanna Mysore from L&T. They changed the contours of the top management but the level just below needed to be addressed by transitioning hundreds of old-timers in leadership roles into retirement. Like many other similar groups, ABG had an ambiguous retirement policy with seniors often continuing indefinitely. Santrupt took measured steps and on 30 September 2000, he had 366 people retiring at one go. It took meticulous planning and strong support from the chairman to accomplish this. The retiring group was informed two years in advance that they would retire in September 2000. Santrupt left out the top ten or twelve seniors who managed the different verticals from this exercise to ensure top-level support for the implementation of the policy. Santrupt was scheduled to be out of the country but laid down a careful plan for everyone to follow. On D-Day, only one person

refused to hand over charge in Kolkata. The staff locked up his room
to make him see reason. Many had tried to use external influence to
have their retirement deferred but at the end, the departures were quiet
and dignified. The fear of an exodus once the retirement dates were
announced proved to be unfounded because the retirement terms and
health benefits were excellent and would kick in only if a person served
till the retirement date.

Santrupt also got Chairman Birla to meet around sixty or seventy key
upper middle managers who had been identified to take on important
roles. They went through training for their new roles. The news made
headlines in the *Economic Times* and Santrupt got a call from Kumar
Mangalam the next day, asking him to come in. As he walked in with
trepidation, wondering if the end of his tenure was nigh, Birla said
that his grandfather, B.K. Birla had called for the first time since the
death of his son Aditya to comment on how Kumar Mangalam ran
the businesses. He complimented his grandson on the 'appropriate and
bold' move. The thirty-three-year-old Kumar Mangalam said that he
felt relieved. Santrupt, then thirty-five, also showed great deference to
his peers, all older than him and insisted on going to their offices instead
of them coming to his. He was also the recipient of great courtesy from
many leaders who helped him survive and learn. The courtesy shown
by Kumar Mangalam in arranging a lunch for Santrupt and a colleague
at the Birla farmhouse near Bengaluru or Donald Stewart, the CEO
of Sun Life Insurance in Canada's Toronto, coming down all the way
from a high rise to the ground floor to see him off after a meeting were
all lessons on human dignity and respect.

After a decade as HR head of ABG, Santrupt's leadership qualities
were recognized and he was offered the CEO's role of the carbon
black business. He considered it carefully before agreeing. After his
appointment as CEO was announced, Santrupt wrote to his colleagues
in the business appraising them of what to expect six months in
advance. By 2011, the carbon black business had acquired Atlanta-
based Colombian Chemicals, a company significantly larger than
ABG's carbon black business. As this dual responsibility worked out
well, Santrupt was put in charge of yet another large global business—
the group's chemicals business. The CEO's mantle of yet another large

global business, as an additional responsibility, was a radical shift, but Santrupt excelled in such transitions with increasing complexities. He had moved from Odisha to Mumbai to London and back; from academia to industry; and from an MNC to an Indian family-owned business environment and contributed everywhere. The trick was in preparing himself and his new constituency. Santrupt's decisiveness helped him manage multiple leadership roles. If he thought a decision was incorrect, he would go back and correct it without vacillating.

Leadership was a special skill as Santrupt was taught in 2000, when the retirement policy was being implemented at ABG. He was in the US for his Eisenhower Fellowship programme, where he interacted with some legendary figures, including General Charles Krulak, chairman and CEO of MBNA Bank, the largest issuer of credit cards in the US at the time. Krulak had led the US Marine Corps earlier. When Santrupt asked how he transitioned from the armed forces to banking, Krulak said that any idiot could learn banking but leadership was 'not everybody's cup of tea'. Santrupt realized that leadership was a separate domain and if one had leadership traits, one could lead in any sector unless it was a totally technical space.

Santrupt also left a mark on the philanthropic side of the Aditya Birla Group. A conversation with Nobel-winning economist Amartya Sen inspired him to give education a push and create a new position of chief education officer and an umbrella organization called Aditya Birla Public Schools (ABPS). Today, the group manages fifty-two schools under ABPS across India, with some of the best infrastructure in the country. Santrupt also connected with the external public, especially with his professional peers. In 2000, he had been awarded by NHRDN with the Seasoned HR Professional of the Year Award and later became president of NHRDN for three years. He tried to nurture institutions within the NHRDN organization, creating regional presidents to rejuvenate the regional chapters and travelled to many of them. NHRDN apart, Santrupt served on the Worldwide ERC, a global body of mobility professionals, the SHRM Certification Commission and as a fellow of the National Academy of Human Resources, USA. Besides, Santrupt worked on CII committees. His greatest impact was on NHRDN. As chair of a government panel on revamping HR in oil

PSUs of India, Santrupt helped prepare a report on how HR should move in this industry space. He was also an independent director on the board of ONGC.

Santrupt turned several things in his favour. That he had a sparse staff at ABG meant that he needed to know the nuts and bolts of every function. He personally checked out accommodation for senior leadership just as he defended a senior director's compensation package at board meetings. The group has grown well beyond its early contours and employs 1,40,000 people from 100 nationalities in thirty-six countries. Half its revenues come from outside India. As a key figure at ABG, Santrupt addresses groups of 2500 youngsters and takes Q&A sessions with them. Yet he regrets that the complexity of his role prevents him from staying as closely in touch with the people as he was earlier. What he did, however, was to start seeking feedback through an organization-wide annual survey covering a cross-section of people to stay connected and responsive.

Faced with a challenge like Covid-19, the group decided to not cut jobs or salaries across companies. Santrupt is ensuring that the carbon black business becomes a net-zero emitter of greenhouse gases by 2050, which will be a first in the industry. It would align the business with the Paris Agreement on the framework for climate change mitigation. Beyond that, he has taken on the mantle of working with the Aditya Birla Science and Technology Centre to create pathways for all group entities towards the same goals. This initiative will surely leave one more imprint of Santrupt on the Aditya Birla Group, much after he has finished his tenure.

Changing goalposts, moving targets and not settling for just what is on one's plate has been Santrupt's way of leading his professional life. The job that he signed up for at ABG became more complex by the day and this was engendered by Santrupt himself, because complex work needed to be done to meet organization goals. Complexity is something that Santrupt relates well to, given the multifaceted members of his extended family and exposure to different schools as a child. Perhaps that is why Santrupt seeks out complexity, whenever things seem to become simple and easy.

* * *

Satish Pradhan

Intense learner and passionate doer

Constantly learning and thriving in the world of HR, management, conservation and community

Satish Pradhan (Satish) was chief group human resources, Tata Sons, till May 2013 and adviser to the group from May 2013 till January 2015, before becoming an independent consultant in areas of leadership, CEO coaching, organization strategy and design, among others. Apart from creating a unique HR function for the group, he built on the legacy of the two fifty-year-old institutions—Tata Administrative Services (TAS) and the Tata Management Training Centre (TMTC). Satish currently serves the Governing Council of the Tata Institute of Social Sciences, co-chairs a global HR innovation network with Walt Cleaver and is the convener of the Social Innovation Conference of the Pune International Centre. He was on the board of the Bombay Natural History Society and an adjunct faculty at TISS Tuljapur. Prior to joining Tata Sons in April 2001, he was with ICI Plc in London at their head office as organization design and development manager (group human resources).

Satish has a master's in history from Delhi University and is a fellow of the Chartered Institute of Personnel Development, UK. He has worked in public and private sector companies including the Steel Authority of India Ltd, CMC Ltd, ICI India Ltd, Brooke Bond Lipton India Ltd (now Unilever India), ICI Plc. in various leadership roles. He was on the boards of the National Payments Corporation of India and Tal Manufacturing Solutions Limited till 2020, Tata Autocomp Systems Ltd, TGY Batteries, Tata Services, Computational Research Laboratories and on the Strategic Advisory Board of IIT Roorkee, among others. A speaker and adviser, Satish has received many awards and a DLitt. Besides, he has passionately worked in the conservation and community spaces.

The spirit of nationalism was still in the air in 1955 when Satish was born in Bombay. His family was steeped in the uplifting influence of the Sarvodaya movement, building schools and housing, including India's first housing cooperative, the Shardashram Co-operative Housing Society, where the Pradhans lived. His mother, Kishori, daughter of a Marathi poet with a master's in literature, taught at Shardashram Vidyamandir and later worked as a probationary officer in the juvenile justice system at Tihar Jail. A cosmopolitan perspective was brought to the family courtesy father Bhaskar, who had served in the British Army with the Bombay Pioneer Corps in Digboi, Assam alongside the Chindits, prior to joining the Revenue Service in a transferable job that found the family living in a rented apartment in Karol Bagh, Delhi.

The ecosystem of migrants and traumatized post-Partition refugees, in a unique social context and psychological infrastructure, was not lost on the child then preschooling at Holy Child School. The next move was to St Xavier's, standard II under the watchful principal, Fr Thomas V. Kunnankal. He loved the slender pocket money to buy his lunch and became conscious of the difference between his economic status and those of his classmates, but without any rancour. He went on to St Xavier's, Jaipur with Fr Richard Pereira as his principal who encouraged Satish to stand up to the bullies when he complained about being ragged. The principal cared enough to equip him for these slings and arrows of life, as Satish realized later.

His unprepossessing achkan-dhoti-topi-clad Sanskrit teacher, Pandit Hukum Narayan, who cycled to work, impressed Satish with his value-oriented lessons, focusing on the maths and science of literature, which would guide the mind to appreciate the literary aspects, hit the bullseye in Satish's mind. Meta thinking and frames of thinking became very important for him. Meanwhile, Fr Wilzbacher moulded minds with his fancy notebook, enunciation of English words and handwriting, which the boys emulated. They worked on weekly essays that he made them write, rewarding the best endeavour with an opportunity to transcribe the essay in 'Wilzy's' notebook. This pursuit of excellence was engendered by other members of the faculty as well. Satish's older brother, too, was a cool act to follow. Satish enjoyed art and had drawn something special and excitedly presented it to his teacher, G.G. Brandon, who was rudely dismissive. Satish was upset and anxious when he was called to the principal's office the next day. Brandon was there and in the presence of the principal, apologized for his behaviour, attributing it to a personal problem that had nothing to do with Satish's drawing. The demonstration of humility and fair play moved the boy deeply.

Over his father's transfers from Delhi to Jaipur and back, Satish stayed with Xavier's, experiencing camaraderie, sportsmanship and learning to accept loss and victory. Satish's most enduring memory was the leadership demonstrated by Karni Singh, school captain, NCC squadron leader, cricket captain and ISC topper, who did poorly in an important school match and realized how sorely he had disappointed his fans. Trudging back to the pavilion, he picked up a disappointed little supporter in his lap; a gesture that sent a poignant message about facing up to life's disappointments, which got embedded in Satish's mind. Jaipur also added another language, Marwari, to Satish's repertoire, comprising Marathi, Hindi and Punjabi while Xavier's impacted him with its outstanding basketball team and liberal arts department. The latter determined his choice of subject, history, at Delhi University. Satish had won a prestigious scholarship for his graduate programme but St Stephen's, his brother's college and his college choice, offered him philosophy because he did not have the qualifying marks. Hindu College, the second choice, offered him history. Professor Rajendra Prasad there, helped him quickly crystallize his thoughts, asking him to pick between the subject or college of his choice.

Satish opted for subject, walked out of Stephen's, got into history at Hindu College and into a vibrant world of interdisciplinary sharing of knowledge, encompassing art, literature and music.

The flute-playing Debashish Chakravarty, a senior at Stephen's, got him hooked to Indian classical music and its many nuances. Ravindar Pal Singh, university shooting champion and avid birder, dragged him for birdwatching at the crack of dawn. These varied experiences got stored in his mental operating system (OS) as embedded software even as he studied modern India and Chinese history intensely for his master's. Fate intervened in the shape of a bike accident in the middle of his final exams. Satish suffered a spinal compression that laid him up on his bare back on a hard bed for six months at his parents' place in Bombay. He had scored well enough in the ten papers and scraped through his master's but the six months were cathartic, affording Satish the luxury of pressing the pause button to review his life. Satish's enduring realization was that 'shit happens'; how one deals with it is what matters.

Back on a career track, Satish's brother and sister-in-law had both gone into the administrative service with enormous pressure for him to follow suit. However, he opted for JNU on a Junior Research Fellowship for an integrated MPhil PhD. The scholarship made for a comfortable life but Satish had problems with his dissertation proposals, which did not resonate with the primarily leftist mindsets at JNU. Upset with the lack of intellectual freedom, he wanted to get out and sat for competitive examinations: the RBI Grade B selection exam, and the SBI, ONGC and SAIL examinations. He was accepted by all but the first telegram came from SAIL asking him to report at the Rourkela Steel Plant on 15 January 1979. There he met the remarkable Sacchidanand Pandey, the chief personnel officer. The plant was a veritable cauldron with some 40,000 people and Satish was to engage with everyone as he settled for HR, working with the APO Manpower Planning Cell and special officer, IR. The work culture at grassroots was challenging, the manpower-deployment convoluted, with reserved posts, humongous numbers of khalasis sans any job description, and redundant positions, categorized from LI to L7.

The sheer volume of work and keeping tabs on the massive physical registers was befuddling. Satish arrived early in the workers' bus for the 6 a.m. shift, went around the plant, reported to his boss around 8 a.m., often accompanying him for a second round. Getting in early helped him sort out his day, a habit that helped him over his career. Trudging to different shops of the plant meant not just his feet but his body and head getting 'fried'. On the bright side, there were learnings in every tamasha; some deadly serious. A contract labourer died under the shunting engine but the workers held on to the body, demanding employment for the dependent, at two grades higher than was sanctioned. It was a rattling experience, with the corpse lying there for thirty hours, as the workers yelled for ten times the statutory compensation. Satish could not go beyond what the rules permitted. Finally, the administration accepted all the demands. As the ambulance carried the body away, Satish wondered what the purpose of the prolonged drama was; revisiting his own values to sort out his mental muddle. He realized over time that there was a deeper purpose to allowing all this haranguing.

There were other telling dilemmas: a suicide in the plant where the suicide note was removed lest it jeopardized compensation for the deceased's widow. Satish tried sorting out the mess. He had sympathy for the widow but there was wrongdoing involved and suppression of the truth about a death, which went against his professional grain. After much confabulation and Pandey's intervention, the matter was investigated internally; later, a case was prepared for compensation. The matter was resolved with the greatest empathy possible, bringing mental peace and enormous learnings for Satish, though the moral dilemma lingers.

There was more learning and theatrics at the National Joint Steel Union Wage Negotiations. Pandey and his counterparts from the five plants sat at the table with a member of Parliament (also an Indian National Trade Union Congress leader) and a Centre of Indian Trade Unions leader, among other stalwarts. The ACPM, the DCPM, the senior personnel manager and the deputy personnel manager sat in the front rows with the juniors at the back, ready with files, calculators and a stack of blue note slips to scribble comments on. Those would be passed around in a curious protocol. Offers, demands, counter-offers, counter-demands, back channels, 'reading' the wild card players on the negotiating table, patience, quick thinking, quick estimates, delaying, stalling, made the negotiations a saga, rich in learning as much as in imponderables.

SAIL's sales and marketing department (Central Marketing Organization) was represented by the CHRO, S.P. Bhatia, a hail-fellow-well-met kind of person. He asked Satish if he would like to join the CMO, Bombay, where he needed a Marathi-speaking person. Satish found the prospect appealing but Pandey painted a realistic picture for him. Bombay (West Region) HR had to deal with shipping and transport, with some 40,000 *mathadi hamal* (contract labour) in the docks and in the stockyards of twelve branches of four states. In addition, there were departmental employees, the federation of workers with different unions for Jabalpur, Pune and Jaipur, apart from the CITU union leaders at the Bombay regional office. It was like a spider's web and one had to manoeuvre carefully. Rourkela's challenging experiences provided the perfect scaffolding for this intense job, brimming with non-formal learning, as he handled enormous responsibilities for one so junior; an assistant manager, personnel handling a senior manager's work and reporting to the general manager (West). IR managers came over from Calcutta to support him for negotiations. Otherwise, Satish fended for himself, with his mentor, Bhatia, six levels his senior. Every facet of his being got stretched to the point of getting torn and screams became a metaphor for life. Satish got shoved out of his comfort zone by miles.

Satish contracted Computer Maintenance Corporation (CMC) for training his colleagues. There he met the top management and Neeta. These were fruitful meetings. He married Neeta and was offered a job. In a completely different milieu, out of his IR-centric life, in a non-unionized organization as a 'personal specialist', permanently based in Bombay, in the information technology space. The job was too good to be true. Sure enough, upon joining, Satish found the top HR leadership quitting and was left to manage on his own till a director in charge of HR was appointed a couple of years later. He got cracking, building his own HR team from scratch with a mix of talent from the top-ranking management campuses. At the campuses, he was upfront about the low CMC salary on offer but promised the best learning ground and a happy environment. His boss called him an 'idiot' for taking that line in 1982, when all top FMCGs were talking money and perks. Satish, nevertheless, managed to recruit twenty-four people, mostly for sales and marketing, who worked magic for the company.

The HR recruits, from IIM Ahmedabad, XLRI and TISS, were more than just interns; they were teachers to Satish, especially when designing a pitch for the CMC managing committee on rolling out a revised performance management system with skill-building for line managers at the operating level and more. The youngsters had both the depth and width of learning and the knowledge to deliver on the promise, compensating for any shortcomings in Satish's bandwidth to deliver. Satish helped himself to a new universe of knowledge. He also produced a valuable policy manual and was pleasantly surprised to discover during his stint with the Tatas, when CMC was acquired, that most of the document remained valid. By the end of this stint, Satish had come to grips with systems design, corporate HR, organizational development and got networked with the larger HR cosmos.

Meeting influential people like Raghu Ananthanarayanan, professors Pulin Garg and Indira Parikh, V.M. Vartak, the ICI training manager, Zahid Ganjee, Rajan Brijnath and Aroon Joshi was enriching in more ways than one. An attractive offer to take over as HRD head of Dunlop in Calcutta followed. Satish accepted, only to be sorely disappointed with the appalling variance between the promise and facilities on the ground.

Thankfully, within six months, there was a phenomenal offer from ICI as a training manager, initially for India and later for APAC. Satish engaged with a fascinating spectrum of learning, covering diverse geographies and spaces from fertilizers to explosives, rubber chemicals, chemicals, paints, fibres, films, surfactants, speciality chemicals, agro and pharma. Empowering bosses and mentors from India and overseas, tutoring from people like Abhijit Gupta, Ganesh Jejurikar, apart from Mike Gibbs and Steven Glowenkowski from the UK made for exciting times. The roguish Irishman, Peter Edmonds, an amazing facilitator and trainer, spiced up proceedings. ICI's many verticals demanded specific expertise. Satish mastered the contexts to deliver training modules across the spectrum, picking up from top-of-the-line modules, marrying them with ICI's existing modules and designing his own. These he launched for in-house training and for ICI JVs in APAC. Global research in diversity, equity and inclusion for a core development programme for all ICI managers and especially to equip ICI for expanding its footprint to Asia-Pacific got him into the amazing world of Geoff Tudhope.

Tudhope was working with sixty people from the ICI universe to crystallize a development plan for presentation to the director. Satish's learnings from this fascinating facilitator were immense, especially about not making the messaging from the pulpit prescriptive. Tudhope motivated his team to deliver and Satish experienced the humility of the teaching process; there was zero arrogance.

By the end of day four, a model was ready for presentation, which Satish was asked to anchor. The prospect filled him with excitement and trepidation. As he pitched the philosophy of integration with differentiation through a new design architecture for execution across all geographies, he was asked if each region would be reinventing its own wheel. Satish's response—that the wheel would be universal but with regional connotations because it would have to roll on different soils; it could be corrugated for some soils and smooth for others, but it would be an ICI wheel that could roll anywhere—won a smile from Tudhope. As the audience clapped, Satish knew that he had pulled it off.

There was other critical messaging absorbed from this experience: that speaking from one's heart would drive success, as would sticking to one's beliefs; and that communication was about getting the message across, without which the purpose of any presentation was lost. Satish's top-notch performance expanded his scope of work and he navigated through multiple HR issues and addressed other functional resources, as he developed a global competency framework. Later, in his second stint at ICI in London, he developed this into an online Global Development Toolkit on Lotus Notes. The functional standards were aligned to a core that was universal for all managers by level and by functional streams of growth. Satish secured the buy-in of the functional and regional leadership resource committees worldwide because the model had to go live within a year. There was also his own training job in India and the Asia-Pacific to manage.

Crucial to the success of the global assignment was mobilizing voluntary and discretionary contributions of people. Satish dexterously networked, getting people to do things with no authority to demand; extracting help by volition in much the same way as he used hierarchy to get things done. The programme was signed, sealed, delivered and kicked off around the time he made his second mistake. Beguiled by the spiel from the recruiting team, he joined ICIM (now Zensar Technologies), hoping to put his elements of learnings, a bit of IR, a bit of system designs and learning and development under one umbrella as the CHRO. He was disappointed to find that the role was only a partial one, and quit in about a year and a half. R.R. Nair of Lipton's tapped him for the impending Brooke Bond-Lipton merger that K.K. Dadiseth and Sushim Mukul Dutta were actively planning. Dutta wanted an external resource to obviate any Leverization of the merged entity. Apart from a new, integrated culture, he wanted the combined bottom lines to hold. Brooke Bond was the bigger and more profitable entity with turnover and profits around Rs 2200 crore and 400 crore, respectively, and Lipton's around Rs 1600 crore and Rs 150 crore, respectively). Dutta wanted the A+B to hold; a remarkably simple statement encapsulating an enormous demand. It was a new ball game for Satish, who only knew M&A through his readings about the Ciba-Geigy merger.

The cadres of the merged entities had moved in; Lipton with green filing cabinets and Brooke Bond with cream ones. R. Gopalakrishnan soon took over from Manfred Oeschger as the managing director. Over the next three years, Satish worked from 8 a.m. to 3 a.m. every day,

Saturdays, Sundays and holidays included, with the highly-talented K. Ram Kumar (HR manager), and K.S. Kumar (compensation and benefits). The sheer administrative paperwork, the challenge of sophisticated thinking, the design, the planning, the perspective setting, drove the adrenaline while Nair gave him space for independent initiatives. Satish launched into an exciting gamut of activities, designing the structure, processes, workflows, transitions, talent management, while managing integration and softening the consequences of paring down the numbers from 1100 to 700. He prepared a dossier on every individual and customized a fair deal for every pink-slipped person. Many colleagues were unconcerned about how the soft side of the parting was being managed but Satish was no knives and daggers person.

It was a lone, uphill task settling every individual case with his boss. The algorithmic formulation from finance needed humanizing. Satish tried to be mindful of everyone's unique circumstances—sick parents, college-going children and such others, interacting closely with finance to get support for the parting packages and became au fait with that aspect of the business. Exhausting though this exercise was, Satish had an optimum structure in place in eighteen months and the multidimensional experience prepared him for future challenges at ICI. Tudhope was wooing him to join the head office team in ICI London's Millbank Office. Satish inducted K. Ramkumar as a VP HR for ICI India, handed over the India charge to him and he moved as group organization design and development manager in the London HQ. Tudhope played a stellar role in getting Satish acclimatized with his new world, while encouraging him to do the heavy-lifting to manage the large swathe of divestments and acquisitions. Managing the mergers, settling differences between the senior management that queered the pitch for the overall business—expanding each business to twice or thrice its size—meant a beehive of activity with new learnings in every nook and cranny.

The nature of the business was changing—from fertilizers, a high-volume-low-margin business to speciality chemicals, where the margins were significant. Satish acquired a 360° perspective of the emerging multilayered business and diverse business cycle oscillations. Everything got built into Satish's capability structure, including handling acquisitions that were turning sticky. Integration problems with National Starch (NS) had Satish presenting his perspective on how ICI could make the NS operations more resilient. He explained where the acquisition would be headed if it went for the business-as-usual scenario, creating a visual delta of value-enhancing growth, with structural choice built into the business side that would make for lucrative bottom line situations, provided the right capital expenditures were in place along with the right human resources. Elsewhere, he hived off units that made little business sense, such as ICI Learning with high-powered people (£50,000 salary bracket) in different continents. It saved the company some £20 million and he did it with panache, because Satish was flexible enough to manage the boundaries of rigidity, managing trade-offs that left everyone better off.

His third bucket of accomplishment at ICI was designing a leadership development programme. Over twenty days, he checked out the best institutions in Europe and the US to pick the best resources for an advanced management programme. The exercise built Satish's own capability to deliver the specific value that any company needed. He studied the field inside out, examined facilities from Harvard to GE's Crotonville centre at close quarters; attending classes and grasping every dimension. The visits also reinforced his faith in team competency more than mastering every aspect himself. This meant recognizing and nurturing talent; even fighting for them. Amidst the frenzied action at ICI, Satish was pleasantly surprised to get a call from Gopalakrishnan, his former boss at Levers, about an opening at Tatas. They met up over masala dosa and Kingfisher in London, when Gopalakrishnan outlined the job requirements. Things moved pretty fast thereafter, the sense of responsibility towards his and his wife's ageing parents was probably the deciding factor because the Tata position was for Bombay. The plummeting of salary from the ICI UK expat assignment standards to the meagre Tata salary structure was unsettling, but his middle-class mindset about not allowing money to overly influence choices helped.

Ratan Tata made the entry easy, astutely saying that he expected Satish to gain acceptance in the first year for he realized the importance of building the foundation, given the short-lived tenure of the previous Bombay House head of HR for the group. Over a heart-to-heart chat, Satish promised Tata that he was not a quitter. He was committed to making a significant difference to an organization with such a rich heritage but he had no illusions about how tough it would be dealing with 300 managing directors, each with his own achievements and accomplishments. Satish's mental algorithm was about negotiating the twists and turns and delivering value over his tenure, circumventing obstacles and carving out spaces where he could make an impact. This made the journey enjoyable and his commitment to Tata sustained him over the tenure. Gopalakrishnan was supportive to begin with but there were significant differences in their assessments of what the situation demanded. Satish also sensed an organizational alienation from HR. The grapevine had it that his predecessor had estranged the HR teams from their CEOs in a bid to consolidate HR's dominance. He combatted this stigma that affected the heads of HR of individual companies and turned things around, converting alienation to alignment. He wanted an enduring HR legacy without any self-aggrandizement.

Gaining acceptance in an abstract sense was translated to action with the rubber hitting the road and Satish meeting as many people as possible to get their perspectives. He drew on the sagacious counsel of Noshir Soonawala, the non-executive vice chairman of the group, carving out niches where he could deliver value. They met often, just to chew the fat. This helped Satish retain his sanity amidst the cross-currents of divergent views and even criticism. Soonawala's insights into the business aspect of things were brilliant and the respect that he commanded within and outside the group was inspiring. He understood HR and often told company leaders to check with Satish when firming up business decisions.

For Satish, this represented the value that he was bringing to top-level thinking within the group where every unit needed unique treatment within the unifying framework. Rallis or Voltas were as old as Tata Sons itself and Satish quickly learnt lessons in both organizational and social psychology and never trampled on individual identities to create a meta identity. He took a subtle route to create a self-propelling unifying framework and secured buy-ins for the role that HR was playing. It also meant giving HR respect and the space to impact their companies; freeing them from the fear of being steamrolled into accepting all orders from the top. Satish summoned the energy from different sources in the group and consolidated them at the centre, retransmitting it through effective organizational design. Satish also made telling choices. He recalls betting on Mukundan, a young but not-so-experienced

TAS product for Tata Chemicals. Mukundan's varied experience and competent running of the Mithapur plant made him ideal for the global head of soda ash position, when the Tatas acquired overseas companies with different technologies. This eventually prepared Mukundan for the MD, Tata Chemicals position. Alongside, he created a road map around levels of work for developing talent, using the model for early recruitment and injecting greater substance into the Tata Management Training Centre courses.

Drawing on previous experiences, especially ICI, he designed leadership programmes at three levels; the first with three Harvard professors for the top tier, featuring Nitin Nohria, Das Narayandas and Krishna Palepu. Such Tata stalwarts as Ravi Kant, Noel Tata, Natarajan Chandrasekaran, among others, attended the Strategic Leadership programme. The second was a two-module offering with C.K. Prahalad and other Michigan professors for executive leadership—a five-day course, followed by another five days after six months. The third was for young emerging leaders, with Harbir Singh of Wharton and others like Prashant Kale of Rice University and some from IIM Ahmedabad. Satish worked on the design, pulled in the faculty and the Tatas owned the red thread. By the time Satish retired, he was executing a homegrown programme with integrated design, delivery and content in a hands-on initiative. An innovative experiment was a consortium leadership programme along with Prof. Yuri Boshik of Theseus Business School from the south of France and with partners like Boeing, ABB, Li and Fung, ANZ Bank and a few others.

Finally, Satish pulled TAS up by its bootstraps and went back to campuses, establishing a foothold there and was richly rewarded by recruitment: batches of thirty a year in three years and sixty a year in five years, all from the five to ten premier campuses. Learning from the TCS experience of its academic interface programme led to a vibrant networking with campuses, with cross-learnings from them, courtesy advisers making quiet, behind-the-scenes contributions that made TAS talent future-ready and the Tata leadership ready to accept the quality that TAS presented. Satish also built teams and sidelined some who brought dissonance. This could be enervating but it helped Satish achieve a change in the conversation about HR and within HR though not by authority nor pressure from the top. People appreciated that HR was not grabbing centre stage but only focusing on business outcomes.

As he achieved a balance between praise and unwarranted blame, he evolved, often drawing from experiences from his childhood and youth that were embedded in his 'operating system'. Serving at Bombay House was essentially about bringing value to the position without the luxury of being able to leverage authority. Standing up to bullying as a boy may have helped him when the environment turned palpably hostile. He did not quit, despite allurements, because he believed that his biggest failure would lie in his detractors getting him to quit.

Satish dug in and deepened his connections with his own people in HR, with line managers, a very vital stakeholder group, and his secretaries. In them he found enormous strength through their networks and their ability to manage his often-complicated schedules, keeping the wheels of work lubricated and moving. Going to great lengths to 'connect', he would leave office in time to make it the same evening to join a programme at company sites like Mithapur and such others and be back at his desk the next morning, showing support and getting face time with the ground troops. His abiding belief in the infinite potential of human beings deepened, driving his zeal to nurture people. He evaluated, was occasionally judgemental, balancing it all with his philosophic assessment of how the individual was moving through the system. Satish first figured out where he was positioned within the system and banked on the strengths that he derived from that position. He honestly appraised talent, egged it on to reach its pinnacle or gently spoke the harsh truth, when the resource was a misfit for the role. Every assessment was invested with an ample dose of positivity to nudge up performance.

It was the role of a coach and a mentor rolled into one, founded on objectivity and guided by a moral compass, which Satish fine-tuned after retirement. He has injected his rich learnings and constructive support into his independent consultancies, focusing on leadership, CEO coaching, organization strategy and design and taking speaking assignments. Satish's bandwidth to assess current complexities and future unknowns is remarkable as is his ability to engage with positions that ran counter to his own beliefs. Professionalism was not about sticking to the letter of the law or being self-righteous; it meant bringing values to the role, admitting mistakes or accepting the other's point of view. Ram Kumar had once taught him well over massive arguments that helped Satish put some distance between his emotions and the reality, helping Satish revisit his mental framework from another perspective and make a fair decision.

As he has learnt from his colleagues, Satish has shared with the HR profession, working closely with the Chartered Institute of Personnel and Development, UK, the Society of Human Resource Management, USA and with NHRDN, where he served as regional president for western India for two years.

Through all of this, learning has been the name of the game for Satish and each career move has been akin to a child learning to play a new game; training in the present and looking at the future. Satish has never viewed the process as a reinvention of self but about learning the ropes to do every job well. He reframed the issues mentally, assigned priorities to them and knew exactly what he was expected to do.

* * *

Saurabh Dixit

Innovating and navigating around tight corners

An invisible and multifaceted contributor to enterprise-building and scaling-up.

Group president (chairman's office) of the Adani Group till a few years ago, Saurabh Dixit (Saurabh) has over thirty-five years of diverse experience across industries, developing HR systems and practices, especially for the Adani group. There he looked after top management and senior executive level recruitment and was also actively associated with the new business initiatives of the group such as Adani Wilmar Refinery, Mundra Port and SEZ, Agri-Logistics, Adani Energy and Adani Power. Saurabh was instrumental in establishing the Adani Knowledge Centre for conducting in-house training programmes. A silent institution-builder, Saurabh also contributed greatly to NHRDN and the Adani Institute of Infrastructure Management. Prior to joining the Adani group in 1997, he was the vice president (HR) in Reliance Industries Limited.

After completing his schooling in Fiji, Saurabh did his BSc and MSW from Baroda's M.S. University, a PGDBM from the University of Liverpool,

UK and a graduate programme in industrial and personnel management from the Institute of Personnel Management, UK. In 1985, he received the British Council scholarship for doing the certificate in training and internal consultancy at the University of Leeds, UK. Saurabh has extensive experience in conducting training programmes and teaching as a visiting faculty in various B-schools.

At fourteen, Saurabh Dixit suffered a personality reversal. A boy who won prizes for public speaking became an introvert. At ten, representing his Bhavnagar school, Saurabh had won an oratory competition for Saurashtra schools and colleges, speaking on the subject of small savings schemes. This was a great feat for a child who had been struck with polio when he was just a year old. He had only his mother to take care of him because his father, Atisukh Dixit, a senior Bank of Baroda (BOB) officer, was posted in London for three and a half years. His grandfather, a retired doctor, became a constant companion, entertaining him with stories about the mischievous child Sri Krishna and also teaching him basic etiquette. Saurav had easily shrugged off the setback and had turned into a champion elocutionist. Asked by his headmaster what he wanted as a reward for bringing honour to his school, Saurabh asked for a day's holiday for the entire school; just as it celebrated birthdays of famous people.

This was in Bhavnagar where the medium of instruction was Gujarati; English would be introduced in class VIII. In class IX, when Saurabh was thirteen, his father was transferred to Fiji to set up a BOB branch there. Saurabh was admitted into an English medium school there and his world turned upside down. The bubbly thirteen-year old, used to being among the best in his class, was unable to communicate and chose to withdraw into a shell. At the library with his tutor in Fiji, Hari Ram, he was asked to borrow a couple of English books meant for toddlers. It took Saurabh two years to pick up the language and four years to gain some proficiency. Brother Walters, a Christian priest, showed him the trick of listening to tapes and committing stuff to memory while going to sleep.

When he appeared for his Senior Cambridge examinations, Saurabh's English skills had improved substantially and he got an A in the language. This struggle told him that he could back himself for a self-turnaround and develop leadership traits, which he had been demonstrating for a while. Walking back from school, he would escort a bunch of younger children home, even though it delayed him. Passionate about this role, Saurabh would often carry the shoes of his little charges as they walked. He observed his father setting up a greenfield project just as keenly, following discussions at home. Among other things, he saw his father help Panasonic set up its business in Fiji and selling more televisions in the Pacific island than it did in the US. Saurabh understood that doing business with a company or a person meant helping them find solutions.

Saurabh returned to India to do his graduation at Maharaja Sayajirao University in Baroda, where he was considered a foreign student given the Fiji domicile. He got involved in the Overseas Students Association and other extracurricular activities. He was part of the university's Sangeet Sabha, helped to organize cultural programmes and also started managing a band that was much appreciated. Academics took a back seat though, as Saurabh failed in his examinations. Thankfully, the system allowed him a re-take and he cleared all the subjects, having set a dubious record of graduating in physics almost without attending classes. The neglect of studies continued with Saurabh occasionally jumping out of class through a window and became a serious problem when he was studying for his master's in social welfare instead of science. Saurabh continued bunking classes, going for his first MSW class after ten days. The teacher, Indiraben Patel, who was aware of his reputation, denied him entry and later agreed to let him attend classes only if he got an A grade in his first semester. Saurabh took up the challenge and studied hard for his A grade. It changed his habits and turned him into an academic success. It was from his uncle, Bharat Dixit, who was the head of the personnel department at Nocil, that he learnt about HR.

Post graduation, Saurabh got his first job with the Calico Mill as a computer programmer, but his father persuaded him to study further. It turned out to be a double bonanza, for his academic fortunes truly turned around as he won a gold medal and also met his future wife while doing this course. His father was then posted in London and Saurabh went there to do an MBA from the University of Liverpool. He had also got a job with the Bank of Baroda but did not take it up. The same position, of personnel officer, was open when he returned to India and

Saurabh applied and got the job with a posting at the central office in Mumbai. He did not enjoy the stature of being his father's son. He met the HR head of Tata Electric Companies (TEC) socially one evening and that led to an offer from TEC. His salary would be more than double and though his father was unhappy with the switch, Saurabh joined TEC, embarking on what was nothing short of an adventure.

Even before Saurabh was assigned a role at TEC, an opportunity opened up with Ratan Tata. He had returned from the US and was running Nelco and needed someone to handle human resources. Saurabh was assigned to Nelco and while he was excited with this opportunity, the experience was disappointing. Tata himself was not sure about the changes he needed to make at Nelco and kept rejecting the new organization charts that Saurabh was creating. Saurabh sought to be reassigned back to TEC in a move that he would live to regret. While he was at TEC, he had a memorable encounter and a lesson in humility from Ratan Tata's father, Naval Tata, then vice chairman of the Tata Group. It was raining heavily and he had seen the lights on at the TEC office from his home that was adjacent to the office in Sterling Theatre building. He came to check and found Saurabh working alone. He had not eaten anything. Naval Tata returned home and sent over coffee and sandwiches for Saurabh within fifteen minutes.

In 1975, Saurabh moved to IPCL. He had been advised that out-of-turn promotions and increments were not possible within the rigid PSU frameworks, but one could land a larger job profile. Saurabh realized its import later when he was assigned to work with the IPCL chairman, Srinivasan Varadarajan. It was almost like being an executive assistant with a focus on HR and Saurabh by now had realized the mistake that he had made with Tata. Varadarajan asked him to do research as he drafted new policies and get feedback from the senior management and other stakeholders, even building consensus through negotiations, before presenting. He had worked without going through this rigour when he was presenting organization charts to Tata in Nelco. Saurabh was now assigned a major reorganization project, not the usual tinkering with people and processes, but preparing a new organizational structure. Not too many heads of verticals were on board, but some colleagues from these departments were his peers and MBAs and helped him negotiate his way forward, finally coming up with a plan acceptable to most.

Varadarajan was in Brazil and had planned to discuss this in detail at a meeting on a Sunday. He arrived in Mumbai but his flight got cancelled and he reached Baroda by road on a Friday evening after a thirty-four-hour journey. He went over the plan the same evening and started work on it again on Saturday morning at 8 a.m. By Saturday afternoon, the plan was ready and final and the scheduled meeting started. Varadarajan amazed Saurabh by hardly referring to notes because he remembered every detail. Varadarajan was a hard taskmaster and the combination of hard work and logical flow of thoughts at work was a lesson then and there. Saurabh learnt the value of these simple virtues. As he gained Varadarajan's confidence, Saurabh became the back channel for discussions with the officers' association and was also the youngest member of the team representing the management during formal negotiations.

There were exciting events too, especially when the then Prime Minister Morarji Desai was dedicating the IPCL plant to the nation. Varadarajan's wife needed to be present at the factory and with fifteen minutes to go, Saurabh realized that no one had sent her an entry pass. He promptly went to Varadarajan's home and brought the chairman's wife over to the factory as a pillion rider on his scooter. It was always important to think on one's feet. Saurabh also picked up the art of working with data first-hand from Varadarajan and tried to develop his ability to commit things to memory, preparing himself thoroughly for meetings and thinking his positions through, logically. Saurabh also learnt never to tread on the toes of the senior leadership of the company. Even so, after Varadarajan retired, Saurabh was unsure of his future at IPCL, spurred by an unpleasant incident over his visit to the US on a Rotary group study programme. The programme was very educative and involved staying with many families over six weeks, adjusting to their cultures and lifestyles. He had to speak a great deal and became adept at public speaking at the highest level as the programme also opened his eyes in a different way about public sector units.

The problem occurred just before he had to leave. Varadarajan had approved his tour but the finance department brought up an objection just two days prior to his departure. Since the programme involved accepting the hospitality of his hosts, the finance department wanted him to get prior government clearance. Saurabh tore up his application to his company and proceeded on the tour, resigning from IPCL upon his return because he did not want to continue in an environment where the chairman's decision could be overturned for no good reason. He had developed the spunk under Varadarajan just as he had learnt to accept the long hours, working throughout the day and going home with him to conclude the discussions. Saurabh promised that he would treat his people with greater consideration and be a better time manager himself.

Meanwhile, there was an offer from Navin Fluorine of the Mafatlal group; Varadarajan had talked to Arvind Mafatlal about Saurabh before he completed his tenure at IPCL. Saurabh now got the opportunity to work with such human resources processes as talent acquisition, sensitivity training, building up mutual trust among the managerial teams by creating activities that involved the families, among others. He also got independent exposure to training and development and organization building. Saurabh felt at home with this execution role having earlier worked on the administrative aspects of HR and thought this was his calling. He executed a critical project for which he had to enlist the support of the trade unions. Snack packets made at the company canteen for workers at 20 paise apiece were being re-sold outside the factory for Re 1 to buy illicit liquor. There were no limits on the number that a worker could buy. Saurabh got the unions to agree to stop taking the packets out of the factory but had antagonized the wives of managerial staff who lived in the company colony next door. They protested the end of almost free snack supplies for their homes.

In 1983, Saurabh moved on to polyester yarn manufacturer Petrofils, with a home posting at Baroda but at a reduced salary because this was in the cooperative sector. Many in the top management were from IPCL and Saurabh had to start an HR department. I.T. Bhatt, an industrial relations veteran, was in charge of personnel management and did not welcome Saurabh's intrusion. Saurabh took on the challenge of being unwanted with the support of the chairman and managing director, V.N. Jikar, who allowed him to develop programmes to develop people. Saurabh organized a six-day family programme for workers and their spouses and a 'Three Module Programme' covering all employees in two years. The results were unbelievable. Saurabh also successfully introduced a KRA-based appraisal system and a group target setting with group rewards in a continuous process industry at a threshold limit of 102 per cent capacity utilization, beyond which rewards were payable. The highest capacity utilization achieved was 153 per cent. Saurabh also learnt to accomplish things under Bhatt's radar, making friends with the man in charge of recruitment and helping him in whatever way he could. During a strike at the unit, Saurabh got a free pass from the trade unions as he generally worked on development and related issues and was allowed to move freely. He used his freedom to help Bhatt through the strike and then slowly got into his good books. Saurabh had figured out that since he could not choose his boss or colleagues, he would have to find ways to work with them. Meanwhile, an incentive bonus scheme paying a bonus for productivity above 102 per cent was worked out in contrast to the standard PSU bonus paid at productivity above 60 per cent to 70 per cent. Petrofils won an award from the National HRD Network and his work was appreciated by the management, and he was sent to Leeds University for a course on internal consultancy.

In 1990, Saurabh received an offer from Reliance Industries as Deputy General Manager (same rank as at Petrofils) and he joined the organization despite having apprehensions regarding his upward mobility given that peers would be older and entrenched in the system. Nevertheless, he was elevated to vice president at Reliance in 1995, the youngest VP in the company. At Reliance, his first task was to regularize personnel files because people worked without appointment letters, saying that they worked directly with Reliance chairman, Dhirubhai Ambani. Saurabh managed to regularize everyone on the payroll and moved on to talent acquisition because many big names were being hired for the Reliance corporate office. They were accustomed to fancy offices and other facilities that Reliance's small Mumbai office could not provide. Saurabh took them around the spacious facilities at Patalganga and then to the small chambers of Mukesh Ambani and Nikhil Meswani in Mumbai. Once they saw the size of the offices of the company leadership, they were more amenable to accepting the space allotted to them.

The Jamnagar refinery was coming up and Saurabh was deputed to the Jamnagar project and had to hire for the refinery, targeting candidates from public sector units. It was difficult because people were unsure about taking a gamble on Reliance, a private sector firm. Also, the hiring process sans advertisement was new for them. Saurabh's first target was to get supervisors to run the refinery. He went to Mathura to hire from Indian Oil Corporation's Mathura refinery, setting up his office at a dhaba (tea/food stall), opposite the IOC staff colony. He took over the dhaba for two days and was a one-man army, meeting IOC employees, assessing them and making job offers right there. Half the accepting numbers did not join up but around a third of the initial supervisory staff at Jamnagar refinery was hired at this Mathura dhaba. Word spread to other PSU refineries too and soon many others joined. Saurabh was picking up lessons from his bosses too. At Jamnagar, he saw his boss V.V. Bhat spotting a large commercial building near the proposed refinery site with just one barber's shop. Bhat walked into the barber's and over a chat, while he got a rather unnecessary haircut, picked up all the information about the building. Soon the largely-unused building was converted into a guest house for Reliance. Saurabh learnt about visualizing something that was not there and then creating it.

In 1998, Saurabh moved to the Adani Group where, at fifty, he was one of the oldest employees. Most of the senior managers were in the thirty to thirty-five-year range and Saurabh switched over to a mentorship role as group president HR, also the head of corporate communication and, shortly after, head of the chairman's office too. He was recruited to mentor Gautam Bhai and other leaders, which was a big responsibility as he slowly worked towards transforming Adani from a trading organization to a conglomerate. Saurabh developed succession planning found that some fifty traders reported to Gautam who was engrossed in trading. He had to extricate him from that. Part of this mentoring was to show the top honchos how valuable timeliness was and why mindsets needed to change. Discussing a Mundra tender, the group talked for seven hours to save Rs 1 lakh and Saurabh explained that for a project involving capital of more than Rs 100 crores, time was money. If needed, the company should pay a bonus to achieve project completion before the deadline; something that he had learnt in Reliance. He had also developed a knack for figuring out what costs had to be controlled and got CAs together to monitor outstandings, called monthly meetings and presented the monthly performance of each trading desk. There were difficult tasks that he executed for Adani, including pink-slipping people who had to go, even though it upset him emotionally. Some thought that he was a man with no heart but he handled the partings sensitively and remained friends with most of them.

Adani was then an export-import organization with 225 employees with a turnover of Rs 2400 crores and getting ready for the Mundra port to be opened in the year 2000. There were the top three people managing the project and Saurabh coordinated the process with the management to determine who would be the boss. The next nightmare was to manage the inauguration for which 2000 people were invited and Mundra did not have the infrastructure for this. Saurabh and the administration head, S.S. Bhatti, pressed a couple of Boeing 737s, seven helicopters, seven train compartments and 25 AC buses into service. Saurabh had managed large gatherings for Reliance in the past and had seen his father deal with arrangements for Bank of Baroda's fiftieth anniversary, but the Mundra programme was much bigger. As the head, chairman's office, apart from being the HR head, Saurabh had to play multiple roles in a rapidly growing family-owned company that was trying to professionalize. He also had to help with building Adani Wilmar Ltd, a 50:50 joint venture in edible oil between Adani and Wilmar of Singapore, which has become the largest Indian edible oil company.

In 2006, Saurabh helped develop the blueprint for an institute of higher learning, the Adani Institute of Infrastructure Management (AIIM) and got the much-esteemed Bakul Dholakia, who had just completed his tenure as director, IIM Ahmedabad, on board. AIIM was involved in establishing policies and processes and strategizing for growth, and Saurabh invited Mrityunjay Athreya to help develop an organizational vision, holding follow-up conferences to carry forward the vision. Saurabh initiated a three-day offsite annual conference, with each business presenting its performance of the past year, its proposal for the next year and the upcoming five years. The Adani management strategically decided to hire a large number of engineers, MBA, CA and ICWAI students directly from colleges, train them for a year, making them au fait with the company, business and trade, and imparted soft skills as well. The trainees were rotated in three businesses for two months, followed by an internal selection done by the businesses at the end of the year. This has worked well for the group and created an Adani Culture over a period of time.

The canvas became bigger for Saurabh who was involved in developing an LNG/CNG company distributing piped gas in two major cities of India and setting up operations in seven more cities a year after. He also helped develop an organization for developing special economic zones in India, a BPO company and a groceries supermarket, which was sold to Reliance in 2007. Right through his career, Saurabh moved on when he felt that he had served his purpose and was not adding value to the role or to himself. Naturally entrepreneurial, he took on jobs and converted them into profit centres. Greening up Mundra, Saurabh built a nursery, which started making profit on its own. In 2008, Saurabh sought a change in roles at Adani, gave up the HR portfolio but continued with the chairman's office and took up the challenge of interior decoration in many Adani buildings. In 2012, Gautam Adani entrusted him with conducting workshops for the Adani family, which he did sensitively over three months, involving both the older and younger generations who were present together, as he got problems to surface and got them resolved over dialogue. Saurabh felt a sense of belongingness with the family.

In 2016, Saurabh retired, having spent a lifetime thriving on solving problems, innovating, often stepping on the toes of influential people and paying the price for it. Going by one's heart and mind is good for the soul and risk-taking enhanced the creative juices within him. Risk-taking and side-stepping obstructions are par for the course when working in senior positions on new greenfield projects as he did towards the latter part of his career. Saurabh found his ideological home at Adani, going on to different things when a project was accomplished. Once he had his heart's fill, Saurabh hung up his boots and severed connections with work. It was time to reconnect with friends and family, tinkering with electronic gadgets, joining music and drama clubs, creating travel plans for himself and friends or informally advising people, just to amuse himself.

Someone for whom work was pleasure, it was time to make a business of pleasure; of being happy.

* * *

Shrikant Gathoo

Perennial achiever

Facilitating decision-making with exceptionally high achievement orientation, mellowed by spiritual bent of mind

Shrikant P. Gathoo (Shrikant), former chairman of Petronet India Limited and Petronet CCK Limited and director, HR, Bharat Petroleum Corporation Ltd (BPCL), has been an outstanding HR professional demonstrating leadership in the oil, energy and gas space where he rose to be the business leader. Apart from his sharp analytical skills, Shrikant brings to the table his expertise in strategy, business planning, talent management, succession planning, information technology, corporate governance and board processes. Besides, he has extensive experience in business as well as in information technology.

Shrikant holds a postgraduate degree in management from the University of Pune, is a fellow of the LEAD International Institute and did his International Directors' Programme–Certification from INSEAD. Before joining BPCL in 1986, he worked with Bharat Heavy Electricals and NTPC. At BPCL, he led initiatives in the areas of employee relations, employee development, benefits administration, administrative facilities, services and projects, besides real estate, corporate social responsibility and sports.

A fauji for a father meant a life of transfers for Shrikant Gathoo. His eleven years of schooling meant travelling from posting to posting across India. Academics apart, this made for a fascinating education and, though an average student, the sheer diversity of experiences and deep learnings from different influencers and friends made for a solid foundation for the child growing into adulthood. Shrikant did his school finals from the Kendriya Vidyalaya, Jodhpur, in 1974, and stayed on in the city for his graduation with commerce. The family's nationalistic background impacted him just as much as patriotism and a culture of service came with the lineage.

Shrikant excelled at athletics and basketball and had a yen for poetry and writing. He demonstrated an innovative spirit by starting

Sahityaki, a literary association, for kavita and shayari (poetry in Hindi and Urdu) with zero resources. Seeds of becoming a people's person were sown when he became the secretary of the college student's union. The brilliant Prof. N.K. Maheshwari, who became the principal at a very young age and wrote a textbook on cost accounting in his twenties was a strong influence, touching a chord in Shrikant heart and mind with his observation that he could easily become an all-rounder if he took studies a little more seriously. Shrikant could become a chartered accountant but wanted to pursue something where his people skills could be put to use. He had not heard of the IIMs and chose to do his master's in personnel management with HR from Pune University that was within the family's means.

The course helped him understand how his natural inclinations could become useful in real life and the field work brought to the fore the underlying HR person in him. Shrikant had opportunities to interact with union leaders such as Gajanand Gokhale (Koyla Shramik Sabha–HMS), who was next to George Fernandes in the field of railway unionism and got involved in union negotiations. The first major fight was with Gokhale and the German managing director, who was offering a 14 per cent bonus. The agitating workers demanded 20 per cent, choosing to go in for a fight. After three months of strike, they had to settle for an 8 per cent bonus because the company was debilitated by the strike and could not go beyond 8.33 per cent. Shrikant had learnt his lesson. Everything was about 'timing' and negotiators should know when to act and when to withdraw, a lesson that he spent a lifetime honing. He understood the collateral concerns around the core issues at a given point of time and learnt to strategically pick the enablers and disablers to achieve the desired ends.

Shrikant worked on the art of energizing the enablers and neutralizing the disablers right from there. He also stayed in a basti (shanties) with the workers in Kalyan for a couple of months during his field work at Century Rayon for a first-hand experience of their lives. Datta Samant was at his peak and it was just as well that Shrikant became familiar with Samant's ways for he would soon be in an HR leadership position dealing with Samant at his militant worst. Samant led the workers of the Kamala and Phoenix Mills in a long-drawn but infructuous strike.

The workers never got their provident fund, gratuity or their final dues and the regrettable denouement rankled with Shrikant, even though he was not involved with this strike. The mills made way for malls and his conscience does not permit him to go to them; the injustice done to the workers remains unacceptable.

Shrikant had two options for a career; the Tatas in the private sector or BHEL in the public sector, where Venkataraman Krishnamurthy was chairman. There were 2000 applicants for the BHEL positions and twenty were selected; Shrikant was one of them. He promptly read two volumes of BHEL's personnel manual on its system orientation for fascinating learnings. His induction was unique too. His boss, K.S. Saini, who was on deputation from the Steel Authority of India (SAIL), met him on day one and asked him to take the office car and driver and go round the city, have a good time, get some lunch, see a movie and report to him in the evening at the guest house. For a week, Shrikant was given no work because Saini was checking out his ingenuity to suss things out for himself and also to get him to know his way about in the city. HR was often asked to figure out which organization would best serve a sudden need and where it was located. It was important for HR people to be in the know.

At the end of the week Shrikant reported all that he had done, was complimented and asked to create his own job profile, for working at the power project sites as well as the headquarters. Accompanying Saini to a site where there was a strike, Shrikant found a confronting crowd with an abusive and threatening union leader. Saini calmly told the union leader that he was using a criminal's language; criminals were dealt with on the streets and not in conference rooms. The man soon calmed down, did the traditional namaste and the dialogue began. Shrikant picked up the art of telling the union leader, in no uncertain language, that respect begets respect and unless the welcome to Saini's chamber was reciprocated with cordiality, things would not proceed. Saini also let him handle tricky issues independently; one where the contractors ran away from the site. Having his boss's backing worked wonders for Shrikant's confidence. Saini was the master negotiator and Shrikant was a quick learner in his three years at BHEL, before moving on to NTPC, a public sector start-up.

Shrikant, among the early joinees, was totally impressed by R.V. Shahi, the chief operating HR functionary at NTPC. He was keen to work at a project site and got a Korba posting for five years where he acquired a 360° perspective of doing things from scratch, including setting up a colony. K.K. Sinha, his boss in Korba, was a visionary vis-à-vis the living environment that he wanted for the employees and their families, his own included. He brought in the Kendriya Vidyalaya and DPS—thanks to Mrs Sinha's insistence that she would not move unless there was a DPS at Korba!—and a 75-bed multispecialty hospital. Setting up a new location including a township was another enormous learning opportunity and Sinha was very empowering. He told his team that as long as the intention was right, clear and honest, it would be fine. What he discouraged was any form of personal aggrandizement. Perceptively, he stayed away from naming any initiative after a person because of the likelihood that the next person would kill the initiative. Shrikant ensured that his personal investment in any agenda never came to the fore even when he was giving it his all; it would not do to have it perceived as Shrikant's agenda. It had to be perceived as a generally beneficial scheme.

That Srikanth evolved into an empowering person over the years was because of his phenomenal bosses. The NTPC ecosystem bred and fostered trust. Its liberating environment was enhanced by the fact that nothing had been laid down; Shrikant set things up from scratch. His first assignment was to hire 2000 people for the Korba project and his team spent the first six months establishing a foolproof selection process that would be immune from political interference, which was approved by the management committee. Shrikant went for a massive recruiting drive, diligently putting away ministers' slips in his drawer, setting up the plant personnel department to develop an outreach to people in the project site and got a pure project experience. The motto was to deliver on every promise but never to overpromise. Decisions at NTPC involved thousands of crores in rupees and impacted thousands of lives in terms of employment as the company spread its wings from one plant to fifty at present and made for valuable learnings.

For Shrikant, there were emergent issues on the personal front, though. His son was not getting 'metro quality education' and his father-in-law developed a heart condition that needed medical attention in Mumbai. A BPCL advertisement with two alluring lines: accommodation in Mumbai and opportunity for creativity and innovation, was most opportune. These expressions, commonplace today, were unheard of in job advertisements in the seventies and Shrikant was instantly attracted. He was the first candidate to be interviewed by the full panel, sent for his medical tests and get selected. Twenty-eight-year-old Shrikant joined the refinery of BPCL, where he worked for the next thirty-one years. BPCL meant a new role every three years and, over his life, Shrikant did eighteen roles across companies. He was posted as head of HR (west), a refinery, for implementing SAP and as head of the lubricants SBU.

The move from refinery to marketing was fraught with sensitivity because the two were different legal entities in the past. Burmah-Shell refineries was an Indian company under the Indian Companies Act, while Burmah-Shell oil storage and distribution was a London-registered, pound sterling company. Removing the trust deficit between the two was Shrikant's first priority. He brought to bear all his people skills, encouraging ventilation of thoughts and attentively listening to them, without pushing his point of view. Establishing endearing connections was the first step, followed by a dialogue around the best way to create a united perspective. By then, the other person was made to feel that the outcome being pursued would be a winning proposition for him as well. Shrikant witnessed the amazing transformation in the workplace as wariness made way for warmth in the working environment. The greatest learning was that gaining acceptance of his colleagues was fundamental to doing his job and he practised coming across as a forthright and clear-headed person to gain acceptance.

Shrikant's success was evident in the increasing numbers who made him their first stop when something troubled them. Shrikant conscientiously communicated that his interest in the problem was genuine, he listened patiently and guided people in their best interests. That was the core of being a good HR person, just as people connection was the key HR responsibility. Indeed, Shrikant could be quite disarmingly humble because he focused on touching every employee positively. Making change happen at an individual level across all rungs in the company, however, meant hard work. Workaholic that Shrikant was, he pulled it off; never leaving his desk without addressing every pending issue with his meticulous discipline. Shrikant collected his thoughts about what he had to accomplish over the day before leaving the house, and got things moving urgently so that they got done by the close of day. His secretaries placed his files on a five-rack tray in order of importance and he dealt with them accordingly before leaving for home with a clear conscience.

He was equally disciplined about not taking his work home because he wanted to spend quality time with the family. He went on wonderful vacations to company-owned holiday homes in lovely locations, recharging his batteries that had to be recharged given the long and harrowing fights with the unions. The big disruption arrived post nationalization in 1976-77, when Burmah-Shell became BPCL and people wanted Burmah-Shell wages. Hardly a battle that could be won over dialogue, Shrikant braced for a settlement in court, on ground and through legislation. The Datta Samant-led union went for a six-month long strike, which was pretty much in keeping with the strained IR climate of the time and it led to realization of criticality of legislative intervention. Painstakingly engaging with parliamentarians and the law-making process for six months, in extreme confidence, to have an act of Parliament to set aside the law of succession, whereby Burmah-Shell wages did not become binding on BPCL, gave Shrikant heartburn and acidity. He took antacid shots at the medical centre for such sustained critical nocturnal engagements but achieved a new wage regime for BPCL with the public sector scales. Salaries dropped for 40 per cent of the people while 60 per cent benefitted. Critical to the process was getting Samant to agree to a court-adjudicated settlement and call off the agitation. Thus, while matters were fought at courts, Shrikant made working relations as amicable as possible, extending the cordiality to the families of those he fought in court and attending social functions at their homes.

Around 2008, there was growing concern about the control panels at the Mumbai refinery being manned by non-management staff. The sophisticated computerized system in the control room is usually run by chemical engineers, who not only control the system but also introduce changes for process improvements. A distillate yield enhancement by 1 per cent, for instance, would lead to a Rs 100 crore+ improvement of profit and only chemical engineers could do so. Elsewhere, the union recalcitrance was addressed by the police physically removing the workmen from the control panels but Shrikant wanted a negotiated settlement to avoid such unsavoury experiences. A painstaking five-year-plus negotiation with a plethora of unions followed. Shrikant fine-tuned his art of marrying diplomacy and power and deploying both these weapons with skill, given the sharpened HR person that he had evolved into.

Another major anomaly lay in worker wages being open-ended; many got higher salaries than the chairman, directors, general manager and managers. Also, the unutilized portion of medical benefits could be carried forward without a cap. These were untenable legacies of the past and Shrikant pared them down. Elsewhere, new work clauses had to be introduced without deflating workforce morale; the carousel had to work non-stop, with rotating shifts; working hours at the office had to be increased from thirty-six to forty hours; and from forty-five hours to forty-eight hours in operating locations. Shifting the regime of outsourced truck-loaders to in-sourced resources, while driving productivity and with zero-loss of man-hours was tricky, but Shrikant had insights into every aspect of the organization. He was now given business roles outside HR for nearly ten years with bottom line responsibilities.

Heading the lubricants division, he had to double revenue and quadruple profits under the aegis of a strategic 'Project Destiny' mission. Not only did this sharpen his profit and loss sensitivity and make him cost-conscious, it motivated him to continuously reinvent himself. Reinvention was the name of the game as he got thrown into Project ENTRANS, the most edifying and humbling experience of his life, when in 1999, Chairman U. Sundararajan asked Shrikant to work on a SAP implementation programme. He was clueless about the work, which involved learning the core of how the entire organization functioned and getting 100 BPCL members SAP-certified at the huge cost of between Rs 1.5 lakh and Rs 2 lakh per person. Despite scepticism, Shrikant insisted that no bond, guaranteeing continuance with the company, be taken. No one quit till the end of the programme because there was a moral bond to complete the project. Under Shrikant's lead, the initiative achieved the distinction of registering the fastest SAP implementation in the world, with all modules being implemented at the same time across 376 locations. More to the point, it demonstrated Sundararajan's faith in his HR man. The perceptive chairman realized that the challenge was not the technology but the mindset and the people dimension. He had no qualms about putting a man with neither IT nor business background in charge, only because he was a people's person, brushing aside Shrikant's own reservations.

Shrikant established personal rapport with the CEO of SAP in Germany to smoothen the passage and managed with the dilapidated Indian telephone infrastructure of the time, and had servers linked through satellites across India. Shrikant pulled it off as he did a slew of such challenging assignments for a decade in several aspects of BPCL before returning to HR. He learnt to encourage youngsters in his team to seize every opportunity to work outside HR and spend five to seven years in a line or a P&L role. Alongside, he aligned HR's focus to BPCL's business objectives and initiated a Project Sankalp to create a five-year strategy. He invited his former chairman, Sundararajan, to facilitate the process, which he did with great intensity of passion. In November 2011, Shrikant was elevated to the BPCL board and created strategies for HR to deliver effective solutions through an 'Integrated career development framework'. It would make people ready to take on leadership roles and to step into the shoes of retiring leaders. His grooming for succession was largely based on Ram Charan's *The Leadership Pipeline*, mapping key competencies of people with scope for a 360° feedback. He reinforced this with a talent management team of the top 200–300 people, managed by the chairman and directors, with their unique strengths identified for further training for future postings. These would also be cross referenced with their achievements of performance targets and lived corporate values.

Shrikant's Leadership Development Centre with seven mandatory training programmes for top positions ensured that anyone eluding this rigour would have even confirmed promotions held in abeyance. This was about empowering them to change gears from 'managing self' to 'managing others'. New roles were preceded by people having to perform two out of the three roles in which they were responsible for managing others. These checks and balances ensured that no one became a functional head without working in two regions or a business head without working with two businesses. Promotions would often be preceded with an empowering posting to familiarize the person with the geographical locale or the business role; facilitating a smooth ascension into the senior position without having to flounder in unfamiliar terrains.

To the board, Shrikant clarified that the HR head's job was all about empowering the CEO to achieve organizational objectives. The BPCL board had such eminent thought leaders as Prof. Samir K. Barua, Prof. N. Venkitswaran and Prof. Jayant Varma, and Shrikant used them as a sounding board for his ideas before formally putting up the proposal for the board's insights. They also served to have a balanced approach within the board. Shrikant tapped into the strengths of every board member, benefiting enormously from their contributions. He also had to groom the top deck and did so by conscientious empowerment, ensuring that people had access to the top minds in the business. Professors from INSEAD, Ross School of Business and IIMA, among others, spent time with them, often engaging at the board level. High-potential people with established competencies from junior management were identified and those from middle management were fast-tracked.

Fast-tracked promotion was exemplified by a 2009 TISS graduate becoming a chief manager by 2018; covering five promotions, from management trainee to assistant manager to deputy manager to manager to senior manager to chief manager, in nine years. This was very rare in the public sector but crucial for BPCL because 50 per cent of the top management would be superannuating in a couple of years. Building up the next rung of leaders was a business imperative, otherwise the company would face a massive talent and company-specific knowledge gap. Lateral talent injection had its limitations and the fast-track process was immensely useful. For talent-mapping, Shrikant took recourse to technology, mapping around 4000 people, creating a one-page data sheet on each, that the talent council processed. It moved the chosen few faster, organized specific exposure to targeted roles and relevant training. Shrikant also set up a centre of excellence within every business with twin mandates to groom people from basic to advanced to specialist to expert on the one hand and usher in 'next practices' on the other.

Even the brightest functional trainees went through the paces to imbibe BPCL logic and processes to obviate possible errors if they were not well-versed with the internal processes. The centre's thorough training and exposure empowered them to create the next set of practices to keep up with the times. Shrikant had some of the brightest operating people running the centre of excellence. For the millennials, Shrikant used a different line with forums dedicated to the young; one being 'Ideas', which has been running for almost two decades. It funnels innovative ideas and has now become industry practice with more than 2500 ideas coming in every year with the best one winning the chairman's trophy. One winning innovation came from a young girl, no more than four months old in the company, who developed an app in four weeks for customers, practically on a zero budget. A leading IT company had agreed to do it at a huge cost and in seven months, while the youngster did it in almost no time and delighted the customer. Dealing with millennials meant reformatting Shrikant's own mind because they wanted entirely different things—global holidays, not holiday-home vacations, for instance. Shrikant believed in customizing for the new generation in what was essentially a cafeteria approach that gave them a choice.

There were equally tricky issues around engaging with those he overtook as he moved up the ranks. Shrikant brought to bear his genuine concern for his colleagues to the workspace and ensured that harmony at a personal level was never disrupted even when the other person felt wronged in not making the grade that Shrikant had. Even from his position of seniority, Shrikant kept connected with people at the grassroots following BPCL protocols. Going to a field location with a sales team, for instance, he would sit alongside the sales officer if he was driving, allowing the spirit of informality to prevail. The territory manager would follow in another car and the junior colleague could feel free to talk without his boss's presence. Such trips provided excellent listening posts. That he knew people personally made a difference; he gave everyone space to perform and felt for them like a caring mother. It was also customary to have the whole team over for dinner when he visited operating locations and that gave him time with the youngsters. He spent time chatting with them, sitting with each of them individually for a few minutes, encouraging them to open up. Over the years, Shrikant had developed a well-defined reporting process, with quarterly reviews and monthly regional reports for each function that he would peruse. Nothing missed his attention or escaped his memory and if later reports varied from the earlier stated position, he would catch on.

For every business, there were strategic objectives that he drove himself or monitored personally. It was a conscious effort to know what exactly was going on because sometimes things panned out differently from what was planned; sometimes unexpected hurdles troubled the implementation. Shrikant had the humility to appreciate the fallacies in planning and the flexibility to change course. Elsewhere, he pushed through unpopular decisions gracefully and without his ego coming to the fore. He also worked meticulously with his board colleagues for grooming potential people who could succeed the current leadership so that the Public Enterprises Selection Board had a competent pool to select from. The talent review panels at various levels did so for successors to business heads, regional heads and territory managers too, taking full advantage of Shrikant's integrated career development framework, identifying and training people. They were sent for top global leadership programmes and given exposure to the board for which they had to make presentations. It helped them grow in confidence and learn how to handle the board. The target was to ensure a sufficient talent pool for clear succession.

In his 'will do, can do' approach, he found inspiration from his father's fauji spirit that taught him not to waste time asking irrelevant questions but resolutely doing things that clearly had to be done, whether it was taking on the implementation of SAP or obstinate unions or selling lubricants. He also read a great deal about the thoughts of powerful and even spiritual thinkers. Among the training programmes that BPCL sent him for, was a life-shaping one by Prof. S.K. Chakravarty on spirituality in management at IIM Calcutta's Centre for Human Values. It provided him with a powerful mental framework through an amazing experience; in a situation with no telephone or television and having to spend time with oneself; it was a little bit like Vipassana, focused on silence and self-study to help one turn inwards. It was a great source of personal empowerment for Shrikant, who realized that

India's contribution to the science of management was through the spiritual route.

Shrikant supplemented it with alone time during his early solitary morning walks and meditation, and brought much of these internal learnings to his workplace. There is so much inside that evades exploration but the more one does so, plunging the depths of spirituality, as it were, the more lasting the learning becomes. For HR, it was always critical to place people at centre stage and serve as a vehicle to guide their success without ever making HR or its head the centre point. Even today, people call him for his counsel and his approach remains the same; placing them in front of a mirror as it were and guiding them towards sounder decision-making about issues that are bothering them. Post retirement, he continues to share his wisdom with company boards as they shape their people's policies and programmes.

Facilitating sound decision-making is what energizes him as do his inner motivations. A competency assessment exercise gave him a 99 per cent+ on achievement motivation, which can push someone to extremes, but Shrikant's spiritualism has mellowed this. The rest was about doing what the hour demanded, backing it with his full might without ever trying to put 'brand Shrikant' forward.

* * *

Sridhar Ganesh

The HR Superstar

Sharing his wisdom, helping people realize their full potential in business and community

Managing director and CEO, Adrenaline Systems Limited from 2017 to 2021, Sridhar Ganesh (Sridhar) headed HR at Cadbury India and, later, HR in the Africa–India–Middle East region for Cadbury Schweppes Plc. He was director, learning and development, EMEA, managing Cadbury's L&D across businesses in Europe, the Middle East and Africa. Returning to India, Sridhar, for nearly seven years, led the HR function as group director HR in the Murugappa Group and as lead director for this diversified group.

An alumnus of IIM Calcutta, post his innings with Murugappa Group, Sridhar worked as professor in strategy in Loyola Institute of Business Administration, Chennai, sharing his vast experiences as a business leader with young MBA students. With specialization in business strategy, leadership development and presence and communications, coaching leaders for business roles continues to be his passion. For the Calcutta boy, a people's person who ventured to Bombay and the UK, life is coming full circle, in his home city, Chennai, trying to give back to society by helping special children with their livelihoods, teaching English to children in Tiruvannamalai and contributing to other social causes.

Sridhar Ganesh was born in Calcutta. The hub of managing agency houses and top engineering firms, Calcutta of the fifties and sixties was a great place to be growing up in, particularly if one's father served with such a firm. Things were pukka for the child, with a chauffeur-driven Morris and all the frills of the plush 'boxwalla' culture that defined corporate life. As purchase manager, Braithwaite, his father was a man of stature within the community and the secretary of the well-regarded National High School in South Calcutta that Sridhar attended. Growing up was joyful, especially as the sixth of seven siblings with a role model in his big and strong eldest brother, who was an oarsman at the rowing club on the Dhakuria Lake and a cricketer to boot. His sister's Enid Blyton collection brought familiarity with the English language and the cosmopolitanism of his environment was making him a well-rounded person; something that would be immensely helpful in professional life. Then tragedy struck.

His father's death was a cataclysm devastating his mother and leaving the children in a state of upheaval. The tragedy created a great bond though, and collectively engaging with a world that had literally come crumbling down, especially for his mother, deepened the fraternal feeling between the siblings. His older sister, then twenty, made her three younger brothers her little charge. Finances were not entirely strained because of his father's pension. There was a house in Chennai that was sold to enhance the family coffers but frugality had come to stay. The eldest brother was employed by Braithwaite and sent for a two-year stint in the UK. Sridhar realized that he had to fend for himself and life would henceforth be about second-hand books, self-reliance, hard work, resilience and living within one's means. These became his subconscious mantras.

Sridhar was interested in history and geography but loved science, getting through school with a high second class (a first-class in Calcutta was not easy to come by in those days). Maths was not the favourite subject though 80-85 per cent was par for the course for the family that focused on academics. Home, at Jatin Das Road near Triangular Park in South Calcutta, was a three-room affair—no designated bedrooms, dining or drawing room—with vegetarian fare but no great disciplinary demands. There was childlike joy in playing gilly danda (stick and stone), pittu (seven tiles), kabaddi and cricket (batting, not bowling), the standard fare in most Indian neighbourhoods and getting all starry-eyed with Park Street. A visit there was like going to 'England' because Park Street of yore was as impressive as European cities. Going there meant dressing up for the occasion while wondering if one was meeting sartorial standards. Sridhar yearned for a St Xavier's blazer for his college fest but his sister did not have the resources.

Sridhar's heart was on doing medicine but he did not have the qualifying marks. The boy, whose hero was Edison, settled for science at St Xavier's. More than academics, he was drawn by the outstanding French-Belgian Jesuits, whose humility and dedication deeply impacted him. He visited them in their private chambers occasionally and felt elevated; as if he was with a Nobel laureate, awed by their exemplary discipline and simple living. Academically, Sridhar managed to get an average of 60 per cent over the three-year degree course and made an abortive bid for MSc in physics. He did not understand the subject and was a man in search of a future when he heard about IIM Calcutta. With four or five friends, Shridhar prepared for the entrance examination and cleared it, to embark on an exciting and novel learning experience with a batch of ninety-odd students. The IIT Madras graduates did remarkably well in all quantitative subjects and the non-engineers got coached by other A-grade students. Faculty adviser, the charming Prof. Kamini Adhikari, with her perfect English accent, taught organization and administration, and Shridhar had the privilege of her mentorship, discussing various models and even doing a summer project under her.

Sridhar's batchmates fancied sales, marketing or operations, as did his older brother, a senior marketing professional in Brooke

Bond (now a part of Hindustan Unilever) who was nudging him to follow in his footsteps. Sridhar was fascinated by other subjects and heavyweights such as professors Gouranga P. Chattopadhyay who taught transactional analysis, the much-travelled Nitish De who taught personality development and was referred to by the likes of Indira Gandhi, and Mohan Kumara Mangalam. Nitish De posted reports on his work with the public sector on the faculty notice board and Mrityunjay Athreya posted his generally dissenting response. Such high-calibre professors influenced Sridhar to go in for HR. He had the knack for building relationships, easily relating to those coming from south India, speaking Tamil, Bengali and English with ease. He became the 'Placement Rep' for the institute and a much-sought-after person by his classmates, particularly in the final year.

This distinctive positioning among students served as a confidence-booster, as Sridhar dined with the prospective employers as the intermediary for the students. He ended up impressing some who made him job offers and Sridhar settled for the multinational engineering firm GKW, because it was Kolkata-based and offered a princely Rs 900 a month. A caring and nurturing boss, D.V. Kapoor, head of training, made it worthwhile. His classmates went into flashier marketing roles and pulled his leg but Sridhar had found his métier. When Arun Banerjee, head of forgings at GKW, asked him to do a team-building workshop to get the quality and production people in the thirty-five to forty age group to become more cohesive, Sridhar applied his learning of the Johari Window on real people. He ran a well-regarded programme at the Kenilworth Hotel, addressing a session on self-image vis-à-vis others, for colleagues in quality and production. Over an engaging heuristic exercise, he helped them jointly plan a way ahead. Deeply appreciative of his programme, Banerjee renamed the Johari Window as the Sridhar Window. Kapoor, his boss, was a very happy man. Sridhar went on to design a series of initiatives for junior management training programmes as well. In his programmes, subjects were distinguishing between attitudes and behaviour, establishing the relationship between the two; the art of winning respect and trust; leadership behaviour; giving an excellent account of himself even while learning the ropes. Then came a tough but distinguished assignment as executive assistant to the chief general manager, personnel, Nirmal Guha Roy, for a 'three-year wage settlement' with the unions. Sridhar was grateful for his maths, as he carried out innumerable permutations and combinations manually for a whole year in a world without computers. The unions thought he was an important man and came fishing for information. The real reward was coming close to Guha Roy, 'a man from the old school and gentleman to the core; well-mannered, soft-spoken with a keen business focus'. Guha Roy took a keen interest in Sridhar, coming over for chats about his career, issues in HR, leadership for business, employee relations, productivity and costs, among others, that Sridhar found energizing and perspective-building. He preferred the softer side of HR work but Guha Roy pushed him to develop IR competencies for well-rounded career development. Sridhar's reward for a job well done was being assigned as IR officer at the dreaded Currie Road factory, part of the Sankey Pressing Precision Division, with its militant unions and troubled IR history. Eyebrows went up when the young man was sent there, but Guha Roy mentored him as he went through the paces, literally shaping him for an IR career, demonstrating great faith in his competence and driving him on, without saying as much.

The twenty-three-year-old had not seen more acrimonious people, 1100 strong and prone to violence. His boss there was D.P. Ray, who sat in an air-conditioned cabin, while he had a cabin with a fan, handling complaints of every kind. He observed Ray handle difficult situations and thought that he would have dealt with them differently because he had picked up interesting cues from the line managers. A colleague in the IR department, around forty years of age, who had been angling for his job, gave him a testing time, escalating issues relating to the quality of food, uniforms, wages, PF loans and such others, essentially to give him a hard time! One worker turned up, as Sridhar recounts, bare-bodied wearing pantaloons of sorts, held up with a string, probably just to irk him.

Another workman seeking a loan from his PF account had a transforming impact on Sridhar. He dismissed the loan-seeker for being ineligible, having claimed the privilege the previous year, but the union leader, Ajit Kundu, barely five feet tall, confronted him with a question: 'Is it your job only to tell him that he is not eligible or, as a qualified man, to find a solution?' This very powerful question disturbed Sridhar about the bigger purpose of his role and, indeed, life. Kundu had taught him to look within; something that would guide him throughout his life. Other learnings came from the industry-based extracurriculars such as inter-corporate management talent (young managers) competitions by the All India Management Association (AIMA). Sridhar and a couple of colleagues represented GKW and won the AIMA Young Manager Award. They went on to win at the regional level at Patna but agonizingly lost in the finals to Metal Box and Abbott Laboratories. Sridhar learnt to face disappointments and take them in his stride. Life looked up as Sridhar got married and got an offer from the Sundaram Clayton (TVS group) in Madras with the carrot of a two-wheeler! Guha Roy advised him against it because TVS would be too much of a culture shock for him. He would have to remove his shoes if he went to see the big boss and attend pujas, something that was alien to the corporate culture that Sridhar was accustomed to. Sridhar heeded the advice and everyone was happy, even the testy colleague, who realized that Sridhar was good at handling the irate unions. He also had a knack of making friends with the workers on the shop floor and got to know what was afoot.

Meanwhile, Arabinda Ray, formerly with Metal Box, had taken over as the managing director of GKW's steel business, and noticed him at a training event. Sridhar was asked to do a manpower planning assignment for the Indian Institute of Packaging at Mumbai. He did it with aplomb and won the industry's recognition, along with a job offer from Metal Box. Sridhar switched jobs, going on to Metal Box as assistant personnel manager for the metals unit in the densely industrialized Hide Road area, where C.D. Menon was the personnel director. Metal Box was a bigger company with 2100 employees and his fondest hope was that his life in the morning would not begin with dealing with the likes of scantily-attired workers. The management was more sophisticated and its perks way better. Culturally, there was more of the boxwallah than the hard-nosed engineering GKW. Sridhar got a Rs 28,000 loan to buy a car (as opposed to Sundaram's offer of a two-wheeler) and was surely moving up in life! His daily commute was upgraded from a staff bus (in GKW) to a carpool but the unions were worse and the days far more stressful. Handling this real kettle of fish needed great patience and manipulative skills, the unions having got away with indiscipline, impertinence and impudence. They were saucy at best; vulgar at worst and always devoid of respect. Sridhar handled the challenge with great dexterity between 1978 and 1984, having mastered the art of getting the unions to agree to produce more without being begged for it and addressing rampant insubordination. Union members going to the senior manager, refusing to do something, were called out as Sridhar engaged with them on behavioural issues. Humility was a matter of pride and not shame he said, as he addressed their social life ethos and the different ethos that they brought to the workplace. In the process, he got insights into value systems that differed from his and learnt to deal with them with courage. Sridhar was becoming a gutsy IR man, displaying raw courage and becoming a hardened individual when it came to things patently unacceptable. Not only did he gain in self-confidence, the experience also widened his perspective on how the quality of engagement reflects on productivity at the shop floor; what succeeds and what fails. Sridhar had experienced both.

Some union actions were patently mischievous. Sushil Acharekar, his works manager, called him at 6 one morning to say that work in the 700-strong morning shift had not started because the unions were protesting the small-sized rasgulla served in the canteen for breakfast. They demanded a 'due slip'—a document of promise to make good the size on a subsequent day! Sridhar was there by 7 a.m. and took a hard line of 'no work; no pay'; his self-assurance conveying to the unions that he would brook no nonsense. Once they realized that he was quite unruffled by their shenanigans, the workers returned to work and Sridhar scored big time. After a four-year stint at the metals unit, Sridhar became the personnel manager at the Paper and Plastics unit, in fulfilment of a long-cherished ambition. A smaller unit with about 300-odd workers, it was beset with more acute challenges of productivity and business profitability, giving Sridhar a different experience, more insights into business and the role of costs and productivity in shaping margins and profits.

The competitiveness of the unit remained a challenge, but its IR issues were somewhat under control when Sridhar was called by the director personnel, Menon, to move to the head office as the management development manager. He would now review and revamp the job evaluation of senior roles as the business context had changed considerably from the last evaluation. Sridhar was deputed to learn and be trained by Hay MSL, the UK consulting firm and returned to refine the existing Hay Evaluation of some jobs in Metal Box. However, the promise of the role did not materialize because Metal Box was going through difficult business challenges, leading to a pervading sense of negativity across the company. Sridhar sensed this early and looked for options, initially taking up the Jenson and Nicholson—the paint company with an iconic tag line, 'Whenever you see colour, think of us'—position as staff and development manager. Shortly after, he met Biji Kurien, the charming managing director of Berger Paints, at a seminar at IIMC, Joka and, in 1985, at around thirty-four years of age, Sridhar became head of HR at Berger Paints (general personnel manager) with an air-conditioned car, a telephone and club membership to boot! Life's ambitions seemed to be getting fulfilled. Subir Bose, a 1974 IIMA graduate, was the general sales manager in a great peer group , considered to be the change leaders. Sridhar served there for seven years, getting a better understanding of the business. He got inspired, and had the humility to be mentored at times by Rehana Haq, a 1980 XLRI graduate, who was manager, staff training. Rehana showed him the way to process work and soon Sridhar completed his professional training with Indian Society for Individual and Social Development (ISISD) under the leadership of Pulin Garg and Indira Parikh.

Then came the seven-year itch and the lure of a job with Cadbury's. The star attraction was the brand. The conversation with Aroon Joshi, the HR chief, was just as significant as was the discussion with C.Y. Pal, chairman and MD. Both envisaged a 'management and leadership development oriented' role for him, with little to do with IR. In late 1992, Cadbury's had both chocolates and ice creams (Dollops) as part of its portfolio; another big attraction! The reality was very different. Sridhar's first assignment was to manage a Voluntary Retirement Scheme (VRS) scheme for Cadbury's Thane factory, paring down 200 of nearly 2000 people. The challenge was compounded by the resignation of the general manager-IR for having been passed over for the job. His hope of taking over from Joshi had been belied. These were not promising circumstances for Sridhar because downsizing in principle went against his grain. It was also paradoxical that while he was trying to engage with the business, his primary focus was on disengagement of a large number from what was considered the mother factory!

The second time around, it was to shut down Cadbury's ice cream business, under the brand name Dollops. Frustrated at the turn of events, Sridhar even reached out to his professional friend, Ivan Mathias, then heading HR in Shaw Wallace, for a job. Jayanti, his wife, told him that it would not behoove him to quit the company and that he should face up to the task and challenge.

Yet, there was a lot troubling him about Cadbury's amidst a rumour that the company was shifting its base to Delhi. A sense of uncertainty pervaded the air and the initial years were made more challenging with the unions labelling him as someone who had come to close factories. The unions complained to his predecessor Aroon Joshi, about a Madrasi, unlike Joshi, being unsuited for the job. They did not realize that Sridhar had had his IR baptism in Kolkata where the unions had given him all the training that he would need. Sridhar was relieved that he had handled the VRS competently. In the midst of these unsettling conditions, Sridhar completed his professional accreditation with the ISISD, a unique experience challenging his beliefs, questioning his 'shoulds' and 'should nots' as he was made to come to terms with himself in his totality by Pulin Garg, one of the ISISD founders. Garg was reputed to be a terror and extremely difficult to get along with. Sridhar was not spared the agonies of learning with him but came out with deep reverence for the man. Garg played a huge role in his understanding of what 'being human', and all that came with it, meant. He challenged Sridhar to examine issues around his self-beliefs and his needs for autonomy, goading him to go beyond his reactive self and deal with his challenges. It was painful and confusing and Sridhar wanted to withdraw, overcome by bouts of self-pity and tears, feeling that he could not take all this any more. He persisted for three years to complete his professional membership, did a few other labs in between, wrote almost forty pages of review and earned his membership, to his abiding delight. Sridhar considers Garg among the most significant influences on his life; a coach, not classical in style, but a human being with all his idiosyncrasies, driving Sridhar to relentlessly explore and find newer meanings to himself. He came to the realization: 'I am this and more.'

Back at Cadbury's, the boss from Cadbury's UK, Neil Hawkins, gave Sridhar a pat on his back for his work on the VRS at the Thane factory accomplished with minimal blood-letting and without disrupting relationships with both unions and the workmen. Hawkins was clearly fond of his Indian head of HR, spending considerable time discussing VRS and other matters with him. The importance that this gave Sridhar within the company was another confidence-booster. In any event, he had good equations with his colleagues, Rajeev Bakshi, head of marketing; Niraj Goyal, head of operations and Deepak Sethi, head of sales, who were supportive of HR. More than anything else, there was a sense of bonding and working together. At home, his wife was a constant source of encouragement. Thus fortified by his personal conviction, boss's confidence, supportive peers, he fed his gleanings back to himself and realized that he was 'seen as a decent guy', helpful and not into politics. Sridhar's innate humanity came to the fore during the bomb blasts in Mumbai, when he was the last to leave the office, taking six colleagues back with him, dropping them home in his Contessa. It was his Calcutta (now Kolkata) background that gave him the inner conviction that every challenge can be met if one is prepared to put in one's best.

Within Cadbury's, Sridhar initiated several changes in processes and practices to humanize the workplace after the VRS bruises. The use of a formal performance management system to measure employee contribution (performance) in relation to one's goals was the first major change that Sridhar introduced. A.F. Ferguson, with Anita Ramachandran as its head, was brought in as consultants to work on a formal job evaluation system. UK helped him initiate many other progressive measures, including an accelerated development programme, offering training outside India for young managers and building a new organizational culture that was more open and transparent. Cadbury's soon assumed a young look, thanks to the young management team and marketing and sales talent being recruited from the IIMs. It also had an expat managing director and finance head. The second VRS became much easier to handle as young professionals came to the fore—Sharad Gangal, Harsh Bhosale, K.S. Harish, Raju Nalbalwar, Kanika Sagar, Somna Singh and V.J. Rao, were in his team around 1995 and Cadbury's was doing well as an organization. The marketing efforts started to bear fruit and the Dairy Milk cricket advertisement with Shimona in the lead was a runaway success. Creating his new team became one of Sridhar's most satisfying achievements. Rajiv Bakshi had taken over as managing director and sought to open up Sridhar's sphere of operations. He asked him to handle exports to Bangladesh and Sri Lanka; the latter was a tough ask. Head of operations, Niraj, was tasked with overseeing the northern region as the company wanted everybody to have a customer-facing target. It was suggested that he should take on line responsibility, which was the route to becoming the CEO. Sridhar was clear that he wanted to support line managers to become CEOs; was proud of his function, and HR was not a support function but critical to organizational growth. Nevertheless, the export challenge was a great teacher. Addressing an unfamiliar terrain needed great sensitivity and understanding that he would only acquire with time. His Sri Lanka campaign boomeranged because he had Indian, bindi-wearing models for the advertisements there, which did not resonate with the Singhala culture. Another major lesson among many was around managing discount-seeking distributors and customers with different mindsets about profitability. Everything was about learning and getting HR insights. Sridhar travelled, explored different cultures and learnt a lot about their uniqueness and the similarities, coming to the conclusion that people are not all that different across the world.

After another seven years, Sridhar was contemplating his future in the hierarchy and realized that he should have responsibilities beyond India. He made an impressive HR presentation on challenges and the way forward to the supervisory director and got an international assignment in 2000. He had an interesting offer from the Murugappa Group in Chennai as group director HR too, but the opportunity to work overseas was more exciting. The Cadbury's UK job was a challenging one as director HR for Africa, India and the Middle East, based in Birmingham in the UK. The India portfolio remained with him for some time, till Radha Menon took it over. Sridhar was then made the L&D head for Europe (Ireland and UK were not part of Europe for the business), Africa and the Middle East. Sridhar loved L&D but, beyond a point, the role and assignment ceased to be engaging because it was difficult to create an impact long-distance, particularly in learning, when follow-ups became challenging. It was one thing, having a concept to share but quite another if one did not have the wherewithal to make it happen. Sridhar reflected and wondered how to shape thinking in remote markets or impact the culture of the management team. These challenges affected Sridhar's effectiveness, but the UK tenure also taught him many things both personal and professional. He recognized the power of thinking and planning before doing. The focus on outputs as distinct from inputs and, of course, personal discipline in leading one's life independently were great learnings. At another level though, he felt HR as practised in India was perhaps deeper and people-centred, as opposed to being systems-centred with people connect at a discount.

By 2004–05, Sridhar was longing to come back, when Sarosh Kuruvilla, husband of Rehana, Sridhar's colleague in Berger Paints, put in a word to M.M. Venkatachalam of the Murugappa group. This was the same offer that Sridhar had turned down prior to going to the UK. He was invited to meet A. Vellayan, followed by several meetings, a chat with the corporate board members and the endearing chairman, M.A. Alagappan. Sridhar was offered the role as the group HR director. It suited him because his elder brother and sister were in the same city and he knew the language, though he had fears about how he would be received in India. He need not have worried, for it was like homecoming with chairman Alagappan warmly welcoming him and helping him settle in. It was an unforgettable experience. Sridhar was presented with a larger corporate role and shifted gears from managing only single-company operations to those of a $5-billion group with several units and a strong brand. Murugappa also had several big CEOs, each very powerful and autonomous but was on an even keel with no great emergencies, save for day-to-day transactional issues.

Sridhar turned his attention to value addition, focusing on the difference that he could make. Murugappa's values and beliefs were of 1970s vintage and, as his boss suggested, they had to be contemporized. The idea was strongly supported by N.S. Raghavan, founder–director of Infosys, who served on the Murugappa corporate board. Companies do well to consider values and beliefs when times are good and look within to ask what they stood for. Sridhar went through the exercise and came out with the Five Lights imagery values, encapsulated in an O&M video on the Murugappa group. The values exercise energized Sridhar and he found it a great vehicle to reach people across the group. Another big initiative was the digitization of the performance management process across the group senior management. Moving from a paper-based process to a digital system called for support in terms of education and hand-holding. Every bit was centrally orchestrated and became the standard process for the group to follow.

The Management Development Centre received an impetus through a business leadership programme run in partnership with IIM Bangalore. It was a source of great satisfaction at the programme level, but Sridhar believed that it could be more effectively leveraged, given its potential to support the talent pipeline. As a trained coach, who had conducted many 'Growing our People' programmes at Cadbury Schweppes, Sridhar saw the opportunity to introduce a similar theme here with many managers trained over a series of two-day programmes. In partnership with the Coaching Foundation of India, Sridhar had many HR leaders accredited as coaches to support their business needs. The competency framework received a relook and a new set of competencies for various levels was drawn up and launched, giving him great satisfaction despite some failures.

The group adopted a formal career development process and competency-based assessments to grow the middle managers. These involved self-assessment and 360° feedback along with a personal development plan. Great attention was also paid to employee communication, engagement and digitization, though 'coaching' did not take off. It continued to be an unfinished agenda. Sridhar was personally very conscious of the difference that individuals made at the workplace and set clear priorities for all. He delegated work down the line to capable young professionals who were taught to gain 'clarity of purpose' and did not get involved when he thought that things could be handled at the local level.

Between February 2007 and December 2013, Sridhar had done another seven-year stint, as Murugappa's group director, HR; the last two under a new chairman, who was more of a 'day-to-day' man. Sridhar liked working over a perspective, feeling uncomfortable with a myopic approach to HR. He had the likes of Anand Mahindra talking to the company's leadership team about 'purpose'. The talk was much admired and an attempt was made to internalize it through vision workshops. Sridhar's Indian company experience was turning out to be rewarding. He had autonomy and professional freedom that he had not experienced before. The leadership of individual companies and the directions they set for themselves was another process that Sridhar admired. At a personal level, relationships with his team and employees across the group were fulfilling, but Sridhar wanted to quit at the end of his contractual period. An offer from the Loyola Institute of Business Administration in October 2013, to be professor, strategic HR, OB and chairperson of its Management Development Centre provided an interesting interlude after a lifetime in the corporate world. After a four-year stint, he moved on, taking over as the managing director and CEO of the Chennai-based Adrenalin Systems Limited in December 2017. As the GKW management trainee stepped into the MD's shoes, it was a satisfying feeling.

As he approached the end of his stint here, Sridhar focused on wider areas of knowledge; reading the Bhagavad Gita, for instance, while keeping up the practice of meeting and connecting with people. He has taken up mentoring both at a functional level as well as young managers across industry. Life's fascinating experiences have been too compelling not to share, and Sridhar has put pen to paper and written two books: *Reflections on Mindsets, Leadership and Personal Change* and *The HR Superstar*. Meeting people, factory visits, sitting with unit heads and helping them formalize their own 'challenges' are what interest him. Coaching leaders for business roles continues to be a passion. He is equally passionate about social causes, helping special children with livelihood options by producing gift items and selling them to corporates, teaching English to children in Tiruvannamalai, among others.

For the people's person, a Calcutta boy who ventured to Bombay and the UK life is coming full circle, back to the land of his mother tongue, trying to give back to the society that built him.

* * *

Vineet Kaul

Vineepedia

Inspiring people with his unmatched perspective of labour laws and personal connect with the who's who of corporate India

Vineet Kaul (Vineet), after over a decade-long tenure comprising the first seven years as CHRO of Metal Sector/Hindalco followed by three years as

adviser to Group HR in the Aditya Birla Group, is currently adviser for the newly established School of Management by Birla Institute of Technology (BITSoM). As Hindalco's chief HR officer, he led the global HR function for the $18-billion metal business of the Aditya Birla Group, with a workforce of 36,000 employees, including 11,000 based outside India. He also set up a Shared Services Centre (SSC), talent councils, and achieved HR process excellence and HR audit for the group. Earlier, with Philips India as executive director and vice president, HR—Indian Subcontinent, he led such change initiatives as restructuring of businesses, managing a paradigm shift in people processes, setting up a software development company in Bangalore and a shared services unit in Chennai for Philips' global operations. Vineet was appointed to the Philips India board and inducted into its Global HR Council.

Vineet did his master's in social work from M.S. University, Baroda and started his career as a management trainee with Tata Motors, working in various roles across the personnel function. Later, he joined Eicher Motors as chief of HR and TQM, and led initiatives on total employee involvement and quality that were adopted across group companies. He introduced workers' training at Mitsubishi factories that helped them imbibe good work practices and culture. Vineet has also served as president of the Employers Federation of India. Besides, he won the HR Excellence Award of the National HRD Network and was recognized as the Best HR Professional by the Centre for Industrial Relations and Social Development. He was on the CII National Committee for HR and IR 2004 and the President, Mumbai Chapter, National HRD Network 2000.

A Kashmiri mathematician with an interest in music, Som Nath Kaul, taught in several schools in pre-Partition India, giving his son Vineet wondrously varied schooling—from a primary school for the underprivileged (because Som Nath liked the devoted Christian lady who ran it); followed by the army-run King George's School (military school) at Belgaum from class V. Vineet, born in Srinagar in 1955 and lived in Belgaum from 1957, was socially at ease with friends from both elite and army families. He was delighted with King George's that had three football grounds, two cricket grounds, four hockey grounds, one swimming pool, two basketball courts, three courts for volleyball, tennis and squash for a school of 360 children and did well in sports, apart from excelling in public speaking and winning awards for general knowledge. Things changed dramatically with his father's deputation to Khadakwasla for two years, where Vineet found himself at a Hindi medium Kendriya Vidyalaya, though he wrote his exams in English.

For the rest, he ran the eight-kilometre cross-country, was a good bowler in cricket, played reasonable volleyball and felt proud to see his father perform on stage. The once every-two-year visit to Kashmir, changing trains thrice and then taking a bus added colour to an interesting childhood that was enriched by avid reading. Vineet developed a yen for history, literature and economics; all horizon-expanding experiences, as life itself injected flexibility and adaptability into his persona. A 90 per cent at the All-India General Knowledge Test and an 80 per cent at the UNO's won him plaudits. His principal, impressed with his talk on the UN, asked him to present a news bulletin every day. This meant listening to the news every evening, referring to newspapers and preparing a bulletin for school the next day. It was a well-rounded boy who completed class XI.

His brothers had chosen their careers; the eldest graduated from Fergusson and the second was doing engineering in Hubli, close to Belgaum. They lived in a hostel, which cost his father a pretty penny. Yet, when Vineet wanted to go to Fergusson too, Som Nath agreed, despite the expenses. He took early retirement at fifty to access his provident fund and gratuity, which he used to finance his children's studies. Vineet realized this great sacrifice of quitting a government job to educate his sons.

Three years at a hostel pursuing graduation with honours at Fergusson opened up newer vistas. Eating chapattis made of Milo, coming under PL 480 grants from the US in India's ship-to-mouth era, free time after 8–11 a.m. classes, diverse friends from Pune to a Bangladeshi boy, raising funds for Bangladesh's freedom struggle, representing his university in ball-badminton at an inter-university tournament in Kerala (discovering that the girl shuttlers from other teams were better) and delving deep into Maharashtra's agrarian society for an NSS project were vista-widening exposures. An ebullient Vineet emerged as a natural leader, protesting against unfair practices and leading the students' agitation to have the hostel fee hike withdrawn; not by aggression but by dialogue. Vineet was getting into politics, first winning a position at the college gymkhana elections and emerging on the wider stage—the National Student Union of India. As a member of the newly-formed executive committee for Pune, he mingled with the likes of Priya Ranjan Dasmunsi, the Youth Congress president, held discussions around the position propagated by the Akhil Bharatiya Vidyarthi Parishad and Marxist thinking, becoming a public speaker in the process and getting reported in the media.

Lessons and exams often took a back seat as Vineet gradually turned anti-establishment. The JP movement, the influence of Rashtriya Swayamsevak Sangh (RSS) leaders, attending the All India Student Leaders Conference in Delhi in January 1974, meeting the flamboyant Arun Jaitley, who was managing the conference, Ravi Shankar Prasad, Laloo Prasad Yadav and many such from universities across India, made for fascinating perspective-building. Secret meetings with the intelligence wing on their tail, friends telling him that he was crazy, prompted him to confess to his father about his activities. Som Nath advised his son to do what he thought was right!

Feisty in his protests against wrongs, Vineet and a few friends reported a leaked question paper to the vice chancellor of the university in 1974. When no action followed, they went to the *Maharashtra Herald* and handed over the leaked question paper for the next day. The paper flashed it, keeping the source anonymous. The examinations were cancelled and rescheduled. Some guessed the source and such colourful doings made him rather popular. After graduation, he went to Baroda, where his family had moved, keen on doing simultaneous master's in political science and law. The University Grants Commission (UGC) did not permit enrolment for two courses. Vineet walked up to the VC when he was stepping out of his car and presented the problem. Taken aback to be thus accosted, the VC said that he could do nothing about the UGC rules. Vineet settled for a master's programme in social work, with a specialization in labour welfare and personnel management at the Faculty of Social Work, Baroda, in a class of about thirty-seven to thirty-eight. Far less cosmopolitan than Fergusson, the college, however, followed the American system, supporting students in their fields of study with excellent in-house and visiting faculty.

The field work in the first year at a correctional school of 200 children resonated with his NSS social work. Understanding their case histories, engaging them in sports, taking them on outings and on their family visits, while trying to figure out how to rehabilitate them with normal families, meant a deep engagement with the socio-economics of the correctional homes. His past caught up with him when the local student leader recognized him from the Delhi meet. Word got around about his politics; also about his inherent honesty. Vineet did not refer to books even in open-book tests and a professor realized that he was the only student who did so. There were some unhappy brushes with the authorities and run-ins with rival groups too.

The second-year fieldwork took Vineet to Hindustan Brown Boveri (ABB), where an empowering personnel manager allowed him into meetings and exposed him to other industrialists at a community service project. Given his background, Vineet gave excellent advice and collected data on 1250 families over weekends, involving his friends and impressing everyone. The Brown Boveri CEO wrote to his dean in appreciation and made a job offer too. Vineet did well in his finals, standing second in the university and got shortlisted for a job with Telco (now Tata Motors) Pune in 1976. This was a new ball game and his first assignment involved recruiting 1000 people a month for supervisory and workman jobs for the new Telco lines. He had to identify them and organize interviews. His workday ran from 8.30 a.m. to 7 p.m., after which he screened applications. Vineet ensured that the candidates sitting outside had ceiling fans; having been one like them a couple of months ago, sitting on a cement bench without a fan.

Vineet was quick to detect that something was amiss about the process where twenty-five candidates appearing for technical operators' positions were made to do a lot of work in the factory. A dozen were shortlisted and only two got selected. The line managers were getting a lot of work done for free as trade tests and Vineet protested. Matters went up to his superiors for streamlining the process. He got exposed to more such corporate chicanery at the personnel/IR department. Telco, in 1976, had 2000 people at Chinchwad and around 3000 in Pimpri; the bonus was disputed by the union and hence handed over by the cashiers to the employees. Vineet became the cashier's smoking buddy and was allowed to sit in his room. He discovered to his dismay that everyone was scaling up the number of bonus takers on a particular day. More curious cases came to his plate: overcrowding in the canteen, lockers for the workers—when the lockers purchased exceeded the number of workmen!

Setting things right involved engaging with a lot of people but trying to reorganize the poorly-run canteen meant disruption. Vineet wanted the sambar–idli coming at the same time so that people did not drink up the sambar before the idli arrived and demand to be served again. This impacted work. The canteen staff were often inefficient and undisciplined. So resentful did some become of Vineet that they assaulted him in an unprecedented action. The offenders were suspended and the canteen workers retaliated by refusing to serve people on the shop floor, resulting in a strike. The administration initially resisted but finally withdrew the suspensions to settle issues. An upset Vineet promised to make the guilty pay and built up cases against the eleven assaulters. Over fifteen months, he had all eleven terminated with the orders upheld after three years in court. This was not about a personal vendetta but about instilling discipline. The canteen demanded all his creativity, especially when a cockroach was spied in the food, with eighty to ninety workmen staring at it. It could snowball into a big issue so Vineet calmly ate the cockroach, insisting that was just spice, before exiting and spitting it out. How he did it, he does not know, but with one's back to the wall, one innovated. There were innumerable such situations over the eleven and a half Telco years.

In 1977, a new union leadership wanted each worker to operate only one machine instead of three machines grouped together in the gears section, bringing work to a standstill on the issue. Vineet, as personnel officer, decided to take action and served charge sheets to seventy-three people on the machines. No one was suspended at first but, when suspensions started, there was a strike. Vineet was in the thick of things and matters were resolved with the Maharashtra government's intervention and adjudication. Vineet also kept watch on slack security guards and sleeping shift in-charges, hobnobbed with people at the community centres, got invited to popular gatherings and began to understand their ecosystem. In the process, he built a rapport with the union, the managers and with people at the individual level. He also worked well beyond his responsibilities in sorting out all kinds of problems with out-of-the-box solutions.

The auto division found it hard to get people to fit large tyres. Vineet looked around and learnt that major petrol pumps had skilled tyre puncture repairmen/fitters. He recruited seven or eight of them who were delighted to work for Telco. There were other complex issues when Telco Pune recruited some 950 ex-servicemen for the foundry and auto divisions; physically strong, disciplined and mature, given their twenty years of service. However, they got volatile and disruptive and even an ex-colonel, brought to head the divisional operations, could not manage the situation. Vineet quickly grasped the source of discontent, thanks to his schooling and having military studies as a subject in college. Army men were used to hierarchy; a JCO, an NCO, among others, resented Telco placing everyone at the same ex-servicemen grade. Vineet and his boss talked to them and figured out fresh fitments; moved the senior people into supervisory roles, used some as counsellors, some Air Force technical people were moved to quality control, some were moved to stores and white-collar jobs. Vineet learnt how intent and good moves got derailed by inadequate understanding of mindsets and ethos.

The Telco Pune HR boss, V.D. Mehrunkar, a gold medallist in economics, was a former deputy labour commissioner in Indore, who quit the government for industry. A risk-taker, he gave Vineet a long rope but instilled in him a respect for the law. His auto division line boss, V.M. Raval, was a tough, demanding man but Raval and Mehrunkar had an excellent rapport and exemplified excellence in the HR–line working relationship. Vineet spent time building relationships with operational managers and was, of course, on good terms with his peers, workmen and the unions, getting enmeshed into their culture and language. He shed his 'outsider' status to become the only non-Maharashtrian in the IR team. These were initial days for the new plant with productivity and efficiency as the desired outcomes and Vineet and his line colleagues had to work hard to get things going. Those were also the times when Data Samant was making an entry into Pune and Vineet and his colleagues strove to keep him at bay, counselling unions and telling people not to join external unions.

In hindsight, he believes that was wrong. He had a brush with Rajan Nair too, whom Telco had suspended. Around August 1987, Vineet had accepted a job with Birla Yamaha Limited as head of personnel, when Nair landed up at his house, saying that Vineet ought to stay back even though he had destroyed his happiness. Vineet never could figure out why Nair wanted him to stay. He moved on to Birla Yamaha, with 750 employees; tiny compared to Telco. It had one factory on the Dehradun–Haridwar Road and a marketing team in Delhi, but presented a culture shock for Vineet, who was reporting to the president. Things were in an instant whirl. The buck stopped with him at Birla Yamaha. The explosive Uttarakhand movement meant fending off groups demanding funds. Two presidents quit within a year and a half, local recruits had to be introduced to an 'industrial culture', while the local versus outsiders (people from the plains) animosity was an HR nightmare. Developing people processes, policies, building a work culture, training from the basics, supervisory development, building management and initiating a workforce value system made for terrific learnings. However, the remoteness of the location started gnawing at him. He felt isolated from professional associations.

A meeting with Eicher's Anil Sachdev (an ex-Telco colleague), prompted a move to Eicher Motors, Indore, the joint venture with Mitsubishi, with its subculture of excellence around productivity and quality. The ecosystem was invigorating with HR heads from different Eicher companies exchanging information, collectively focusing on people engagement and communication. An overseas training at Mitsubishi for quality saw his function expanding to both HR and quality management (TQM). He and his CEO, S. Sandilya, were both based at Pithampur and addressed the issue of an unsettled contingent of people transferred from Faridabad, and Vineet turned to Japanese solutions. Japan brought in Filipinos to overcome its manpower shortage and got them to conform to Japanese work culture. Eicher employees, sent to train at Mitsubishi's Kawasaki plant in Japan, returned motivated. Many of the learnings at Eicher Motors went into the creation of Eicher Consultancy Services (ECS).

Eicher Motors, of course, had its own HR ethos and ECS clients would spend a couple of days seeing how things were done there. The likes of Crompton, Cadbury's and Godrej spent one or two days at Eicher Motors, learning about the bonding of workmen with the Japanese single-mindedness of focus. Not meetings but presence on the shop floor, where Japanese production methods were actually practised, mattered. Vineet had an independent role and began to shape things, and revamped core HR processes such as performance management and compensation. Further, Indore's management association opened Vineet's world to other professionals. He felt stimulated. A couple of years later, Sandilya and the Japanese wanted him to take over as the manufacturing head. Even with his familiarity with the auto space and understanding of engineering, Vineet chickened out. That was an opportunity lost. Around this time, Vineet started getting giddy spells with a sharp drop in his haemoglobin count. He needed hospitalization to have it restored but there was no clear diagnosis.

It was 1994, and as per Eicher's policy of rotating its managers, Vineet was to move to a Bombay position with ECS. This did not materialize because Eicher Motors was not ready to release him and personal reasons prompted him to consider other offers. He chose Philips where he would head corporate HR, handling recruiting, compensation, training and HR administration at the head office, reporting to the director HR. Philips had eleven locations with two large clusters in Pune and Calcutta, and Vineet was effectively No. 2. ER/ IR were the HR Director Kris Ramchandran's responsibility. Times were complex; outside the Shivsagar Estate Philips office, a union banner screamed: 'Human Resources Destruction Department'. Inside were three floors occupied by an overmanned Philips with innumerable ER issues. Vineet was au fait with Philips' history and Ramchandran asked him to handle some 100 letters of complaints. He analysed them and shared his thoughts on remedial measures that were implemented immediately with some positive impact.

Vineet then plunged into addressing productivity issues but ran afoul of unions, who rushed to the authorities and courts at the drop of a hat. They even questioned Vineet's air-conditioned car (paid for by himself), in what Ramchandran called 'white collar terrorism'. After six months, 80 per cent of his job was to look after ER and IR for all eleven locations and Vineet started to tire out quickly. This time it was correctly diagnosed and he went through a major surgery. He survived an unnerving experience but was back into crisis management at Philips, which was losing out in the marketplace. In effect, Philips had stood still while the world moved on. Only unionized salaries mounted. Thanks to double DA linkage, their salaries escalated even without an increment, while an engineer's emolument remained at only 60–70 per cent of the pantry man's. The interfering unions objected to even managers having soup and sandwiches for lunch because the change of menu had no union sanction. Company transport ferried only the unionized staff, not the management. Addressing these issues meant getting abused. While Vineet felt physically and mentally shattered, he was too tough to take it lying down.

The sale of a unit to Videocon, which refused to take the entire manpower, was stymied with government institutions voting against the resolution at the AGM in Calcutta. To the media, Philips was a tainted multinational, alienating its assets and treating people like chattel. The truth got suppressed in the ongoing dialogue. Bengal's CPM government wanted Philips to continue these units despite inefficiencies and losses, and Vineet had a major brush with the Labour Minister. It took months of dialogue to get everybody around, including the Amsterdam headquarters that wondered why Philips was paying VRS to let go of people! The sale of the Shivsagar Estate office too got stuck because the union would not let go of its office there, which it claimed to own. Vineet tricked it out under the guise of office redesigning. All hell broke loose and the slogan-shouting union came to Vineet's house, ready to fight with him; but no law had been broken. Kris, the CEO, and Vineet created new locations for the back office (Vashi) transferring the excess manpower there and a front office (Andheri), where the required people were posted. Matters went right up to the Supreme Court, where Philips finally won the case.

Vineet's refusal to accept the tyranny of people got around and he was invited to workshops to share his experiences and learnings. He also got the Philips management to open through town hall dialogues with all 4000–4500 employees talking to the entire management once every four months. Vineet anchored live proceedings (webcast) over sixteen VSATs that his IT colleagues helped set up, achieving a major rapprochement over a year. Unanswered questions were addressed in a booklet within ten days; an effort commended by the media. The visiting global board was delighted to attend a session and wanted it to be replicated in Amsterdam. After years of bad press, Philips figured in the Hewitt Best Employer list. Vineet restructured job grading in line with group principles, rolled out a robust talent management process and revamped the L&D programmes. Such progressive work got Philips on the Best Employer list for two years. Its software campus got listed in Great Places to Work.

Some good intentions went awry though. Under the Defined Benefit Superannuation Scheme (DBSS), managers got about 75 per cent of the last drawn salary as pension. People became eligible at age forty-eight. Several companies had changed DBSS to Defined Contribution Superannuation Scheme (DCSS). Vineet worked with the actuaries but erred in the fine print, as he changed from DBSS to DCSS and secured 100 per cent consent of eligible employees. He had not bargained for any drop in interest rate, which caused considerable reductions in the pension benefit under DCSS. This was among his biggest blunders. In 2001, he addressed the case of surplus unionized employees earning twice as much as the engineers and worked out an excellent separation scheme. However, in the rush to close it, he overlooked a couple of words, cleverly put in by the union, conveying that discounting rates would apply though the computation was based on a frozen figure. The uncorrected version was mischievously announced by the union. Philips went to court to correct it and rebut allegations of wilful deceit. Its case was finally upheld at the tribunal level, subsequently at the high court and was followed by an out-of-court settlement.

Vineet's most important contributions were being part of the initial team for pathbreaking the Philips Innovation Campus, from which it continues to benefit, and setting up the Shared Services Centre (SSC) for finance, based on Scope International Pvt Ltd—the shared services centre of Standard Chartered bank in Chennai. The SSC brought forty-eight accounting centres to Chennai and impressed every global Philips CFO. Chennai developed into a 600-seat centre, covering Asia, Europe and the US. It had the entire global operation moving to India by 2005 and sold to Infosys at a whopping profit in 2006–07. As Vineet soaked up Philips' good global practices, he also got the global team to pick up Indian practices in learning, for example, sometimes blending the two systems. Philips' performance management system was global, for instance, but Vineet amended the six-grade job rating system by introducing two middle grades as was appropriate for Indian operations. He was in the forefront of business restructuring/divestments and acquisitions too. The management recognized his contribution and he was appointed to the Philips India board.

Vineet was on an autopilot mode in Philips, when he got a call from Santrupt Misra, HR director at the Aditya Birla Group, offering him a position in Hindalco, which had taken over Novelis. The prospect of managing a gigantic operation, sprawled over twenty locations in India, and four greenfield projects with an outlay of Rs 40,000 crore, was exciting. Vineet said yes and joined in 2008. On day 2 of the twenty-day induction, he was called in to 'observe' a discussion on a problematic unit, when he chipped in with two observations. Before he realized it, he was in the middle of an assignment under the managing director; his induction defenestrated. Hindalco's complexities were huge; its mother unit at Renukoot came up in 1961 but it had eight to ten acquired units and three or four companies. Their subcultures and strengths presented major integration challenges, compounded by diverse local conflicts in states like Orissa and Madhya Pradesh on the one hand and understanding leadership needs on the other. The leadership oversight and integration of Novelis into Hindalco and the group processes was enriching as Vineet worked through a change in the terms of the various business and functional heads' movements as per their requirements.

The enormity of the assignment—the metals business, which he was looking after, accounted for about 50 per cent of the group turnover—and the culture shift, given Hindalco's courtesy deficit, were forbidding. Though never humiliated personally, he was galled to see his colleagues being hauled up unceremoniously. He addressed it by enhancing delivery quality to obviate complaints, working fourteen hours a day, becoming more operational in his style, checking and double-checking everything, often with no value addition; only to maintain the credibility of his team and manage the expectations of leadership. Integration too ran into thick walls; Indal versus Hindalco, aluminium versus copper; with varying perks and compensations. Creating a seamlessly neutral structure took two years, as benefits from five different systems were rationalized into one. The integration and team-building with Novelis, with a global spread, took a few years. Vineet followed up by driving transparency through open dialogues and sharing market data to enable employees to understand how numbers were arrived at. He dealt with objections to such openness and was well-rewarded by improved engagement.

Alongside, Vineet created opportunities for senior people to visit different units and broadened their perspectives, keeping in mind the bigger roles envisaged for them. He personally handled senior-level recruitments even in remote locations that were riddled with local-level interference. There were leadership demands for appropriate manning on the projects on the one hand and the unemployability of locals on the other. Vineet got companies like People Strong and TMI to help with the bulk-hiring but handled senior recruitments internally.

Over enormously detailed planning, beginning with recruitments, preparing frameworks, manuals, working with local groups, project teams for local operations, including HR people for different units, Vineet prevailed. He built his own grapevine connect that, along with the formal channels of information, gave him early-warning signals of impending trouble. This is why he planned his day well—factoring in unexpected developments—completed his scheduled work and always created time to talk to people and international colleagues outside office hours. These conversations helped in bonding with colleagues, improved his information bank and often helped him hold his ground. He advised his teams never to yield ground when they were in the right. Over the years, he became a master of his craft and impacted professional bodies like CII and NHRDN. He also internalized knowledge from his interactions and the networks that he built, serving as president of NHRDN Mumbai. Vineet was felicitated as Seasoned HR Professional in 2012.

Multifaceted training, including visits to globally-best facilities, supported by D. Bhattacharya, his vice chairman and managing director, top technology, interesting practices picked from Novelis, cross-learnings from downstream organizations, even while encouraging independent initiatives and operations, comprised his challenging workday. There were special hurdles at project sites, local challenges, especially around greenfield projects with land losers, and governments and political parties getting involved. At Aditya Aluminium, Lapanga, in Jharsuguda, the locals complained, not quite truthfully, that they were not being hired. Vineet had to deal with an arrogant collector who wanted his officers to sit at interviews and offered other hare-brained schemes to manage local dissatisfaction to pre-empt a law and order problem. It took enormous patience to address the collector and the agitators, as Vineet convinced them that all employable people from their villages would be considered. At Silvassa, where manpower in the foils business had to be downsized, despite a seven-time MP locally calling the shots, he achieved the desired results.

The thirty-five-year-old Kalwa plant with a Datta Samant union had to be wound down due to business reasons. Vineet pulled it off with endless hours of negotiations, finally settling for a VRS. In three months, Vineet had everyone out but had to handle questions in the state assembly thereafter as the miffed local authorities felt outwitted. Different stakeholders had to be managed with tact and patience without ever breaking the law and Vineet knew how. However, such tactics failed while closing down a Telangana foil plant in 2013. A 1980s Supreme Court order disallowed Hyderabad factories within 10 km of the Himayat Sagar Lake, but companies got two-year NOCs and continued. Vineet notified that operations were being scaled down for want of an NOC and announced thereafter that the 230 employees would be transferred, after discussions with them. On the day the transfer letters were issued, however, people became violent. The plan backfired when the labour minister (with the home portfolio as well) in the new state of Telangana, a local trade-union strongman, issued a permanent NOC in writing. Vineet was stuck with a plant that the company did not want, which was subsequently sold as a going business.

Vineet mastered the art of tightrope-walking, managing people and egos in organizational interest and nurturing the HR team. He held periodic meetings, where some 160 people in various HR units met to share their learnings. He teamed up with colleagues at Novelis to ensure their success. Vineet started a monthly call with HR heads and teams through WebEx with everybody dialling in and an HR connect programme with line managers to enhance their understanding of HR processes and communicate the good that HR was doing. Alongside, Vineet started an online grievance system, whereby every grievance got logged, which was rolled out across the company. His theory was that organizations thrive on communicating good ideas and initiatives so that nothing got bottled up. It was just as important to have excellence recognized. Vineet started 'PRAISE', an initiative ensuring instant recognition from the manager and exposure for everyone getting praised, even in the remotest corners. Every employee was engaged in such initiatives as Vineet got people talking the HR language, finding excellent traction and appreciation.

While never holding people back if they found greener pastures, Vineet suffered heartaches of payroll paring, especially when employees were paying the price for market obsolescence. Sometimes, friends had to be sacked too, causing a different kind of discomfiture, but Vineet explained his reasons for the decisions. People sacked for misdemeanours were presented with the evidence before being released. At other times, as with Philips in Calcutta, he organized training programmes at the District Industrial Centre to empower the outgoing employees with new trade skills. He was firm in fighting white-collar terrorism or any exploitation of the management, though.

Pre-retirement, Vineet detached himself from the enormous space that he straddled. He had people in place for various functions and gave them time to settle in while he was in charge. However, the company asked him to stay on to help with group-level strategic initiatives and guiding business heads and CHROs. The upcoming telecom joint venture also needed guidance and kept Vineet busy for three years as adviser, group human resources. He called it a day in March 2019 after four decades and more of impacting HR in five leading Indian corporates. Post this stellar corporate career, Vineet is now busy setting up a world-class management institute serving as an adviser for the School of Management launched by Birla Institute of Technology (BITSoM).

In 2018–19, Vineet became the president of the Employers Federation of India and continues to be an HR adviser and a mentor to senior HR professionals and business leaders, over a wide canvas of human resource issues. For them, Vineet continues to be inspirational with his unmatched perspective of labour laws and personal connect with the who's who of corporate India that has won him the sobriquet of Vineepedia!

* * *

Visty Banaji

Leader on the road less travelled

Reading, researching, reflecting, and experimenting to discover newer answers rather than flowing with the current

Having spent around half a century in human resources, Visty Banaji's (Visty) contribution to the blue-chip companies that he served with is only matched by his contributions to enrich the profession. Beginning as a TAS officer in 1973 with the Tata Group, he worked with Telco (now Tata Motors) at its Pune complex, driving manpower planning at the corporate level in 1980 and then leading Telco's corporate HR function. After twenty-four years in Telco, Visty joined Alstom in India in 1997 as executive director (HR) and, later, on an international assignment in Paris as leader of Alstom's global project for reengineering key HR processes and supporting them through the deployment of a state-of-the-art HR management system. In February 2003, Visty joined Godrej Industries Limited as executive director and president of Group Corporate Affairs. He led corporate HR, strategy, corporate communications, legal functions and IT for Godrej Industries and associate companies till 2010. Visty left Godrej to start his own HR firm, Banner Global Consultancy, in March 2010.

Visty is a member of the CII National Committee on Skills and Human Resources and of the HR Committee of the Employers Federation of India, He received the Pathfinders Award 2006 for Seasoned HR Professional at the 10th National Conference of the National HRD Network. Visty was responsible for crafting a 'Fair Organization Code', following a discussion at the National HR Committee of CII that such a code could provide a starting point for any organization keen to create a bulwark against unfair or unscrupulous practices. A strong proponent of the rights of SCs, STs, the physically challenged, religious minorities and women in organizations, Visty also contributed in the development of NHRDN's HRScape, a comprehensive set of critical competencies for HR professionals covering technical and behavioural competencies.

Getting into the prestigious Tata Administrative Services (TAS), the management cadre of the Tata group at nineteen was a godsend for Visty Banaji. It also caught him unprepared. TAS had two yearly intakes at the time; the summer intakes were management graduates generally from the cream of the IIM pass-outs. The winter batch brought in the diversity; the graduates from top foreign universities like Cambridge and Stanford. Still a teenager in 1973, Visty was neither, having studied in Nagpur University's Hislop College for a bachelor's degree in literature, philosophy and psychology. The college was notorious, its wild students would even rough up the teachers and served as the playground for petty politicians and local thugs. Visty's fate was no different as he got into trouble, beaten up for standing up to the college toughies.

Both his school and college had, however, brought the NCC (Air Wing) to Visty and helped him learn to get along with people from very diverse backgrounds, giving him the rudiments of leadership, making him adept at swearing in a variety of languages and permitting him to indulge his love for flying and aircraft; traits that he assiduously cultivates even today, save for flying. What Visty brought to the table as a young joiner to TAS was a lifelong habit of taking on an impossible goal, the ability to think big and a penchant for rejecting established norms. As a young man, Visty was keen on science and set up a laboratory at home to conduct his own experiments.

Visty came from a middle-class family, the son of an Indian Airlines officer and a schoolteacher mother, who went on to become the principal of the J.N. Tata Parsi Girls High School, where Visty studied because it allowed boys till class seven. He went to the St Francis de Sales High School, Nagpur thereafter. His mother was a big influence in his school days but gave him the freedom to choose his subjects in school and college, his profession and his life partner. Intra and inter-school elocution contests, as well as the NCC, transformed Visty from a very shy, reserved child to one able to mix and speak his mind in larger gatherings. This had long-term lessons, the key one being that one could overcome innate traits like shyness. Also that, even as a leader, one should be able to do the toughest physically demanding jobs oneself.

NCC also provided him with a continuing practical challenge to lead mostly older people without having any real authority over them. Visty studied science enthusiastically till class IX, was keen on qualifying for the National Talent Search Scholarship and experimented in his home laboratory. He was (and is) interested in blowing things up and managed to produce acetylene in the lab, a combustible gas, and set fire to it. The explosion could have been fatal but he continued his pursuit, reading his elder brother's science textbooks. He asked a scientist in the neighbourhood college for a project to do and he found that he was given a project that was quite a boring one. Visty saw the scientist himself involved in pretty routine work and that killed his zeal to become a scientist. Such routine work was not the kind that his scientific heroes had done.

Visty loved reading his mother's books on literature from his school days. Having given up on science, Visty decided to go in for BA in literature. Philosophy he added as a means of understanding literature and psychology as a way to putting philosophy on a firm foundation. In this too he showed a trace of rebellion, moving away from the prevailing norm of meritorious students pursuing only engineering or medicine. College made for tumultuous times but Visty had three anchors. First Zavera, whom he met in college and started dating in 1971, getting married in 1975.

Second, the continued association with the NCC Air Wing. After gliding, he went on to powered flight and got his solo wings. Third, the books that he read voraciously, which were a source of pleasure and profit. Visty also became the president of the literary society of the college. For his final exams, Visty encountered a stroke of luck. Due to rampant cheating, the final exam was cancelled, which was a blessing because he had erred in a statistics question. That would have brought down his total score in the exam and Visty made no such mistake in the re-exam. He was third on the university merit list.

Around then, Visty also began to read and question all religious beliefs. He did not find logical answers in religion and turned agnostic for life. In the process, Visty also questioned what everyone seemed to accept, and developed the capability to think differently from the crowd. Abandoning religious beliefs in his early teens was traumatic in many ways as it took away one of life's moorings but taught him at least two lasting lessons. First, one should accept the truth established only after careful reasoning, howsoever personally unpalatable or unacceptable to anyone else, including those one respects and loves. Second, it is possible to think differently from everyone else. This progressed to a questioning of the median of general belief and ended with the conviction that the herd is usually wrong.

Visty was clear that he needed to follow his passion, regardless of what the crowd was following, seriously considering a career in the Air Force. He applied to the National Defence Academy because the life of a commercial pilot did not appeal to him. The Air Force appeared to be full of adventure and he loved flying. However, the petty politics while he was in the NCC Air Wing, as a senior under officer put him off, especially when his glider met with a mishap on landing. No one was injured but the investigation that his instructor was put through was a case study in futile bureaucratic blame-pinning.

A disillusioned Visty was then asked by his uncle, the principal of Elphinstone College in Mumbai, to do his postgraduate. Visty lived with his uncle and went into post-graduation in philosophy but quickly realized that if he went on to become a philosophy teacher, he was unlikely to have the standard of living that he desired or be able to support his prospective life partner. Their neighbour in Nagpur, who was the head of the Empress Mills (the first Tata unit) guided him to try for the Tata Administrative Service (TAS). Most TAS officers were placed either with the Indian Hotels Company Ltd (Taj Hotels) or Telco. Telco in Pune, in the midst of its expansion, was then considered an exciting place. Visty had found his vocation.

As a young entrant to TAS, Visty faced the challenge of proving himself, which was compounded when he was placed at the Telco, Pune (now Tata Motors). The company was led by the towering Sumant Moolgaonkar and the director in charge was another technical genius, Sharad Jakatdar, whose executive assistant, Visty became. The MBAs who joined TAS were all aware of their own goals and targets and which branch of management they wanted to pursue. Visty was not sure what he wanted to do. For a non-engineer in Telco, the choices were limited. The prime possibilities were IT or HR. He gravitated towards HR as he had a psychology background and has been with it ever since.

What changed was the beard that Visty had sported. He had shaved it for the TAS selection but decided to grow it after joining Telco to look a little older than twenty. In many ways, the stint at Telco became a part of his management education as he worked with very talented mentors, including Jakatdar, Arun Maira, K.R. Mondkar, J.E. Talaulicar and Sumant Moolgaonkar himself. Almost five years into his Telco stint, he got to do a six-month course at IIM Ahmedabad. Initially, his career progress was slow but that was neutralized by his fast progress later as he grew to lead HR within the same organization.

The first few years at Telco were all about learning from mentors, especially Jakatdar, V.S. Mahesh and Arun Maira. The last two were from TAS and great influencers. Mahesh was a great HR visionary with good political skills and Visty learnt how to survive tricky organizational undercurrents from him. Arun Maira was a visionary and organizationally adept, and had an uncanny ability to look at old problems in a 'new way' and then see them through to a solution. For instance, when everyone was looking at linking the workers' remuneration with output, Maira thought of linking it with skills.

Apart from mentors, Visty also learned from his subordinates. He spent time at the shop floor every day and learnt the nuances of factory operations from the engineers there. Being the youngest among his peers right through his career in Telco and often younger than his subordinates was occasionally a challenge. Coupled with the lack of an engineering or an MBA degree meant overcoming more obstacles. To make matters worse, he was from TAS that many people resented for the head start it gave. In 1978, Visty got the opportunity to attend the six-month management education programme in IIM Ahmedabad. After attending this programme, Visty became more confident about his understanding of management theory. What he did not learn at IIMA, he learned on the job.

His responsibilities included hiring and Visty got his first experience of mass-production process planning for HR. Being in a plant, he was open to the secondary hazard of dealing with industrial unrest too. The hiring role also brought occasional pressures and pulls from seniors that he had to learn to ward off. After his return from IIMA, Visty was keen to practise his newly acquired non-HR learning and got transferred to work as Arun Maira's executive assistant before moving to corporate HR in Mumbai. He thrived here, making significant contributions to this role in which he spent seventeen years. When Visty took on this role, it was not a regular corporate HR function, with no great expectation from this position. For instance, requests for manpower would go to the MD and wait for his approval. Visty changed things around and analysed the rationale for the request before putting his recommendations on the file that went to the MD. To do this exercise, Visty set up an industrial engineering cell and went on to attempt an analysis to make senior-level promotions more equitable and substantive as well. For obvious reasons, these did not add to his popularity with the senior people who were unused to being questioned.

Moolgaonkar was an inspirational leader and backed home-grown innovation. He led people like Visty to believe that, to make a difference in the world, they needed to serve the country and by working in Telco, they were serving the nation. They were inspired to apply their minds and come up with ideas, and experiment instead of running to consultants. Visty revelled in this environment and came up with many new initiatives that were unique at the time. Some of these, like climate surveys, assessment centre-based fast-track career progression and the creation of a non-engineer officers' cadre, were all indigenously developed by Visty and his team. Besides coming up with these new programmes, he also had to persuade the directors to accept these new policies and programmes.

Telco was a political space and the position Visty held had little formal authority. He had to cultivate peer relations, maintain proximity to power and, finally, depend upon objectivity and influencing abilities. The experience remains the biggest corporate influence on Visty, Telco having nurtured him from age nineteen and provided hands-on professional education. Moolgaonkar's sensitivity to the impact of corporate actions on society, ecology and industry was also greatly impactful. Moolgaonkar involved communities around the plant and made people policies that helped uplift them.

Visty continued to read, to access new ideas or generate them. He read three journals in particular, *Personal Psychology, Journal of Applied Psychology* and *Administrative Science Quarterly* regularly and indexed the good articles, making notes in his personal notebook. The idea was to constantly challenge himself and his team to try and innovate and walk that extra mile, so fired up was he by the superordinate goal of working for the nation by working for Telco, which gave him a strong bias for action.

Working along with team members in creating and executing these ideas, Visty was helping develop his people. Although he personally never went abroad from Telco, he sponsored many to go and participate in relevant programmes. Many of his subordinates became CHROs in other large organizations and some even commercially marketed these tools. Visty believes that he was blessed with fantastic teams and never felt threatened by his team members because there were always fresh domain conquests to be made and passed down for consolidation.

In the first five years out of the seventeen as the head of corporate HR at Telco, Visty created a base by making Corporate HR a genuinely contributing function. He built a team, added the industrial engineering and corporate learning cells to his team and provided HR support for the non-plant people, who were left out of HR programmes. The next seven years were about the pioneering initiatives. In the last five years, after Ratan Tata took charge at Telco, there was much opportunity to learn from outside consultants. Visty was also involved in the project that culminated in the creation of a group HR function for Tata.

However, he also realized that if he needed to understand other geographies and the way true multinationals worked, he would need to move beyond Tata. Visty joined GEC Alstom as country HR head. It was a much smaller company in India but, as a member of the Global HR Committee, he got the international exposure he wanted. It also represented new learnings. Many parts of GEC Alstom's India business were in bad shape. Going against his principles, Visty was a party to downsizing the workforce even though he held that, at the collective level, overmanning was a failure of management strategy and manpower planning for which it had no business to make the lowest levels pay. The emotional turmoil of downsizing was not something that he could accept as he believed that, at the individual level, there ought to be pre-signalling about a role becoming redundant at least six months to a year in advance to minimize the suddenness and trauma, allowing people to take a dignified way out.

Visty's next assignment was at Alstom's global head office in France as a project director responsible for implementing Peoplesoft's Human Resources Management System (HRMS), reporting to the global HR head. The idea needed to be sold to each and every business head and this was another great learning experience both in terms of working across geographies and in understanding how an MNC functioned in a matrix organization structure. Alstom was also transiting from the traditional country manager-led structure to a globally verticalized business organization. In the new structure, individual businesses in the country did not report to the respective country managers but to the global headquarters of those businesses. The HRMS project involved working with a team of people from different nationalities; they were British, French, German, Australian, Vietnamese, American,

Filipino and Indian. Visty's challenge was to inspire them all for this project. His one advantage was that each member had volunteered to be in the project. At the time, the company was going through an intense crisis and most programmes were getting axed, but the HRMS project survived.

This global exposure also rounded the rough edges to Visty's personality; rooted out the Indian habit of talking loudly, making him much more global in style. His early experience of learning computers from his subordinates in Telco came in handy. Visty had the modern manager's skills of working with his own hands rather than depending upon support staff. However, as this project moved towards its end, Visty thought that he would return to India but not to his old job at Alstom India. He chose to make a career move to the Godrej Group in 2003 as executive director and president. Visty found Adi Godrej's vision very exciting and enjoyed working with him.

Though a transition from an MNC to a family-controlled company, the culture at Godrej was not very different. Visty's mandate was to professionalize the HR function in the group with a small team and everyone was aligned to the agenda. The organization had little politics and once Adi Godrej approved something, one just went ahead with implementation. Visty implemented many substantive initiatives in areas of talent management, climate survey and the performance management system, among others. These pertained to the basic needs of the organization and had to be implemented. They represented original thinking and were not cut-and-paste jobs taken from some MNC. Adi Godrej always insisted on a critique of his proposals or ideas and those of others and never accepted or gave a blind or blanket nod. Visty was also given responsibilities beyond HR, which initially included strategy and corporate communications that were later substituted by IT and legal.

Over the years, Visty developed his own style of picking out talent and was fiercely inward-looking, focusing his entire energy within the organizations and avoiding outside recruitment by ensuring talent development from within. He identified apolitical, wackily bright sloggers who were willing to sacrifice and believe in them, stretching them beyond their own beliefs. He insisted on having HR head positions in all Godrej units reserved for internal youngsters, whom he supported from the sidelines. He also had rules for hiring, taking after Napoleon Bonaparte, and never picked from elite institutes only. Some of his best picks have been from a variety of unusual backgrounds.

The idea was to make extremely high, even unrealistic, demands given their age, maturity and backgrounds, which tied in with the stretch philosophy. He would excite them about the vision and then delegate excessively, which became very important in a group or HQ role. Visty considers his former team members, who went on to become exceptional leaders, his greatest contribution to enhancing the quality of HR practice in the country. There were also some path-breaking programmes and the art of understanding the different ways of looking at issues.

Visty did not care for the external connections that one makes in a position such as his, being rather dismissive of those who spent their time in professional bodies. If he did some good work, it would get known over time. Nevertheless, Adi Godrej pushed him to the CII where he joined the National Committee on HR and met some very impressive business leaders like Rajendra Pawar, founder of NIIT; B. Santhanam chairman and MD of St Gobain India and T.V. Narendran, MD of Tata Steel. However, he never took up any office in the professional forums but was felicitated by the NHRDN with the Seasoned HR Professional Award in 2006.

As the younger Godrej family members began to get involved in the business, Visty felt it was time to move on. In 2010 and at the age of fifty-seven, he chose to take early retirement, having groomed a successor within the organization. Throughout his career, Visty allowed external situations to change him internally as his workplaces moulded him into a slightly different person; every working day. A great emotional and mental agony that has possibly spurred him on is the sense of his own ignorance, compared to how much there is to learn in every conceivable subject. Strangely enough, this anxiety has been combined with an even more irrational confidence that he can acquire the missing expertise by independently applying himself, reading, reflection, experimentation and, a little after halfway through his career, the Internet. Even while working for seventy hours a week, he would keep the first hour or two in a day for his own learning and development.

The chronic fear might have been borne out of tracking the frontiers of the disciplines; the giants leading that charge. Visty jocularly suggests that part of the confidence in catching up might come from the relative disinterest in the corporate world for fundamental intellectual pursuits. Always keen to apply his enormous knowledge into practice, Visty attributes his ability to innovate in HR to his exposure to fundamentals of psychology and reasoning. He gained acceptance by ensuring absolute impartiality through structure and decisions and did not get lost in day-to-day transactional routines by assigning these tasks to his deputies as he dwelt upon the concepts and doing new things right through his career and learnt from the greats.

A five-week-long programme in 1989, titled 'Integration of Knowledge', with eminent physicist and nuclear scientist Raja Ramanna as the programme director was amazingly insightful. It brought in the best subject matter experts from a variety of disciplines as faculty; from history, philosophy, sociology, literature and computer sciences. Today, Visty continues to share his wisdom as a consultant, as a columnist, apart from pursuing his passion for photography and his love for wildlife. He is also a keen follower of the latest developments in aviation, is a regular at aero shows and also makes the most of his hobby of photography at these events. His old teammates still keep in touch and catch up with him over drinks, a true indicator that people were truly inspired working with him.

For Visty, the most lasting legacy one could leave is through people carrying one's values and approach in their careers as well as through processes and programmes that one exemplifies. That is the essence of human resource management.

* * *

Vivek Paranjpe

Sagacious with feet on the ground

Integrating life experiences with spiritual wisdom

Consultant and executive coach, Vivek Paranjpe (Vivek) has been an adviser on matters of strategic HR and business transformation to the chairman of

Reliance Industries Limited since 2003 and led the group HR function from 2009 to 2013. Vivek has more than forty years of experience in India and overseas; sixteen of them with Hewlett-Packard, with the last role as HR director for the Asia-Pacific region, based in Singapore. He held several important positions and was a part of the team responsible for the acquisition and merger of the Compaq Corporation.

A science graduate with honours from Pune's Fergusson College, and a postgraduate from XLRI Jamshedpur, where he was a Gold Medallist, Vivek started with Hindustan Lever in 1975 and worked in blue-chip companies like Johnson & Johnson and ICIM before joining Hewlett-Packard. Vivek received the NHRDN President's Award and has written two books.

Vivek Paranjpe failed in his first year in college, not once but twice; his young dreams of becoming a doctor had long been shattered and he faced the prospect of starting his life as a peon at a bank. The family was hysterical with anxiety, but this was the wake-up call to turn his life around, withdraw from politics, keep his reading habits alive and keep his commitment to his father, an important functionary at the Bank of Baroda (BOB), that he would study; for Vivek wanted to be a boss, not a peon. Vivek kept his promise and when he did graduate in five years (not three), he was the topper at Fergusson College, Pune. Academic struggles were not new to Vivek. Following his father's transferable job, he switched from Delhi's Hindi-medium Bal Niketan School at Karol Bag to Nagpur's English-medium, Saraswati Vidyalaya. Conversational English bugged him, even when he studied human resource management at XLRI.

Childhood memories featured stories about the family deeply rooted in RSS ideology—his father being a pracharak (propagandist)—bearing the brunt of the aftermath of Mahatma Gandhi's assassination, though before he was born. For the rest, a bi-monthly family trip to Chandni Chowk with parents, chaat and a movie were the main attractions. It was his father's colleague at BOB who recommended that Vivek be allowed to join XLRI when he cracked the entrance examination. No one had even heard about XLRI within the family or its close circles and it was an expensive course, but better-informed friends of his father said that completing the course would place Vivek in a senior leadership position quickly. XLRI not only gave him an understanding of human resource management but a couple of quick stints at top multinationals, providing great learning for the youngster.

In effect, XLRI familiarized him with the realities of Indian society, especially with assignments in industrial sociology under Prof. Nilima Acharji. The first was to interview 100 beggars in Jamshedpur. Vivek completed only twenty but the experience was enriching as he sat down with the beggars on the street of Bistupur to conduct the interviews. His second assignment was to observe construction workers to get a feel of their living conditions, which Vivek did for eight to ten days. The bitterness of the daily life cycle; the husband and wife fighting after returning home from work, sometimes dead drunk, others giving a little opium to their children to make them fall asleep quickly at night and fight their hunger during the day; was overwhelming. It was excellent education and there were tears in his eyes when he presented his findings at XLRI.

Vivek also became a favourite of Pritam Singh, a Fulbright scholar, who had returned from the US to join XLRI. He was a very modern man, well-dressed, who even permitted smoking in the class, great with communication and with greater depth of knowledge. Vivek annoyed him by asking too many questions and Singh would ask him to come to his house, where they ended up talking on a range of subjects from epics like the Mahabharata and about the Indian ethos and life in general. Singh's household was simple; his wife sat on the kitchen floor and cooked simple roti, subzi and dal that they shared for dinner, sitting on the floor. Over discourses and dialogues, Vivek completed his post-graduation with flying colours, as a Gold Medallist from XLRI. A job with Hindustan Unilever (Hindustan Lever then) followed under V.V. Ginde, deputy personnel manager at HUL's Sewri factory, where Vivek went for his initial induction and training. Ginde was an expert in industrial relations and labour laws and a strict disciplinarian too, who asked Vivek to shadow him for six months. Vivek reached Ginde's house in Mahim at 8 a.m. and travelled to the factory. En route, Ginde shared a lot of practical knowledge on the realities of handling workers. Having lunch together provided opportunities for more learning.

Ginde's boss was Umrao Bahadur, the factory's personnel manager, a warm-hearted father figure, from whom Vivek got an understanding of how HR's role was that of a business partner. Vivek was posted in

Taloja as factory personnel manager, reporting functionally to Bahadur, who visited the plant. Vivek spent nearly half a day showing him all the beautification done through horticulture, elaborate security systems and the impeccable housekeeping. At the end of it all, Bahadur pointed out that if beautification was all that was required, he could have appointed a retired army officer at half the salary to do the job just as well, if not better. He explained to Vivek that the real role was to understand the HR challenges of the unit, the priorities of the business head and then align HR actions to support the business head as a partner.

Pritam Singh, Ginde and Bahadur had all treated Vivek like family and he picked up abiding values from close interactions with them. He also went through several training courses and was assigned to work for a start-up project within the company at Taloja.

Vivek had to set up the HR processes from scratch. Excellent though the learning was, Vivek realized that HUL traditionally brought line function leaders to head the human resources function and this did not suit his ambition of 'being the boss'. He left Levers for a Johnson & Johnson position at its Mulund, Bombay, plant, where he got a good grounding in industrial relations, witnessing violence during labour disputes. Much of his time there was spent handling police cases, running around from courts to police stations or addressing workers at gate meetings. At age twenty-eight, Vivek had jumped jobs once more, joining the Hotel Corporation of India at double the salary.

The Hotel Corporation was a fully-owned subsidiary of Air India and a hotbed for IR issues and political interference. His work was mainly around handling disciplinary issues, long-term settlements, bonus issues, productivity-related matters and such like. However, he had to deal with the underworld and political figures, meeting the infamous don Haji Mastan and the Shiv Sena supremo Bal Thackeray a few times too. Other experiences included having to reduce the workforce by some 300 and Vivek had workers falling at his feet either to save their jobs or escape from disciplinary issues. Their stories gave him sleepless nights.

His father's transfer to Mumbai as general manager at BOB meant living at home. His family realized that he had acquired an unusually abusive manner of speaking, using the choicest Marathi expletives even in his regular verbal communication. Vivek's father pointed out to him that by being foul-mouthed, Vivek was digging himself into a career hole and would never be welcome at the corporate office of a respectable company. Once again, Vivek accepted his father's challenge and addressed the bad habit because he wanted to return to a corporate function. He was lucky to get selected by an old British firm, ICIM, though at a lower salary. Vivek recalls shouting at a tea boy for his sloppy service using Marathi abuses but peer pressure worked wonders, and Vivek adjusted to the customs and traditions of a corporate office, editing out the colourful swear words from his vocabulary.

At ICIM, Vivek reported to P.K. Nair, to whom he owes his corporate indoctrination, working as manager, learning and development. After two years, the UK head office insisted that he take on the mantle of the compensation and benefits manager, an entirely new position. Nair and Vivek examined the job description sent by the UK and figured out what knowledge and skills Vivek would need for the new role, and mapped out his skills and the skill gaps. This helped them determine the courses that he needed to attend to bridge the gap. Accordingly, Vivek attended several excellent training programmes. With two years in L&D and another two in compensation and benefits, preceded by eight years of IR, Vivek had evolved into a well-rounded HR professional. He also started teaching at the Jamnalal Bajaj Institute and the Narsee Monjee Institute, returning to academia and creating an impressive profile.

Such complete exposure made him ideally suited for Hewlett-Packard (HP), then starting its business in India. ICIM, too, was sold to an Indian promoter-led group and Vivek was not sure if he would enjoy working outside the MNC environment. At HP, Vivek came into his own, literally. He was HP's first employee in India and set up many processes that shook the bigwigs of the Indian IT industry with the manner in which HP did its business; its ideas of an 'HP Way' of doing business was not only about being honest in its practices but also to promote honesty and trusting behaviour. Working under Suresh Rajpal, a great leader who gave Vivek complete freedom within certain boundaries, Vivek soon learnt to translate the HP Way into everyday practices. Values and beliefs of the company are important but putting them into practice is difficult though very important for building the right culture. In HP's case, it began with trust and Vivek was asked to break the typical Indian factory practice of frisking workers at the entry and exit points.

Another typical practice in India was to have a component of compensation as medical reimbursement, which would be tax-free. Employees across Indian companies presented fake bills that the employers passed. Vivek was asked to avoid such components that encouraged employees to submit fake vouchers, even if that cost the company more. It was ethical with its recruitment policy too and when N.R. Narayana Murthy, the founder–chairman of Infosys, complained to HP's global headquarters about sharp HR practices employed by Vivek to lure Infosys employees away to HP India, HP ordered an investigation into the complaint. Two auditors from the US came to examine the complaint but found no foul play in the way Vivek had conducted himself. However, the entire experience demonstrated the lengths to which HP would go to maintain its honest culture. These provided Vivek with an exceptional ground for learning business excellence practices. Soon, Vivek became an auditor and was auditing HP businesses across the world.

HP had adopted the Malcolm Baldridge model of Business Excellence (BE) and Vivek went through the BE training modules, learning the rigour of BE audits and becoming a certified BE auditor. HP India also decided to adopt the CII Business Excellence model based on the European Foundation for Quality Management (EFQM) model, which ensured that Vivek received in-depth exposure and training in all facets of business excellence and the depth and breadth of the HP businesses across the world. Suresh Rajpal's leadership of HP India won it the Chairman's Award and the CII Business Excellence Award. As he mastered business excellence, Vivek learnt how to be an effective business partner and qualified to become an internal assessor for business excellence to assess many global HP entities. After he returned to India, CII used his services as a lead assessor for many years to assess various leading Indian corporates. Vivek's career was on a sharp incline, having been identified as a high potential talent (HiPo) early on and he was on the radar of the global HR chief, Pete Peterson. HP invested in Vivek's development and was asked to groom his successor in India to move on to global responsibilities. Vivek groomed Himanshu Jani.

Vivek was posted in Singapore as diversity head for Asia–Pacific. He travelled extensively for this role, attended global meetings in Europe and in the US, and got trained on LGBT issues by Stanford professors. After a successful stint as diversity head, he was elevated to lead HR and the quality function for South-east Asia spread over six countries that employed 20,000 people. Eventually, he took on the mantle of regional HR head of the Asia–Pacific region. He found getting acceptance from the hostile Chinese and the Australians in the organization a challenge because they were unused to an Indian boss and even his former peers in India were diffident with him as their boss. Vivek had to overcome these barriers by working harder and smarter, as people began to recognize his capabilities and acceptance followed. HP's strong culture and systems helped him too.

Then came the dotcom bubble of 2000–01 and HP, which had almost never terminated an employee as a part of downsizing, asked Vivek to restructure and reduce the Asia–Pacific headcount by 6000. The entire exercise was planned with full involvement of global HQ and carried out over five to six months with matters handled in a very humane way. Outplacement agencies were engaged to help people find alternate employment. Even so, it was traumatic to announce the massive downsizing and his wife, Mugdha, who he had married in 1976, was like a strong anchor, counselling him by saying that he was not hurting anyone for a personal, selfish reason. None of these learnings had, however, prepared Vivek for the challenges that presented themselves as Carly Fiorina took over as the CEO of HP in 1999. Not only did she replace the HP Way but, with the subsequent merger with Compaq, created chaos in the HP ranks. Within a few weeks of joining HP, Fiorina introduced what she called 'rules of garage', announced through circulars across the company, leading to anxiety and confusion all around.

Nobody really understood what she wanted and Vivek believed her actions were a good example of how not to bring about a culture change, especially when one was a values-led company (HP) and another (Compaq) had a cowboy culture, where actions and results mattered most with people and processes the least. Also, HP was highly profitable while Compaq was bleeding and was an easy target for the acquisition. Fiorina, new to HP's values, wanted to push the merger irrespective of the vast cultural differences. Vivek's next assignment was another difficult exercise 'member of clean-room', designed to prepare the organization for its merger with Compaq in 2001. Structurally, HP was a vertical organization and its top talent resided in the headquarters and regional offices. By contrast, Compaq was a horizontal, decentralized organization in which the top talents resided at the country level. After the merger, most of the top positions at the country level went to the Compaq people, who were result-oriented and not necessarily process and people-oriented leaders. This led to the exodus of senior talent from HP.

Vivek had to convey these changes personally to people, many of whom he had known for years. He also had to deal with the tough trade unions in Korea and Malaysia. Many HR people quit HP and were replaced by Compaq's HR professionals. Vivek decided to take early retirement as well and return to India in December 2002. Always deeply influenced by the Indian scriptures, Vivek planned to retire at the age of fifty, the age of Vanaprastha as in the Vedic scriptures, after discussing things with his wife. Shivaji Bhosle, a professor of logic and philosophy and retired vice chancellor of Marathwada University, played an important role in guiding Vivek from his go-getting ways to following the mantra for a fruitful retirement. However, he insisted that Vivek remain connected with his profession too.

On his return to India, Vivek was introduced by Tarun Sheth to Reliance Industries and soon he took up a position of an adviser in the company. He liked this new advisory role as he was not in the rat race and could afford to call a spade a spade. Between 2003 and 2009, Vivek was involved in setting up two Reliance businesses, Reliance Infocomm and Reliance Retail. Then came the big move as he was asked to step into the shoes of the redoubtable V.V. Bhat, Mukesh Ambani's key person, when he passed away in 2009, an interim HR chief. Bhat's style was unique and he was extremely capable, but Vivek explained to Ambani how he would be different at the outset and secured his support, moving on only when a full-time HR head was inducted. Though Bhat was a veteran at Reliance, Vivek had worked for six years in the chairman's office when he took over as HR head and was quite familiar with the Reliance culture. Getting a budget approval of

Rs 40–50 crore for a specific legitimate spend was never a big problem if one was a trusted leader in Reliance. Vivek felt the need to establish a diversity function that entailed a spend of around Rs 40 crore. Such infrastructure as ladies' toilets in some factories and crèches had to be created and a team for the diversity function had to be appointed and trained. Ambani gave Vivek a carte-blanche approval. On another occasion, Vivek got approval to upgrade a workers' housing complex, a long overdue initiative. These helped Vivek earn acceptance at Reliance even from those who were accustomed to Bhat's style. On his part, Vivek travelled a lot to connect with people.

Early in his career, Vivek had wanted to speak at professional forums and had attended many programmes, though as a participant. In Mumbai, he regularly attended the Bombay Management Association programmes. Suresh Rajpal of HP encouraged his senior team to be visible in professional forums and had assigned Vivek to the Indian Society of Training and Development (ISTD) and the Delhi Management Association (DMA). Vivek became the vice president of the DMA. For nearly a year during 2004–05, Vivek was the CEO of NHRDN and met senior HR leaders in the country, rebuilding the contacts that he had lost during his overseas stint. Vivek also put in place rules of governance and defined the roles of key stakeholders in NHRDN. He realized how difficult it was to implement these ideas in an organization where everyone was a volunteer. They were far too busy to have the time to devote to such work and NHRDN would need a very strong secretariat to become impactful. He served as a member of the board of NHRDN. In 2010, Vivek was felicitated by NHRDN with the President's Award for his stellar contribution to the HR profession .

It was important to share his extraordinary experiences and Vivek wrote two books in the late eighties, largely based on his teaching notes on labour laws and manpower planning. Influenced by Vivek Patwardhan and N.S. Rajan, he started blogging, mostly on spiritual matters, which he stopped because he was not making any original contribution. Instead, he started writing a column in *People Matters* magazine, responding to career questions. From the day he turned his back on the prospect of becoming a peon at Bank of Baroda, Vivek raised his game, again and again, to move forward. ICIM's Nair altered his outlook by challenging him to do a job through an alternative process. The exposure to business excellence at HP and the foundational training in quality management helped him to learn to prioritize and create processes and organizations to handle routine work. Strong processes and efficient people were needed to handle the routine work. HP India was one of the early adopters of EFQM, a business excellence model. Attending several programmes under its aegis, Vivek got a perspective of looking at the business as a whole. He began to see himself as a business leader; an integral part of the management team, taking a deep interest in subjects such as finance and customer satisfaction.

When Kewal Khanna, business head of the Test and Measurement Group asked Vivek to do a two-day off-site programme to get his leadership team more committed to improving customer satisfaction, given the rising customer complaints, Vivek suggested they do the diagnostics first. Kewal and Vivek went around the country and met twenty-five customers to understand the problems. They soon realized that a training programme was not the solution. They needed to look at the complete process of delivering customer satisfaction and make appropriate process improvements. Reinvention was an instrument to use for continuous development. To shake people out of their complacency, Suresh Rajpal brought in brilliant speakers from various disciplines like Jairam Ramesh, Subramaniam Swamy, a few Indian army generals and other thinkers to address top HP India leaders. Exposure to such brilliance was humbling in many ways. They provoked the need for self-reinvention and unfroze complacency. Even to this day, Vivek holds following wise people to gain knowledge to be his motto.

Jairam Ramesh, then environment minister, was particularly brilliant in the depth of his knowledge and transformational with his out-of-this-world presentation. It opened up people's minds. Vivek personally felt there was so much more to do and that they had just scratched the surface.

This also helped Vivek unfreeze and reinvent himself. It made him humble too, for Vivek had realized that when you believe that you have arrived is when you freeze and stop growing.

* * *

Yogi Sriram

The self-directed HR leader

Constantly challenging himself to learn wider and intriguing subjects

Yogi Sriram (Yogi), until recently senior vice president, corporate HR, Larsen & Toubro Limited, has forty-four years of experience in HRD functions and leads a world-class institute of project management. A passionate promoter of management and HR development through various forums like the All India Management Association and the National HRD Network, Yogi's areas of interest are succession planning, career sculpting, team coaching, talent management and change management.

After pursuing his education from SRCC, TISS, FMS and the University of Delhi, he got accredited in psychometric testing techniques, completed a diploma in training and development and a certificate course on 'Appreciative Enquiry' from Case Western Reserve University, Ohio. Yogi was the first HR professional to become a fellow of the AIMA and has received the 'Best HR Professional Award' from the Maharaja Sayajirao University, Vadodara. He has published in international journals and is on the board of many professional bodies.

Conventional wisdom says that there is no better teacher than life itself. Yogi Sriram never felt the need for a mentor or a role model as he learnt from his own experiences, many of them the hard way. Losing his father at the tender age of fifteen was Yogi's first brush with reality. Yogi's father, a doctor, was a high-ranking official in the Indian government's ministry of health. His parents pandered to all his demands; he went to Delhi Public School on Mathura Road, considered among the best schools in the capital; his family hobnobbed with VIPs and life was all about attending Diwali parties and Republic Day parades in the 'Babu City'. All this changed with his father's sudden demise but Yogi's resolute nature helped him to deal with the void, picking himself up during his adolescence without leaning on anyone for support. He learnt to make his own decisions and rely strongly on his own instincts, even as he built up a personality with determined resilience.

Yogi knew his mind and made clear academic choices, giving up commerce for economics for his graduate degree programme at the

Sriram College of Commerce (SRCC) just because he loved the creative possibilities in exploring 'conceptual' studies and found accounting to be dull. Yogi also refused to give in to the pressure from his mother to get into the Indian Administrative Services (IAS) and opted out of the MA course in the Delhi School of Economics as well, though he had cracked the entrance test. Yogi decided to pursue management studies in a delayed decision when every MBA school had closed admissions except the Tata Institute of Social Sciences (TISS). Yogi got in for the Personnel Management and Industrial Relations (PM&IR) course. TISS was a serendipitous discovery and the career choice of pursuing a master's programme in PM&IR was self-driven.

His academic pursuits after TISS were either guided by his natural determination or by some external provocation. His initial love for law, especially labour law, had been kindled at TISS by Professor Kudchedkar; it developed following a result of a property dispute with an MNC; and grew strong, especially around labour law at ACC, leading him to a formal degree. At NTPC, a taunt by a senior finance colleague that HR personnel were neither capable nor qualified to handle finance or understand numbers led to an MBA in organizational behaviour (OB) and finance from the Faculty of Management Studies (FMS), Delhi University as well. For big career decisions, Yogi relied on his intuition and gut feel and he always loved challenges. Never a 'fantastic' student in school, Yogi ranked within the top quartile of his class but stood out in co-curricular and extracurricular activities, excelling in sports, especially boxing and cricket, and was a state-level chess player. He was also exceptional in art, in both drawing and painting and indeed with several creative pursuits.

A toy train bought by his parents from Hamley's in London and several Meccano sets that Yogi owned as a boy spurred his interest in physics and mechanics. He loved to tinker with mechanical gadgets and electrical circuits, which became a lifelong passion. His father's passing did impact his persona. From a brooder, daydreamer and carefree child, he became extremely focused on his career. Despite his keenness for science, he did not take up engineering because of his love for conceptual and hands-on knowledge, which he thought engineering institutions could not provide. After joining SRCC in Delhi, Yogi again shifted gears, changing to economics as he found concepts like an 'indifference curve' far more intriguing than accounting, his original choice. The highly competitive atmosphere of his college and the success of his batchmates made him determined to do well in life. He finally found his calling in HR management and there was no looking back after joining TISS.

In 1977, Yogi joined ACC Ltd as the personnel and welfare officer in a cement plant on the foothills of the Shivalik range, near Chandigarh. An unexpected turn of events changed his position. His supervisor, K.N. Prasad, fell ill and, at twenty-two, Yogi was the de facto head of HR of this cement unit in Surajpur, near Kalka, with around 6000 workers and a large, open-face limestone mine attached to it. The responsibility came with perks of a five-bedroom bungalow in Chandigarh as his official accommodation, when all he possessed were a guitar, a large wooden box with his clothes, a Nutan stove and his Bullet (Royal Enfield 350cc motorbike). His voice echoed in the near-empty living room, but ACC provided opportunities for professional growth. G.L. Govil, head of staff and industrial relations division, taught him the ropes of IR and labour laws over interactions at ACC's headquarters, Cement House, at Churchgate, Mumbai. It included basics like drafting of circulars and legal processes for compliance that were copiously detailed. Yogi's first hands-on experience in dealing with an IR issue involved an incident with contract labourers. The union leader of the unit stormed into his office and scattered a plastic container full of kankar (small stones) on his desk. The well-built man with large hands, otherwise endearing in his interactions with Yogi, spoke condescendingly and threateningly as he complained of the kankar in the dal (a lentil soup) for the workers in the factory's canteen, cautioning Yogi to watch out.

Despite his youth and zero prior experience of dealing with worker agitations and tantrums, Yogi coolly stood his ground, pointing out that disrespectful behaviour was not acceptable, regardless of the age difference, though he promised to look into the matter personally. Over time, he won the affection of the factory workers as well, who respected his fair and structured ways of working. Yogi never displayed one-upmanship and felt genuine empathy for the contract workers who often lived in very modest conditions in the nearby villages. He forged a personal connect with them by visiting them at their pind (village) to share a meal or a glass of chhass (buttermilk) over small talk.

He learnt a smattering of Punjabi and even saw his first Punjabi movie, *Pind di Kudi*, organized in the township. When he left ACC in 1978, the workers gave him a touching farewell, moving the unflappable Yogi to tears.

The second big lesson at ACC was on labour laws. Yogi had the experience of dealing with arbitration proceedings under Section 10A of the Industrial Disputes Act early in his career as part of the negotiations between the cement industry federation, led by the legendary G. Ramanujam, co-founder of the Indian National Allied and Cement Workers Trade Union Congress (INTUC) and his then boss K.N. Prasad, who was well-versed in IR. While Ramanujam represented the workers' federation, Yogi represented ACC in Jaipur as a part of the employers' federation. Prasad was the other representative of the employer. At the age of twenty-two, Yogi was sitting across the negotiating table with industry veterans and navigating the conversation with logical arguments about how the yearly dearness allowance (DA) to the workers should be pegged at a level, without flinching under pressure or getting intimated. He could do this with such confidence because he had prepared well and charted out a clear strategy for implementing his plan.

Another hilarious incident during his 'bright-eyed and bushy-tailed' days at ACC taught him an invaluable lesson around understanding the culture of an organization and the people in it before implementing changes. He suggested to his Punjabi boss, O.P. Walia, that the cooking medium used at the company's canteen be changed from vanaspati (hydrogenated fat) that Yogi had read was bad for the heart. He misread his boss's grunt as a go-ahead and he had the cooking medium changed. An uproar followed because in Haryana and Punjab people were used to food cooked in Dalda (a popular vanaspati or hydrogenated vegetable oil brand), which enhanced taste and was cheaper than desi ghee (clarified butter). Workers complained to Walia that the 'young boy' had ordered this change in the canteen and Yogi earned a reprimand.

These initial learnings were invaluable while managing many sticky situations in his career. In Dabur, the management left it to him to tackle one of the ugliest strikes by contract workers in the Sahibabad unit. The tension had created rifts between the workers and the employees, which was intensified by the presence of a group of contract workers who were particularly difficult. Yogi ironed out the differences in his inimitable way and forged great bonds with some of the workers who are still in touch with him. Dabur taught him a great deal. Workers periodically switched off power at the factory and Yogi had to cajole this very young group of workers back to work, handling the situation on his own and taking longer to resolve it. He did not ask for help nor was any offered and in hindsight, he believes that being stricter would have helped. The point is that making real change happen needs a coalition with other stakeholders.

Yogi's NTPC experience, reporting to R.V. Shahi, the former power secretary who was a director there, was outlook-changing. Yogi credits Shahi for his structured and logical thinking abilities, inculcated through the innumerable debates the two would engage in, on diverse topics. A bunch of short stints with some of the top companies across multiple sectors, including a few MNCs, followed as Yogi gained experience over a wide canvas—from industrial and manufacturing companies like ABB and BP to consumer and hospitality companies like Dabur and Indian Hotels Company Ltd, including a three-year-plus stay with Larsen & Toubro Ltd (L&T), where he later returned for his swan song. All these were high-impact jobs and helped Yogi broaden his own horizon and take his development to a different level, giving him exposure to an MNC, responsibilities across regions and into a consumer-facing industry.

From 1985, Yogi served as CHRO in different organizations for over thirty-three years. His first role as a CHRO was at the age of thirty in Shriram Refrigeration Ltd, which was later acquired by the US-based compressor manufacturer, Tecumseh. The company was headquartered in Hyderabad but Yogi was posted in Delhi and reported to Raj Pandit, the president. Siddharth Shriram took a keen interest in HR and Yogi had considerable interactions with him as well. He was still in his thirties when he had joined that company and both his bosses became important influencers for him. He also worked for two other group companies during this stint. An amusing exposure to cultural diversity and inclusion challenges within an organization came at Shriram where senior employees brought dabbas (tiffin boxes) from home. Yogi walked into a small cubicle where his colleagues were eating with his dabba, wanting to break the ice and mingle with them as the new HR manager. The room was filled with the aroma of turnip pickle, typically eaten in north India and the cultural difference between Yogi and the rest was apparent. Small wonder his request to join the group was turned down with a brusque '*Yahan jagah nahin* (There is no room here).' Yogi was surprised and disappointed with the snub but Raj Pandit helped him to fit in.

At Shriram, Yogi helped to straighten the existing systems and procedures and brought structure to most of the HR practices. His meticulous ways pleased Pandit, who depended on him for many things. People noticed that the HR role was getting a lot of attention from the senior leadership and Yogi's importance increased too. His structured methods of functioning helped him to tackle difficult situations though they made him look quite punctilious and fussy, as Yogi became extremely meticulous and punctual. Such traits irritated his wife at times but helped him earn the respect of his colleagues. Yogi was also extremely well served by the brilliant Rajesh Mehrotra, along with an excellent team. Mehrotra is currently executive vice president (HR) at Godfrey Phillips India and others like Husnain Zaidi, Pramod Fernandes and P.C. Rajiv are all tall HR leaders of today. At British Petroleum, Yogi had an entirely different experience of leading the HR function across forty countries. He would hop from flight to flight and travel the entire world—right from Sierra Leone and Cape Town in Africa to Myanmar and Istanbul in Asia—to understand and learn about the cultural nuances and regional challenges like the black empowerment policy in South Africa, Omanization ('sons of the soil' quotas for employment in Oman) or Emiratization (having more Emirates citizens in the workforce) issues in the Gulf, among others.

This experience was not just educative but, as the CHRO, he also learnt to be extremely alert and disciplined as he juggled responsibilities across time zones and dealt with multiple stakeholders. At BP, he also learnt how to negotiate what he calls 'an incorrigible matrix of accountabilities' and be self-directed as this was quite different from an organization structure that had a single point of responsibility. The Taj Group meant a paradigm shift from engineering processes and shop floors to encounters with spotlessly attired general managers talking about luxury hotels and brands like Gucci. He picked up the nuances of customer service through his dealings with annoyed customers as he observed and learnt. The practice of housekeepers scanning dustbins for crowns of beer bottles in order to understand the customer preference for beer brands, or how chambermaids held bedsheets from four corners and dropped them with the precision of a slam dunk while making the bed as they needed to ensure there were no creases on the sheet that could offend a fussy customer were inspiring. He got to understand molecular gastronomy and rebadging people when a hotel was taken over. Business to customer (B2C) was an entirely different ball game.

Over the years, Yogi realized that CHROs could not be fitted into a stereotypical mould given their multidimensional roles. Sometimes they needed to delegate responsibility and move things more through influence than power. In other instances, they would need to be control-oriented using the key that works for a particular situation, making it an art rather than a management science The 'one size doesn't fit all' norm is particularly true for large conglomerates like L&T that are highly diversified with multiple business interests and thousands of employees. The CHROs of such large conglomerates are responsible for the entire group's HR and must work hard to ensure that the policies are more evolved. HR heads of divisions in such structures need to develop a hard line reporting to a central HR rather than mere faint dotted line reporting or zero-reporting structures.

The biggest challenge for CHROs of such diversified conglomerates is to keep in touch with a large employee base at a personal level and understand their pulse. Yogi believed these two objectives cannot be met through employment engagement programmes or surveys, so he devised a unique way to do it at L&T by creating enough opportunities for employees to mingle. He interacted with employees across ranks and levels in places like company guest houses or car pools. They loved to talk to him and he loved to hear, which is how Yogi managed. If analysed through the lens of David Kolb's multiple learning models that can be used to gather knowledge, Yogi's learning as a CHRO was through a myriad of experiences and the practice of keeping his ear to the ground. He also believes that his habit of intense reflection and self-analysis helped him to improvise on his decisions and draw up priorities. He would bounce off his thoughts with the seniors and juniors alike, which allowed him to look at situations from different perspectives. He usually dealt with all his paperwork and emails in the evening in order to keep aside time during the day to meet people. For example, in Taj, he would sometimes walk into the kitchens to talk to the chefs or in ABB, Dabur and L&T, he would just visit offices or plants to speak with the employees and workers.

It is just as important to listen to the chief executive officer but not to accept his/her words as sacrosanct. A strong HR person needs the backbone to challenge what is incorrect with data and evidence to justify the objections. Listening to the voices of his HR colleagues mattered just as much because framing HR policies in large conglomerates such as L&T with multi-generational employees needed multiple perspectives. Yogi's three-pronged strategy helped him to make decisions and prioritize. First, he established a twenty-six-member HR council, comprising functional leaders from all the independent group companies, which met every quarter to weave a common HR agenda. Second, he had many task forces that helped him to understand the priorities while carrying out the job. Third, he closely tracked the organizational data and studied the current trends. If a metric showed that the company was losing a lot of middle management people to competitors, he would be worried.

Yogi's intuition and his natural disposition to depend on his instincts also saved the day for him many a time, but the intuition was always informed by knowledge and experience. Yogi always associated himself with critical aspects of the businesses and mingled with 'people who knew their domain'. This helped him to understand complex issues and garner technical knowledge on various subjects. Over the years, Yogi's methods evolved with changing times and his own experiences. Earlier, there was little diversity or variety, no Internet nor today's digitalization. In his early days at Shriram, essentially a product company with an assembly-line set-up, the main tasks of the CHRO would include personnel management, leading employee relations, doing performance appraisals, running assessment centres, among others, with loads of paperwork and HR decisions based on extensive interactions with business heads. The yardstick for modern-day CHROs is very different with new-age technologies such as data analytics providing varied metrics that aid HR policy formulation.

During his first stint with L&T, there were debates with the senior leaders about bringing in differentiation and a more aggressive performance-linked pay structure. The company then was hierarchical, a cadre-based company with an egalitarian compensation structure. Yogi made a presentation to the corporate management committee on moving out of this cadre-based increment system and introducing an aggressive performance-linked pay, that could be 1x, 2x and even 3x to 4x of the normal increments as per performance. He was almost booed out of the room for his proposal. Surviving the criticism and maintaining his stand took a lot of energy and courage on his part, along with a good measure of humility not to overstate one's convictions. His stance on a variable pay structure based on a 'forced choice bell curve' at L&T was diametrically opposite to the views he held at his earlier organizations. During his seven years in ABB India, he was passionate about equal increments across the board, about using appraisals only for development and team-based appraisals, and such others.

Deeply influenced by Stephen Covey and his *Seven Habits of Highly Effective People*, Yogi evangelized teamwork and advocated team-based performance processes. He even told the managing director, Arun Thiagarajan, that he would quit if the system of performance appraisals was changed to a variable structure. He was vehemently against the concept of rank and yank and force-fitting employees on a normal distribution curve, having been deeply influenced by the work of Edward E. Deming, particularly Deming's biography by Mary Walton. While the system was not changed at ABB at his insistence, Yogi himself changed his mind completely after joining L&T because, for a poorly performing company in diverse businesses and an extremely diversified shareholding structure, a fixed compensation structure was not the most viable option. It would not work in the way it had worked for ABB, which had adopted a TQM (total quality management) approach and team performance processes as a philosophy. TQM met with initial resistance at L&T with critical comments on the validity of results from the assessment centres by senior business colleagues. Yogi opened up the assessment process to the senior leaders, negotiated every assessment process and test, and sought alternatives when resistance was strong, to carry the day.

Yogi's key experience during his second stint at L&T came from being executive vice president, HR for two large business divisions, power and hydrocarbons. In addition, Yogi assisted A.M. Naik in talent acquisition for senior leadership positions for group companies. He took on the mantle of the CHRO for L&T only after his predecessor M.S. Krishnamoorthy retired and found many peers suddenly reporting to him. He ensured that he never treated them as reportees but as equals or friends and partners, basing the relationships on mutual respect. At L&T, Yogi got to understand the pain points of its MD and CEO, A.M. Naik, when running a company that was not doing well. The share price was low and Yogi could see at his first workout (a six-monthly meeting of L&T leaders), an organizational development exercise with the entire top management in one place, that many businesses were stressed. Under such circumstances, Yogi rethought this paradigm and concluded that theories had to fit a context and that the context for a business that was at 'a low' would be different from the business context in ABB that was on 'a high'. He readjusted his thinking, appreciating the need to differentiate.

Shareholders would hold on to their investments only if the company performed well and business, team and individual performances were equally important to preserve shareholder value. Accordingly, Yogi implemented three crucial changes at L&T. First, a differentiated performance appraisal process, Framework for Linking Appraisals with Incentives and Rewards (FAIR) that continues at L&T for over eighteen years now. Second, assessment centres with consultants conducting the assessments, with about 19,000 assessments conducted through them covering managers in four distinct levels of the organization. Third, the most painful introduction of a VRS scheme for managers and officers in 2001, the first in L&T's history, to trim down personnel cost by about 10 per cent and eliminate role redundancies. These changes contributed in helping L&T's share price grow exponentially. Such fundamental changes went against L&T's grain and needed deep engagements with the top brass, with seven out of the eight senior members of the management having rejected the VRS proposal. L&T's CMD, Naik, was persuasive as he championed the VRS, showing its benefits to his colleagues and helping Yogi to push it through. Yogi developed a close working relationship with Naik during his years at L&T and continues in an advisory capacity after retiring in 2020.

There are responsibilities on the professional front too, with Yogi heading the NHRDN chapter in Mumbai and the Bombay

Management Association (BMA) at the same time, as president in the past. Back-to-back meetings and conferences of both, ensuring success, managing BMA's fund crisis, were attention-demanding. Thanks to his peers at NHRDN, Yogi jointly shouldered the responsibilities and made his stint successful. On the professional front, Yogi pushes for differentiation even in the HR function. He does not believe in generalists and says that an HR career should be shaped like a wine glass, where the base is like broad-based management education, followed by the stem that should be like seven to eight years of specialization, followed by wider responsibilities. Even as CHRO, one should be the master of at least one area, says Yogi, who continues to extricate his junior colleagues from a generalist mentality. The ability to manage meetings is another skill that he likes to share. This is derived from the authority of knowledge and experience to handle people pushing their own agenda or making impractical suggestions at meetings. Yogi allows these diversionary tactics some free run before moving the agenda and guides the meeting towards the desired conclusion, allowing them the freedom of their positions while they fall in line with the majority. HR, he insists, should have the evidence to back its opinions and boldly express them. This means mental and physical discipline. Turning up late for meetings is unacceptable in Yogi's books.

It is this mental discipline that allows him to enjoy his diverse interests today. His penchant for Meccano sets and scale-model trains has grown, as he works on converting analogue trains into digital ones in a small workshop that is a part of the dry area outside his kitchen. In the drawing room at his Mumbai home, Yogi has set up scale-model train tracks, along the walls, close to the ceilings. He has a shelf in one of the bedrooms with model railway stations and working signals and tests his newly converted digital trains on these tracks. Mentally young and agile, Yogi interacts with younger colleagues and reads interesting and intriguing subjects. He is fascinated by the idea of phenotypic age that measures a person's rate of ageing and how old one is as per that model, vis-à-vis the chronological age or the number of years one has been alive. Other eclectic pursuits range from gender socialization and how the concept of gender forms in the minds of children or learning Python as a language for understanding artificial intelligence. Besides, Yogi has a keen interest in photography.

The obstinacy of youth has been converted to resilience and maturity, enabling Yogi to reverse his own stance on issues, and become flexible enough to work with others on meaningfully intriguing subjects that may well alter the face of the HR profession in India. As chairman of a committee that has senior HR professionals and heads of key professional bodies, Yogi has floated the concept of a certification for a chartered professional in human resources (CPHR), along the lines of a chartered accountant. The idea is to have the Parliament pass an act, much like the existing acts for CAs, cost and works accountants and company secretaries, which will make it mandatory for every company to employ a CPHR in a statutory role. It will define qualifications for a CPHR and a process for education and conducting examinations. The plan envisages the creation of a regulatory body like the one that regulates chartered accountants. The position of the CHRO has been growing in importance and this might give the CHRO a status similar to that of a CFO.

If Yogi succeeds, this will be one of the most impactful contributions from him to the profession of human resource management.

3

Baking of Leaders: Crucible Experiences

A crucible is a testing moment that normally has a transformational effect on the individual. The impact reveals itself in many forms; new insights, self-realization, self-discovery, change of outlook, a reaffirmation of one's beliefs or a changed belief and such others. Each contributes to the building of the individual. This often involves reformatting certain critical aspects of one's thinking and approach to challenges. It is through a series of such new awareness—some intuitive and some practised—acquired through a crucible and other experiences that the leadership talent gets baked.

In our interviews with the thirty eminent HRLs, we discovered a slew of intense experiences through which they learnt and evolved into the impactful personalities that they have become. Bennis and Thomas (2002) identified such experiences as crucibles, a transformative experience through which an individual comes to a new or altered—but always an improved—sense of identity. These intense experiences could be positive or traumatic. In their life journeys, through family, academic, social or work environments, our HRLs have undergone several crucible experiences, each leaving its rich and unique imprimatur, as it were. Reading these stories has familiarized you with the vibrant persona of these HRLs but, more importantly, it has given you insights into the messages that they have internalized from their struggles and the exciting aspects of their own journeys.

Truth be told, both of us knew these HRLs rather well or so we believed. Over the years, we have worked closely and frequently with most of them in professional forums. It was only during these interviews, running into six to eight hours each, that we uncovered what lay beneath the accomplished exteriors; what a wealth of formative experiences lay in the deeper layers of their lives, shaping them. We knew about some of their work, thoughts and desires and were au fait with their public image. Listening to their personal stories first-hand, with some of them consciously letting down their guards, was a truly intense learning experience for us. It worked both ways with the interviewer and the interviewee caught up in an immersive process with some HRLs sharing deeply emotional personal experiences for the first time.

After thoroughly understanding these stories, we began to look for a broad pattern underpinning them, despite the varied nature of the experiences. Our quest was for a common thread between these multifaceted crucible experiences. If there were none, we had to explore more to understand how each one of them got baked as HRLs of exceptional quality; achieving what they did or impacting the way they did. In this chapter, we share our findings on these broad patterns. Our objective was to decipher commonalities in the processes that baked our HRLs and also to highlight unique situations that some of them faced and how they impacted the baking process.

From our analysis of thirty case studies, whereby we had isolated the crucible experiences, we found some emerging patterns. These experiences could easily be classified on the basis of the context or settings in which they occurred, the sources of the crucibles (persons and situations that caused these crucibles) and the nature of these crucibles. The classifications or categories are not mutually exclusive but make for a convenient device to convey our understanding of the baking process.

The settings or the contexts that we identified fall into the following categories:

A. Family (including early childhood);
B. Schools and colleges;

C. First organization and first job;
D. Subsequent roles and organizational experiences; and
E. Professional bodies

Classifying them on the basis of the sources that had a key role in creating these crucible experiences, we identified the following:

F. Parents (families and extended families);
G. Teachers;
H. Bosses and other role-setting members (first boss, other bosses and seniors, mentors, coaches, colleagues and juniors); and
I. Self-directed crucibles

Classifying them on the basis of the nature of the crucibles, we identified the following:

J. Handling industrial relations;
K. Role-taking and new initiatives;
L. Stretch jobs;
M. Setbacks and reverses; and
N. Volunteering for social causes

The following sections present our findings. In presenting them, we followed a different sequencing as below:

A. Crucible of the family;
B. School and colleges;
C. Influence of their teachers;
D. Learning from the crucible of their first jobs;
E. Learning from their bosses;
F. Learning from stretch jobs and business roles;
G. Crucible of industrial relations;
H. Learning from setbacks and reverses;
I. Challenging the status quo and leading new initiatives;
J. Role-making;
K. Baking through high-quality training programmes;

L. Investing in developing the self;

M. Engaging with professional forums; and

N. Crucible of volunteering for social causes

A. Crucible of the family

We started with the impact that parents, families and early childhood had on our thirty HRLs and their influence on the baking process.

It is well-established that the education within the family contributes to the overall upbringing of children, preparing them to receive external stimuli of a different nature, which is crucial for the formation of a balanced personality. It facilitates a state of preparedness for leading independent lives and developing leadership qualities. The HRLs covered by us came from widely varying family backgrounds. Some were affluent, based in major metros; some came from very influential homes in small towns or villages; others came from very modest families, and some struggled to make ends meet. Irrespective of their socio-economic background, the families provided richly experiential environments, where parents or others from the family were role models, anchored in values and often committed to serving larger causes. The families also gave reasonable freedom to our HRLs to pursue their interests. These were the key factors impacting the baking of their characters and the value system that governed the HRLs' universe.

Some specific experiences from our case studies illustrate these points.

R.R. Nair (RR), was born in a relatively affluent family with his father (rising to the position of a secretary in the Kerala government) teaching him that humility and honesty were key to becoming a credible person. He also imbibed the deeply religious environment in the family and was particularly fond of his father, mother and his eldest brother.

D. Harish's father was the production head in Dunlop. He later became the HR director in Union Motors and subsequently, president of the NIPM. To Harish, his father has been a role model. He observed his father handling people from all walks of life, including union leaders, with dignity and respect. He also saw father refusing to entertain people who brought even a 'box of sweets' in acknowledgement of a perceived favour. He was just as impressed by his father never humiliating a worker but appealing to their hearts if they were recalcitrant. These had a lasting impact in shaping Harish's mental model and were baked within as his personal values.

Anil Sachdev, an army child, learnt to adjust to frequent transfers. Active engagement with such national events as the traumatic return of the martyrs from the war in coffins, to their weeping widows, brought out the compassion in him. Raising funds for war widows, marching as a bugler in the funeral procession of Jawaharlal Lal Nehru at the age of eight, writing a play when seventeen to raise funds for army wives and singing patriotic songs around the dinner table have all baked courage and compassion along with a feeling of nationalism in Anil.

Hema Ravichandar's father, a Kerala cadre police officer, was posted with the home ministry in Delhi. She studied in Delhi's Mater Dei and at Lawrence School, Lovedale in Ooty, a boarding school. The importance of a good education was considered supreme in the family. Hema's mother served as her role model from her childhood. Early in life, she encouraged Hema to express her views, irrespective of the stage, often giving Hema and her brother topics to talk about and then asking them to prepare and make short presentations during dinner. She would help them with material to read for the presentations. Occasionally, she would share poetry for them to read and explain it to them, to help them grasp the deeper meaning. In the process, Hema developed a keen interest in understanding larger human issues.

Saurabh Dixit was born and brought up in a VIP family with his father holding an important portfolio at the Bank of Baroda. Saurabh won the first prize for his school in an elocution competition and when asked by his school headmaster what prize he would like for bringing this honour to his school, his considered answer was a day's holiday for the entire school because he considered himself to be a VIP like his father. Over the years, Saurabh had developed a sense of importance about the job that he was holding and the need to do it well.

These are just a few examples. In all, we had fifteen HRLs from 'well-to-do' families. They were sustained by family rituals, role-modelling by parents and engagement with the broader social or national agenda: Hema Ravichandar, P. Dwarkanath (Dwarka), Anand Nayak, Anil Sachdev, D. Harish, Rajeev Dubey, RR, Saurabh Dixit, Yogi Sriram, Marcel Parker, Satish Pradhan, Shrikant Gathoo, Anuranjita Kumar, Pradeep Mukerjee and Aroon Joshi.

Others, like Kishore K. Sinha, Pratik Kumar, Vivek Paranjpe, Santrupt Misra and Visty Banaji grew up in relatively smaller towns or villages, where their families had rather eminent positions for various reasons. Kishore's father had been friends with the children of India's first President and freedom fighter, Rajendra Prasad. As a man with strong anti-British political leanings and an imposing appearance (tall, broad shoulders, largish moustache), Kishore's father found it tough to land a job in British India. It was only after Independence that he landed a job in Ranchi as a bank officer. However, he was well-regarded in the village as 'Billu Babu' and his children were well taken care of. Kishore's abiding memory was how Hindu and Muslim families in the village would stand by each other in times of distress and participate in each other's festivals in happier times. Kishore's upbringing prepared him to be an inclusive leader and commit himself to larger causes.

Santrupt's father was a professor with a rich grounding in social sciences. For Santrupt, that was much more valuable than material wealth. He was also a liberal social crusader, who never imposed his views on others. He would also seek legal redress to undo perceived injustice. One such unresolved case had even cost him an administrative services career. The one lesson Santrupt learnt from his father was to never boast about achievements. His mother's side of the family had medical doctors and PhDs, and his mother herself was a public servant who invested in Santrupt a sense of respect for women.

These families, too, baked the characters of our HRLs by their role-model behaviour, while also connecting them to larger causes in support of society and the nation.

Some HRLs grew up in modest families. Ashok Balyan, Raghu Krishnamoorthy, S.V. Nathan, Niddodi Subrao (N.S.) Rajan, Dileep Ranjekar, Chandrasekhar Sripada (Chandra), Anil Khandelwal, Aquil Busrai and Sridhar Ganesh were deeply grounded in strong middle-class values.

- Ashok's father was a shahar kotwal—a policeman with 100 sub-inspectors under him—who refused a Rs 50,000 reward for having rescued an industrialist's daughter! This act was embedded in the psyche of the child and baked the priceless value of not expecting rewards for doing one's duty. His father's love for sports, ingrained in him, made him pursue sports throughout his academic career and institute sports in the company that he would lead in the distant future.

- Rajan's early childhood in a middle-class rural family, with a yen for learning, had his father instilling in him a respect for people. It was a lesson that his father held him to even later in life as Rajan was reprimanded by him for scolding the peon (Mohan) for not getting him the English newspaper. 'What is the difference between Mohan and you? Only opportunity,' was the sharp remonstrance.

- Dileep's father served with the police department. His family gave him all the freedom to choose a career. Dileep acknowledges that he learnt how to be upright and to figure out ways to deal with circumstances, adversarial or otherwise, from his father.

- Aquil was raised amidst financial hardships in his early childhood, living in a small 10x7 feet room with his mother. With his father passing away when he was only eleven years old, it was left to his mother to make both ends meet by stitching, giving tuitions and trading some consumer products. Aquil himself gave private tuitions and shared food with servants, even when there was very little to go around, a trait that came naturally to him. His mother's self-reliant nature and dignified way of living, despite such humble means, inspired Aquil to inculcate similar virtues in his own life.

In these nine families of relatively modest means, the parents were the role models and they baked strong human values in the HRLs early in their lives. These stayed with them right through. These illustrate how the baking of leadership qualities—resilience, empathy, courage, along with values like honesty, service and independence—starts from early childhood with the environment created by parents as well as their personal conduct. In more adverse circumstances, when one of the parents is absent, as in the case of Aquil or frequent transfers, as in the case of Nathan, societal influences or those of the extended family or the doubled influence of the single parent create the nurturing environment.

- Nathan had a very modest beginning with his family living in a single room in Chennai, where his father worked. After his father moved to Calcutta for better prospects, Nathan lived with his uncle in Chennai for two years. His mother, Bhageerathi, a school topper, had been unable to pursue higher education, given the many mouths to feed in the family. Things were no better for her daughter, Nathan's sister, Jayanthi, who had cracked the IIM admission test but could not pursue management education because their father could not afford the financial burden. Nathan wonders how things would have changed if women like his mother and sister had been supported in their education. They would not only have changed their own lives but made the world a better place. These experiences of how women were dispossessed in a family made a deep impression on Nathan and he was committed to looking out for women in his career; helping them to pursue their aspirations whenever possible.

- In Sridhar's case, the death of his father resulted in him having to fend for himself, become frugal and work hard.
- Yogi's loss of his father at the tender age of fifteen left him with a void but, thanks to his resolute nature, he picked himself up without leaning on anyone for support. Yogi also learnt to make his own decisions and rely strongly on his own instincts, even as he resolutely developed a determined and resilient personality.
- Saurabh was afflicted with polio that affected one side of his body. It was his mother who cared for him because his father was posted in London at the time and returned only after three and a half years. The other constant companion was his grandfather, who not only told him stories about the child Sri Krishna's mischief but also taught him basic etiquette that was to be of great importance in life.

One of the first important patterns that we discovered was that, regardless of the family's socio-economic circumstances, our HRLs were shaped by family rituals, role-modelling by parents or influential elders and the family's engagement with the broader societal and national agenda.

B. Schools and colleges

Schools and colleges impart not just knowledge and skills but, by providing early exposure to the external world and facilitating engagements with it, richly invest the youngsters with attitudes and values. They also provide opportunities to exhibit, activate and build leadership qualities through sports and extracurricular activities. Teachers have a tremendous impact on students at all ages with their human touch. The institution's infrastructure, facilities, its prevailing culture, the values that it promotes, the camaraderie, the discipline, the cocktail of activities, projects, programmes and the ability to be disciplined and yet carefree cannot but leave lasting impressions on a youngster. Much of this is often taken for granted while assessing what impacts the making of great leaders. They get acknowledged only upon deep reflection. During our interviews, we attempted to facilitate some reflection on the impact that their schools and colleges or other institutions that they attended had on our HRLs.

Our constituent HRLs went to different kinds of schools and colleges, ranging from the vernacular village school to eminent ones in major metros, but most of them pursued post-graduation studies in highly-reputed professional institutes. Regardless of their stature, these schools exposed them to community service, drew their attention to national causes and provided them with opportunities for well-rounded development through academic and extracurricular options. They got the intellectual space and a degree of freedom that helped our HRLs to choose their paths and evolve.

- Kishore went to a village school with a swadeshi flavour. Students often went on early morning processions through the village with the Indian tricolour, singing inspirational songs. It had a Gandhian touch and students would learn various crafts during the second half of the school day. He even marched to Nalanda, some thirty-five to forty miles away, in a group of 100 boys, singing songs. The Farakka dam over the River Ganga was under construction and boys between twelve and fifteen years of age were sent over to serve by donating labour (shram daan). Thousands of children from various places across the country came together to get a feel of nation-building that the dam represented. Kishore was developing an interest in understanding the larger agenda of a developing nation.
- Ashok went to a small village school where he sat on a floor mat through classes I–II and then trudged four kilometres to reach the Chaharwati Intermediate School, Akola for class III and IV.

The school had only one teacher for everyone. The fun lay in the loads of extracurricular activities because sports ran in his veins and that made him use sports for strengthening human resources in companies that he served.

- Pratik's father was the chief inspector of factories in Bihar in the sixties, which meant a life of transfers every couple of years. Getting thus transplanted from one place to another was a fascinating experience and Pratik was enchanted by new schools, new friends, comfortably adapting to new circumstances, playing with children from all strata of society, with no questions asked about the background. He learnt to fend for himself, stand up for his friends and, of course, to play cricket. There were holidays too, especially one pan-India tour in 1962 that was as engaging as it was educational. These helped Pratik to become an inclusive leader.

- Santrupt's formal schooling only began at the age of seven, when his father moved to Angul. It was not a smooth transition and Santrupt went from a school in Angul to one in Sambalpur and, finally, to Cuttack's Secondary Board High School. Such changes made him action-oriented even when he was in school; earning the sobriquet of 'safai mantri', as he made a habit of picking up straws that littered the road to school, making a makeshift broom and cleaning up the classrooms. Quick to learn from failures, Santrupt mastered the art of public speaking after he failed to speak for even thirty seconds at a Rotary Club event and went on to win prizes for debates in school and college. He joined the National Cadet Corps (NCC), learnt to do menial work like polishing shoes and would help carry people's luggage during train journeys. Santrupt understood dignity of labour, learnt to overcome obstacles and establish an expanded role for himself to serve the organization.

- Aquil learnt the biggest lessons in people management when he joined the Boy Scouts at school. The scoutmaster, Dr Kotwal, was a big influence on Aquil, instilling a sense of excellence in the boys. His deep involvement with every individual and sharp observation skills were exemplary. Here, Aquil also got to know boys from different backgrounds and communities—Chinese, Parsis, Marwaris and Bohris. Many came from rich families and lived in bungalows. Aquil visited their homes and welcomed them

to his home as well. The group would assemble every Thursday
at St Thomas Church on Free School Street, in full Boy Scouts'
uniform and soon Aquil was leading a patrol of seven boys. He
tried very hard to make his team the best and Aquil himself did well
enough to win the President's Scout badge. These early experiences
convinced Aquil about his leadership capability and gave him the
confidence that he could achieve excellence against all odds.

- Visty joined the NCC, which gave him exposure to the nuances of
  leadership early in his life. He enjoyed this and rose to the level of
  a senior officer.

Likewise, Nathan, Dileep, Chandra, Anil, Rajan and Vivek went
to modest schools that, nonetheless, were instrumental in baking
their characters, which stood them in good stead as they grew to be
eminent HRLs.

- Vineet, by contrast, went to the famous Lawrence School at
  Sanawar and the army-run King George's School from class V. The
  school had three football grounds, two cricket grounds, four hockey
  grounds, one swimming pool, two basketball courts, three courts for
  volleyball, tennis and squash courts for a school of 360 children. It
  was a delight for the boy, who did well in sports but also developed
  a yen for history, literature and economics; all horizon-expanding
  experiences. Life itself injected flexibility and adaptability into his
  persona. A 90 per cent at the All-India General Knowledge Test
  and an 80 per cent at the UNO's won him plaudits. His principal,
  impressed with his talk on the UN, asked him to present a news
  bulletin every day. This meant listening to the news every evening,
  referring to newspapers and preparing a bulletin for school the next
  day. This had all the ingredients to bake Vineet into a well-rounded
  boy by the time he completed class XI.

Pradeep, Hema, Anuranjita and Marcel went to affluent boarding
schools that baked their leadership capabilities, marked with
independence, discipline and respect for people. Even at the college
levels, HRLs who went to modest and relatively lesser-known colleges,
grew by immersing themselves in sports, libraries and extracurricular
activities, leveraging the freedom that they enjoyed.

- Dileep enrolled himself for BSc with zoology, botany and chemistry at the Ahmednagar College, an excellent institution set up by the Barnabas Family. It had a beautiful chapel and a large library with more than one lakh books and over 100 cubicles for individual studies. Making excellent use of the academic freedom, Dileep became a voracious reader of Marathi novels in particular. An excellent auditorium there gave him exposure to theatre personalities, including the famous Prof. Madhukar Toradmal, a member of the faculty at Ahmednagar College. His classmates included Sadashiv Amrapurkar, who had acted in much-acclaimed Bollywood films such as *Ardh Satya*. The gregarious Dileep developed a large circle of friends, evolving with a sense of independence and excellent people connect that became his forte in life.
- Chandra, disappointed with the rejection by St Stephen's because of his vernacular background, enrolled at the Central University in Hyderabad that, over time, influenced his thinking through poetry. Its rich library was his window to a world of literature. The CIEFL (now the English and Foreign Languages University, EFLU) with its phonetics lab helped him to speak English without an accent, which added to his self-confidence. Chandra was baked afresh by his college experience.

HRLs like Raghu, Rajeev, Yogi, Marcel, Anuranjita, Anil, Aquil, Vivek, Vineet, Anand and Satish and others evolved through high-quality academic environments, supplemented by extracurricular activities that reputed colleges offered.

- Anand served one day a week at a rural dispensary and visited old age homes to cheer the residents, sometimes singing for them. The food-for-work programme at Hasan that he attended for a few weeks early in life deepened his proclivity for service.
- Raghu was a bundle of activity from his early school days, learning a great deal through extracurricular activities. He excelled in table tennis and his competitive spirit was honed by participating in TT contests. He gave an excellent account of himself at state-level championships as well as in debates and quizzes. Travelling with his college team widened the circle influencing him, making for rich learning experiences at Nizam College, Hyderabad. It was peer

influence more than anything else that stoked his ambition to raise
the bar for himself.

- Pradeep was at Mayo College, Ajmer, a boarding school, for some
  time. This stint made him independent. He made important choices
  about his school board examinations independently in class VIII. IIT
  Kharagpur was yet another liberating and learning phase. Pradeep
  won the prize for the most enterprising 'fresher' as he would always
  help out with organizing stuff. Pradeep continued to demonstrate
  this streak of independence and enterprise later in his career.

Going to such eminent colleges as Nizam, Bishop Cotton,
Fergusson, St Xavier's, Hindu, Shri Ram College of Commerce,
St Stephen's and Indraprastha College baked our HRLs to grow into
well-rounded leaders. Save for a few, they pursued post-graduation in
highly-reputed professional institutes such as XLRI, TISS, IIM, Leeds
and Yale, although the choice may have been a matter of coincidence or
courtesy a gentle nudge from a friend, a well-wisher or a teacher.

- Anuranjita was all set to go overseas after her undergraduate
  studies at the Indraprastha College, Delhi, but her professor,
  Mrs P. Kapoor, inspired her to go in for a management degree. She
  went to XLRI instead of going to the US. Such was the influence
  of her professor!
- Vivek had registered for studying law when he came across an XLRI
  advertisement. It was somewhat expensive but his father's senior
  colleague at Bank of Baroda endorsed the institution, observing
  that, after an XLRI education, Vivek would land himself a big
  job with several people reporting to him. This was consistent with
  Vivek's own aspiration and he made it to XLRI.
- Pradeep followed his father's colleague, an HR man with Tata
  Power, to apply for TISS, to pursue a course that prepared him for
  a career in human resource management.
- Sridhar's heart was in medicine, but having failed to qualify in
  the entrance examinations, he pursued undergraduate studies at
  St Xavier's. There he heard about management education for the
  first time. Along with four or five friends, he sat for admission to
  IIM Calcutta and cracked it.

- Dileep, who had done his MBA from Pune University, discovered during his first job interview that his MBA had very little brand value. When he came across a catchy TISS advertisement by chance, he made a dash for it.

Financial straits forced some to pursue their post-graduation in lesser-known universities or colleges.

- Kishore moved to Patna to study economics at Patna College and graduated among the top ten in the university. He qualified for XLRI but, without the resources to pursue studies there, he settled for a Patna University course in labour and social welfare that charged all of Rs 11 a month, which the family could afford.

There were others who pursued post-graduation in other disciplines but came into HR.

- E.I. George, the psychology teacher, who had RR spellbound, persuaded him to go to IIT Kharagpur to study industrial psychology.
- Satish, keen on history, opted for JNU on a junior research fellowship for an integrated MPhil–PhD programme, only to get disillusioned by the academic environment there. He then sat for competitive exams and joined SAIL.
- Visty, after doing graduate studies at Hislop College, Nagpur University, with literature, philosophy and psychology, moved to Mumbai to do his master's in philosophy. He realized that it would do little to enhance his career prospects and, on the advice of his neighbour, who worked at Empress Mills, joined the prestigious Tata Administrative Services.

We are tempted to conclude that the institution one went to did not matter as much as the kind of experiences that the institution offered in the baking of our HRLs. Some institutions like XLRI—more so the teachers there—provided the crucible experiences, as the next section indicates.

C. Influence of their teachers

Apart from the influence of their schools and colleges, our HRLs were deeply impacted by what their teachers taught, the way they taught and their personal conduct. These made for abiding impressions. The teachers helped to bake the right values and professional temper that were life-changing for the HRLs, who generally excelled in their studies. Some, who did not, saw sense after suffering reverses from taking studies lightly and, appropriately counselled by the teachers, were propelled to change their attitude. Eventually, they too got into the business of excelling academically. The HRLs were meaningfully influenced by their peers, particularly in making the right professional choices.

Anuranjita's psychology professor, Dr (Mrs) Kapoor influenced her to give up her plans for higher studies in the US and join XLRI instead. It was life-changing for her. Likewise, at IIMA, Hema and Raghu were deeply influenced by the T-group sessions facilitated by Prof. Pulin Garg and HR subjects taught by Prof. T.V. Rao, as they opted for HR as a profession. At the IIMC, heavyweight professors as Gouranga P. Chattopadhyay, who taught transactional analysis and Nitish De, who taught personality development, influenced Sridhar to go in for HR. Several HRLs from XLRI, such as Aquil, Nathan, Vivek, Pratik, Harish and Rajan were influenced by Prof. Nilima Acharji there. Her teaching approach made for deeply immersive experiences and invested them with a sense of empathy for the underprivileged, which baked their mental make-up. They developed a deep respect, compassion and a sense of fair play when it came to the blue-collar workers. Vivek, for instance, was required to interview beggars and live with construction workers and made an emotional presentation on his findings at XLRI.

The personal conduct of the teachers and their connect with their students contributed considerably to the baking of their characters.

- Prof. Pritam Singh of XLRI often invited students to his home and shared his thoughts with them over dinner.
- At St Xavier's College, Sridhar was deeply impacted by the disciplined lifestyles of the French Belgian Jesuit priests.
- At MS Baroda, Prof. Indiraben Patel confronted Saurabh with a challenge: only when he got an A would he be allowed to attend her classes.

- Ashok got interested in chemistry courtesy Prof. P.I. Ittyerah's engaging storytelling style.
- Prof. N.K. Maheshwari told Shrikant that he could easily become an all-rounder if only he took studies a little more seriously. Shrikant pulled up his socks and took a hard look at academics, never to look back.

These were all life-changing encounters and messages.

- For Chandra, the fantastic Prof. Mangesh Vital Nadkarni of linguistics and phonetics at the CIEFL (now EFLU) with its phonetics lab, almost wove a magic wand, as he helped Chandra to speak English without any accent. This process singularly baked Chandra's self-confidence for life.
- Fr D'Souza, the XLRI director, cancelled an event because the students were making a ruckus, even though a guest was present. He gave the students a tongue-lashing the following morning, asking the noisy students to own up. Pratik, among the five or six who did, was summoned to his room but only to be complimented for their honesty. Thanks to Fr D'Souza's conduct, Pratik understood the lasting value of having the 'courage to own up' to one's mistakes.
- Prof. McGrath at XLRI never 'taught' but interacted and created an environment of self-discovery and self-learning. The ability to listen and provide psychological space to people, be it a colleague, direct report, union leader or shop floor worker, has been key to Anand's people connect. In St Joseph's College, Bangalore, Anand was inspired by the Jesuit priest, Father Peter Ceyrac SJ, a Frenchman, who had made India his home for more than forty years. He exhorted students to: 'Stay on and work for the people of your country. Only rats desert a sinking ship.' Such passionate patriotism made Anand stay on in India unlike many of his friends who were headed overseas in search of better lives.

Most Jesuit institutions focused equally on academics and community service, working with the poor in urban slums and rural areas, getting students to spend a couple of weeks during every school and college vacation at rural work camps under their watchful eyes.

These experiences instilled the spirit of 'service to others', which was of seminal value in Anand's upbringing. He was imbued with a caring nature that extended to all fellow human beings, alongside his academic pursuits in missionary institutions, and stayed with him   all his life. Anand ensured that no worker under his watch was exploited.

- Maths was Santrupt's weak point even when he secured 800 marks overall in class 11 but failed in two maths papers. His maths teacher, Vishnu Prasad Jain, fetched up to their home on a bicycle at 4.30 a.m. just to counsel him and shore up his self-confidence. That gesture was inspirational and Santrupt went on to secure 95–96 per cent in both his maths papers thereafter.
- At St Xavier's School, G.G. Brandon, the art teacher, apologized to Satish, in the presence of the principal, for his unwarranted outburst that had nothing to do with Satish's drawing. Brandon's demonstration of humility and fair play had a lifelong impact on Satish's psyche.

These are a few examples of how role-model teachers, by their approach to teaching, the power of their lessons and by their personal conduct, made a deep and enduring impact, influencing the HRLs at all stages in their lives. They propelled them to excel in studies and make correct career choices by baking their world views and helping them to embrace outstanding values that determined their thoughts and deeds throughout their lives.

D. Learning from the crucible of their first jobs

First jobs offer a lot of learning opportunities. McCall et al. (1988), in their classical and often-quoted study of successful executives, observed that the most important driving force was the job challenge faced by these managers. The experiences of the first job and other early jobs lay the foundation for subsequent competency-building and leadership action. In another classical study of the formative years, Bray and associates at AT&T found management success to be associated with the first job challenge and assignment stress and unstructured assignments (Bray et al., 1974). McCall et al. also presented a body of evidence indicating the significance of the first job and early careers in preparing the stage for later success. We observed the same in our HR leaders.

- Shrikant Gathoo was among the twenty selected from 2000 applicants for a BHEL position. Upon joining, he read two volumes of BHEL's personnel manual on its system orientation and found the learnings fascinating and significant. Shrikant was a quick learner and in his three years at BHEL, before moving on to NTPC, Shrikant assisted his boss, Sinha, to set up a township, among other things. That was an enormous learning opportunity. The first NTPC assignment was just as rewarding, Shrikant had to hire 2000 people for the Korba project and spent the first six months establishing a foolproof selection process that would be immune from political interference.

- A change in jobs often catapults one into a new sphere with every experience providing new learnings. Shrikant's case demonstrates that he was in a constantly learning mode at BHEL, NTPC and subsequently, in BPCL. Some new learnings were path-breaking in nature, as Shrikant engaged painstakingly with parliamentarians and the law-making process for six months to bring about a legislative change around the law of succession. It needed an act of Parliament to set aside an earlier act, whereby Burmah Shell wages did not become binding on BPCL that had taken over Burmah Shell. In his 'will do, can do' approach, he found inspiration from his father's fauji spirit that taught him not to waste time asking questions but to resolutely do whatever had to be done, whether it was taking on the implementation of SAP or irate unions or selling lubricants. McCall et al. (1988) emphasized that jobs (first-hand experience) seemed to be the best development tool.

We found that most of the HRLs started their professional careers with structured, accountable jobs. In a few cases, where the jobs themselves were routine, the HRLs were able to convert them into meaningful learning opportunities, rather than cribbing about them. Often, routine assignments are treated as a waste of time. In fact, in recent times, some HR leaders have observed that HR has no future if the HR staff reduces themselves to doing routine work that could be done by machines. That attitude will render their jobs replaceable with the emergence of AI presenting a very legitimate threat. Not all our HRLs got routine assignments. When they did, our HRLs did not treat them as humdrum but extracted value from them as well.

We do not consider industrial relations assignments as routine because they are emotionally challenging, particularly in the Indian milieu. However, maintaining attendance records, files of appointments, performance appraisal data, training programme data and such data maintenance and record-keeping are considered routine. Such routine tasks can, however, provide insights that help one to make a difference:

- The first challenge that Saurabh faced at Reliance was to regularize the personnel files. Many files did not even have appointment letters and many said they worked directly with the Reliance chairman, Dhirubhai Ambani, himself. He learnt a lot about streamlining systems and also about people.
- Dileep was placed in charge of a factory with 800 employees.
- Vineet, in Tata Motors, was responsible for hiring nearly 1000 workers every month.
- Dwarka was assigned to Usha Sewing Machines in Kolkata with 10,000 employees. He learnt the nuances of his job by closely observing his boss, Chanchal Raj Singhvi.
- Nathan was posted at ICI Ennore and had to handle the unhappy task of managing VRS.
- Rajan, unlike other HRLs, started his career in field sales with Ranbaxy.
- At DCM, RR learnt by observing his boss, Paul. Among other things, RR was assigned the task of reading articles and papers and sharing the summary with Paul. RR, who also organized and ran training programmes for the DCM employees, used the programmes to educate himself. They amounted to tremendous learning.
- Vivek was mentored for six months by Ginde, the deputy factory manager at Sewri, before being posted as factory personnel manager in Taloja.
- Rajeev had a structured, six-month induction with the Tata Group and then another six-month induction at Tata Steel, in the finance and marketing functions.
- Harish got the opportunity to work on several HR-related subjects at Sundram Fasteners, often pushing the boundaries for the company. He tried to apply his knowledge to create new systems.

His work spanned from performance management to career planning and from developing a matrix for evaluating interviewees to talent development.

- Harish had a great boss in Sambamurthy and learnt a great deal from him. The relationship soon developed into one of a trusted mentor and protégé.
- Ashok's first job was at the R&D department with the Shri Ram Institute for Industrial Research in Delhi. His long hours of research on polymers and plastics in December 1972 at the laboratory got him two patents that stand to his credit.

Confronted with routine jobs, some of the HRLs converted them into deep learning opportunities rather than moan about them.

- One of Aquil's first tasks was to fill up information cards for every worker. The work seemed boring at first but when he went about meeting the workmen and their leaders, he realized that it had familiarized him with every detail about almost every employee, including the trade union leaders, which was an enormous advantage.
- Kishore did not recoil from the mundane assignment of maintaining employee records in his first job. He managed to extract many insights from these employee profiles.
- Pradeep's routine task of allocating resources, as per the submitted requirements of project managers, was not treated like a mindless exercise. Pradeep made sure that he examined the requirement and developed a point of view for informed decision-making. He did not act as a mere postman.
- Visty, in his corporate role at Tata Motors, was responsible for putting up the manpower requests to the MD. Instead of just forwarding the requests, Visty examined and analysed them before sending them up with his recommendations on the file. To facilitate the process, Visty set up an industrial engineering function in the company.
- Transferred from the training function to the position of AGM personnel at Bank of Baroda, corporate office, Anil Khandelwal found that there was no real job allocated to him. Anil utilized the

time to go over the files of other bank officers and made himself a valuable resource to the chairman. So much so that whenever any 'people' decision was required, he would be asked to chip in given his encyclopaedic information about people.

- Hema never shied away from the transactional and routine as she found that 'data mining, for example, considered by many as transactional, delivers diamonds of information as nuggets'. She found the transactional interventions to be as important as the strategic ones. As she said: 'That is the philosophy that I have lived by through my career. But I have consciously worked on providing bandwidth and capacity to deliver on the transformational.'

Our HRL case studies indicate that, irrespective of the structured induction, their keenness to learn baked them as leaders. These HRLs found merit in even routine jobs as they converted them into learning opportunities to get a better grasp of the company and to learn the business in-depth. This narration bears ample testimony to the importance of the first jobs even when they appeared to be routine. They represented early career challenges in building HR leaders or, for that matter, any leader.

The foundational elements in early career experiences pertain to building self-confidence, identification of potential and execution abilities. For some, they offer opportunities to become innovative, develop out-of-the-box thinking and the ability to execute them. These experiences have had lasting impacts on the baking of our HR leaders. All of them remembered their first jobs with a sense of fulfilment. The first-job crucible experience often depends on the approach that the person takes. The other significant messaging for organizations is that they need not shy away from giving routine and difficult jobs to entry-level executives because they can build a great deal more by way of leadership skills if they plan systematic reviews with them and assign managers who can be mentors and influencers.

E. Learning from their bosses

As they progressed in their careers, bosses played key roles as mentors in all cases. Such bosses were supportive, inspiring, demanding and served as role models, taking a keen interest in developing the HRLs. The characters of the boss varied but by observing them and being guided by them, our HRLs were rewarded with transformative experiences.

Supportive bosses:

- Pratik was supported by Paul and Premji when it came to honouring campus commitments, even though circumstances had turned adverse.
- Kuldeep Chandra, head of chemistry, was of outstanding support as Ashok plunged into the job of unpacking new equipment lying unused.
- Arun Maira's encouraging style impacted Anil Sachdev.

Bosses as mentors:

- Pratik learnt etiquette from Siddiqui in HMT.
- Ashok learnt a lot from S.N. Talukdar, a brilliant geologist and a super exploration man.
- Moolgaonkar inspired many and convinced people like Visty to believe that to make a difference in the world, they needed to serve the country and that by working in Telco, a home-grown company, they were serving the nation. They were also inspired to apply their minds and come up with ideas and conduct experiments, instead of running to consultants. Moolgaonkar constantly walked that extra mile and was passionately charged by the superordinate goal of working for the nation by working for Telco. Visty not only learnt about community development from Moolgaonkar but photography as well.
- Visty learnt how to survive tough situations from Mahesh.
- Harish benefited from the mentoring of his boss, Sambamurthy, who was like a father figure to him.
- Anil Sachdev benefited from the early influence of Mahesh, who persuaded him to join Telco. Anil also saw and imbibed Arun Maira's encouraging style.
- At Eicher, Anil learnt the essence of humility from Vikram Lal and developed the ability to genuinely connect with workers on the factory floor.

Demanding bosses:

- Paul moulded Pratik's thinking, decisiveness and ability to cut through the clutter, improving his responsiveness at Wipro. He also taught him to look at the business dimension.
- Jain was an amazing boss who would walk up to Pradeep rather than summon him to his desk. He guided Pradeep about the need to think about the decisions being taken and then to come up with recommendations.
- Dileep, in the corporate office of the consumer products business of Wipro, working under P.S. Pai—a tough, demanding and mercurial boss—learnt the art of grassroots management, including good housekeeping at the plant.
- Raghu recalls learning from an Irish boss, an empathetic as well as tough taskmaster.

Role model bosses (learning by observing them in action):

- Shrikant observed his boss, Saini, dealing with an abusive union leader in the conference room. Saini calmly told the irate leader that he was using a criminal's language and that criminals were dealt with on the streets and not in conference rooms. He succeeded in getting him to behave.
- Nathan learnt from the ICI senior bosses that one should carry one's attaché case and not expect the bearers to do so, as was the custom in many multinational firms. Nathan learnt never to encourage subservience or be overly reverential.
- Ganesh Jejurikar taught Nathan the art of gracious hospitality, as he personally looked after the candidates, including Nathan, offering tea and biscuits during interviews at ICI House. Jejurikar also showed class when he insisted on paying for minor repairs done in his company accommodation.
- Raghu's early exposure to great bosses in Escorts and Niki Tasha inspired him to dream big. Being allowed to interact with seniors, despite being relatively junior in the organization, gave him opportunities to watch and imbibe.
- Raghu, as CHRO of the global sales force, was part of Jeff Immelt's quarterly meets and benefitted immensely from exposure to top-level minds.

- Yogi, reporting to R.V. Shahi, the former power secretary, who was a director at NTPC, credits his boss for helping him develop structured and logical thinking. This he inculcated over the innumerable debates that the two would engage in on diverse topics.

Unpleasant bosses:

Good HRLs have learnt as much from good bosses as the poorly-behaved ones. Occasionally, some did come across bosses who were unpleasant and not supportive.

- Towards the end of his tenure, Kishore's relationship with his new chairman soured and he quit using the age issue as an excuse. The point was that Kishore was uncomfortable working with the person and chose to part ways.
- Rajeev Dubey sensed cracks in his relationship with the new chairman of the company and ultimately quit but not before imbibing deep learnings from his unpleasant experience.
- Satish found his views at variance with his boss on some issues of import. While quitting was an option, he stuck to the commitment that he had made to the Tata supremo himself that he would not be a quitter. He was determined to find avenues to make significant differences to the organization and found ways to navigate through choppy corporate waters and make meaningful contributions.
- Chandra had his share of pleasant and abusive bosses. He had a shouting, insulting and humiliating boss, with whom no cordial interpersonal relations were possible. The constant boorish behaviour, which bordered on attempted humiliation, hurt his self-esteem. Chandra drew upon his inbuilt resilience to handle such depredations. He had developed it over the conscious process of self-transformation from a rural boy from an indigent background, through his journey into mind-liberating literature, into an accomplished HRL.

Reflective learning, confronting, adjusting and even quitting were some of the strategies used by our HRLs in dealing with difficult bosses. There is no uniform way of dealing with a difficult boss, but our HRLs used their intellectual and emotional devices and past experience to address unpleasant bosses and grow in stature, as it were. Indeed, they leveraged these experiences to learn and build themselves.

Clearly, good bosses bake and shape the destinies of HR leaders by recognizing their potential, giving them freedom and empowering them with opportunities to create new systems and processes. They also help develop new capabilities and invest their juniors with the self-confidence required to make a difference in the company and to their own personas.

F. Learning from stretch jobs and business roles

Our interviews indicated that job changes and challenging new assignments provided good crucible experiences. When a professional, trained in a particular function, is given a role in a different function, it creates a crucible experience. Some of our HR leaders were given line jobs on functions that they had not handled before, creating new learning opportunities for them. Some were given difficult jobs that stretched their roles. These included dealing with mergers and acquisitions. All of them were crucible experiences and built them up with new exposure, new insights, more self-confidence and understanding of the business. These, in turn, strengthened their HR leadership skills.

As HRLs progressed through their careers, they went through a slew of stretch jobs offering challenges and learning opportunities. In many instances, they were given the opportunity to do a stint in line positions through which they got first-hand exposure to business realities. There are some outstanding instances of line exposures providing truly crucible experiences that baked the mental model of the HRLs.

- For Rajan, the journey was the other way round. He started in sales and then moved to the recruitment business, consulting business and, finally, became the CHRO of Tata Sons, at the very top of the organization.
- Rajeev came from a line function, having run a company as MD, to the role of CHRO at Mahindra's.
- Ashok successfully worked for ONGC in Nagaland and Assam, increasing production and reducing cycle time, overcoming serious challenges, including terrorist threats. After his successful innings in refineries, he was moved to the CHRO position.

- Shrikant was moved as business head of the lubricant business and was later assigned to lead the company-wide IT initiative.
- Aroon was given the additional responsibility of running the Metal Box Bombay factory when the factory manager died.
- Anil Sachdev was sent to Eicher's Faridabad factory as the works manager with 1000 people working there and a production manager many years his senior. It was both a humbling and a richly-rewarding experience, especially working with the unions.
- Anil Khandelwal's transition from a staff to a line role is another fine example. Largely in the personnel and training function for a long part of his career, Anil was given the first opportunity to lead a difficult zone in banking for the first time as a DGM. He did a great job and was posted to another troubled zone. There, he surpassed all expectations as business manager of a difficult industry like banking and was rewarded with the position of executive director. He went on to become chairman and managing director of first, Dena Bank and then the CMD of Bank of Baroda.
- Santrupt took on the responsibility of leading two large global businesses in addition to continuing with his Group CHRO role.

By doing these business roles, HRLs also developed new perspectives about the HR role itself.

- Pratik, as a business head, recognized that HR needed to shed its self-restraint and develop muscles to talk straight to the boss. It would simultaneously have to sustain its ability to listen and be perfectly aware of what was going on, without being ostrich-like about its position. As the genuine custodian of organizational value and culture, HR could not remain a one-way street. It needed to engage with and mould every individual in a manner that would best suit the person and the role.

Our HRLs were also thrown into managing numerous mergers and acquisition situations that were just as stressful. The stories of Vivek, Chandra, Satish, RR and Dwarkanath provide detailed accounts of the M&A challenges that they addressed, as they leveraged their experience and capabilities to deliver the desired outcomes while learning significant lessons themselves.

- Satish's management of the Lipton and Brooke Bond merger provides a detailed picture of such an experience. He had a clear mandate from the chairman who wanted the A+B to hold in terms of revenue and profit. This remarkably simple statement encapsulated an enormous demand, particularly for Satish for whom it was a new ball game altogether. He only knew M&As through his readings about the Ciba-Geigy merger. This was thus a big-stretch assignment that unleashed a beehive of activity with new learnings in every nook and cranny. Over the three years that Satish managed the merger, he worked from 8 a.m. to 3 a.m. every day, Saturdays, Sundays and holidays included, with the highly talented K. Ram Kumar (HR manager) and K.S. Kumar (compensation and benefits). The sheer administrative details and the paperwork, the challenge of sophisticated thinking to guide an excellent design, the planning and the perspective-setting drove the adrenaline, while Nair gave him space for independent initiatives.

  Satish launched into an exciting gamut of activities, designing the structure, processes, workflows, transitions, talent management while managing integration and softening the trauma of the paring down of numbers from 1100 to 700. He prepared a dossier on every individual and customized a fair deal for every pink-slipped person. It was a lone, uphill task settling every individual case with his boss. The algorithmic formulation from finance needed to be humanized. Satish tried to be mindful of everyone's unique circumstances; sick parents, college-going children and such personal circumstances and interacted closely with finance to get support for the parting packages. In the process, he became au fait with that aspect of the business. Exhausting though this exercise was, Satish had an optimum structure in place in eighteen months. This multidimensional crucible experience prepared him well for future challenges at ICI in a global assignment.

Business roles and M&As apart, HRLs went through many stretch-job crucibles during their years in HR itself. Each one of our thirty cases provides a comprehensive account of the challenge.

- Raghu, as the CHRO of GE's aviation business, contributed to turning around the business by getting people to take pride in being a part of the distinguished workforce that worked in manufacturing for the defence sector. He defined and created the unique culture needed for the business and used different strategic tools to get the mojo back into the business through workshops, where people discovered the purpose of their being and the aviation business.

- The GE Training Centre, Crontonville, offered more opportunities to Raghu to innovate and win. As the chief learning officer there, he created a process of exposure to succession planning for the top positions. Then, through interactions with the board members, he worked out a 'profile' of the GE leader for the 'future'. He facilitated and developed leaders by taking them to unusual places like Antarctica, Normandy and even Cuba to help potential future leaders confront the unknown.

- Yogi was saddled with stretch at the age of twenty-two, right when he had just started his career in ACC, as his supervisor fell rather ill all of a sudden. Yogi found himself at the helm of HR of the cement-manufacturing unit with 6000 workers; a crucible that taught him hard lessons in industrial relations.

- In 1988, after terrorism was rampant in J&K, Marcel had the onerous responsibility of concluding a long-term settlement with the strong unions and the locals very suspicious of outsiders. In the process of handling this stretch responsibility, Marcel learnt the importance of navigating his way through external and internal politics. He discovered that by being transparent and firm, he could win the confidence of both workers and unions.

- During his stint with Sterling Holidays, Nathan discovered that people had to be convinced to work for a timeshare company. He had to sell the idea of the job to the candidate and then train them to sell timeshare. Nathan felt that it was important to sell some timeshare himself and started doing it in right earnest, approaching everyone he came across, even a co-passenger on the train, with the concept. In the process, he learnt about the challenges that selling the concept would involve and also discovered unexpected capabilities in people with unusual backgrounds, which he could work with. He started appointing them in HR leadership roles.

- At Reliance, in the crucible of a rapidly changing business ecosystem, Chandra realized how different phases in corporate growth needed qualitatively different roles for CHROs. It is not a unifaceted role and the skills, competencies and mindsets need to be dramatically overhauled with the changing business challenges. The HR person was the gardener at the developmental phases of companies. At later phases, when the company demanded increasing efficiency, saving costs, fixing people into roles and even downsizing, the CHRO, who may have been a perfect fit for one phase, could turn out to be the worst for the other. Chandra learnt the importance of versatility in a CHRO.

- At Philips, Vineet's challenge was to make the management more transparent. He organized town hall dialogues with all 4000–4500 employees every four months, personally anchoring the live proceedings over 16 VSATs. Unanswered questions were addressed in a booklet within ten days. This path-breaking effort was commended by the media as well as the visiting global board who wanted it to be replicated in Amsterdam. Alongside, Vineet handled the restructuring of job grading in line with group principles, rolling out a robust talent-management process and revamping L&D programmes. The crucible of these challenges that Philips was facing pushed Vineet to think creatively, to launch a multitude of innovative initiatives that finally catapulted Philips to a position in Hewitt's Best Employer list.

Stretch jobs come in a variety of avatars, often appearing to be traumatic at the outset. Indeed, no development occurs without a lot of sweat. Our HRLs took these challenges on their shoulders, used their imagination, treating them as learning opportunities to emerge as far more capable people than they were at the outset. They were truly crucible experiences that engendered a comprehensive enhancement of their HR capabilities.

G. Crucible of industrial relations

The classic study of the development of 191 successful leaders from different corporations by McCall, Lombardo and Morrison (1988) has a chapter, 'Trial by Fire', in which they observed that mastering challenging assignments is related to management success. A similar observation was made by Douglas Bray and associates in AT&T (1974). In terms of crucible experiences, all our HRLs, with the exception of Rajan, had first-hand exposure to dealing with industrial relations of blue or white-collar grassroots-level employees. This is particularly interesting as HR professionals quite often get inducted in corporate offices these days and grow in their careers without having any exposure to dealing with grassroots-level employees. Once they have had such experiences, they have found them to be humbling, among other things. There is no substitute to experiencing this first-hand.

- Sridhar recalls a workman coming to him for a loan from his PF account. Sridhar first dismissed the loan-seeker saying that he was not eligible as he had already claimed the privilege the previous year. The diminutive union leader, Ajit Kundu, challenged him with a question that bowled him over: 'Is it your job only to tell him that he is not eligible? You are a qualified man. Is it not your job to find a solution?' This powerful question disturbed Sridhar for days and made him question the bigger purpose of his role and, indeed, life; a truly transformational impact.

Stories shared in this book provide vivid accounts of such crucible experiences of HRLs dealing with grassroots-level employee issues that made for transformational experiences for them. These may be categorized as experiences with unionized or not-unionized employees, such as the white-collar workforce that Hema dealt with at Infosys and Pratik at WIPRO.

- Early in his career at TVSE, Pratik was confronted with the task of downsizing seventy to eighty employees. These were the very people that Pratik had been personally involved in hiring in the recent past. Pratik was in a quandary about how he would sack his own recruits. They had become friends and the prospect of betraying them made him lose sleep. He tried to do it with the greatest sensitivity, but some getting the pink slip got abusive while others sought help as they looked for alternatives. Pratik shared his own home with many of them and found accommodation for the others in his friends' homes.

- Aquil was confronted with the unpleasant task of terminating a peon for high absenteeism. The offender's pleading and crying made the situation tougher. Pushed by the labour adviser, Aquil talked to the employee and learnt that he was taking repeated leave to take care of his ailing wife. Aquil salvaged the situation but got him to promise that he would henceforth be more regular.

- While matters between management and unions were fought at courts at BPCL, Shrikant focused on making working relations as amicable as possible. His outreach included having cordial relations with the families of those he fought in courts and attending social functions at their homes. It was an enormous tussle that Shrikant managed, while fine-tuning his art of marrying diplomacy and power and deploying both these weapons with dexterity and intelligent manoeuvring. These had helped Shrikant evolve into a sharpened HR person.

- Kishore was thrown into an industrial relations crisis at Usha Martin Black at the very beginning of his first job. 'It was baptism by fire for me; I learnt at the deep end of industrial relations and all its nuances, including the relevant legal provisions.' Kishore also worked through the militant trade unionism of West Bengal of the 1970s, when labour agreements would often get signed under the threat of physical harm and there were stories of a manager being pricked with pins till he agreed to sign on the dotted line.

- Another telling experience for Kishore was when a lockout notice was issued and 150 workers were terminated. The police opened fire after some people were injured by arrows that were shot at them. A trade union leader died and the plant remained closed for three months, opening only after the government intervened. These IR experiences prepared Kishore for dealing with all kinds of crises in his career. He was fair, firm and fearless.

- Industrial relations has been a part of the baking process even for those who worked in MNCs like HLL. Harish faced his first strike at the Hindustan Lever factory; a thirty-five-day closure that ended in terms favourable to the management. When the workers returned, Harish did not want them to feel defeated but arranged for garlands to welcome them back. His innovative ways got noticed and he was transferred to Coimbatore which had four unions and eighteen strikes in fourteen years. Harish successfully handled this as well. He went on a training programme to the UK and also visited a Manchester tea factory that had high productivity. Back at the Whitefield Coffee Factory for eighteen months, where his mandate was to make it the best coffee factory in three years, Harish was building the momentum toward this, when the top management decided to close the factory. Harish had the unhappy task of getting the 110 workers to quit and handled the separation with great sensitivity, designing an innovative separation package.

- Assigned to the Unilever London office for a global project that involved driving enterprise culture worldwide along with Prof. Wayne Brockbank and another expert from the Netherlands, Harish returned home on completion of the global stint as head of industrial relations. He brought abiding pride to the job, reshaping worker relationships from the confrontational to the consultative and broadening the IR manager's role to that of a plant HR role. This was about raising the stature of the profession and pride in their jobs.

- Gheraoed (a sit-in demonstration where management personnel are not allowed to leave) by the workers, after returning to the office from the courts, where he was taking care of the legal proceedings, Pradeep sat through the gherao, interacting with the workers who sat around him in protest. The secret was in removing all animosity from the dialogue and Pradeep soon became a hero of sorts in the company.

- As the general manager (town services), Rajeev had to constantly grapple with issues of law and order in the township. He recalls reaching the town office one morning to find an angry mob of women, children and elderly people shouting slogans of 'Rajeev

Dubey murdabad' because the electricity supply to an unauthorized colony had been cut off. On another occasion, he was sitting in his office with the superintendent of police, when he received news that there was some violence against the town division officers doing a market inspection. In retrospect, Rajeev believes this to be among the finest and most challenging assignments that he had handled and were the stepping stones for bigger assignments.

- For Vineet, eleven and a half years at Tata Motors was one large and intense crucible of experiences that prepared him for all IR crises that he would ever have to deal with and got him to use his immense creativity and courage. This crucible experience at Tata Motors literally baked him for successfully managing much larger and complex IR challenges as well as the wider HR agenda in Eicher, Philips and Hindalco.

- Aroon learnt from Dayal that HR was not about doing mara-mari (fighting). It was about assisting managements to obtain the spontaneous cooperation of workers for achieving the organizational goals. After the eight-month strike at Cadbury's, Aroon ventured to organize a very comprehensive training programme to give the workers an understanding of the business. This included a business simulation game and market visits where the workers got a first-hand feel for the challenges that the company was facing in the marketplace. Over thirty to forty batches, the programme covered the entire workforce of the Thane factory, not only giving the workers an understanding of the business realities but also strengthening the worker–management relationship.

So much so that the workers decided to organize a thanksgiving programme through a Satyanarayan puja. The workers collected funds for their puja and Aroon raised a matching contribution from the company. It was a beautiful occasion with the most recently married worker couple performing the puja. There was a play after which the internal union leader, Vishwas Ghatge, gave a speech. He picked up some soil from the ground and swore that there would be no more strikes. There has never been a strike at the Cadbury's Thane factory since. The transformation was complete.

- Anand worked toward a mindset change across the organization, through a host of initiatives, whereby unions would not be considered as adversaries but partners and stakeholders in the enterprise. This new mindset brought about a veritable transformation in the way the management related to the union leadership. There was greater willingness to share the gains of productivity more equitably with employees, to be transparent in administering rewards and be more open to discussing with unions the need for and implications of changes in technology and work practices. The relational philosophy shifted from the adversarial to one based on the commonality of purpose and alignment with a shared vision.

Both Aroon and Anand show how to handle IR situations such that they led to complete turnarounds in worker–management relationships, driven by a collaborative spirit. In Anil Khandelwal's words, 'Trustful IR environment is a prerequisite for embarking on HRD interventions.' One cannot have sustainable benefit from any HRD intervention unless it establishes a collaborative and trusting IR fabric in the company. These crucible experiences of dealing with people at the grassroots are truly paradigm-shifting as they build compassion and establish connections with the realities of the people whose well-being is the core responsibility of the HR professionals; the raison d'être of the HR profession.

One cannot learn this by sitting behind the computer screen in a corporate office, as our case studies emphasize. The clear message is that being baked into a well-rounded and effective HR professional means that one must go through the crucible of IR experience. Crucible experiences in handling employee relations issues put to the test the leaders and their ability to deal with the masses and difficult situations. They also bring about a human orientation in the leader. They are equally a self-confidence, courage and conviction-building source and bring out the hidden talent, challenging the HR person to test out new ways of influencing the very critical resources that form the backbone of any corporation.

H. Learning from setbacks and reverses

Not all experiences are winning ones. Over their long careers, HRLs also encountered setbacks, failures, unpleasant assignments or those that involved doing things contrary to their personally held beliefs and values. Our HRLs took these reverses in their strides and learnt from these crucible moments as well. One has examined earlier how Harish, Nathan, Kishore, Satish, Rajeev, Anil Sachdev, Anuranjita, Pratik and Raghu have encountered such setbacks and unpleasant assignments. Each one of them took these crucible experiences in their stride and helped themselves to great learnings from them. Some dealt with them by paying heed to the advice from their well-wishers—family members, former or current bosses, mentors and friends.

- In an incident in Korba, under pressure from trade unions and local leaders, the general manager caved in, against Kishore's better judgement. Asked to suspend three officers who were members of the editorial board of the NTPC House magazine, Kishore carried out the instructions but simultaneously tendered his resignation. He proceeded to Delhi to meet his bosses at the NTPC headquarters, where he met some of his former bosses, including M.R.R. Nair. Nair strongly reprimanded him for resigning in a huff, advised him to withdraw his resignation and stay put in NTPC. Finally, the NTPC's general manager for personnel and administration, R.V. Shahi, told Kishore that he would need someone like him at the Delhi headquarters. Kishore heeded his mentor Nair and his boss Shahi's advice, withdrew his resignation and moved to Delhi from Korba.

At the NTPC HQ, he received a hero's welcome that took away his sadness. B.P. Thakur, to whom he was to report at HQ, greeted him by saying, 'You are our hero indeed.' Renu Rajpal from the Power Management Institute wanted to write a case study on the Korba incident. All this made him feel that he was not alone and that people at large were with him.

- Rajeev, who had managed to bring Rallis to cash profits and had been acknowledged as a 'turnaround' man publicly at the annual

Tata Group CEO meet in 2002, had no alternative but to put in his papers when cracks started appearing in his relationship with the new chairman of the company. Rajeev took this unfortunate development in his stride with great elegance. A senior board director, who was very close to the Bombay House top brass, told Rajeev that he had earned respect for the dignity with which he had handled himself during this episode. Ratan Tata said: 'If you have made up your mind, I can understand and respect your decision. However, if in future you wish to come back, you will be welcomed with open arms.'

Parting with the Tata Group shook Rajeev to the core and tested all his inner strength, values and belief systems. Initially, he felt victimized but several rounds of conversations with family and friends made him realize that in life one is not a victim of another's actions. In the ultimate analysis, one is the creator of one's own destiny. Rajeev's father explained to him that outcomes in life are not only the result of what the individual does. Often there are several factors at play that are totally beyond one's control and knowledge.

Rajeev showed Agrawal a copy of the Bhagavad Gita in which his father had inscribed: 'There are five factors that produce results. Your effort is one of them.' He had the pages in the Gita marked out. He also advised his son not to lose his equanimity: 'Do not become arrogant when you experience success and do not drown in sorrow when things do not go your way.' This advice was life-sustaining for Rajeev who focused on being honest to himself and to others, taking success and failure in his stride. One other big lesson that Rajeev learned from his Rallis experience was that he had possibly not understood nor paid enough attention to the politics of the situation. He had not spent enough time with the board members and other relevant actors in the larger ecosystem, in the naïve belief that his actions would speak for themselves.

- During his days in GE Capital's back office in Asia, Raghu Krishnamoorthy had to pare the payroll by 1500 people after the financial meltdown. One pink-slipped person committed suicide by jumping off from the sixth floor of the office. Raghu got a poor performance rating as he had not been culturally sensitive or empathetic while carrying out his difficult mandate. Raghu learnt his lesson on the importance of cultural sensitivity through this error in judgement.

- Anuranjita was passed over for a promotion in London when the entire office was expecting her to be promoted along with some of her peers. The others got their promotions but hers was deferred. This shocked her to the point that she offered to resign immediately. The following day, Anuranjita was unsure about going to work but she did. After discussions at home and office, she decided to seek the counsel of a career coach. The feedback from her office and the coach was that while Anuranjita did well in her work, she had not been able to manage the office atmosphere or the ecosystem very well.

  In other words, she was a victim of office politics. There were also some surprising comments about her in a 360° review that she could not identify herself with. While indulging in office politics may sound somewhat negative as a trait, Anuranjita notes that managing the office environment is equally important for career advancement. With the guidance of her coach, she went out to rectify this situation, identifying friends and allies at the office and creating alliances and friendships. The coaching succeeded and soon the deferred promotion came through.

These stories indicate that such crucible moments are not unusual in one's career. In these moments, one needs to listen to the well-wishers, apart from drawing upon one's own life skills. Kishore, Rajeev and Anuranjita benefited from such wise counsel that came from family members, mentors and bosses. Good advice from well-wishers helps to tide over adversities with equanimity, making each of them a deep-learning experience. HRLs like Anil Sachdev and Pratik dealt with such crucible moments on their own strengths and values.

- When managing the Eicher factory, Anil Sachdev signed a long-term settlement with the unions and discovered to his horror, much after the agreement had been announced to the workers, that there was an error in the calculations, which would jeopardize the company's interest over the long run. Anil had built great trust and rapport with the union and directly appealed to them to withdraw the agreement and amend it. The union saw reason and the agreement was withdrawn. Such unconditional union support during this crucible moment was overwhelming and Anil's close bond with them deepened further.

- At TVSE, Pratik was upset when he had to pink-slip the very people that he had hired. He took it upon himself to host some of them at his own house and for others he found places with his friends till they could overcome the crisis created by their loss of jobs. Pratik dealt with this crucible moment by looking after those affected by the company's decision to the extent possible. It taught him that the real values of the company were quite at variance with its stated values and left a deep scar on Pratik's psyche. The lesson was that reality could be vastly different from what appears on the surface.

Most of the HRLs have gone through the crucible moments of reverses and setbacks. They have dealt with these fires with advice from well-wishers or on their own. Irrespective of how they handled them, going through these crucible moments have positively impacted their mental model.

I. Challenging the status quo and leading new initiatives

Our HRLs invariably challenged the status quo, seized opportunities and had the courage and competence to lead new initiatives. All of them were quick to seize the moment and champion the change.

Satish, Visty, Vivek, Dwarka, Ashok, Raghu, Sridhar, Anand, Hema, Saurabh, Dileep, Yogi, Marcel, Nathan, Chandrasekhar, Santrupt, Anil Khandelwal, Shrikant, Vineet and Aroon, among others, were challengers and change-leaders in their respective organizations.

- Santrupt, in his role as CHRO of the Aditya Birla Group, closely observed the legacy and traditions that were the hallmark of group practices. Some deeply-rooted practices included hiring siblings of employees and indefinite retirement age.
- Satish literally burnt the midnight oil during the Lipton–Brooke Bond merger to understand the personal circumstances of each of the 800 employees being asked to quit and custom-built the separation packages to take care of their unique requirements. He did not take the easy option of just announcing a VRS policy, as is conventionally done, to deal with large-scale separations.

- Quite early in his career in Burmah-Shell, Aroon challenged the practice of hiring overqualified people as operators. He was able to persuade his boss, Jack Trigg, that overqualified people are usually trouble, not a virtue and that the Senior Cambridge or matriculate is an adequate qualification for the operator. Aroon was nothing if not gutsy. Elsewhere, he challenged the conventional way of making the can and, by keenly observing shop floor practices, he figured out that the body-maker himself could do the setting, instead of wasting time waiting for the setter. Nobody in the factory wanted to experiment with this approach because it was not the practice even in the UK. Nevertheless, with his shift in-charge friend, K.K. Thomas, Aroon got two people, who understood the body-maker's work and let them set. They did it in twelve hours, then improved it to eight hours and further to six hours. The objecting manager was convinced about working with the new approach and the productivity of the department improved by around 60 per cent.
- Harish wrote a white paper on why the attrition in HR was high at Levers, pointing out that the top HR job was always given to a line manager and not to an HR professional. He made some specific recommendations for changing this practice, which were discussed at the board level and approved. This led to the appointment of HR professionals as CHROs in Hindustan Unilever, making a break from a long-standing tradition whose time had passed.
- Anuranjita remembers a consensus at RBS around removing a senior Polish manager. She investigated and found that the man was a highly-respected leader in his market and that the decision to have him removed was driven by internal politics. She decided to disagree with the decision and push back hard.

HRLs serve as business partners as well as employee advocates. They constantly observe and challenge what needs to change and then marshal support from the key stakeholders to lead the change.

J. Role-making

Regardless of their given roles, our HRLs pushed to make their roles relevant, contributing and meaningful. In the process, they evolved further and grew in stature and eminence within the profession.

Udai Pareek (1980) calls this role-making. All our HRLs did this to varying degrees.

- Santrupt was appointed as CHRO of the Aditya Birla Group without a script to follow, no definitive direction, no prior experience and not even the guard rails. When he arrived at Industry House to join the group, his team consisted of one person, an old computer and an office next to a stinking toilet. For Santrupt, the entire group was the crucible where he had freedom and the challenge to develop his role. Writing on a completely blank sheet of paper, Santrupt built a team and moved forward, steadily rising to a level of eminence. This he achieved by sheer dint of his relentless and thoughtful actions over the years, with all the passion and commitment that he could muster. His only fuel was his comprehension of the larger aspiration of the group, with his honesty of purpose keeping him going and on track.

- When he joined Philips, Vineet was only responsible for the corporate HR function; handling recruiting, compensation, training and HR administration at the head office, reporting to the director HR, Ramachandran. Industrial relations was not his portfolio, nor was union management. However, asked to handle some 100 letters of complaints by Ramachandran, he analysed them and shared his thoughts on remedial measures. Those were implemented immediately with some positive impact and also catapulted Vineet into the deep end of industrial relations. IR became an integral part of his role in Philips and this expanded role provided the crucible in which Vineet thrived. It helped him grow over the years.

- Dwarka had an almost clean slate to build the HR edifice with its own processes and rules for the Max group. Indeed, Dwarka was the first person to start working out of the newly-created Max Corporate Group Human Capital Office to bring to fruition Analjit Singh's vision to build HR as an enabling function and not a controlling one. The mandate was also to build the verticals for quality, people, governance and strategy. Dwarka hired people for quality, strategy and legal verticals, quickly focusing on building the right culture that would respect people, be benevolent in nature and honour commitments. With the clear but very broad definition of the aspirations, Dwarka embarked on crystallizing his own role; one that was quite different from the one that he had played as GSK's CHRO. He had to be mindful of the unique context of Max and design the architecture of the CHRO role, HR policies and processes accordingly.

- Sometimes it takes provocation from the boss to get into role-making, as was the case with Vivek at the Taloja factory where he was posted as factory personnel manager, reporting functionally to Bahadur. Showing Bahadur around the plant over nearly half a day, including the horticultural beautifications, the elaborate security systems and the impeccable housekeeping that he had accomplished and possibly expecting a pat on his back, Vivek got a jolt. Bahadur pointed out that it was not for an XLRI graduate to get these things done; a 'retired army officer at half the salary would do just as well a job, if not better'. Bahadur explained to Vivek that his real role was to understand the HR challenges of the unit, the business priorities of the business head and align HR actions to support the business head as a partner. That provocation showed Vivek the path forward on what his role ought to be.

- Dileep, fresh out of TISS was appointed as the Wipro factory personnel manager for operations with close to 900 people (permanent and non-permanent), in a taluka in Jalgaon District with a population of a lakh. The stated agenda was to professionalize people and processes and to position the organization as one with high integrity and values. It also involved picking up the art of managing the ubiquitous factory inspector in those days of 'inspector raj'. Dileep learnt everything earnestly through hands-on experience. When he joined, the union negotiations were in the final stage and Dileep represented the management there, signing a historical agreement. This was literally the crucible of fire in where Dileep's professional persona was baked. The sincerity of purpose, Dileep's core values of being 'fair and firm', his sense of ownership and drive toward a larger purpose with an independent mind helped him do the right things at the factory.

- On joining the Metal Box factory in Bombay, Aroon mingled with people and realized that while the personnel department was powerful, it was not very popular. He made friends with people in management as well as workers and some union leaders over chats and discussions to set the stage for warmer relations. Thereafter, at a three-day HR conference in Calcutta, where all the branch personnel managers were present, Dayal, the head of HR, explained that the true role of HR was all about assisting the management to obtain the spontaneous cooperation of workers for achieving the organizational goals. Dayal also asked Aroon to read *Glacier Metal*, *The Human Side of Enterprise* and *Men at Work*, which he would discuss with Aroon on his next trip to Bombay. Aroon's mind was transported from the minutiae to the big picture. *Glacier Metal* explained it all beautifully and Aroon decided that he would have to educate the management on its role and that of HR. Aroon's keen observation of what was happening on the ground and Dayal's guidance prepared him to embark upon his role as HR manager with a new perspective at the newly-established Deonar factory.

The stimuli can come from any source, as these crucible experiences of role-making demonstrate. Our HRLs were provoked, guided or given a broad definition of aspirations. Sometimes, the crucible was wide open and clear for the HRLs to figure out the way forward. In all these scenarios, our HRLs were guided by their own values, sincerity of purpose, understanding of the larger context both on the business and people fronts, as they crafted their roles appropriately.

K. Baking through high-quality training programmes

HRLs also learn from excellent training programmes. Many of our HRLs got deeply impacted by attending high-quality training programmes, some quite early in their careers in India and abroad.

- Five years into his Telco stint, Visty got to do a six-month course at IIM Ahmedabad. This addressed his nagging concern that he was not an MBA while all others in TAS were MBAs from highly reputed management institutes from India or abroad. The course gave Visty greater confidence vis-à-vis his understanding of management theory. Another impactful five-week programme in 1989 was 'Integration of Knowledge' with the eminent nuclear physicist, Raja Ramanna, as its programme director. The programme had the best domain experts from a variety of disciplines—experts in history, philosophy, sociology, literature and computer sciences—as members of the faculty.

- Visty was charged with the new knowledge about concepts and put them to good use, doing new things right through his career. Even while working for seventy hours a week, he would keep the first hour or two in a day for his own learning and development. He was particular about reading three journals regularly: *Personal Psychology*, *Journal of Applied Psychology* and *Administrative Science Quarterly*. If he came across good articles, he would index them and make notes in his personal notebook.

- In charge of organizing a series of top-quality programmes at DCM, RR ensured that he attended them all. A two-week programme by David Clarence McClelland kindled the 'desire to excel', while Prof. Pulin Garg's programme for all senior DCM executives for teaching/mentoring the management trainees taught him self-reflection. He persuaded Paul to let him do a course with Kenneth Benne on OD to help him resolve intercultural problems between people in projects and operations and helped himself to a superb exposure to the concept of OD.

- Kishore attended several strategic training programmes in leading B-schools such as Michigan, where Dave Ulrich and Wayne Brockbank were professors and C.K. Prahalad sometimes lectured.

- Kishore, Saurabh, Raghu and Santrupt recall tremendous benefits they got from the Rotary, Eisenhower and Fulbright study programmes that exposed them to thought leaders and successful business leaders in the UK and the US.

- While at Metal Box, Aroon attended the train-the-trainer programme at IIM Ahmedabad, spearheaded by Tarun Sheth. This was his first acquaintance with the T-group. Aroon attended the three phases of an internship announced by ISABS to become a T-group trainer. This led to organization development and Aroon followed up with a two-month internship at NTL, learning from Richard (Dick) Beckhard and others to see how OD interventions are done. He also spent an evening at Portland (Maine) to hear Carl

Rogers. These shaped Aroon's thinking and beliefs, influencing his workplace decisions and actions.

- During his years in Cadbury, Sridhar completed the three-year professional accreditations programme of the Indian Society for Individual and Social Development (ISISD). This experience was unique, challenging his beliefs and questioning his 'shoulds' and 'should nots'. For Sridhar, the ISISD programme, driven by Prof. Pulin Garg, one of the ISISD founders, was the crucible of learning through which he was driven to relentlessly explore and find newer meanings and come to terms with himself in his totality.

These training programmes proved to be learning crucibles that baked and prepared the HRLs for their impactful careers in the human resource function.

L. Investing in developing the self

Our HRLs spent a good deal of their time and effort to build themselves right from the beginning. Some such as Chandra, Aquil, Nathan, Harish, Santrupt, Marcel, Visty, Rajan and Anil Khandelwal have demonstrable reading habits. Some are also writers and share their knowledge through articles, LinkedIn posts, Facebook posts and in social media. Noel Tichy observes that a great quality of leaders is to have a teachable point of view. Some of our HR leaders have authored books and articles in magazines.

- Anil Khandelwal, Aquil Busrai, Anuranjita Kumar, Harish and Rajan are authors of books and read books, articles and papers to develop themselves.
- In his early years, Kishore Sinha engaged a coach to learn the skill of rapid reading and also learnt 'counselling'. His rapid-reading abilities facilitated a life of continuous reading to keep himself updated.
- Visty invested in self-learning and development even while working for seventy hours a week. He always kept the first hour or two in a day for his own learning and development.
- Dwarakanath introduced reverse mentoring by younger people and kept himself abreast of new knowledge.

These are just a few illustrations and almost all our HR leaders have been reflective learners, using various sources as learning.

M. Engaging with professional forums

Professional bodies like NIPM, ISTD, NHRDN, CII, AMA and its LMAs have played a significant role in developing the management profession in India, as in the west. The Ahmedabad Management Association was started by Vikram Sarabhai even before the IIMs came up. The AIMA's presidents served on the IIM boards. The CII and its committees played a major role in the growth and development of industry in India. These bodies offer enormous opportunities for networking, benchmarking, developing young professionals, influencing best practices in industry, encouraging knowledge-sharing and setting professional standards. They provide the best opportunities to explore, discover, experiment and nurture leadership competencies. Across the world, the most influential academics and practitioners participate, encourage and sponsor various events organized by these bodies. The SHRM in the US, CIPD in the UK and ASTD are known for their contributions to education, training and setting standards in HR and L&D, for example. Participation and holding positions in these bodies is considered an indicator of high professional standing.

All our HRLs have been actively involved in professional forums. They also seized opportunities to learn by interacting with other senior professionals even as they spread learning. Besides playing leadership roles in professional forums, some wrote books, developed standards, organized conferences, introduced good governance practices, designed new curricula and collaborated with professional education institutions and universities. They also consistently took the initiative to self-learn by reading, writing, speaking and teaching.

Volumes can be written about the contributions of some of the HRLs, who are too modest to talk about their contributions to professional bodies. Dileep, Pratik, Pradeep, Shrikant and Visty are among those relatively less involved in the professional forums but focused their energies in other deserving directions.

- Visty concentrated on the organizations that he worked for, while frequently contributing to magazines, newspapers, conferences and social media to share his knowledge. He holds that one's accomplishments have a way of getting known in the community. Adi Godrej pushed him to work with CII, where he joined the National Committee on HR. Visty acknowledges meeting very impressive business leaders like Rajendra Pawar, founder of NIIT, B. Santhanam, chairman and MD, St Gobain, India and T.V. Narendran, MD, Tata Steel.

All other HRLs richly benefited from such forums even as they made rich contributions, growing in stature and networking with fellow professionals. Some even got their career breaks through their association with professional bodies.

- RR was active in professional forums quite early in his career, thanks to his boss Paul and, over time, rose to be the vice chairman of the Delhi Management Association. RR recalls being fortuitously asked to introduce Ranjan Banerjee, then personnel director of Hindustan Unilever, as the speaker at a conference. Banerjee asked him to stay in touch. Six months later, he was called for a formal meeting at HUL, where he met Tarun Sheth and was hired as the selection and training manager. He replaced Sheth, who was moving to another role in the company.
- Sridhar and a couple of colleagues participated in the inter-corporate management talent (young managers) competitions of the All India Management Association, while at GKW. There was the joy of winning the AIMA Young Manager Award, followed by another win at the regional level of the competition at Patna and the disappointment over losing in the finals to Metal Box and Abbott Laboratories. The agonizing loss came with the lesson that one had to take success and disappointments in one's stride. The other good thing that came out of such industry-level participation was that Arabinda Ray (formerly with Metal Box), who had taken over as the managing director of GKW's steel business, had noticed Sridhar at a training event and asked him to do a manpower-planning assignment for the Indian Institute of Packaging at Mumbai. Sridhar did it with aplomb and won the industry's recognition along with a job offer from Metal Box. Sridhar switched jobs, going on to Metal Box.

- Anand's first and abiding love has been ITC but he enriched himself by interacting widely with the HR fraternity across the country. The opportunity to learn from fellow HR professionals was stupendous and Anand was just as generous about sharing his rich learnings from the ITC experience with the profession. His persistent support of NHRDN was marked by two key messages: that HR's role was far more crucial for a developing country like India and that there was the need to extend it well beyond one's organizational boundaries. In his drive for a new identity for HR in this expansive and inclusive world, he conceived of an exhaustive programme for NHRDN in 2004.

The best HR minds in the country were drawn into designing the programme. This was followed by interactions with HR managers to enhance their understanding of strategic frameworks, models, and the logic and process of linking HR strategy to organizational vision. HR strategy would also be aligned to the organization's competitive strategy and goals for the purpose of enhancing enterprise value. The other key objective was to develop senior professionals as strategic CHROs, learning and imparting the art of providing leadership in a competitive and customer-centric world. This programme continues to be organized to this day and is arguably the most exhaustive HR development programme in the country.

Like Anand, other HRLs have benefitted from their fraternal interactions while also contributing to their growth, enhancing the stature of the HR profession in the country and the quality of the professionals themselves. The two are mutually dependent.

Aquil, Santrupt, Rajan, Dwarkanath, Yogi, Rajeev, RR, Harish, Anuranjita, Vivek, Vineet, Chandra, Hema, Saurabh, Kishore, Ashok, Anil Sachdev, Anil Khandelwal, Nathan and almost all the HRLs were associated with NHRDN as presidents at the national level or at its chapters or as members of the executive boards. They not only brought about paradigm-shifting changes to the profession and the professional bodies but contributed to the process of baking the minds of many young HR aspirants with their mentorship and guidance.

Serious and committed engagement with the professional bodies by our HRLs meant that the younger professionals had access to rich sources of learning. When the profession demanded, they took on the responsibility of selflessly delivering to a specific need. They inspired other professionals and helped streamline governance or in the designing of new structures and systems for the development of the professional bodies. Our HR leaders gave to the professional bodies, received much more in return and then they paid them back to develop others and grow talent.

N. Crucible of volunteering for social causes

When the opportunity came up, HRLs were quick to support and volunteer for social causes. Often, they sought out causes to nurture and grow.

- At the prime of his career, when only forty-nine, with a long corporate career still ahead of him, Dileep quit the corporate world and took the plunge into heading the Azim Premji Foundation as a full time 'founding CEO'. Dileep's passion was education and he chose to use education as the foundation's 'overarching strategy to contribute to social change'. His guidelines for running the foundation were steeped in the mission of infusing professionalism to balance the ideology-driven space with an injection of realism. He sought to mould mindsets, bring together the scale and legitimacy of the government, the passion of civil society and the performance, quality, result-orientation and the talent of the corporate sector.

- Raised in an environment of service to the community from his childhood, Anand lived up to his childhood promise. The family was focused on serving to make a difference to the lives of the less privileged, thanks to the inspiration provided by Anand's father, who served in government with integrity and commitment; and his mother, who devoted a lot of her time to community service. This family influence apart, the Jesuit priests who ran the educational institutions that Anand studied in were an immense source of inspiration for community service right through his school and college. After completing his bachelor's degree at St Joseph's College in Bangalore, Anand took a year off to engage in voluntary work with a student organization, working full-time to organize leadership and work camps for youth from all over India.

Fighting against injustice and working towards building a just and equitable social order became a priority in Anand's life from that impressionable age.

During his years in ITC, Anand embarked on a process of reimagining HR, whereby it would shift from a policy-driven approach to a strategy-driven one. HR policies and systems would be geared to enhancing employee well-being as well as customer value, with a telling impact on the bottom line. Yogi Deveshwar taught Anand an important lesson: 'If we can grow our businesses exponentially, create surpluses and invest these surpluses to build infrastructure for new businesses—more hotels and more factories and create more new engines of growth—we would be able to create sustainable livelihoods for millions of these people. The more value ITC creates, the more we can do to enable the disadvantaged sections of our society to live better and more wholesome lives.'

This powerful insight influenced Anand's thinking dramatically and the realization dawned that the role of HR must extend much beyond the enterprise. The question he posed to himself was what did HR need to do to look beyond the shareholder, to look to making growth inclusive. Anand got the deepest sense of fulfilment from his role as mentor of 'Mission Sunehra Kal' from its inception in the year 2000 until his retirement in 2015. With his chairman's total backing and support, Anand initiated a comprehensive intervention to take the company's CSR agenda forward, making significant contributions in the areas of social and farm forestry, livelihoods, women's empowerment, watershed management, wasteland development, value-added agriculture, drinking water and sanitation, health and hygiene, supplementary education and skill development.

Over his four decades and more at ITC, Anand's world view shifted from being anti-capitalist and pro-socialist to a more pragmatic realism. If a society values democracy and democratic values, it must believe in the market economy that made it possible to engineer a congruence between creating surpluses while simultaneously creating and enhancing social and environmental capital. This was prompted by the understanding that economic activity is necessary to generate livelihoods that enable people to live with economic and social dignity. Anand carried on in the same spirit at Samraksha, an NGO that he has been associated with since 2006. Here, too, he is making a difference to vulnerable lives, helping the process of empowering people to take charge of their own lives.

Dileep and Anand are two outstanding examples of successful HR leaders committing themselves to social causes. Other HRLs have taken different routes to serve social causes:

- Satish is committed to the conservation of nature and has served on the board of the Bombay Natural History Society for fifteen years.
- Marcel serves on two school boards and does coaching and leadership-development programmes at some Christian community schools and hospitals, and with teachers, doctors, nurses and NGOs.
- Sridhar is passionate about social causes, supporting special needs children with livelihood skills by helping them produce gifts items and selling them to corporates. He also teaches English to children in Tiruvannamalai and is involved in other social activities as well.
- Aquil tries to give back to society by engaging with youngsters and helping them to skill up. He also engages with his own Bohra community, working pro bono, helping with skill development, communications, goal-setting and dealing with government issues. He recalls looking after shoes during Muharram gatherings at the tender age of ten. With time on his hands, Aquil focuses on service and loves to multitask. 'If you want to do something, it will get done, even if it is at 3 a.m.,' he says. He does not like compartmentalization or straitjacketed competencies and wants to create 'change agents' in society, as he has been all his life.
- Anil Sachdev works with the Chinmaya Ashram and its schools and is promoting education through his own institution, SOIL.

Every HRL has been contributing to professional bodies, which amounts to making contributions to society at large, because all these bodies are not-for-profit and serve social causes.

In fact, all our HRLs are volunteering; contributing to social causes in what is emerging as a virtuous cycle. The deeper their engagements with these causes, the more meaningful the causes become, inspiring them to give even more. The crucible of giving for social causes is baking the HRLs' hearts and minds toward creating a more inclusive world view, which is self-perpetuating.

Summary

Family backing has been of paramount importance to our universe of thirty HRLs, followed by the influence of the academic institutions that they attended and their teachers. The mentorship continued under the bosses that they worked for. Equally influential were their peer groups and others with whom they had the opportunity to rub shoulders, both within and outside the organizations that they served in. These HRLs evolved into seasoned professionals who took initiatives to constantly learn from the people and the situations around them. In the process, they have invested their selves with the gift of seeing beyond the obvious and seizing opportunities; of creating enhanced roles for themselves and hugely impacting people and organizations that they have worked with as well as the profession itself. For them, it has been learning without full stops; learning, evolving, reinventing themselves and contributing towards making a difference in the world around them.

Their journeys through these crucible moments baked certain values and a set of competencies in the HRLs as will be described in the next two chapters of this book.

4

Competencies of HR Leaders

What are the competencies exhibited by HR Leaders (HRLs) in our study? What are the values exhibited by these leaders? These two facets are being explored over this and the next chapter. Some of these competencies have most certainly helped them to become what they are; others were possibly baked through the various crucibles that they passed through. As we documented the case histories, we also looked for indicators of various competencies based on which the competencies were inferred. As outlined by McClelland (1963), Boyatzis (1982) and Spencer and Spencer (1991, 2010), competencies are an underlying characteristic of an individual that causes superior performance or causes leadership in action.

These underlying characteristics may be knowledge, attitudes, skills, motives, traits, values, self-concept and such others. As we prepared the case studies, we explored for these underlying characteristics to infer the competencies from them for the thirty HRLs. A total of 584 characteristics were identified and some embraced overlapping competencies. We then labelled them and classified them under certain well-known and recognizable competencies. In all, we identified forty-seven such competencies and classified most of these 584 indicators. We parked aside a few that did not exactly fit into these forty-seven.

These were further reduced to twenty competencies after consolidating similar competencies and classifying them.

For example, a competency like people leadership has many sub-competencies including interpersonal competence, team management, handling difficult people including bosses, cross-cultural sensitivities involving dealing with people from different nationalities, developing competencies of juniors and others, personal qualities including skills like humility and inclusiveness, empathy, encouraging and empowering others, confrontation and conflict management skills and such others. Similarly, competencies like execution skills, functional competencies and business knowledge and acumen too are multidimensional.

This exercise sought to answer the following questions relevant for this study:

1. What kind of leadership competencies are exhibited by these HRLs?
2. Which of these seem to be critical or more frequently exhibited in making them leaders?
3. How do these competencies compare with other models across the globe?

The central plot of this study of how these competencies got baked and by whom is partially answered in the previous chapter on crucibles with the case studies themselves presenting evidence of the same.

Identification of critical competencies through studying our HRLs' life journeys goes a long way in establishing a framework for developing such competencies in others. The competencies so identified may also help in suggesting course content and curricula for HR and or business schools. If they are formed in the early years and they cut across professions, the lesson would be for schools and colleges to create experiences that would build these leadership competencies.

These twenty competencies seem to fall into the following five categories that we call the five families of competencies: Business, Functional, Personal, Professional and Social leadership.

A. Business Leadership

This pertains to an understanding of the business, its key drivers, trends, competitive landscape and their connection, obvious or subtle with HR deliverables. Business leadership also includes the ability to integrate diverse disciplines to deal with the pressures and pulls of the businesses that may be often contradictory. This family consists of two competencies:

1. Business Acumen

The HR function must be sensitive to the business goals and business realities. People are recruited to accomplish organizational goals, to achieve the vision and mission of organizations, often to create newer ones or take the original vision to newer levels. Together with founders, CEOs and the top management, HR plays a great role in making employees feel that they work for larger organizational goals than annual targets and KRAs. This enhances workforce commitment and makes work more meaningful and enjoyable. An HR leader must learn about business, customers, marketplace, suppliers and all other stakeholders besides the employees themselves. This requires the CHROs to acquire knowledge about the business that they are working with and to create a sense of purpose and partnership in all employees. We found that all our HRLs were business-driven in our analysis.

At least eleven case studies presented evidence of HR leaders with global exposure demonstrating a global mindset. They were seen to exhibit vision and thought leadership and view a broader picture and longer-term perspective. Not only did they think big but they also influenced the business leaders with HR thought leadership often using global benchmarks. They came up with HR strategies and policies keeping in view the business as well as the people context.

2. Integrating Ability

This refers to the ability to establish interdisciplinary connects courtesy their own eclectic minds and supplementing it with their understanding of interdisciplinary solutions to problems. Eighteen HRLs indicated this and it includes:

- Integrating cross-functional work and navigating proposals at the board level and at global academic institutions;
- Integrating multiple cultures;
- Integrating and managing production;
- Integrating with respect for workers;

- Demonstrating an ability to integrate diverse agendas;
- Understanding and balancing opposing views;
- Aligning the HR agenda with business needs;
- Architecting HR processes in coordination with the desired culture;
- Taking a balanced view of HR with a healthy respect for all other functions;
- Balancing between people and business and staying objective and empathetic;
- Balancing individual and organizational needs;
- Having the big picture in view, observing the interplay between different elements perceptively and then plugging in the strategic elements around it;
- Serving as the bridge between a mercurial boss and the rest of the people;
- Building close relations with line managers, including the CEO;
- Building consensus and negotiation, when necessary through informal discussions;
- Managing interdisciplinary work by a demonstrable ability to play multiple roles and multiple functions;
- Integrating interdisciplinary work by a demonstrable ability to smoothen the process with greater knowledge of line functions.

B. Functional Competencies

This family consists of the following five sets of competencies:

1. HR Functional Skills

HR functional skill includes knowledge of talent acquisition, talent management, compensation and benefits, learning and development apart from knowledge of industrial relations theories and practices. Almost all our HRLs were professionally qualified in one field or the other even at the entry-level or acquired them soon thereafter. They have all demonstrated excellence in one or more functional skills. About twenty-five mentioned this directly in the case studies. The functional competencies that surfaced in our discussions include:

- Industrial relations primarily meant being good at handling irate unions, the ability to deal with grassroot level employees and knowledge of the labour law. It also encompassed genuine interest and capability to partner with grassroots level employees to constantly come up with 'win-win' solutions;

- Managing compensation and benefits, which included the ability to create the compensation structure and manage wage negotiations;
- Designing and organizing HR interventions for business results;
- Having a strong interest in finance and customer satisfaction;
- Working with data obtained 'first-hand';
- Organization development skills;
- Talent management skills, talent identification, including the ability to identify high-calibre talent, ability to recognize talent and nurture it, talent development, based on their inner potential and setting up talent management processes, policies and creating a culture of talent multiplication;
- Change management skills, which our HRLs exhibited in ample measure. They constantly engaged in driving change, as clearly demonstrated by at least fourteen HRLs.
  - The indicators included: leading change, leading from the front when required, managing change by persuasion and dialogue than by authority, showing the ability to change HR policies around, demonstrating their ability to induce better performance by pulling the right chords in people, change leadership, accelerating the pace of change through institutional practices, revamping HR systems and practices. Finally, it meant the ability to reshape the basic character of management–worker relationships from confrontational to consultative.
- Communication skills demonstrated by our HRLs included the ability to communicate with clarity, with appealing articulation of policies and issues to enthuse employees to be committed to their work; communicating tough decisions in a soft, humane manner; talking to the media and engaging in public speaking. Some HRLs excelled in public speaking. It also included the art of asking the right question while interviewing, and convincing the other side about taking difficult decisions.
- The courage of conviction was a competency clearly demonstrated by most of our HRLs. They dared to challenge the status quo, speak out and take a stand when required, besides taking tough decisions and creating win-win outcomes while simultaneously sustaining trust;

- They communicated effectively to establish and show linkages between HR practices and business strategies.

2. *People Leadership*

The most critical and consistent competence indicated by our HRLs is their people skills or people leadership skills. The HR function deals with people; managing individuals, teams, departments and the entire workforce, which means dealing with people with different points of view, different statuses, levels, backgrounds and mindsets. Integrating them into a cohesive whole is always a mammoth task. The people leadership skills of the CHRO and all HR professionals are constantly challenged and every HRL in our universe gave evidence of their people management skills. These included interpersonal competence with the ability to encourage and empower juniors as well as other employees. This was supplemented by a knack for setting a climate and culture of empowerment, based on their ability to invest in developing others. They had an equally keen sense of conflict management, managing differences and establishing a climate of mutual respect and collaboration.

- Our HRLs were exemplary listeners, skilfully tuning in to people as they communicated, providing them with psychological space—be it a colleague, direct report, union leader or a shop floor worker. They were adept at finding something to appreciate in a person, building a relationship, making friends and maintaining the relationships. One thing that they meticulously avoided was talking down to people.
- Some were good at building relationships with senior people, including even difficult business people. They deftly managed disagreements and difficult interactions.
- They were also skilled at managing relationships and social interactions across all levels of employees in the organization.
- They were people-centric and saw things from the 'employee perspective'. They encouraged ventilation of thoughts and attentively listened to them, without pushing their own point of view, thereby establishing endearing connections.

- Almost all of them handled difficult industrial relations situations as indicated in the crucible moments and lessons.
- They demonstrated cross-cultural sensitivities; dealing with people from different nationalities (nine cases).
- They demonstrated their ability to invest in their juniors and other staff. It began with spotting talent and then designing special development plans, training and retraining the HR staff.
- They had strong team management skills, the ability to create camaraderie in the workspace and to build strong teams with the same elan as they built consensus, allowing debates over issues and options.
- Many demonstrated humility and inclusiveness by not being judgemental or judging people just by appearances or through a single prism, be it qualification or present position. Equally, they related with people from all strata of society and sought diverse views.
- Some of our HRLs demonstrated high empathy, maintaining amicable working relations.
- Many were good at encouraging and empowering others. They empowered employees to take charge and evolve as well-rounded individuals, giving them opportunities to work independently. They gave credit to others to get their peers on board with their ideas. Alongside, they consciously encouraged innovative thinking.
- Some HRLs exhibited dexterity in confrontation and conflict management. This included being competitive; confronting stressful and disruptive situations or potentially volatile situations with equanimity; sorting out differences respectfully and not allowing differences to blow up into ugly fights; not fighting shy of confronting people to uphold company values; standing up to bullies and encouraging people to unburden themselves of their troubled thoughts.

3. *Strategic Thinking (17) and Analytical Skills (11)*

Strategic thinking is a very critical competence for HRLs. Scholars like Dave Ulrich have maintained for many years that HR is a strategic business partner. A lot of what any organization does and can do depends on the quality of talent the organization has at any given point in time and the extent to which the organization is willing to invest in developing talent. 'Make or buy' decisions in HR have always been tricky and often the top worry. They concern many CEOs as the answers are not simple and easy. This competency deals with both HR strategies and business strategies.

The competency indicators emerging from our thirty HRLs include:

- Designing three-pronged strategy of the HR council, setting up task forces and data monitoring;
- Respecting other functions and demonstrating an ability to navigate through multiple HR issues and addressing other functional resources;
- Ability to conceptualize HR initiatives in dealing with changing business needs;
- Ability to develop HR strategy involving line managers;
- Ability to transition from adversarial relationships to collaborative relationships with workers/trade unions;
- Ability to work out win-win solutions while dealing with powerful people;
- Ability to marry diplomacy and power and deploy this skill meaningfully;
- Navigating challenging battlefronts with finance, marketing and other such corporate functions;
- Ability to quickly analyse issues, seeing through dilatory tactics, games and coming forward to solve problems;
- Leveraging the knowledge and wisdom of thought leaders on the board to resolve issues;
- Ability to deal with moving goalposts, changing contexts and challenges.

The analytical abilities indicated by eleven HRLs include:

- Attention to detail with an eye for detail;
- Analytical skills;
- Willingness to spend time with people at a personal level and the knack to break barriers to help with their formal and informal needs;

- Having logically flowing thoughts and the ability to penetrate deeply into an issue.

About nine of the HR leaders presented evidence of possessing exceptional ability to deal with external stakeholders skilfully. These external agents that they dealt with included government inspectors, labour and unions (whose support was enlisted), law and order in managing a township, M&A partners, officers' associations, politicians and bureaucrats, the underworld to prevent disruption in work. These comprised the bunch of external stakeholders that they successfully managed, apart from dealing with their own unions and managing IR situations.

Some of our HRLs also demonstrated entrepreneurship and entrepreneurial skills.

4. Systems Thinking and Technology Savviness

Systems bring predictability and professionalism into any organization. As organizations grow and expand, the numbers on the payroll increase. Systems help in aligning employees spread across diverse functions, business units and geographies. Recruitment, onboarding, manpower planning, performance management, promotions, training and learning sponsorships, employee benefits and such facets of the HR universe are put into a system, making human resource management easier. In recent times, many HR systems are being automated, bringing in a lot more objectivity, transparency and consistency; reducing the time that line and people managers have to spend on them, thereby leaving them with more time for more productive and futuristic issues.

Our analysis indicated that many of the leaders are system-driven and technology savvy. There is direct evidence in twelve cases about their systems orientation. The indicators of this competence include:

- Designing and building HR processes and systems;
- Preparing policy guidelines and manuals;
- Designing leadership programmes at different levels and strategic HR programmes for the next generation of HR leaders in the country;

- Designing the structure, processes, workflows, transitions and talent management, while managing integration;
- Creating and establishing processes for information dissemination and responsiveness during times of turbulence in the business environment;
- Designing systems like climate survey, fast-tracking career progression, creating career cadre, setting up assessment centres and policies for master craftsmen.

5. Decision-Making (7 cases)

This skill, indicated by seven of the HRLs, includes the ability to make choices, take independent decisions based on complete information and taking tough calls. Though our analysis indicated this as an exclusive skill for a few of them, one can reasonably emphasize that all our HRLs had sharp decision-making skills. The various choices they made included changing or not changing jobs, taking job-rotation opportunities, shifting geographies, taking up new responsibilities and such others, which are clear indicators of their decision-making capability.

A clutch of HRLs (13) demonstrated excellent execution capability. This indicator includes traits such as action orientation, getting things done—sometimes even without the authority to do so—implementing decisions with speed, working hands-on, efficiently organizing events, and unravelling complex issues without getting lost in the labyrinth. Some HRLs demonstrated these while handling the separation of employees, making the parting soft with their supportive touch and being sensitive to the impact of separation on the person. These HRLs also showed their drive and commitment when multitasking and demonstrating their result orientation.

C. Personal Leadership

Ethical sense was consistently demonstrated by all HRLs along with a strong sense of ethics in all their actions. Their ethical conduct comes out consistently and clearly in most of the HR competency models. The strong sense of ethics reveals itself in their actions of being fair, honest, upright, transparent and consistent. Many of our HRLs demonstrate these qualities in more ways than one. About twelve of them indicate that they were very fair, focused and firm. In about twelve cases, this competency included being fair and firm with new hires, and firm handling of all union matters but in an equitable manner.

One of them maintained that he was extremely aggressive while articulating this sense of ethics, even 'obnoxiously so', especially when dealing with the authorities, if the situation so demanded. He was able to take tough calls being focused on the business drivers and on solving the problems of his people. He also practised tough love as the chairman, being strict with deliverables and yet considerate and supportive of people.

Some showed qualities that made them accepted and respected by people, they built trust with stakeholders, including promoters and delivered on promises; they were dependable. In a few cases, our HRLs were objective and data-driven with an ability to look at issues with clinical objectivity. Being open-minded and transparent invested them with a spirit to fight for anything that they thought was correct. A few also demonstrated their ethical sense by being outspoken, emphatically placing their points of view and indicating their penchant for rejecting established norms. HRLs with such high ethical sense exuded a sense of high credibility and are considered so by people at all levels of the organization.

Hard work and high energy comprise an interesting competency observed in most of our HRLs. About sixteen of them considered their high energy levels and ability to put in long hours as a core strength. They demonstrated their preparedness to live a hard life and work hard, to the extent of being workaholics. Even more remarkably, their energy seems to have been sustained over a long period and they remained tenacious and persevering.

Innovation has been a hallmark of about nineteen of our HRLs, who have demonstrated exceptional innovativeness in some form or the other. They are innovative in spirit, have the gift of thinking out of the box and are happy to try solutions in the following spheres, while also demonstrating their creative abilities:

- Innovative in establishing newer ways of engaging people;
- Innovative in their HR practices;
- Innovative in eliminating redundancies of excessive staff and variable pay;

- Innovative with their messaging and communication;
- Generally willing to try new approaches to all issues;
- Working well beyond their responsibilities in sorting out all kinds of problems with out-of-the-box solutions;
- Designing innovative development programmes;
- Innovative with introducing new processes like an incentive scheme for a bank and job evaluations;
- Original thinkers, not given to looking for industry benchmarks when faced with a fresh problem.

Learning agility has been a strength of about twenty of our HRLs, who indicated their strength as listeners and learners. The indicators emerging out of our interviews include:

- General learning agility;
- Learning all the time from different people/sources;
- Learning by observing;
- Learning from being a voracious reader, particularly of travel fiction;
- Seeking professional help from external professionals;
- Seeking support from seniors and gaining acceptance;
- Listening with patience;
- Reading books and reflecting.

Problem-solving and process-orientation skills were indicated in about twelve case studies. The indicators of this competency include:

- Ability to run the business from an analytical perspective and be in their element around the HR issues that the business faced;
- Rebuilding the employer brand;
- Ability to cut through established norms and solve problems;
- Ability to flag issues;
- Ability to find solutions despite challenges and adversities;
- Process orientation;
- Ability to see the means–ends relationships and balance the two.

Adaptability and resilience were in strong evidence in fourteen of the cases. The indicators of this competence presented by our HRLs include:

- Ability to navigate the way forward even amidst adversities;
- Ability to adapt to new situations and turn them around;
- Agility of thought or ability to think on their feet to deal with unusual situations;
- Ability to manage ambiguity and ambiguous situations.

Self-management and rejuvenation as critical competencies of leaders are indicated by a large number of researchers and scholars. For example, Peter Drucker and Daniel Goleman's emotional intelligence and leadership concepts are based on this. In our study, this competence is reflected in our leaders as self-confidence, self-reliance, self-worth and renewal. These competencies were in clear evidence in at least twenty-two HRLs. The indicators include:

- Self-confidence;
- Self-development by constantly questioning oneself: 'What value am I adding?';
- Self-reflective and managing one's ambition so that it did not get in the way of the bigger goal;
- Introspective in nature;
- Ability to take an unbiased view of the company;
- High sense of self-worth;
- Self-assured;
- Self-aware of one's strengths and weaknesses, which includes an understanding of what one is good at and what is not one's forte. One HRL realized that he was not good at resource optimization but good in the organizational development phase;
- Self-confident to the extent of being a daredevil and meeting rebel leaders; not succumbing to terrorist pressure for a ransom;
- Well-rounded and self-confident;
- Ability to improve oneself too;
- Self-discovery and self-learning;
- Self-motivated;
- Self-reliant;
- Self-renewing, courtesy one's ability to look at things afresh, arriving at realizations about old policies that needed to be changed;
- Ability to reinvent self to stay relevant to the changing times.

D. Professional Leadership

Networking skills and networking with others is a critical competence in recent times. It helps the leader to discover new areas of work (including conflict areas) by being in touch with customers, employees, professional bodies, experts and other knowledge givers and sources of wisdom. About twenty of our HRLs have this with their networking spread over:

- Networking with the US consulate to get visas for employees;
- Networking and engagement with professional forums;
- Networking to connect with the public at large;
- Networking to connect with workers;
- Networking to connect with people both at the grassroots as well as with senior bosses;
- Working in professional forums like NHRDN, ISTD, CII, AIMA;
- Networking to leverage all available resources like the resident knowledge in independent directors to bounce off one's ideas;
- Professional networking and brand building.

E. Social Leadership

Social sensitivity, sharing, commitment to service and a sense of responsibility are clear traits in many of our HRLs. Peter Drucker maintained that all good leaders have a high sense of social responsibility and contribute to the larger good. In the book, *Effective People*, T.V. Rao (2015) described an effective person as one who is constantly trying to discover one's own talent and applying it to make a difference in the lives of others. The doctors, teachers, social workers, civil servants and film actors reviewed in his book, all give evidence of making a difference in the lives of others. While most of our HRLs have worked to make a difference, there is direct evidence that some of them have made it a special focus of their work; working for the larger goals of society. In at least a dozen case studies, there is direct evidence of social contributions or thinking of larger issues and attempts to contribute to them. The indicators of this include sensitivity to social issues, creating a shared services centre for the future, sharing knowledge, creating not-for-profit organizations, working for the larger good and promoting larger causes.

HRL Competencies in Existing HR Competency Models

There are several HR competencies models across the world. In this section, we examine whether our HRLs meet the competencies as per the framework of these models. Our analysis indicated that the thirty HRLs exhibit most of the competencies outlined by various professional bodies and scholars in the field across the globe.

Institutional Managers: In the view of the authors, they meet the criteria laid by McClelland and Burnham on institutional managers (McClelland and Burnham, 1996 and 2003). According to them, some institutional managers recognize that they can get things done inside organizations only if they can influence the people around them. Thus they focus on building power through influence rather than through their personal achievements. Such institutional managers are the most effective and their direct reports have a greater sense of responsibility. They see organizational goals more clearly and exhibit greater team spirit.

Socially-Conscious Leaders: Peter Drucker wrote in *Drucker on Leadership* (Cohen, 2020) that 'Leadership is the lifting of a man's vision to higher sights, the raising of a man's performance to a higher standard, the building of a man's personality beyond its normal limitations.' Practising social responsibility is of equal importance to practising integrity and is equally essential. Significantly, one need not abandon organizational efficiency or profitability; one just needs to be ethical. To be socially responsible is a part of good leadership (Cohen, 2020 on Peter Drucker).

Spencer and Spencer (1993, 2010), refer to such managers as human service managers who display fourteen generic competencies. We found that the competencies outlined earlier from our thirty HRLs fit well into this Spencer and Spencer list.

Dave Ulrich and team have studied the subject of HR competencies over the last three decades and have published HR competencies since 1987. Their latest, 2021 model (Ulrich, Ulrich, Burns and Wright) outlines five competencies: 1. Accelerates business and results, 2. Advances human capability, 3. Simplifies complexity, 4. Mobilizes information, and 5. Fosters collaboration. Our HRLs have undoubtedly demonstrated these competencies in varying degrees.

The SHRM Competency Model provides the foundation for talent management throughout the HR lifecycle and helps organizations to ensure that HR professionals are proficient in the critical behaviours and knowledge as are necessary to solve the most pressing people issues of today. The SHRM research indicates that the LBIT model largely explains the success of HR professionals. Here, L stands for leadership, B for business, I for interpersonal relations and T for technical knowledge. Our HRLs undoubtedly display the LBIT competencies to a large extent, apart from minor individual variations in each of the components. In general, there is a good fit.

The CIPD's Professional Map has four key elements at its heart: 1. Purpose, 2. Core knowledge, 3. Core behaviours, and 4. Specialist knowledge. An examination of the competencies demonstrated by our thirty HRLs strongly indicates the presence of each and every competency identified by the CIPD.

The NHRDN HR competency model, the 'HRScape', includes eight functional competencies and four behavioural competencies: 1. Credible champion, 2. Diversity and inclusion, 3. Service orientation, and 4. Managing change. All thirty HRLs fit in well with this model and their case studies feature these competencies in abundance.

Functional competencies are emphasized by almost all the competency models as they focus on functional skills. Some list out specific areas, though the functional skills are contextual. All our HRLs demonstrated great strengths in the functional skills and have presented evidence of being good in one or more of the functional skills presented in this model.

Overall, the thirty HRLs display the competencies outlined by the leading HR competency models across the world. They all demonstrated good business leadership, personal leadership, functional leadership as well as professional leadership. Many of them are providing social leadership in a great measure as well and others may soon catch up.

5

Values of HR Leaders

'People with character have a strong sense of values. Having a sense of values means being guided in your thinking and actions by an inner core of standards and abstaining from what you consider as wrong.' (Rao, 2010) In this context, we need to understand what constitutes values and what are some of the values that we have, how our values influence our behaviour and if we can change our values.

'A value is the degree of worth we ascribe to a person, object, situation and behaviour. The higher the worth or perceived worth of that object in our mind, the more we strive to get or achieve it. Thus, if we value money, we try to amass wealth. If we value relationships and people, we are helpful to people and sociable. If we value power, we may look for opportunities that give us power and so on. In the early part of the nineteenth century, scholars formulated what they thought were the six basic values. These were theoretical, aesthetic, spiritual, economic, political and social.' (Rao, 2010)

Theoretical values represent truth and the systematic ordering of knowledge. Those with theoretical values are empirical, critical and rational. Those with economic values focus on wealth and money; those with aesthetic values like creativity and the arts. Those with social values have altruistic tendencies, are sympathetic to others and like relationships. Political values orient a person towards power and politics and drive one to seek power and recognition. Religious or spiritual values may drive the person towards mysticism and a philosophical bent of mind.

OCTAPACE Values

OCTAPACE (Pareek, 2003; Rao, 2013) is an acronym for Openness, Collaboration, Trust, Autonomy, Proactiveness, Authenticity, Confrontation and Experimentation. These values are considered important for organizations to get the best out of their employees. These are also called HRD values. Many organizations are adopting these values. When a large number of people carry these values and organizations promote a culture incorporating them, they have been found to be effective (Pareek, 1981, Rao, 1999, Mridul, 2019 and Prachi et al., 2017).

HRL Values in This Study

A total of 242 values or indicators of values-based actions and ideas were coming out in the case studies of the thirty HRLs. The authors have used these value statements to classify them, using the OCTAPACE value framework of Udai Pareek and T.V. Rao: Openness, Collaboration, Trust and trustworthiness, Autonomy, Proaction, Authenticity, Confrontation and Experimentation, together with other values such as innovation, learning and discipline that appear frequently in managerial and leadership literature. Also, as observed by most competency models, honesty, integrity, trust and trustworthiness come out as dominant values shared by almost all our HRLs. Discipline and respect for people are also consistently held values by these leaders.

The values that characterize most of our HRLs, as emerging from our study, are:

- Trust and trustworthiness were directly evident in twenty-one cases. This includes indicators such as trusting others, being trustworthy and truthful, delivering on commitments, believing that truth will prevail, seeking the truth and being true to it, being upright, walking-the-talk and being highly credible.
- Integrity and honesty were inferred at least in twenty cases that included: being reputed as a good person who treats those weaker

than oneself well, being honest and intolerant of dishonesty and sloppy performance, telling the truth and being prepared to face the consequences, honouring commitments and not making false promises, being apolitical, not misusing proximity, being ethical and not bad-mouthing the employer and such others.

- Disciplined and being fair and firm with people were found in at least nineteen case studies, indicated by such HRL traits as: holding their space and boundaries firmly and not taking any calls even from top bosses beyond committed timings, being fair in decision-making, not getting bound in the policy alone, being fair to women, favouring young people where required, firmly dealing with union-led indiscipline, trying to see things in black and white, diplomacy not being a strength, being frugal and never splurging, being generously appreciative and being genuine and showing gratitude.

- Selfless and respectful of people include being service-oriented, sharing, self-renewing and reflective, which were evident in eighteen cases. Such HRLs respect people irrespective of hierarchy, even critics, respect all functions, respect people's personal time and do not disturb them during the weekends.

- Sacrificing for peers, reinventing self and selflessness include the ability to operate without one's ambition getting in the way, showing no personal aggrandizement, sharing everything and passing on responsibility without feeling threatened, sharing one's knowledge generously and learning with others, and passing on knowledge to the next generation.

- Superordinate goals and higher purpose were evident in at least seventeen cases and include: care for others, ensuring that no worker under one's watch is exploited, being associated with nation-building activities, creating economic wealth in an ethical way to make India a better place, creating happiness in the lives of people and serving mankind while creating wealth, caring for fellow human beings—learnt from education in missionary institutions, doing good for society, being driven by the larger purpose, giving back to society, constantly walking that extra mile and being fired up by this superordinate goal of working for the nation, being liberal with people less economically privileged, wanting to make a difference in the world by serving the country, valuing the poor, keeping oneself meaningfully occupied, being oriented towards the welfare of people, living in India and working for India and not hankering for better opportunities overseas, and being driven by such beliefs that only rats desert a sinking ship.

- Humanitarian values were found in at least seventeen cases and include being humane and caring, being supportive of people, being helpful, caring for others, standing up for others, having the highest standard of work ethic, being compassionate, having socialist views, speaking up for people, being supportive, having sympathy for the underdog and taking a chance with people.

- Talent and people management along with positive thinking were found in seventeen cases and included: deep belief in the limitless potential of people, developing people, deep belief in the dignity of labour, having faith in teamwork, having emotional self-control, being temperamentally balanced, being accommodative with an ability to adjust; being approachable, being adept at boss management, being respectful of women and believing in their potential, being inclusive of differences and being at ease with people from different walks of life.

- Humility was found in twelve cases and this trait included the ability to acknowledge one's mistakes, admitting to having taken a misstep, living a life of dignity even with humble means and showing no need to dominate.

- Commitment and sense of ownership was evident in twelve cases and includes commitment, consciousness about responsibilities, sense of discipline, sensitivity to people, simple living within means and sincerity of purpose. This person works with a sense of responsibility, ownership and care for the role. The person shows situational sensitivity and has demonstrated an ability to navigate through any situation.

- Openness was evident in ten cases and included: accepting a truth as established only after careful personal reasoning and irrespective of how personally unpalatable it may be, assuming that nothing will remain secret, giving freedom of choice to people, showing a positive attitude towards people, having a personal vision to become a better person, not competing with others and treating others as valuable resources.

- Authenticity and transparency were directly evident in ten cases and included a clear conscience, refusal to accept things that one did not agree with and such others.
- Courage and risk-taking alongside being independent was evident in nine HRLs and included: courage to correct a course, courage to own up, the ability to hold one's ground to ensure commitments given to people were honoured, courage to pursue what one felt was right and courage to try out new things.
- Passion for learning was of high value in eight cases and included learning from all possible sources, focused on academics, always a learner, continuously reading books, leveraging adversities as opportunities to make an impact, appreciating value for reading and reflection and treating meta thinking and frames of thinking as very important.
- Proactiveness, initiative-taking and optimism were traits in seven cases that were characterized by: keenness to meet new people and learning from them, not being constrained by policies if they came in the way of dealing with problems, the ability to challenge policy and drive changes in the policy, the ability to organize professional bodies, involvement with professional bodies and launching initiatives to spread knowledge.
- Confrontation is a trait that was indicated in seven case studies that included: fighting for justice, fighting for correcting wrongdoings even if it was with the boss and confronting issues and bringing them to the fore to solve the problem.
- Sense of purpose was evident in five cases; these HRLs were achievement-driven, always followed a standard, saying and doing what was believable, the operational job was about putting HR and its values into practice, affiliative and working towards raising the lifestyle of the family without taking undue risks, ambitious, aiming high and wanting the company's HR to be the best in the world, purposive, with a will-do, can-do spirit and not wasting time asking questions (fauji spirit).
- Empathy, customer and employee-centricity was evident in five cases and included: credibility, customer centricity, empathy that included empathizing with people in lower rungs of society (servants) and employee-centricity.

- Collaborative, with a yen for teamwork, and co-creation in a couple of cases.
- The spirit of experimentation and innovativeness in two cases included: coming up with ideas and experimenting with them instead of running to consultants and being innovative in introducing HR practices.

Summary and Conclusions

Our thirty case studies of HR leaders demonstrate beyond doubt that they are people of character, with high ethical standards and values. Consistent values emerging from these thirty cases also indicate that these leaders value people and have a positive view of human beings. This positive view, encompassing people in general and employees and other stakeholders in particular, enables them to sustain their higher sense of values, self-respect and social responsibility. These traits sit comfortably on their shoulders and lead them to be open and trusting. They invest them with the drive to promote teamwork and collaboration within their workplaces and even outside, especially with the professional bodies that they are associated with. Given their authentic, transparent, trusting and trustworthy nature, they honour their commitments and are proactive, while being humble as well. These are values that could be emulated by future leaders not only in HR but in all professions.

The findings on the values of our HR leaders are in tune with the various competency models of HR professionals across the globe. For example, CIPD maintains that the fundamental purpose of the people profession is to champion better work and working lives. It is about creating roles, opportunities, organizations and working environments that help get the best out of people, delivering great organizational outcomes and, in turn, driving economies and making good, fair and inclusive work a societal outcome. This, in our view, is the core value of the HR profession.

The HRSCAPE of NHRDN lists 'Credible champion' as one of the core competencies required of HR professionals. Credible champion denotes the ability to demonstrate high integrity in personal and professional transactions. It includes the following elements that are essentially values: (a) integrity and fairness, (b) building trust, (c) emotional maturity and (d) being ethical.

(a) Integrity and fairness include the following traits:

- Meets timelines;
- Demonstrates objectivity in transactions and decisions;
- Avoids bringing personal biases;
- Delivers consistently on commitments;
- Sensitizes others about the impact of personal biases;
- Runs the extra mile to deliver beyond commitments;
- Stands for just causes and acts on them;
- Works with stakeholders in creating a culture of fairness;
- Sticks one's neck out on issues based on conviction; and
- Acts as role models for organizational values.

(b) Building trust includes such traits as:

- Maintains transparency in all dealings;
- Shows consistency between espoused and enacted values (authenticity);
- Demonstrates courage and conviction in all dealings (confrontation;)
- Displays integrity in all communications;
- Interfaces with stakeholders with authenticity;
- Helps to institutionalize systems and processes to facilitate two-way communication.

(c) Emotional maturity includes such traits as:

- Demonstrates self-awareness;
- Consciously seeks regular feedback;
- Owns mistakes and takes corrective action;
- Is self-motivated to take action;
- Maintains composure in trying circumstances;
- Defers short-term gratification for long-term objectives;
- Displays equanimity at all times; and
- Acts as a role model in managing intrapersonal and interpersonal emotions

(d) Maintaining ethical standards includes such traits as:

- Influences others to behave in an ethical manner;
- Develops and supports systems for reporting unethical behaviour;

- Identifies and escalates potential ethical risks associated with organizational policies and practices;
- Creates ethical champions across the organization by being an ethical role model; and
- Creates benchmark ethical practices to enhance ethical orientation among employees.

'Fosters collaboration' is among the five competencies identified by Dave Ulrich and team (Ulrich et al., 2021) on the basis of their thirty years of research. This competency is closer to what we present here as a value. As per the round VIII report of the RBL Group: 'Fosters collaboration describes the ways in which an individual can build trusting relationships with others in order to effectively navigate getting things done. First, relationships with others start with an individual's ability to manage their own self by being open to feedback and displaying confidence, humility, integrity and ethics. Second, fostering collaboration entails building trust, working effectively with, and valuing people from different organization levels, skill levels, functions, backgrounds and cultures.'

Our HR Leaders emphatically demonstrate all the professional values of integrity, honesty, honouring commitments, openness, collaborative spirit, trustworthiness, trust, proactiveness and many other values described in all global HR competency models.

6

Lessons from 'Baked' Leaders

The crucible of experiences that HR leaders were baked in hold important lessons for parents, teachers and managers both in HR as well as those in leadership positions in organizations. This chapter highlights the lessons that we find from our study of the baking process of the thirty HRLs.

Our study of thirty HRLs indicates that regardless of the socio-economic conditions of the families, our HRLs were shaped by family rituals, role-modelling by parents and engagement with the broader agenda of society or the nation.

A good part of the leader's values gets formed early in life. Crucible experiences of the HRLs indicate that, irrespective of the family's socio-economic status, the parents can provide the right atmosphere at home to inculcate worthwhile values that will be appropriate and supportive for the person to grow as an effective HR leader. There are specific aspects that shape such value-building:

Lessons for Parents

Rituals and role-model behaviour of family members in terms of the values they display in their day-to-day living generally have a very profound impact.

Families, particularly parents and siblings, need to be mindful that their everyday actions provide the crucible experiences for the growing children, baking their characters for the future. Of particular import are: how they treat each other, how they treat the employees working in the house, how they relate to religion and spiritual aspects of their lives, the recreational activities they engage in, conversations that they have among themselves, conversations that they have with the growing child, how they deal with crises in the family, their attitude towards education and learning activities and how they relate to larger social and national issues. All of these reflect the values that the parents communicate and even demonstrate through their actions in the family. The children experience them and these qualities serve as building blocks for their character.

Our study revealed that parents apart, in many instances, others emerged as the key influencers: an elder sister or brother, grandparents or uncles. These key influencers impact the child even through their intermittent interactions and need to be equally mindful of their role in baking the character of the child.

Lessons for Educational Institutions

The second important kilns where the child's psyche is baked for leadership roles are the schools and colleges. Our study indicated that more than the nature of the institution, it is the quality of experiences that the institution offers that shapes the character of the individual. The academic environment, the presence of libraries and the abundance of extracurricular activities have a positive influence on baking the appropriate leadership capabilities in the students. Right from the primary school to institutions of professional education, there are opportunities to engage the students in a variety of ways; project work, field visits, debates, dramatics, the inclusion of specific subjects in the syllabus, sports, celebration of national festivals and other such extracurricular activities go a long way in shaping the character of the students.

The manner in which the child is disciplined has a significant impact: how the students are treated by the school or college authorities goes a long way in baking their life skills. A student typically spends fifteen to seventeen years—starting at the age of five, from primary school through to completing professional education at the age of twenty-two years—under the watchful (or neglectful) eyes of the academic institutions. These are the most formative years in a youngster's life; when the persona gets baked with appropriate skills and values, when the person gets prepared for the life ahead. Academic institutions thus need to be mindful of their responsibility for not only imparting academic knowledge but also for significantly contributing towards building lasting characters of the students.

The HRLs in our universe going to XLRI or TISS acknowledged that they were deeply impacted by the fieldwork they were required to do during their academic years in these institutes. These were emotionally-moving experiences and their respect for the underprivileged, in particular, went through significant transformation. Working on projects aimed at deepening the understanding of the society—particularly for those who do not have access to sophisticated education and other resources—helps to develop the right attitudes and values for HR professionals and these experiences eventually shape them as leaders. Schools and colleges are where leaders are groomed and much of this is accomplished outside the course papers and are beyond the purview of the syllabus. Every school and college should discuss, debate and create such project opportunities for the students. Activity-centred schools and colleges contribute more toward developing leaders and leadership.

Lessons for Teachers

Teachers have played a great role in several cases in our HRL universe. Role-model teachers profoundly impacted their students by what they taught, their approach to teaching and their personal conduct, influencing the HRLs at all stages in their lives. The influences extended to driving the HRLs to excel in studies and choosing the right profession, baking their world views and helping them to embrace appropriate values for their lives ahead.

The significant lesson emerging from these case studies is that apart from just textbook teaching, teachers have been mentors and coaches, who have helped to bake the HRLs for their lives ahead. Our HRLs have acknowledged how their teachers took a specific interest in nudging them to do well in their studies. In some cases, the way the teacher taught the subject was so absorbing that the student ended up choosing the profession related to that subject.

The stories narrated by the HRLs contain instances of this at the school level as well as later, at the postgraduate level at the IIMs, XLRI and TISS. In some cases, the teachers built personal connections with the students, inviting them home for dinner and discussing subjects of wider interest, thereby shaping their world views. Some teachers even went to the extent of guiding the student in their choice of profession or guided them to altering their choices to areas that would suit them better. Others dealt with indiscipline innovatively, with care and with no trace of personal ego, reinforcing their values of integrity and accountability.

Thus, teachers at all stages in life, right from the primary to the postgraduate level, have had abiding influence by making learning absorbing and exciting, teaching their subjects to arouse curiosity, being role models and also connecting with the students at a personal level, as mentors, challenging them, stimulating their interests and supporting them, thereby baking the character of the students for their lives ahead. This is the greatest success a teacher can have and some of our HRLs have themselves taken up teaching in the latter stages of their lives.

Lessons for CEOs and Managers

First Jobs

The first job, the initial job experiences and the early organizational exposure are particularly impactful and have made a lot of difference in the emergence of leaders and leadership. Some of our HRLs converted even their routine jobs as opportunities to learn about the company and used them to gain insights into the business. Routine jobs represent early-career challenges in building HR leaders. The early career lays the foundations by developing self-confidence, identification of potential, stoking execution abilities and, for some, offers opportunities to innovate and share out-of-the-box thinking. These experiences make a lasting impact on baking the HR leaders for life.

Organizations need to pay special attention to their induction programmes and design them in such a way that the new entrant is encouraged to start the self-discovery process for life, using the organization as a platform. Every manager that the new entrants meet in the first few weeks and every single event they participate in and contribute to goes into the building of their character and values. Induction programmes need to invest one with the art of efficacy and help individuals to be effective in their roles. Induction or onboarding programmes reveal a lot to new recruits and a lot of the assumptions, beliefs and viewpoints that they may be carrying need to be altered and their mindsets redirected towards attaining their potential in the evolving future.

Induction programmes socialize the recruits into their job or role; the first boss or the first few bosses' encounters with them play a significant role in grooming them as leaders. Organizations, thus, need to understand the significance of the first job or the first few jobs in the lives of an individual and plan experiences such that the new recruits can realize their potential. Our HRLs acknowledged that they benefited from their first jobs that had the right blend of challenge, learning opportunity, autonomy as well as support. They had the benefit of bosses who mentored them by helping them to interpret some failures, and both negative and positive experiences enhanced their overall learning. These helped them bring out their leadership potential and baked them for senior leadership roles.

Mentoring Bosses; Leadership Creation

Bosses as mentors and coaches played exceptional roles in their lives, as most of our HRLs acknowledged. As they moved ahead in the profession and business, good bosses baked and shaped their destinies by recognizing their potential, giving them freedom, empowerment and opportunity to create new systems and processes. They also invested them with the self-confidence required to make a difference in the company.

In today's world, the success of CEOs and leaders is largely measured by their ability to create leaders of others around them. Every organization is concerned about fabricating a leadership pipeline or bench, organizing leadership succession through empowerment, coaching and other planned interventions, and creating a culture of continuous learning and development. An important lesson to be derived from our stories of HRLs is the positive role played by their seniors and bosses as mentors and coaches, providing guidance and direction wherever required.

By implication, all those who reach the middle or senior level in the managerial ladder should be able to play this mentoring and coaching role for their juniors. As Noel Tichy (1997) observed, anyone who has a teachable point of view can be a leader and leaders are teachers. Taking this point of view, we recommend all managers to evoke the teacher within and facilitate learning for their juniors. Our HRLs have greatly benefited from their seniors, mentors and coaches and speak with admiration for them.

Stretch Jobs

Stretch jobs contribute enormously to development, especially because of the trauma that they often inject into the workspace. No development occurs without a price. Our HRLs responded to these challenges by both primarily and principally treating them as learning opportunities and building their own capabilities. They have all acknowledged learning and growing by doing demanding jobs that stretched their capabilities. These demanding jobs were truly crucible experiences that helped bake them for future leadership roles.

Project assignments, job rotations and change of geographies have all been impactful experiences in building our HRLs. They take individuals out of their comfort zones and ask them to deliver to a new set of challenges, building resilience, evoking their innovative spirit and widening their socio-corporate horizons, completing them as individuals. Organizations, thus, need to examine their own internal HR processes and identify how they can strengthen the leadership development component in them. Interventions like employee-engagement surveys, organizational-climate surveys, performance-management processes, learning and development activities, task forces, working groups, temporary teams and such others go a long way in bringing out the leadership talent besides getting the work done in specialized areas.

Exposure to Business Roles

In many instances, by doing business roles, HRLs developed new perspectives about the HR role itself. Exposure to business roles has been very immersive and invaluable in baking the mental models of the

HRLs early in their career. Organizations should seriously consider job rotation to business roles for two to three years to develop HRLs. These should be challenging and accountable jobs with clearly measurable deliverables. Several HRLs have reported that such an exposure truly provided them with crucible experience that was invaluable in baking them as seasoned HR professionals.

Significance of Industrial Relations

The stories of our HRLs suggest that to be baked into a well-rounded and effective HR professional, one must go through the crucible of IR experience. In recent years, there has been a tendency to underplay the significance of employee relations or industrial relations. Often, young HR professionals indicate their preference for doing HR roles at corporate offices rather than being in the trenches rubbing shoulders with blue-collar workers. HRLs in our study have acknowledged that they developed as leaders courtesy the IR situations they faced and the manner in which they handled them, learning through every move, nuanced or bold. Even in the services industry, HR professionals need to get assigned to handling employee relations where they have to deal with employees directly at the grassroots level.

Dealing with Setbacks and Failures

The stories of our HRLs indicate that it is not unusual to come across negative crucible moments in one's career journey. Missing promotions, postings in unknown territories, unexpected downturns in business, having to downsize or terminate employees, facing unexpected strikes and such like are common crucibles. Faced with such adversities, those with leadership potential show humility and seek the counsel of wiser, better-informed and experienced people and well-wishers. Such counsel has often equipped them to encounter the challenge with elan. Whatever the nature of the assistance, internal strength or external support, the experience of these crucible moments have impacted their mental model. Not losing courage and sustaining their confidence throughout the challenge, using a coach, a good boss, a parent, reading books like the Bhagavad Gita, listening to good words and using these as learning experiences are lessons that these experiences teach.

Challenging the Status Quo and Leading New Initiatives

HRLs, as business partners as well as employee advocates, constantly observe, review and call out what needs to change and then marshal support from the key stakeholders to lead the change.

Role-Making

Crucible experiences of role-making indicate that, quite often, HRLs are provoked and sometimes receive guidance or a broad definition of what is expected of them and what they should aspire for. Sometimes, the crucible is just wide open and clear and it is for the HRL to figure out the way forward. In both scenarios, the HRLs are guided by their own values, sincerity of purpose, understanding of the larger context, both on the business and the people fronts, as they craft their roles in alignment to the demands of the situation.

Attending Training Programmes; Learning from Various Sources

Some of our HRLs made it a point to get global exposure and exposure to current thought leadership by attending training programmes and also organizing them for their senior managers. These training programmes proved to be learning crucibles that baked and prepared the HRLs for their impactful careers in human resource functions. Almost all our HR leaders seem to be reflective learners using various sources as learning.

Leadership in Professional Forums

Our HR leaders took their engagements with professional bodies seriously as sources of learning. When given any responsibility, they contributed selflessly as well. Professional bodies can often offer what organizations cannot, in terms of kilns that could include opportunities for testing out new ideas, innovative opportunities to inspire juniors, streamlining governance, designing new structures, systems and processes. Such bodies offer an enriching world of mutual support. Our HR leaders too gave generously to the professional bodies only to receive much more in return. They paid back by helping to develop others and grow HR talent.

Professional bodies offer multiple advantages for one keen to demonstrate and share one's talents, or interested in enhancing or multiplying one's own leadership attitudes and skills, or one who is keen to develop talent and leadership in others. These bodies provide a platform where leaders are free of organizational pressures to deliver results, where they can drive their own initiatives and are given the space to experiment. There are limits to independent initiatives in organizations that perhaps are not as restrictive in professional organizations, where there is no telling pressure for results. Also, there is no one forever questioning an entirely independent, self-initiative. What one cannot do in one's own organization can be done in professional bodies that are supposed to further such initiatives.

Such professional bodies also prompt one to make oneself more accountable even when official accountability is low, just as they create the ecosystem for commitment and for developing a keenness to contribute because money is not the primary consideration as they are not-for-profit organizations. They offer platforms for building others as leaders, initiating new areas for research, measuring impact, benchmarking and promoting best and next practices, documentation and other measures to drive professional excellence and elevate professional standards across the board. When one contributes to a professional body, the contributions are lasting and go beyond benefiting a few individuals; they go towards building a profession.

Most of our HRLs have both developed and used their leadership competencies to inject values and good governance through their work in these professional bodies. The authors hold such professional bodies as the epitomes of excellence across the world, which serve as the best platforms for demonstrating and baking leadership talent.

Contributing to Social Causes and CSR

Every one of our HRLs is volunteering to contribute toward social causes in one way or the other. This is the virtuous cycle, whereby the greater their engagement with giving to social causes, the more meaningful their contributions become and the more inspired they feel to give even more. The crucible of giving for social causes is baking the HRLs toward a more inclusive world view that is self-perpetuating.

HRLs as Institution-Builders

Among the most remarkable, yet unacknowledged, contributions thrown up by the case studies is the great capability for institution-building that our HRLs have demonstrated. They have hardly ever been recognized as or even acknowledged as institution-builders, though. Using the framework of McClelland presented in the introductory chapter, our HRLs found unique opportunities in the HR function to meet the criteria laid by McClelland as institution-builders or institutional managers. Almost all of them were organization-minded and felt responsible for fine-tuning and investing the tasks and functions they were given to handle with depth and sophistication.

- All of them were hard-working people and reported liking their work. It satisfied their need for getting things done in an orderly way;
- They were quite willing to sacrifice some of their own interests for the welfare of the organization they served;
- They created a separate and distinct identity for the HR function;
- They created a culture that maximized the use and development of internal talent;
- Many of them performed the synergizing role focused on integrating the use of various functions and resources;
- Several of them presented evidence of having played a balancing role between profits and people, between conformity and creativity;
- Some have performed the linkage-building role where linkages were built between the organization and its stakeholders, including other agencies and society. This was demonstrated particularly during the pandemic;
- Many of them also performed a futuristic role by anticipating the future and with vision, guiding the organization into the future; and
- They also contributed to the impact-making role, whereby the leader ensured that the organization made an impact on society and in the field in which such impact was intended.

Building Others as Leaders

The case studies present evidence that several HRLs had unique perspectives on a number of issues at different points of their lives and took pains to articulate them and put them up for discussion, enabling others to learn from them and progress in their careers. When the situation so demanded, they were happy to learn from the dialogues and review their positions or learn new things altogether. Many of our HRLs are acknowledged for contributing to the career growth of others and also for serving as role models. Our HRLs in their roles of president, general secretary, board member and such positions of influence in professional bodies certainly did a lot to impact others. They created scope for autonomy and problem-solving.

Effective Leaders and Effective People

Overall, our HRLs were effective in what they did. Data from their case studies reveals their qualities as effective people as they worked to make a difference through the policies and practices that they followed. The HR profession and HR roles offer an individual the unique opportunity to make a difference in the lives of others by virtue of being in the profession. HR professionals have no need to search for opportunities to impact through what is nowadays referred to as corporate social responsibility. If every organization is considered a social system in itself, it has an in-built opportunity to make a difference in the lives of others.

By doing their job sincerely and with commitment, HRLs can make a difference in the lives of others if they are empathetic, grateful to people, view other people as possibilities (innovative and capable of generating new ideas and ways of doing things) and respect each of them as born with some unique talent. This is irrespective of gender, caste, creed, cultural and ethnic background, socio-economic status, nationality or state and other diversities in their backgrounds. They are all treated with respect. The HR profession is all about offering opportunities to make a difference to customers, employees, employers, investors and all members of society. Our HRLs collectively demonstrate this.

The Bottom Line

This journey with the thirty HRLs has been an enriching experience for both of us. They have exemplary lessons to offer and we have presented a few outstanding ones; all fundamental to excellence in HR. These we selected after many meticulous reviews of the case studies. We ensured that we captured every significant trait; even nuances. We expect you, our readers, to find other appealing lessons that inspire each of you specifically.

The purpose of this book will be well served if you internalize these lessons, invoke them in your lives and possibly provoke yourselves and others to apply these lessons in situations that the lessons lend themselves to. Hopefully, readers will be guided to develop their own ecosystem of values, their own vision of the functions that they are called to perform in their lives, both professional and social. After all, the overarching lesson that one has learnt is that HR management is about encompassing the entire universe of people within one's scope of influence. If we have been able to impact your hearts and minds, we will consider ourselves gratified.

7

References and Bibliography

Boyatzis, R.E. (1982), *The Competent Manager: A Model for Effective Performance*, John Wiley & Sons, 1982.

Cohen, William (2020), Peter F. Drucker's Leadership: see https://www.corporatelearningnetwork.com/leadership-management/articles/drucker-called-these-two-organizational-qualities-essential (downloaded on 9-9-2021).

Drucker, Peter (2004), 'What Makes an Effective Executive', Harvard Business Review Communication, June 2004, https://hbr.org/2004/06/what-makes-an-effective-executive

Giang Thi Huong Vu (2017), 'A Critical Review of Human Resource Competency Model: Evolvement in Required Competencies for Human Resource Professionals', *Journal of Economics, Business and Management*, Vol. 5, No. 12, December 2017, pp. 357–65.

https://dpglearn.co.uk/blog/human-resources/cipd-profession-map/

https://hbr.org/2003/01/power-is-the-great-motivator

https://www.cipd.co.uk/cipd-hr-profession/cipd-hr-profession-map/default.html

https://www.hrci.org/community/blogs-and-announcements/hr-leads-business-blog/hr-leads-business/2020/09/04/nine-competencies-for-hr-excellence-emerge (downloaded on 26-08-2021).

https://www.shrm.org/learningandcareer/career/pages/shrm-competency-model.aspx (downloaded on 7-9-2021).

Mayne, Theresa (11 March 2021), CIPD Profession Map, downloaded on 7-9-2021.

McCall, Morgan W., Lombardo, Michael M. and Morrison, Ann M. (1988), *Lessons of Experience: How Successful Executives Develop on the Job*, New York: The Free Press.

McClelland, David C. and Burnham, David H., 'Power is the Great Motivator,' *HBR Classic*, 1976, 2003.

McClelland, D.C. (1973), 'Testing for Competence Rather than for Intelligence', *American Psychologist*, Vol. 28, no. 1, p.1, 1973.

Meginley, Dave, (2020) GPHR, and HRCI Chief Business Development Officer: HR Leads Business, September 4, https://www.hrci.org/community/blogs-and-announcements/hr-leads-business-blog/hr-leads-business/2020/09/04/nine-competencies-for-hr-excellence-emerge 2020 (downloaded on 7-9-2021).

Morgan, Jacob, (2020), https://www.chieflearningofficer.com/2020/01/06/what-is-leadership-and-who-is-a-leader/)

Mridul Trikha (2019), Organization Culture 'Octapace', *International Journal of Science and Research (IJSR)*, ISSN: 2319-7064 ResearchGate Impact Factor (2018): 0.28 | SJIF (2018): 7.426, Vol. 8, Issue 7, July 2019, pp. 655–59, https://www.ijsr.net/archive/v8i7/5071901.pdf. Reviews studies on OCTAPACE.

Nikam, Prachi, Suresh Patidar and P.N. Mishra (2017), 'Octapace Culture: A Predictor of Faculty Performance', *International Journal of Advanced Scientific Research and Engineering Trends*, 2(1), Vol. 30–35, http://www.ijasret.com/VolumeArticles/FullTextPDF/123_IJASRET_Octapace_Culture_A_Predictor_of_Faculty_Performance.pdf

Pareek, Udai (1981, 2002), *Effective Organizations: Beyond Management to Institution Building*, New Delhi, Oxford and IBH.

Pareek, Udai (1980), 'Dimensions of Role Efficacy', in J.W. Pfeiffer and J.E. Jones (Eds) *The 1980 Annual Handbook for Group Facilitators*, San Diego, Calif., University Associates, pp. 143–45.

Rao, T.V. (2014), *HRD Audit: Evaluating the Human Resource Function for Business Improvement*, New Delhi, Sage India.

Rao, T.V. (1999), *HRD Audit: Evaluating the Human Resource Function for Business Improvement*, New Delhi, Sage, Response Books.

Rao, T.V. (2010), *Managers Who Make a Difference*, New Delhi, IIMA Books, Random House.

Rao, T.V. (2013), *The HRD Missionary*, 2nd Edition, Ahmedabad, TV Rao Learning Systems.

Rao, T.V. (2015), *Effective People*, New Delhi, Penguin Random House.

Rao, T.V. and Charu Sharma (2011), *100 Managers in Action*, New Delhi, Tata McGraw-Hill publication.

Sinha, K.K. (2014), *My Experiments with Unleashing People Power*, New Delhi, Bloomsbury.

Spencer, L.M. and Spencer, P.S.M., *Competence at Work Models for Superior Performance*, John Wiley & Sons, 2008.

The CIPD Professional Map. Downloaded on 7-9-2021, https://www.coursesonline.co.uk/everything-you-need-to-know-about-cipds-new-2021-qualifications/

The SHRM Competency Model (2016), https://www.shrm.org/LearningAndCareer/competency-model/PublishingImages/pages/default/SHRM%20Competency%20Model_Detailed%20Report_Final_SECURED.pdf (downloaded on 12-9-2021).

Tichy, Noel (1997), *The Leadership Engine: How Winning Companies Build Leaders at Every Level*, New York, Harper Business.

Ulrich, Dave, Mike Ulrich, Erin Wilson Burns and Patrick Wright (2021), 'New HRCS 8 Competency Model Focuses on Simplifying Complexity', 22 April 2021; https://www.rbl.net/insights/articles/new-hrcs-8-competency-model-focuses-on-simplifying-complexity

Ulrich, D. (1997b), *The Human Resource Champions: The Next Agenda for Adding Value and Delivering Results*, Boston, MA, Harvard Business School.

Ulrich, D. and D. Lake (1990), *Organisational Capability: Competing from the Inside/Out*, New York, Wiley. References | 361.

Ulrich, D., J. Younger, W. Brockbank and M. Ulrich (2013a), *HR from the Outside in: Six Competencies for the Future of Human Resources*, New Delhi, Tata McGraw-Hill.

Ulrich, D., J. Younger, W. Brockbank and M. Ulrich (2013b), *Global HR Competencies: Mastering Competitive Value from the Outside In*, New Delhi, Tata McGraw-Hill.

Wright, Patrick M., Mike Ulrich, Erin Wilson Burns and Dave Ulrich (2021), Navigating HR's Impact, HRCS Round 8 Findings: HRCS, The RBL Group and Michigan Ross: file:///C:/Users/Admin/Downloads/HRCS-8-report-final.pdf

Zenger, John H. and Joseph Folkman (2002), *The Extraordinary Leader*, New Delhi, Tata McGraw-Hill (Original McGraw-Hill Edition 2002).

8

Appendices

Appendix 1: Interview Questions

Brief bio sketch—which gives factual highlights.

Who were the early influencers (mentors)—parental, neighbours, school or any other role models early in life.

Higher education—critical incidences, influencers, which had a lasting impact on you.

Early career—first two jobs—critical incidences, which had a lasting impact on you.

Early experience of becoming CHRO—your leadership journey—key activities done, challenges, specific approach you followed—for gaining acceptance and establishing yourself.

Experiences that were intense, unforeseen, which had a lasting impact in shaping your current persona. Nature of these incidents and the specific impacts on your persona.

Experiences of sorting out vital from trivial many—how did you prevent yourself from getting lost in day-to-day transactional matters.

Experiences of dealing with tough emotional issues (firing people).

Experiences of dealing with former peers.

How did you continue the connect with people—even after reaching the very top of the organization.

Experiences of nurturing talents—your approach toward identifying and nurturing other 'high-calibre talents' in the team. Personal philosophy.

Experiences of hearing truth—which may be contrary to own beliefs/convictions.

Experiences of understanding the context and your approach to carrying existing people toward the change agenda.

Experiences of preparing for passing on own wisdom and succession.

Experiences of reinventing.

Readings, conceptual framework—which had a lasting impact on you.

Challenges faced in managing:

Juniors

Line managers

Establishing credibility of HR strategy used

Appendix 2: A Tool for Self-Assessment of Competencies

Given below are a checklist of competencies, competency indicators and values from our study of thirty HR Leaders. Tick mark the competency you think you have to an adequate level, and find those which you still need to develop, consolidate this list, and make an action plan for developing the same. You may also use this checklist for getting 360 Degree Feedback from those who have interacted with you including your seniors, juniors, and colleagues. You can also use this as a five-point scale for assessing the extent which you think you have the competency. You may use the following scale for self-assessment:

0 = I don't have this at all, and I need to cultivate and develop this
1 = I have this to a small degree, and I need to work on it a lot

2 = I have this to some extend and I could strengthen the same in future

3 = I have this to a great extent and with a little more effort I can make it my strength

4 = I have this to a great extent, and this is one of my strong points.

1. Focused: picks one's battles and does not try to change everything
2. Penetrates deeply into an issue faced at work
3. Confident in dealing with mergers and acquisitions
4. Keeps reading books and other material and keeps academic interests alive
5. Can adapt to new situations and turn them around
6. Agility to deal with moving goalposts, changing contexts and challenges
7. Agility to think on his/her own feet to deal with unusual situations
8. Feels comfortable with ambiguity: can manage ambiguous situations
9. Pays attention to details
10. Spends time with people at a personal level, in their formal and informal needs
11. Cultivates a logical flow of thoughts
12. Protects self from politics
13. Is at home with facts and theory
14. Comes up with HR strategy and policies keeping in view the business and people context
15. Can clearly see the connection of quality of engagement with productivity
16. Has service mentality—servant leadership
17. Formulates HR policies as the need arises
18. Ability to pick up performance by pulling the right chords of people
19. Accelerates the pace of change through institutional practices
20. Manages change by influencing—not by authority
21. Leads from the front and dirties hands where needed
22. Can reshape worker relationships—from confrontational to consultative

23. Has skills to change people through dialogue
24. Proud of one's organizations
25. Committed to making a significant difference to any organization where one works
26. Communicates tough decisions in a soft, humane manner
27. Ability to articulate issues
28. Compassion and humility, respecting all, irrespective of their social status and dignity of labour
29. Ability to manage conflict and potentially volatile situations
30. Ability to sort out differences respectfully—not blow up into ugly fights
31. Confrontation skills: ability to stand up to bullies
32. Connectivity: ability to be in touch with people at all levels
33. Connectivity: ability to connect with grassroots
34. Courage to challenge status quo
35. Courage to take tough decisions
36. Creating win-win outcomes
37. Creating linkages between HR practices and business strategies
38. Creative in solving problems
39. Credibility: delivery on promise—dependability
40. Cross-cultural sensitivities: dealing with people from different nationalities
41. Diversity management: ability to manage in different cultures
42. Ability to clarify and build company culture
43. Ability to deal with bureaucrats and politicians
44. Dealing with officers' associations, enlisting support of unions
45. Decision making: ability to make independent decisions
46. Defining and developing culture in the organization
47. Delegating work to younger professionals—trusting them and giving them freedom to work
48. Developing people: ability to groom talent
49. Emotional maturity: high self-regard and emotional maturity
50. Empathy: ability to change frame of reference and understand others' points of view
51. Empowering: choose the right person and leave him/her alone to do the work, does not encourage escalations

52. Empowering: giving credit to others to get peers on board with his/her ideas
53. Energy: speed of action
54. Engaging militant union leaders with empathy, listening and understanding
55. Entrepreneurial
56. Execution: ability to get things done
57. Execution: ability to organize events
58. Execution: action-oriented
59. Execution: gets things done without throwing his/her weight around
60. Firmness: ability to take tough calls
61. Functional: ability to create the compensation structure
62. Functional: HR functional knowledge
63. Functional: respect for the law
64. Functional: strong interest in finance and customer satisfaction
65. Functional: technical bent of mind
66. Global exposure
67. Global mindset
68. Hard-working: working long hours
69. Humility and fair play
70. Inclusive: does not judge people just by appearances/just one prism—be it qualifications, present position, etc.
71. Influence skills: ability to influence people several levels above him
72. Initiative
73. Innovative HR practices, including ADCs, cutting redundancies of excessive staff and variable pay
74. Innovative: willing to try innovative approaches
75. Innovativeness: ability to design innovative development programmes
76. Integrating ability: ability to connect discipline—eclectic mind; appreciation for interdisciplinary solutions to problems
77. Integration: ability to integrate diverse agenda
78. Integration: ability to understand and balance opposing views
79. Integration: aligning HR agenda with business needs

80. Integration: architecting HR process coordinated with desired culture

81. Integration: balanced view of HR—respect for all other functions

82. Integration: balancing between people and business—staying objective and empathetic

83. Integration: Balancing individual and organizational needs

84. Interpersonal competence: the ability to listen and provide psychological space to people—be it a colleague, direct report, union leader or shop floor worker

85. Interpersonal sensitivity: adept at finding something to appreciate in a person and building relationships

86. Learning all the time from different people/sources

87. Learning: seeking professional help from external professionals

88. Manage disagreements: how to surface disagreements with strong bosses

89. Mentoring; ability to mentor and guide others

90. Multi-tasking: can handle multiple tasks simultaneously

91. Negotiating skills without wavering under pressure or getting intimated

92. Networking and engagement with professional forums

93. Networking with people at all levels

94. Objective and data-driven

95. Openness to ideas and views from others

96. Organizing ability—even large events

97. Proactive: Volunteering

98. Problem-solver: Being a problem-solver

99. Process skills: ability to see the means and ends to relationships

100. Productivity improvements: ability to manage productivity improvements

101. Reading: avid reader

102. Resilience: ability to face adversity

103. Result-oriented

104. Risk taker: prepared to plunge into shouldering new responsibilities—risk-taking

105. Self-confident
106. Self-development: constantly questioning self, 'What value am I adding?'
107. Self-reflective: culture—managing own ambition so that it does not get in the way
108. Self-renewal: habit of intense reflection and self-analysis
109. Self-renewal: Introspective nature to take a transparent look at the company
110. Self-worth: high sense of self-worth
111. Sense of responsibility of a HR person
112. Spiritual bent of mind
113. Strategic thinking respect for other functions: ability to navigate through multiple HR issues and address other functional resources
114. Strategic thinking: ability to conceptualize HR initiatives in dealing with changing business needs
115. Strategic thinking: ability to develop HR strategy involving line managers
116. Strategic thinking: ability to transition from adversarial relationship to collaborative relationship—with workers/trade unions
117. Strategic thinking: ability to work out win-win solutions while dealing with powerful people
118. Strategic thinking: art of marrying diplomacy and power, and deploying both these weapons with skill
119. Strategic: using organizational capabilities for competitive advantage as a part of this new ball game
120. Strategic: quickly analyses the issue and sees behind the tactics and games, and comes forward to solve problems
121. Strategic: using thought leaders in the board—past and current
122. Systems and processes: ability to build HR processes
123. Systems orientation with process insights
124. Systems: Designing the structure, processes, workflows, transitions, talent management, while managing integration

125. Systems development: ability to design and develop HR systems like climate survey, fast track progression, induction, integration, competency mapping, incentives, performance management, assessment centre, etc.
126. Systems: using systems and processes for business goals
127. Talent development based on their inner potential—and giving people chances
128. Talent identification: ability to find high-calibre talent
129. Talent: ability to recognize talent and nurture the same
130. Team management: ability to manage peers as direct reports
131. Teamwork: consensus building, allowing debates over issues and options
132. Technology savvy: ability to use technology
133. Time management
134. Versatile: versatility to meet the changing nature of business and challenges
135. Vision: ability to look at the broader picture and has a longer-term perspective
136. Vision: thought leadership
137. Workforce management: ability to manage large workforce with multiple companies
138. Work-life balance: balanced family outings with office work
139. Ability to see the linkages between society, economy, governance, people inside and outside
140. Ability to appreciate and promote philanthropy and CSR

Appendix 3: A Tool for Self-Assessment of Values

Given below is a checklist of values, from our study of thirty HR Leaders. Tick the value you think you have at an adequate level, and find those which you still need to develop, consolidate it, and make an action plan for developing the same. You may also use this checklist for getting 360° feedback from those who have interacted with you, including your seniors, juniors, and colleagues. You can also use the following as a five-point scale for self-assessing the extent which you think you have the specific value:

0 = I don't have this at all, and I need to cultivate and develop this
1 = I have this to a small degree, and I need to work on it a lot

2 = I have this to some extent and I could strengthen the same in future
3 = I have this to a great extent and with a little more effort, I can make
it my strength
4 = I have this to a great extent, and this is one of my strong points

1. Trusting: trusts others adequately and takes them at face value
2. Trustworthy: delivers on commitments
3. Integrity/Honesty: speaks the truth and is prepared to face consequences
4. Honours commitments and does not make false promises
5. Disciplined and fair and firm with people
6. Respects people, irrespective of hierarchy, functions, levels, etc.
7. Shares own knowledge freely and learns from others
8. Lives with superordinate goals and higher purposes like 'creating happiness in the lives of people' and 'serving mankind while creating wealth'
9. Humanitarian outlook: stands up for others, compassionate and supportive
10. People positive: deep belief in the limitless potential of people and at ease with people from different walks of life
11. Humility: acknowledges own mistakes, admits a misstep and is humble
12. Commitment and sense of ownership, conscious about responsibilities, simple living within means
13. Openness: accepting the truth however personally unpalatable it may be
14. Authenticity/Transparency: speaks as he/she thinks, thinking is aligned with promises and talk
15. Learning: always a learner, continuous reading of books and reflecting what was learnt
16. Proactiveness: takes the initiative and is optimistic
17. Confrontation: confronts issues and brings them out to solve problems
18. Sense of Purpose: thinks and acts with purpose
19. Collaboration and Teamwork: believes in co-creation
20. Experimentation and Innovativeness: comes up with ideas and experiments with new practices

Appendix 4: Crucible Experience Planner for HR Professionals

Based on lessons learnt from the thirty HR Leaders, certain kinds of crucible experiences appear essential for growing as an HR Leader. First, we have given some example to illustrate how to use this template. The next table gives the template for self-reflection and planning to get the crucible experiences.

Example:

Sr. No.	Essentials for growing as an HR Leader	Self-Reflection	Self-Score out of 10	Crucible Experience Plan
1.	Exposure to industrial relations	Saw my colleague handle IR situation. But I have had no direct responsibility for IR.	2	Ask my manager for job rotation in IR position.
2.	Working under a boss who is a role model	Worked for three years under a boss from whom I learnt the following: 1. 2. 3.	8	Make a list of role model bosses and keep track of opportunities that may open up under them.
3.	Working under a demanding boss	Had opportunity to work under moderately demanding boss.	4	Make a list of very demanding bosses and keep track of opportunities that may arise to work under them. Work towards seizing such opportunities.

	Exposure to business role	No opportunity to do business role. But I have accompanied my VP sales in her/his field visits.	3	Discuss with my boss the possibility of posting in the business role for minimum two years

Crucible Experience Planning Template

Sr. No.	Essentials for growing as an HR Leader	Self-Reflection	Self-Score out of 10	Crucible Experience Plan
1.	Exposure to industrial relations			
2.	Working under a boss who is a role model			.
3.	Working under a demanding boss			
4.	Exposure to business role			
5.	Senior HR professional as mentor			
6.	Working on a job that stretches my capabilities			
7.	Assignment that gives opportunity to challenge status quo and lead new initiatives			
8.	Assignment into a job role which is not fully structured—giving elbow room for 'role making'			
9.	Active engagement in professional forums			
10.	Volunteering for social causes			

Acknowledgements

This book would not have seen the light of the day without the overwhelming support from the HR leaders who have been featured here and whose stories constitute the core of this work. They candidly shared their stories with the appropriate level of granular details, displaying enormous patience during the long interviews that lasted for several hours, spanning multiple rounds of in-person and, where required, video meetings. They trusted us fully with their personal details with no hesitation whatsoever. Further, they painstakingly went over the draft version of their respective stories, making all the factual corrections and, in many instances, making invaluable changes to the original draft to make the stories more meaningful. Our deepest gratitude to all of them for the priceless gifts they have given not only to the two of us but to the entire human resource profession, as these stories of role model HR leaders will no doubt inspire the next generation of leaders in their development journey.

We are grateful to Dhananjay Singh—Director General of the National HRD Network (NHRDN) and his team from the national office for sharing with us specific information regarding awards and positions held by the HR leaders in NHRDN. The stories featured here would have been incomplete without the mention of these important contributions made by them to the HR profession and the acknowledgement conferred on them over the years by NHRDN.

Further, the voluminous data that we had gathered through our meetings with the HR leaders in our longhand together with several hours of audio/video recordings had to be transcribed. We are truly grateful to CA Deepika Agarwal and her team from RDK Professionals based in Jaipur for completing this arduous task of producing legible transcriptions for us to move forward with our work.

We further acknowledge the invaluable editing support that we received from Aditi Roy Ghatak and Suman Layak who brought in their enormous professional expertise as writers and gleaned from our long manuscripts succinct stories that were both more readable and meaningful. This was the most tedious part of putting this book together. We kept going back and forth, chopping and changing, drafting and redrafting. The work was endless, exasperating and went on for well over a year. We cannot thank them enough for their patience, sustained hard work and the highest level of professional expertise that they brought to bear throughout this engagement.

We must acknowledge the indomitable Radhika Marwah, senior commissioning editor, who read through our long manuscript, saw value in it and quickly responded by tying up all the ends to make this publication by Penguin Random House India possible. We are also grateful to Ralph Rebello, copy editor, for the most detailed and comprehensive copy-editing so mindfully done.

Finally, our gratitude to our better halves both Henna and Jaya for their enthusiastic support, encouragement and patience over the years without which we would not have been able to put this book in your hands.